The Ambedkar–Gandhi De

Bindu Puri

The Ambedkar–Gandhi Debate

On Identity, Community and Justice

 Springer

Bindu Puri 🆔
Centre for Philosophy
School of Social Sciences
Jawaharlal Nehru University
New Delhi, Delhi, India

ISBN 978-981-16-8688-7   ISBN 978-981-16-8686-3 (eBook)
https://doi.org/10.1007/978-981-16-8686-3

This Springer imprint is published by the registered company Springer Nature Singapore Pte Ltd.
The registered company address is: 152 Beach Road, #21-01/04 Gateway East, Singapore 189721, Singapore

Preface

This book was a long time in the making simply because of the rather daunting task that it had set itself, that of bringing out the intense conflicts, between two very good men. There were three important conflicts in Gandhi's life, and these conflicts occasioned, in the Gandhian way, three debates. It is surely significant to take note of this last in our intolerant times for it is from Gandhi that we might learn that non-violence involves more than merely tolerance/*sahishnuta* of those whose ideas are very different from our own. Gandhian *ahimsa*/non-violence involves much more; it involves, a joyous and welcoming engagement with criticism. For Gandhi, it would be violent/*himsanat* (such *himsa*/violence emerging perhaps from an ego-centred mind) to disregard criticism. Gandhi's first debate was with Savarkar, the second with Tagore and the third with Ambedkar. The debate between Gandhi (1869–1948) and Bhimrao Ambedkar (1891–1956) took place between the early 1920s and 1956 (after Gandhi had died and) when Ambedkar embraced Buddhism. I have been very interested in the connections between Gandhi's non-violence/*ahimsa* and his curiosity to engage with the ideas of those who differed most sharply from him. There are not many among us who have such curiosity and desire to joyously (and this is what is so distinctive about Gandhi) enter into an exchange with those who are most opposed to ourselves.

There is so much to learn from the man at the other side of the debate with Gandhi, Bhimrao Ambedkar, who was (as is well known) a liberal constitutionalist *par excellence*. However, what is more important about Ambedkar and perhaps lesser commented upon, and what has made for greater learning for a student of philosophy (like me), has been his very meticulous scholarship. He was a scholar of the Western liberal tradition and paradoxically enough a scholar of ancient Indian texts. Ambedkar had a stunning ability to make an incisive analysis of the arguments in such texts and bring out the conceptual difficulties with such arguments and with the Hindu tradition itself. Though he had tremendous difficulties with the memory of the past his own ability to remember and put together, so much of what he read is inspiring to students of the past like myself. It is well known that Ambedkar was the chairman of the Drafting Committee of the Constitution of India. It is also interesting and "a lesser known fact" (Chakrabarty 2019, viii) that Jawaharlal Nehru had selected the eminent lawyer Ivor Jennings for this task and that it was Mahatma Gandhi's personal intervention which secured for Ambedkar the opportunity to perform this role at the most important juncture of India's history (not *itihaas*).

Having read Gandhi for the most part of my academic career, the debate with Ambedkar has intrigued me for many reasons but most of all for the fact that two good men can come into conflict about things that both seem to agree are important. It has also intrigued me that Ambedkar, the only apostle of justice in our living memory, has called into question Gandhi's integrity and more so his love which appeared so free of attachment to the person of any other. One might recall Akeel Bilgrami's famous argument that Gandhi was not only a "man of integrity" (Bilgrami 2006, 248) but that "his thought itself was highly integrated" (Ibid., 248–249). One might also recall that Gandhian love was a love for the very last person at most distance from himself. It is for reasons like this, among others, that I was led to explore the issues that underlay this exchange and to write the book.

However, before embarking into an account of the incommensurability and conflicts between Ambedkar and Gandhi, it is important to note that many scholars of Ambedkar's life and work have commented on his debate with Gandhi. Scholars including Zelliot (1972), Nagraj (2015), Guha (2012), Vajpeyi (2013), Thomas Pantham (2013), Aishwary Kumar (2015), Nishikant Kolge (2017), Aakash Singh Rathore (2017) and Bidyut Chakraborty (2019) have had something to say about Ambedkar's debate with Gandhi. The important question is why there should be yet another attempt in this book to bring out the central issues in the debate between Gandhi and Ambedkar? While there have been essays or chapters in books (as noted above) and indeed significant books by Kolge (2017) and by Kumar (2015) which have been preoccupied with the Ambedkar–Gandhi debate to the exclusion of all else, this book is somewhat different.

It is for example different from the historian Kolge's (2017) wonderful account of this debate. Kolge taking his *que* perhaps from Bhattacharya's (Bhattacharya 2008) chronological account of the debate between Gandhi and Tagore in *The Mahatma and the Poet,* has made a detailed (and most useful) account of Gandhi's debate with Ambedkar. He has divided this account into five time periods—1915–1920, 1920–1927, 1927–1932, 1932–1945 and 1945–1948 (Kolge 2017, 101) on the basis on the themes (and changes in such themes) which emerged in Gandhi's writings during these periods. This book will not attempt such a historical account of issues and themes. It will instead take its *que* from Gandhi and question "history" itself making a philosophical investigation into the set of notions that formed the basis of the more apparent issues around which Gandhi and Ambedkar came into conflict. The book will not only bring up these more fundamental issues—self-identity, community, justice, *itihaas*/it so happened and history—in a single work, but it will also take up these issues in continuity with the work of previous commentators on the debate. Taking up the discussion sometimes from where others had left it as it were.

This book has chosen to engage with such conflicts instead of seeking their dissolution by an attempt at a retrospective reconciliation of the protagonists. As the book will argue continuity itself (for instance that between the past and the present) let alone reconciliation, becomes a matter of much debate, between Gandhi and Ambedkar.

The book will argue, in fact, that Gandhi and Ambedkar cannot be retrospectively reconciled as they thought from within incommensurable world views and one might say, used the same words to speak very different languages, as it were.

I have been working on this book for a few years during which time I served as the chairperson of the centre for Philosophy at Jawaharlal Nehru University. The shift from Delhi University (which indeed I miss a lot) to Jawaharlal Nehru University delayed the completion of the manuscript by a little. I am very grateful to the support which I have received from my editor at Springer, Satvinder Kaur, whose timely reminders helped me much more than she knows. Abhishek, my erstwhile student and present colleague, was just an email away when I needed his help in procuring relevant essays and texts, and he contributed in his way to my academic endeavours. I would also like to thank another erstwhile student and present colleague Reetu Jaiswal for conversations and interjections. My sister Puja and brother-in-law Samir Yajnik supported and encouraged me to demonstrate how addiction to academic work makes one happy besides all odds. Since I spoke of Gandhi's immense interest in criticism, it would be amiss if I did not thank my own best critic and mother, the painter, philosopher and scholar of the tribes of North-East India, Sujata Miri who, borrowing Gandhi's words for the poet Rabindranath Tagore; has been like a light house or indeed "a Great Sentinel" giving warnings of "dangers lying in the stormy paths of life" (Gandhi in Bhattacharya (ed) 2008, 48) dangers like "Lethargy… Ignorance, Inertia and other members of that brood" (Ibid., 88). She continuously inspires us all to do our very best. I would like to thank my husband the wonderful scholar and Physicist Professor Sanjay Puri who taught me that the pandemic, suffering and even the departure of those who went much before their time should not interrupt academic engagements; indeed that it is such engagements which give us the strength to move beyond every grief. My wonderful kind children, now young men, Nikaash Puri and Akshay Puri, gave me technological support and so very much more, as they always do. I would most of all like to thank my father and very eminent philosopher Professor Mrinal Miri, for the long conversations about philosophy (how it ought to be done properly) and about Gandhi and Ambedkar which both inspired and sustained my intellectual zeal.

New Delhi, India   Bindu Puri
2021

References

Bhattacharya, S. ed. 2008. *The Mahatma and the poet. Letters and debates between Gandhi and Tagore*, 1915–1941, 5th edition 2008. New Delhi: National Book Trust.

Bilgrami, A. 2006. Gandhi's integrity: the philosophy behind the politics. In *Debating Gandhi: A Reader*, ed. A. Raghuramraju, 248–66. New Delhi: Oxford University Press.

Chakrabarty, Bidyut. 2019. *The Socio-Political Ideas of B R Ambedkar: Liberal Constitutionalism in a Creative Mould*. New York: Routledge.

Guha, Ramachandra. 2012. Gandhi's Ambedkar. In *Indian Political Thought: A Reader* eds. Aakash Singh, and Silika Mohapatra, 33–38. London: Routledge.

Kolge, Nishikant. 2017. *Gandhi Against Caste*. New Delhi: Oxford University Press.

Kumar, Aishwary. 2015. *Radical Equality: Ambedkar, Gandhi, and the Risk of Democracy.* Stanford, California: Stanford University Press.

Nagraj, D. R. 2015. *The flaming Feet and Other Essays: The Dalit Movement in India,* ed. Prithvi Datta Chandra Shobhi. Ranikhet: Permanent Black.

Pantham, Thomas. 2013. Against untouchability: The discourses of Gandhi and Ambedkar. In *Humiliation: Claims and Context,* ed. Gopal Guru, 179–208. New Delhi: Oxford University Press.

Rathore, Aakash Singh. 2017. *Indian Political Theory: Laying the Groundwork for Svaraj.* London, New York: Routledge.

Vajpeyi, A. 2013. *Righteous Republic: The Political Foundations of Modern India.* Harvard: Harvard University Press.

Zelliot, Eleanor. 1972. Gandhi and Ambedkar—A study in leadership. In *The Untouchables in Contemporary India,* ed. J. Michael Mahar, 69–95. Tucson, Arizona: University of Arizona Press.

Book Notes

The author has spelt Sanskrit words used by Gandhi and Ambedkar (which appear in quotations from their works) exactly as they appear in their writing. Consequently, in the interest of consistency diacritical marks have not been used for those words throughout this book (except in the glossary). The author has simply followed the style of the original texts or of the translations which have been quoted in the book.

Contents

About the Author

Bindu Puri is a Professor of contemporary Indian Philosophy at the Centre for Philosophy, School of Social Sciences, Jawaharlal Nehru University. Her main interests in philosophy are in the areas of contemporary Indian philosophy and moral and political philosophy. Puri has over 50 papers in edited anthologies and philosophical and interdisciplinary journals including *Sophia, Philosophia* and the *Journal of the Indian Council of Philosophical Research.* She has authored two monographs: *Gandhi and the Moral Life* (2004) and The *Tagore-Gandhi Debate: On Matters of Truth and Untruth* (Springer: New Delhi, 2015). She has seven edited volumes and her eighth and most recent edited volume *Reading Sri Aurobindo - Metaphysics, Ethics and Spirituality* is currently in press with Springer Publications. She has presented over 160 papers and lectures at national and International forums. Professor Puri delivered the prestigious annual 'M. K. Gandhi lecture on Peace and the Humanities' 2017 for the Mahatma Gandhi Peace Council of Ottawa, Canada and the Johnson and Hastings lectures at the University of Mount Allison, Canada for the same year.

Chapter 1
By Way of Introduction: The Ambedkar–Gandhi Debate: Three Fundamental Questions

Abstract The introductory chapter to this book on the Ambedkar–Gandhi debate will bring up three important questions, answers to which, underlay the conflicts between them. These are questions about the relationship between the present and the past and can be spelt out as follows; can one access the past from the standpoint of the present; How should one relate to an emotion (whether such an emotion be in the present or in the past) which overrides all other emotions and dominates one's mental life? And lastly, how ought one to understand and respond to a politics of suffering. This chapter and the book will unpack Ambedkar and Gandhi's very different answers to these questions.

Keywords Present · Past · Emotion · Self · Identity · Community · Justice · Owners · Authors · *Itihaas* · Measure · Four Noble Truths · History · Judgement · Modernity · Tradition · Continuity · Politics of suffering

This is a book debating a continuity in the relationship between the present and the past. Yet in a somewhat paradoxical engagement with the spirit of continuity, it examines the third in the trilogy of Gandhi's (1869–1948) debates (with Savarkar, Tagore and Ambedkar)[1] that with Bhimrao Ambedkar (1891–1956). The book seeks to bring out the philosophical issues that underlay the conflicts which took place between the early 1920s and 1956 (after Gandhi had died and) when Ambedkar embraced Buddhism. There were several issues which had become the subject of conflict between these two good men across 36 years; untouchability, separate electorates, Hinduism, conversion, temple entry, caste, *varna*, history and tradition. However, it is possible to philosophically reinterpret this debate as a series of conflicts about more fundamental issues—the nature of the self, the relationship between the individual self and the community, the appropriate relationship between the constitutive attachments/encumbrances of the self and a conception of justice and the ways in which one can come to the truth about the past (as history or *itihaas*). These issues will be taken up across the following five chapters in the book. However, Ambedkar and Gandhi's contrary conceptions of the self, history, *itihaas,* community and justice

---

[1] The second of Gandhi's three debates was with Tagore and I have made a somewhat detailed study of it in *The Gandhi Tagore Debate: On matters of Truth and Untruth.* Sophia: Studies in Cross-cultural Philosophy of Traditions and Cultures, Vol. 9, Springer 2015. (ISBN 978-81-322-2115-9).

© Springer Science+Business Media Singapore 2022
B. Puri, *The Ambedkar–Gandhi Debate,*
https://doi.org/10.1007/978-981-16-8686-3_1

were properly articulated only as they each sought to grapple with more fundamental questions about the relationship between the present and the past.

The issues more fundamental to the debate between them could be put in terms of the following questions; can an individual access the truth of the past from the standpoint of the present? How should one to relate to an emotion (whether it be in the present or in the past) which overrides all other emotions and indeed overwhelms everything else? And lastly, how ought one to understand and respond to the politics of suffering? This chapter will look at Gandhi and Ambedkar's responses to these questions across its different sections.

1.1   To Access the Truth About the Past

It is very important to an understanding of the debate between Ambedkar and Gandhi to ask whether one is able (or not able) to access the truth about the past from the standpoint of the present. Answering this question involves one's relationship to the memory of the past and how one might access such a memory. One can say that Gandhi and Ambedkar answered this question in different ways. Ways which might perhaps be best described as ancient and modern, respectively. To the ancients like Gandhi thinking from within the "old-world Indian mind" (Bhattacharya 2011, 104) one could access the truth of one's past simply through the memory of it as a passing of all that which had happened in its unique immeasurable singularity. For Ambedkar on the other hand, the answer to the question "can one access the truth of one's past?" was "No, but one can retrospectively pass a judgement/indictment on that past by selecting a measure to write its history". This section will only initiate the discussion on this question (and on its answer) which will be taken up in more detail in the next chapter entitled "Memory history and *itihaas:* Ambedkar and Gandhi".

To begin with, and as already noted, the old-world Gandhi thought that this question could be answered in the affirmative. However he believed that Truth could be accessed without the "measure" of history simply as *satya/*being in the *itihaas* (a composite term *iti* and *haas)* the it *(iti)* so happened *(haas)* of the past. In 1909, Gandhi had explained how one might access the past without the measure of history in a set of fairly dense paragraphs in the *Hind Swaraj.* It was while speaking about *satyagraha-atmabal* or the force of truth/love that Gandhi explained the different ways in which one could access the truth (or indeed not be able to access the truth) of that which had come to pass in one's own past;

> But you ask for historical evidence. It is, therefore, necessary to know what history means. The Gujarati equivalent means; 'It so happened'. If that is the meaning of history, it is possible to give copious evidence. But, if it means the doings of Kings and emperors, there can be no evidence of soul-force or passive resistance in such history. You cannot expect silver-ore in a tin-mine. History, as we know it, is a record of the wars of the world, and so there is a proverb among Englishmen that a nation which has no history, that is, no wars, is a happy nation. How kings played, how they became enemies of one another is found accurately recorded in history, and, if this was all that had happened in the world it would

have been ended long ago. If the story of the universe had commenced with wars, not a man would have been found alive today. (Gandhi 1888–1948, 10: 291)[2]

Gandhi explained the role of retrospective judgement and the place of measure in writing a history of the past. On this view, the historian retrospectively makes an indictment of the past recreating it through the prism of the selected measure. This retrospective judgement and writing of history effectively destroys any access to the truth of the past as it was or had passed as a set of unique individual happenings. The choice of measure (Marxist, liberal, dalit, feminist, Islamic, Hindu, Sikh, dalit feminist, dalit feminist Marxist, dalit Marxist, dalit liberal, dalit liberal feminist, etc.) indeed is what enables the historian juror to distinguish between relevant and irrelevant facts against itself (as measure) as it were. As it destroys the access to the truth about the past, history ensures that the past is recreated as monolithic and unidimensional. For Gandhi, it is the choice of the measure which determines the dominant character (as just, unjust, oppressive, artistic) of the history of the now unidimensional past. It is the chosen measure which determines whether history be read (and the past be seen) in monolithic terms as purely (even solely) a record of wars, of injustice, of oppression of women or the suffering of the untouchables (to mention a few possibilities).

> Gandhi implicitly assumed that history …was a one way traffic, a set of myths about past time or the *atit*, built up as independent variables which limit human options and pre-empt human futures. (Nandy 2009, 59)

What appears lost (to the past, present and future) is the *it so happened* in the past in its multi-dimensional reality. It is the *sat*/being which is lost as that which might have appeared as the truth of the past without a measure or indeed without the need to make a retrospective judgement on that which had passed. Gandhi refers to that which was lost as that which lay in the immeasurability of the unique everyday happenings as they had simply happened in the past;

> Hundreds of nations live in peace. History does not, and cannot, take note of this fact. History is really a record of the even working of the force of love or of the soul. Two brothers quarrel; one of them repents and reawakens the love that was lying dormant in him; the two again begin to live in peace; nobody takes note of this. But, if the two brothers, through the intervention of solicitors or some other reason, take up arms or go to the law-which is another form of the exhibition of brute force-their doings would be immediately noticed in the press, …and would probably go down to history. (Gandhi 1888–1948, 10: 292)

It followed, for Gandhi at least, that the truth about the past should be sought as *itihaas*/it so happened and not as history and that the present should not retrospectively reject/erase the truth of that which had already passed. Gandhi argued

---

[2] Gandhi 1888–1948 refers to the *Collected Works of Mahatma Gandhi*. The volume concerned and the page numbers from which citations from Gandhi are drawn have been mentioned within parentheses. These have been mentioned to indicate the exact location of the quotation in the electronic edition of the *Collected Works of Mahatma Gandhi*. However, for the purposes of reference, it may be noted that I have resourced these volumes from the *Collected Works of Mahatma Gandhi*: Volumes 1 to 98. New Delhi: Publications Division Government of India, 1999. Accessed online in May 2021 at https://www.gandhiashramsevagram.org/gandhi-literature/collected-works-of-mahatma-gandhi-volume-1-to-98.php.

that no matter how severe the retrospective indictment passed by history the present ought to make conceptual space for continuity with the past. For Gandhi, there were difficulties with the making of such retrospective indictments through a selection of measure and the writing of history. The first of these difficulties as already apparent was the loss of truth as the indictment had necessarily to be made from the standpoint of the present, and in Ambedkar's case, through the prism of one overriding emotion that of suffering. The second difficulty followed from the first, in that, the denial of the truth also led to the rejection of the resources of the multidimensional past which Gandhi believed could help mitigate the suffering brought in its wake. This point was connected with the idea that the most appropriate way to work through injustice oppression and grief brought up by the past would be to work through these emotions. However for such a working through of emotions (connected with the past), it was essential to seek the truth of the past without measure and just as it had passed.

One might begin with Gandhi's idea that the character of memory infused by the multidimensional nature of *satya*/the it so happened of life would, in itself, contain resources from the form of life that had been lived, its songs of grief, its modes of worship and the small moments of happiness alongside (the sole preoccupation of measure and history) the moments of injustice, pain and the suffering. The memory of such a past which was as multifaceted as human life itself would contain resources within its own multilayered set of events to help the individual and the community move beyond/work through the over whelming pain and attendant rage that the injustice of that same past had brought. The next section will bring out Gandhi's effort to work through the past by making a creative use of his own over whelming emotions. For the moment, one may note that for ancients like Gandhi a self-willed amnesia built upon the refusal to own the small events in the *itihaas*/ it so happened of the past could be debilitating for the self. Such amnesia would for-close possibilities of drawing comfort from the other less miserable aspects, of the past that was. Nandy gestures towards such other less miserable parts of that which had so happened when he recalls "Nagraj's passionate commitment to the rediscovery –not discovery—of …the diverse, rich cultures of Dalit communities…" (Nandy 2015, xv).

Such a rediscovery of diverse and rich cultural pasts could help the individual (and community) move beyond socially constituted suffering to a future which would be in continuity with the past and the present but not limited by the stultifying injustice and despair of that past. In Gandhi's view, the continuity with one's *itihaas* would keep in place not only the integrity of that which had passed but also the integrity of the self as the person on whom the past, had passed, as it were. It is surely significant that the destruction of the integrity/wholeness of the self that inevitably accompanied the destruction of the past could also lead to a "totally impoverished" (Shobhi 2015, 4) conception of the self as primarily or even solely a humiliated person.

It is important to add the *caveat* that Gandhi's effort to keep continuity with the past would not have to be understood as devoid of reason and reform along the lines suggested by reason. Only, as MacIntyre has argued (1988), one would have to make room for "a tradition constitutive and tradition constituted" (MacIntyre 1988, 10) conception of reason in all its contrary from the "reason" of the liberals. One should note that such a conception of reason (alternative to the liberal one) can countenance critique and reform of, the repository of all meanings that constitutes a tradition, from within the continuity of the same evolving (never static) tradition. In this connection, there will be occasion to speak of Gandhi's understanding of reason (along the lines of the ancients and best understood in terms of MacIntyre's (1988) argument) across the chapters in this book. To make room for such an alternative Gandhian understanding of reason (and justice), one might note that

> ...rationality itself, whether theoretical or practical, is a concept with a history: indeed, since there are a diversity of traditions of enquiry, with histories, there are, so it will turn out, rationalities rather than rationality, just as it will turn out that there are justices rather than justice. (MacIntyre 1988, 9)

Moving on to Ambedkar's answer to the question "can one access the truth of the past" in all its difference from the answer given by Gandhi. Ambedkar rejected the idea that one could access the truth of the past through the memory of that which had so happened. He retrospectively judged the past from the standpoint of the present as beyond redemption. It followed (for him) that the memory of such an unjust painful past ought to be erased and indeed could be erased by a wilful "act of the vanishing of memory" (Nagraj 2015, 155) of the events in the past in their individual immeasurable singularity. The only way to relate to the past after such an act of erasure was by recreating it through history. Ambedkar answered the question "can one access the truth of one's past" by saying that one should make a retrospective judgement on the past by writing a history about it. This writing of history by the nature of the case would have no interest in the truth of the small, individual, everyday occurrences of the past. This was because history by the nature of what it was could only be interested in a retrospective application of measure on that which was specific about the past. The specific would both facilitate its own indictment and become a precedent for law. For Ambedkar, it was the figure of the historian juror as the third party who adjudicated the sins of the past in line with such measure and law. As it was the *socius* and not the singular individual (as unique and not able to present that which could be measured) who could be made responsible for the sins of the past, it followed that individuals could not atone for such sins. There was then no truth to be sought in the past, and all that the past could do was occasion an indictment and a politics of suffering and rage.

Apart from his several works on Gandhi (which will be taken up in the book), one can see the extent of Ambedkar's retrospective indictment of the past even in his "religious" (there will be some discussion on Ambedkar's interpretation of the term "religion" in Chap. 3 of the book) reinterpretation of Buddhism. In *The Buddha and His Dhamma* (2011), Ambedkar had suggested that "Man's misery is the result of man's inequity to man. Only righteousness can remove this inequity and the resultant misery" (Ambedkar 2011, 152). Measuring the past against such an insight, Ambedkar rejected all traditional knowledge and indeed all the knowledge givers of the unjust past;

> Being out of sympathy for their welfare, his (the *savarna* Brahmin's) heart would become established in enmity; and when one's heart is established in enmity, that is unsound doctrine. (Ibid., 155) (the parenthesis are my own addition and not present in the original)

On such a view scholars of the unjust past could not "communicate any knowledge or learning" (Ibid.) or "illumine" (Ibid., 156) others with their "learning" as they were "danger-maker(s)" (Ibid., 155). All traditional religion and traditional knowledge was thereby discredited as "unsound doctrine" (Ibid.) having been produced from a "heart (which) stands fast in enmity" (Ibid.);

> If any man, whether he be learned or not, considers himself so great as to despise other men, he is like a blind man holding a candle—blind himself ,he illumines others. (Ibid., 156)

For Ambedkar, this meant that the unsound past in its all encompassing and over whelming blindness brought no light in its wake and no continuity with it needed to be sought. It followed naturally enough that for him the past with it is traditional knowledge (produced by hearts full of enmity) ought not only to be condemned but erased in its entirety.

1.2 Responding to One's Emotions

1.2.1 Ambedkar: Of Overwhelming Emotions

Ambedkar's rejection of the past and of traditional knowledge through the measure of its practice of inequity (and prism of the attendant suffering) as completely "unsound" (Ibid., 155) might lead one to reflect upon how one should relate to emotions and the experience of emotions (whether these be in the present or in the past) that seem to override everything else. For there are such emotions in every human being's past and present. Those perhaps of grief, humiliation, over whelming love and anger. One might see why this question should seem to be so important to the Ambedkar–Gandhi debate if one considers that Ambedkar and indeed later dalit scholars saw dalit reality as something both understood and lived only through the prism of suffering. This second question (of the three raised in this chapter) "how ought one to relate to overriding emotions?" could lead one to consider whether there could be a reality other than that/outside that of the emotional life? If this question can be answered in the affirmative, it would follow that one should also question whether one might be able to step back from experiences of overriding emotions. Such a stepping back could perhaps help one to understand the emotion and more importantly to understand the reality that lay outside of the over whelming experience of the emotion. This last could make for conceptual and practical space for working through such over whelming emotions. Perhaps even for moving past them to the business of leading lives beyond those experiences and their somewhat lingering influence.

Gandhi and Ambedkar gave very different answers to the question of their own relationship with overriding emotions and their lives took very different courses as they lived out these answers. One might consider that an individual can be overridden by the intensity of a past or present emotion. Tagore a silent interjector in this debate (there will be some discussion on Tagore's interjections in the conclusion) described overriding emotions in his prose and poetry. He wrote (for instance) that the experience of intense emotions distanced the experiencer from every one and indeed from everything else. In such a self-enclosing distance, the experiencer lost the ability to see reality as it existed outside of the emotion concerned. In *The Home and the world,* Tagore (2012) relates the heroine Bimala's imprisonment in her passionate longing for Sandip;

> Where will it all end, I asked myself? Shall I ever recover ,as from a delirium, and forget it all; or am I to be dragged to depths from which there can be no escape in this life? (Tagore 2012, 277)

Tagore brought out, as it were, the blindness that came in the wake of such overwhelming experiences of emotion. One might consider that for a person who is overwhelmed by love or pain reality fades away and evades all his/her thought and understanding just as it evades his/her efforts to live life itself. Witness how one might identify with the following blindness;

> When I came to my room today, I saw only furniture—only the bedstead, only the looking glass, only the clothes rack—not the all pervading heart that used to be there, over all. (Ibid., 350)

For Ambedkar and for much of the dalit movement which followed him, the overriding emotion was that of suffering. Ambedkar had argued that suffering defined dalit reality and it came to constitute the identity of the dalit and the modality of his/her existence in the world;

> As the leader of the Untouchables of Maharashtra, Ambedkar was never free of the consciousness of the suffering of his people. Indeed, for him, suffering is constitutive of the very identity of the Untouchables; it is the modality in which they experience their being in the world—especially since society, from their perspective, is created by and for those with caste. (Vajpeyi 2013, 214)

Ambedkar answered the question about how one should respond to an overwhelming emotion by recommending a holding on to, and identification with, one's overwhelming emotions to the exclusion of everything else. One might consider here that he chose to convert to Buddhism selecting Buddhism (from the other religions he had considered) on account of the pivotal place accorded to suffering by the Buddha. One might also consider that the same necessity of identifying with the overwhelming experience of suffering lead him to reject the traditional Buddhist account of the Four Noble Truths. Such a traditional interpretation was deeply disturbing to him because it suggested that one could deal with the overwhelming emotion of suffering in human life by putting it in perspective (as a link in the twelve pronged chain of the *Bhava chakra*/wheel of existence and) as an experience due eventually to ignorance about the true nature of the self. An understanding of the no self-doctrine of the Buddha would, on more traditional accounts of the noble truths, lead the aspirant/sufferer to transcend his/her experience of suffering and finally arrive at an extinction in *Nibbana*/salvation. Ambedkar argued that suffering could not be and indeed, ought not to be, transcended. As socially constituted and historically specific to a people it needed to be retained at the core of individual being so that it could be redressed by restorative justice and affirmative action as it were. He sought to reinterpret Buddhism as a religion constituted around the experience of suffering and indeed sought to build a community of suffering dalit's around the overriding emotion of suffering.

One might consider in this connection that in his introduction to *The Buddha and his Dhamma* Ambedkar rejected the traditional account of the Four Noble Truths as mistaken and misleading;

> The second problem is created by the four noble Aryan Truths? Do they form part of the original teachings of the Buddha? This formula cuts at the root of Buddhism… The four Aryan Truths make the gospel of the Buddha a gospel of pessimism. (Rathore and Verma 2011, xxix-xxx)

As Vajpeyi (2013) suggests;

> The only thing that then explains Ambedkar's rejection of the Four Noble Truths is his inter-pretation of duhkha—not as individual, karmic suffering, but as collective ,social suffering. In other words, in undermining the Four Noble Truths, what Ambedkar challenged was the notion that all persons, of whatever caste, class, or gender, need to face and transcend their suffering; rather according to him, suffering had to be seen as socially constituted and historically specific, and could be conquered only via a creed that placed suffering at the very center of its entire ethical structure. (Vajpeyi 2013, 214)

This necessity to define the self in terms of an intense overriding emotion led Ambedkar (as mentioned earlier) to reinterpret the Second and Third Noble Truths of the newly accepted faith. On this view, suffering's arising (from craving) and cessation were not to be associated with ignorance of the true nature of the self and the transcendence of the ego and ego driven desire (respectively). The Buddhist belief that eventually there is annihilation of human suffering itself by complete extinction in *Nibbana* had also to be rejected.

> There are certain misunderstandings about the Buddha's doctrine of Nibbana. The word Nibbana etymologically means outblowing, extinguishing. Taking hold of this root meaning of the word, critics have tried to make nonsense of the of the doctrine of Nibbana…Nibbana can never have this meaning. (Ambedkar 2011, 127)

In Chap. 3 of *The Buddha and his Dhamma,* Ambedkar suggested instead that the noble truths were to be reinterpreted as concerned with the class struggle;

> 'Why is this craving or greed to be condemned? Because of this', said the Buddha to Ananda, 'many a bad and wicked state of things arises-blows and wounds, strife, contradiction and retorts; quarelling, slander and lies'. That this is the correct analysis of class struggle there can be no doubt. That is why the Buddha insisted upon the control of greed and craving. (Ibid., 129)

Consequently in Ambedkar's *Navayana,* Buddha was understood to have propa-gated a social rather than a religious message. Such a reinterpretation of the noble truths as connected with strife and the class struggle enabled Ambedkar's *Navayana* to keep suffering intact as the primary modality of the dalit's being.

1.2.2 Gandhi: Putting Emotions to Work

Both Gandhi and Ambedkar were sensitive to the overriding emotion of suffering that lay between their conflicts. Gandhi, however, dealt very differently with the experience of such emotions those for instance of suffering, guilt and love. Like Ambedkar, Gandhi too did not recommend the transcendence of suffering through religious salvation. However whether emotions be of love or of pain, Gandhi suggested putting emotions in perspective in human life by creating some distance between the self and the experience of any/all overriding emotion. *Brahmacharya/*celibacy *satyagraha/*passive resistance and *tapasya/*self-imposed suffering became each, in their own way, very important to such a putting of emotions at a distance from the experiencing self and from thence to a consideration of the Gandhian response to overriding emotions.

It is important to note, in the interest of all that has been said about authenticity and suffering by Ambedkar (and by those who followed in his steps), that Gandhi had his own (very real) experience of suffering and humiliation as a victim of racial injustice and oppression. Gandhi's emotions as a victim of practices of racial discrimination were brought to an intense high in the experience of being thrown out of a train in South Africa. One might in fact align Gandhi's experience at the Pietermaritzburg Railway Station alongside that of Ambedkar's suffering at being thrown out of a lodge at Baroda and Phule's experience of being thrown out of an upper-caste marriage procession in nineteenth-century Pune (Guru 2012b, 123). Gandhi relates the experience at the station in his autobiography;

> The constable came. He took me by the hand and pushed me out ...I refused to go to the other compartment and the train streamed away. I went and sat in the waiting room ...It was winter, and winter in the higher regions of South Africa is severely cold. Maritzburg being at a high altitude ,the cold was extremely bitter. My overcoat was in my luggage ,but I did not dare to ask for it lest I should be insulted again, so I sat and shivered. There was no light in the room. (Gandhi 1888–1948, 44: 174)

What is significant in Gandhi's retelling of his experience of humiliation is perhaps how he stepped back from the darkness and from his emotions of suffering and anger;

> I began to think of my duty. Should I fight for my rights, or go back to India, or should I go back to Pretoria without minding the insults, and return to India after finishing the case? It would be cowardly to run back to India without fulfilling my obligation. The hardship to which I was subjected was superficial—only a symptom of the deep disease of colour prejudice. I should try, if possible, to root out the disease and suffer hardships in the process. Redress for wrongs I should seek only to the extent that would be necessary for the removal of the colour prejudice. (Ibid.)

It is surely significant that Gandhi chose the moment of overwhelming grief not only to step back from the emotion and understand it better but also chose to creatively re-employ the experience of his own humiliation to think of a method to secure rights for all humiliated persons. As he described that method in 1909;

> Passive resistance is a method of securing rights by personal suffering; (Gandhi 1888–1948, 10: 292)

Gandhi seemed to have understood what Tagore had described as the blindness in overriding emotions in terms of their close association with passion. Tagore, one might recall had argued (during his debate with Gandhi), that passion generated by the choice of an experiencer to remain preoccupied with the experience of an overpowering emotion would lead to distortion/blindness; because "we fix our attention exclusively …by reason of some infatuation—be it of love or hate" (Tagore in Bhattacharya (ed) 2008, 70). Reflection on such insights might have led Gandhi to respond to overriding emotions by moments of silence which could help (a person) to step back from the emotion and from the passion to keep it at the centre of one's being. One might recall that this can explain why Gandhi had employed fasting in his own life as a method of reducing "…anger" (Gandhi 1888–1948, 44: 346) and substituting it by a "…clearness of vision…" (Ibid.). Such a stepping away from pain, anger, humiliation and even love was often effected by Gandhi through observing days of silence/fasting. The choice to distance himself from the intensity of strong emotions not only helped Gandhi to understand the emotions better but also helped him to make creative use of those emotions. One might then be able to delineate two aspects in Gandhi's response to overriding emotions. The first, a stepping back from the darkness of an overwhelming emotion, in order to understand it better, and the second, a creative and positive employment of the emotion itself in order to transform both the experiencing self and the "other".

Gandhi responded to different over powering emotions at different times of his life. These included those of suffering, humiliation, guilt/shame and even that of love. His response to the darkness of suffering and pain was to step away from their personal impact and creatively employ the "long burning track" (Tagore 2008, 122) of "sorrows" (Ibid.) in thinking up notions like *satyagraha/* a firmness on truth and *tapasya/* self-imposed pain. Both these notions became a part of Gandhi's method of earning rights by self-imposed suffering. Gandhi made a similar creative employment of the emotions of guilt and shame. It was such creative employment which was brought out at its best in Gandhi's efforts to evoke the shame of the *savarna* Hindu in connection with the removal of untouchability in Indian society;

> As not a few have sensed, like Socrates and Christ before him, Gandhi knew how to use man's sense of guilt creatively. (Nandy 2009, 93)

One might take note of Gandhi's several tours, fasts and arguments to evoke the guilt of *savarna* Hindus in order to effect a transformation of heart;

> …the caste Hindus who recognize that untouchability is a blot on Hinduism have to atone for the sin of untouchability. (Gandhi 1888–1948, 45: 231)

With the vow/*vrata* of *brahmacharya*/celibacy taken in 1906, Gandhi had effected an inner distance within himself from the overriding emotion of love/lust. He went on to emancipate the emotion of love from its unilateral and somewhat overwhelming preoccupation with its particular object—the person who was loved—and who thus came to be at the centre of the lover's being. Gandhi used the emotion of love (once it was thus emancipated from its passion for a singular object) as the universal love inherent in *ahimsa*/non-violence. Such love was put to work in Gandhian notions like *satyagraha,* where firmness about rights was imbued with a love for the opposing other. The transformed emotion of love also inspired *sewa*/service of those most distant from oneself. Such service became central to Gandhi's practice.

> Ahimsa means Universal Love. If a man gives his love to one woman, or a woman to one man, what is there left for all the world besides? It simply means, "We two first, and the devil take all the rest of them". As a faithful wife must be prepared to sacrifice her all for the sake of her husband, and a faithful husband for the sake of his wife, it is clear that such persons cannot rise to the height of Universal Love, or look upon all mankind as kith and kin. For they have created a boundary wall round their love. The larger their family, the farther are they from Universal Love. Hence one who would obey the law of ahimsa cannot marry, not to speak of gratification outside the marital bond. (Gandhi 1888–1948, 49: 420)

Gandhi had realized that unless the experiencer could put a distance between him/her self and the somewhat overriding experience of emotion there would be no way of working through the over powering and debilitating impact of such emotions on the individual, on the past and on the community. Creating a distance could, on this view, also enable one to work through the emotion and its blinding passion to put it to more creative use. One need only consider in this connection how differently the *itihaas* of India might have come to pass if Gandhi had not worked through his own feelings of humiliation and anger in the positive way that he had.

1.3   The Politics of Suffering

The third question important to the debate between Gandhi and Ambedkar concerned the issue of how one should understand and relate to a politics of suffering. This section will examine this issue across three sub-sections. The first will discuss Ambedkar's response to and articulation of the politics of suffering. The second will look at a more recent response to such a politics in *The Cracked Mirror: An Indian Debate on Experience and Theory* (Guru and Sarukkai (eds) 2012a). The third subsection will bring out Gandhi's response to the politics of suffering.

However, before one can ask this question, one needs to ask why it should even make sense to speak about the politics of suffering. Suffering surely belongs to the emotional life of an individual, and there are questions about whether it **can** even be spoken about by another. This for example is largely the burden of Guru and Sarukkai's argument which will be preliminarily raised in Sect. 1.3.2 and will form the subject of a more detailed discussion in the conclusion to this book. The "politics" of suffering can only make sense after suffering itself emerges from the sphere of that which is intensely private (to an individual's emotional life) into the public sphere where it can be seen, spoken and theorized about by people at large. The origin of the idea of the public sphere can be traced back to ancient Greece where the public sphere was conceptualized as being at complete contrast to/from the private realm (Arendt 1998, 28). The English word "idiot" in fact comes from the Greek noun *idiōtēs* signifying a private person, (as opposed to an official) a private citizen or a common man. It later came to be associated with the words "unskilled" or "ignorant" as derived from the adjective *idios* meaning private/one's own. One should recall that for the Greeks, the private realm, was the area which was bound to the necessity of life and was primarily for production and reproduction. It followed that the private sphere of individual life was not deemed as something to be protected from the manoeuvres of institutional power but was on the other hand considered to be a realm of deprivation. In fact "privacy" literally meant being deprived of things essential to humans. These last were the experiences of being seen and heard by other people. The public realm, on the other hand, was the realm of politics, action and freedom. It was the space in which one could be seen and heard by other human beings. The rise of the *polis* in ancient Greece meant that a human being received a life other than and alongside that of a private life. This was a second life, a political life[i] (Ibid., 24).

The politics of suffering in the context of the Ambedkar–Gandhi debate perhaps emerged from the shift of the emotion of suffering and its place in dalit experience from the private to the public sphere in the 1900s. It was Ambedkar who made it most visible in the public sphere in a space where it could be heard and responded to by the polity. Dalit suffering perhaps received another life, a second political life, in the context of Ambedkar's arguments about those who might have the right to represent the suffering of the untouchables in the legislatures which belonged squarely within the public sphere. Such arguments can be traced back to Ambedkar's assertion that the suffering/*duhkha* of the untouchables was different from any other kind of pain in that it belonged to the dalits who had suffered it. Consequently, it could only be understood (and significantly addressed) by those who had experienced the suffering, that is, by the legitimate owners of that social/collective experience of *duhkha*/suffering.

1.3.1 The Quagmire of Suffering: To Be Private/Idios or Public/Politeia[ii]

In his evidence before the Southborough Committee in 1919 Ambedkar had defined the modality of the existence of the untouchables in terms of suffering "The exact description of the treatment cannot be attempted. The word untouchable is the epitombe of their ills and sufferings" (Ambedkar 2014, 1: 256)[3]. Ambedkar brought such suffering into the public sphere by demanding that suffering was not only the modality of the being of the untouchable but that it was inalienable from the untouchables. He argued that any person who had not experienced such suffering could not indeed represent the untouchables in legislatures or in the high offices of government.

[3] Ambedkar 2014, refers to the 17 volumes of *Dr Babasaheb Ambedkar writings and Speeches*. The volume concerned and the page numbers from which citations have been drawn have been mentioned within parentheses. These have been mentioned to indicate the exact location of the quotation in the 17 volumes. However, for the purposes of reference, it may be noted that I have resourced these volumes from Ambedkar, B.R. 2014. *Dr Babasaheb Ambedkar writings and Speeches*, edited by Vasant Moon (set of 17 Volumes). New Delhi: Dr Ambedkar Foundation. Ministry of Social Justice and Empowerment. Government of India.

> The right of representation and the right to hold office under the state are the two most important rights that make up citizenship. But the untouchability of the untouchables puts these rights far beyond their reach. In a few places they do not even possess such insignificant rights as personal liberty and personal security, and equality before law is not always assured to them. These are the interests of the Untouchables. And as can be easily seen they can be represented by the Untouchables alone. They are distinctively their own interests and none else can truly voice them. A free trade interest can be voiced by a Brahmin, a Mohameddan or a Marathi equally well. But none can speak for the interests of the untouchables because they are not untouchables. Untouchability constitutes a definite set of interests which the untouchables alone can speak for. Hence it is evident that we must find the untouchables to represent their grievances which are their interests and, secondly, we must find them in such numbers as will constitute a force sufficient to claim redress. (Ibid.)

Ambedkar was clear that the right to represent suffering could not be shared with anyone *other than the one* who had experienced the suffering. Gandhi as discussed earlier had his own authentic experience of suffering which he had worked through by creatively re-employing it to end the suffering of others as it were. Perhaps such an experience led him to say (without this being inauthentic/in bad faith) that

> I claim myself in my own person to represent the vast majority of untouchables. (Gandhi 1888–1948, 54: 159)

> You are born an untouchable but I am an untouchable by adoption. And as a new convert I feel more for the welfare of the community than those who are already there. …I do not like it from the beginning that the community should be divided into two groups. I will raze to the ground the fort of sanatanists with dynamite if all the untouchables are one and united. I want that the entire untouchable community should unitedly rebel against the sanatanists. (Gandhi 1888–1948, 57: 440)

Ambedkar could not accept Gandhi's claim to represent the suffering of the untouchables. In his view Gandhi could not legitimately claim a oneness with the victims of a suffering which could not be his. In 1931, Ambedkar voiced such a critique of Gandhi during the meeting of the Minorities Committee in London;

> The Mahatma has been always claiming that the Congress stands for the Depressed Classes, and that the Congress represents the Depressed classes more than I or my colleague can do. To that claim I can only say that it is one of the many false claims which irresponsible people keep on making ,although the persons concerned with regard to those claims have been invariably denying them. (Ambedkar 2014, 9: 65)

Ambedkar had articulated the relationship between suffering and political representation at first as/in a demand for reserved seats in legislatures for the untouchables;

> …it was felt that in the case of the Untouchables mere right to vote would not be enough… It was feared that a member elected on the votes of the Untouchables, if he is himself not an Untouchable, might play false and might take no interest in them. (Ambedkar 2014, 5: 351)

However, the relationship of inextricability between suffering and injustice demanded more than simply a limitation which restricted the right to *represent* suffering. This led Ambedkar to add in 1932 that there was need to qualify the right to represent suffering with additional limitations. This lead him, in fact, to replace

the demand for reserved seats for untouchables through a "system of joint electorates" (Ambedkar 2014, 3: 671) by the right to elect representatives "…through
separate electorates of their voters" (Ibid.). It is interesting to note that the text of the
Communal Award (negotiated by Ambedkar at the second round table conference)
specified both reserved seats and the assurance of two votes to the depressed classes;

> Members of the "depressed classes" qualified to vote will vote in a general constituency …a
> number of special seats will be assigned to them… These seats will be filled by election
> from special constituencies in which only members of the "depressed classes" electorally
> qualified will be entitled to vote. Any person voting in such a special constituency will, as
> stated above, be also entitled to vote in a general constituency. (Ambedkar 2014, 5: 332)

Ambedkar's point was that the untouchables could not be represented by those
in whose election the oppressors of untouchables had played any part. This was
because members who had been elected (even in part) by votes of oppressors could
not but **"play false"** (Ibid., 351) to the interest and suffering of the untouchables.
The collective suffering of the untouchables was on this view inextricable from
the injustice perpetrated by oppressors and those who came in the lineage of the
oppressors were suspect on that account. Indeed on Ambedkar's understanding, any
kind of continuity with such a past or, with those who had been implicated in the
injustice of the past, would only perpetuate that injustice.

In this context, it is interesting to note that Ambedkar had himself apprehended
the conflict somewhat internal to the demand for separate electorates. This was the
conflict between the politics of suffering and the politics of democracy. Perhaps one
might describe such a conflict as the quagmire/entrapping predicament somewhat
internal to the idea of a separate/communal electorate in a democratic polity. One
might spell out this conflict to make it clearer. One could consider that if suffering
belonged to the sphere of the political and thereby the public sphere in a democracy
(consider that a demand for representation made sense only in a democracy), it
was no longer private. Once it became public and entered the liberal democratic
space requiring to be represented, it needed to be governed by the principles of the
democratic space. Such principles central to the spirit of democracy involved the idea
of each person counting for one (and not more than one) and the rule of the majority. It
followed from such principles that the victims of suffering could not claim separate
electorates on at least two counts. The first reason was that they could not claim
a double vote and the second that they could not claim that they represented the
will of the majority and should indeed make laws to govern the democratic polity.
This last would have gone against the principle of consent central to democratic
governance; because the existence of the separate electorate would mean that the
untouchable candidates were in fact making law to govern the polity though they
had been elected by only a small subset of the citizens of that same polity. Ambedkar
had himself made arguments against separate electorates prior to the second round
table conference voicing this very same conflict between separate electorates and the
principles of democratic government in 1928–29;

Apart from the question whether separate electorates are necessary to protect separate interests, it is necessary to be certain that there are any interests which can be said to be separate
in the sense that they are not the interests of any other community. In the secular, as distinguished from the religious field, every matter is a matter of general concern to all. Whether
taxes should be paid or not, if so, what and at what rate; whether national expenditure should
be directed in any particular channel more than any other; whether education should be free
and compulsory; whether Government lands should be disposed of on restricted tenure or
occupancy tenure; whether State aid should be granted to industries; whether there should
be more police in any particular area; whether the State should provide against poverty of
the working classes by a scheme of social insurance against sickness, unemployment or
death; whether the administration of justice is best served by the employment of honorary
magistrates, and whether the code of medical ethics or legal ethics should be altered so as
to produce better results, are some of the questions that usually come before the Council.
(Ambedkar 2014, 2: 350–351)

In his presentation to the Simon Commission (Indian Statutory Commission)
in 1928–1929, Ambedkar had himself brought in the afore mentioned principle
of consent central to democratic governance in connection with the communal
electorates which were also separate electorates;

Now, it is an universally recognized canon of political life that the Government must be
by the consent of the governed. From what I have said above communal electorates are a
violation of that canon. For, it is government without consent. It is contrary to all sense of
political justice to approve of a system which permits the members of one community to
rule other communities without their having submitted themselves to the suffrage of those
communities. (Ibid., 354-355)

In a sense such a quagmire between suffering as private to those who own it and its
claim to a public political presence (from which others were barred) is inescapable
by the nature of the case. This is a quagmire that continues into more contemporary
discussions on the owners of experience and authors of theory about such private
experience. In such discussions, it is the proprietors of suffering alone who can be
authors in the essentially shared democratic and public domain of theorizing in the
social sciences.

1.3.2   Suffering: Owners and Authors

Moving on from the quagmire somewhat internal to Ambedkar's articulation of the
politics of suffering (as an essentially private experience that becomes central to the
public realm), it becomes important to examine other articulations of the politics
of suffering in more recent times. To pre-empt the discussion which will follow
in the concluding chapter, it is significant to recall that Guru and Sarukkai have
raised questions about the ownership of suffering and the right to theorize about the
experience of such suffering in the practice of the social sciences. On this view, the
politics of suffering extends into the politics of theorizing about suffering. The latter
rests upon the title to the ownership of the experience of *duhkha*/suffering itself and
the relationship between owners and authors;

> Yes I can …argue that somebody can still claim to have ownership of this experience for the simple reason that it is embedded in this person and someone is the carrier of this experience. (Guru 2012b, 124)

Guru and Sarukkai question "…why this continued distrust of experience in the construct of the theoretical?" (Guru and Sarukkai 2012b, 3) On this view, social science has been developed on the model of the natural sciences. In the same book, *The Cracked Mirror* Sundar Sarukkai reminds us that this should not unduly influence the social scientist who must reflect on the choice before her/him;

> Following the development of the theoretical stance in natural sciences, social science can decide to ignore the experiential and the subject as integral components of theorizing or it can create its own style by building upon these as core elements. (Sarukkai 2012b, 135-136)

On such a view, a social science theory (properly re constituted) would need to involve the subject and his/her experience as integral elements in the act of theorizing. One is already familiar with a long chain of arguments which have made the methodological point that a theorist speaking about the practices of a group should look at them from the point of view of those who are involved in the practices. What is meant by restructuring theory around practice, in Guru and Sarukkai's version of the argument, involves much more than taking a view from inside it. It means that the theoretician *must be inside* the group or a legitimate owner of the experience itself in order to write about it. In addition (on this view), the theoretician cannot be inside the group unless he/she belongs to the group as someone who has been born into the lived experience concerned by being born as a dalit or an *adivasi*/tribal as the case may be.

Guru has brought forth moral arguments to build up an ethics of doing theory which should be reconstituted by responding to the need to articulate experiences in the mind of a group whose experience is being written about. He has argued that the individual self is an encumbered self with a historical memory which can be that of an oppressive past. Such a self is situated in a set of cultural and social practices and has experiences about which he/she needs to theorize indeed, about which, he/she *ought to* theorize. It should be part of the ethics of doing theory to build theory around this need and the moral duty of the subject who has the right to speak.

Sarukkai has (in the same book) examined the term "experience" to argue that what we call experience comes powerfully mediated in, by and through, concepts we already have. There is little or no experience which comes to an individual completely innocent of concepts. Social science theory, which reflects upon experience, is also dependent on concepts, which are, for the most part derived from Western knowledge traditions. This leads Sarukkai to raise ethical concerns about the need to choose the right concepts;

> To do theory is to chose certain kinds of concepts and structures, and this choice cannot be legitimized on an epistemological basis alone but should also be ethically answerable to what is right or wrong in talking about certain experiences. Thus the chosen concepts are not only judged on whether they are 'correct' or not but whether they are also 'right' or not. (Ibid., 153)

On this view, it becomes imperative for the social scientist to ask normative questions about doing theory. One can, for instance, ask—"Who really has the right to theorize in the social sciences? This is a problem that has affected many of us, both in academics and outside" (Sarukkai 2012a, 30). In terms of this argument such a question can be asked about the social sciences in general, the practice of the social sciences in India, and about the social sciences seeking to say something about dalit experience, in particular. Much of the arguments in *The Cracked Mirror* have indeed been preoccupied with the normative concerns relating to theoretical "outsiders" who seek to reflect upon tribal or dalit experience. It has been argued that

> ...speaking for the Dalits (or anybody) constitutes a *jajmani* relationship, structurally involving a patron and a client. In the present case, the *muknayak* becomes the patron, and the 'dumb' becomes the client to define the patron. The patron ,in a very ironical sense, tends to reproduce the Brahminical mechanism of first controlling knowledge resources and then pouring them into the empty cupped palms of Dalits. (Guru 2012a, 25–26)

On this view, there is a necessity somewhat internal to the dalit self to be able to speak about his/her experience. This is also a social necessity one that expresses the need for the dalits to become "the subject" of their own thinking. Guru and Sarukkai also recommend that the dalit ***ought to*** theorize about such experiences. Such insights become the ground for the argument that there is a limitation on non-dalits in that they ***ought not*** to "appropriate" dalit experience by attempting to theorize about it. This last raises more general normative questions—those related to the right to theorize-about another's experience. Guru asks "How ethically sound" (Guru 2012b, 126) such a position might be. He speaks pejoratively in this context of those who "try hard to become the author of somebody else's experience?" (Ibid.)

In such a context, it becomes important to ask what it is to have or experience an emotion like suffering? An emotion one might find is a complex mental phenomenon: it is not just a sensation or mere feeling—it must have a structure surrounding it—a feeling or experience certainly more or less complex—but an experience embedded in a structure of thought and beliefs which enable it to be articulated and thus rendered intelligible and assessable. We also know that an emotion need not be just that of an individual, it is often shared by a group or a community. The dalit experience is shared by the dalits. But one needs to note that Guru and Sarukkai have made the following additional claims: (i) no one outside the Dalit community—particularly people who have been involved in the humiliation and annihilation of the self-respect of dalits—can share the experience; (ii) an outsider cannot therefore articulate the experience with any degree of authentic understanding; (iii) the outsider, thus, is necessarily incapable of theorizing about the dalit experience in order to make the experience generally intelligible; (iv) attempts to theorize about the dalit experience of suffering by the outsider must therefore be necessarily hypocritical or self-deceptive. (v) Such attempts, therefore, must attract moral suspicion, if not outright condemnation. I have very serious reservations about these claims and shall take them up for discussion in the concluding chapter of this book.

However, to pre-empt that argument, one can ask if it is possible to argue (as Guru and Sarukkai have argued indeed) that the inextricability between injustice and suffering in the dalit experience makes for the right of ownership of that experience; in a manner so that those who are not owners (like Gandhi) would be trespassers if they venture to try to understand it? Further, one might also ask if it is possible to question the organizing insight of the argument in *The Cracked Mirror* that the right to speak or theorize about the experience of unjust suffering cannot belong to ***anyone*** who does not own the experience of the unjust suffering/*duhkha* concerned? While these questions will be raised (as already mentioned) in the concluding chapter, one might bring up the quagmire/entrapping predicament inherent to the position that only owners of suffering can be authors of theory about that experience. Consider that on Guru's position only the single person who experiences suffering can be owner of it and the author of any theory about it. Such an experience as Sarukkai explains belongs to the person whose experience it necessarily is. "Lived experience" refers only to "those experiences that are seen as *necessary,* experiences over which the subject has no choice whether to experience or not… Even if the experience is unpleasant, there is no choice that allows the subject to leave or even modify it" (Sarukkai 2012a, 35).

On this view, the experience belongs only to the one who cannot choose ***not to have it***. An experience, which the experiencer ***cannot choose not to have***, cannot belong to anyone else; because it cannot be a *necessary* experience of any one other, than the one person whose ***necessary*** experience it is. Sarukkai paraphrases Guru's claim about owners and authors saying "that only those who experience can theorize implies that only an owner can be an author" (Ibid., 38). On this view, theory cannot be legitimated by establishing a distance from experience. If it is at a distance it will be "vicarious" on two counts. First because it vicariously appropriates the "others" experience and then because the appropriator tries to do theory vicariously as a site to "distribute… guilt" (Ibid., 44) about what he/she has done to the "other" who has been the victim.

Guru and Sarukkai have argued from these premises that the experience of suffering cannot be spoken about or theorized about by anyone who is not an owner. Yet one might consider that if the owner is an author doing any kind of theory, he/she must be able to speak in the context of other experiences significantly like his/her own. More importantly, others must be able to speak about, understand and discuss such experiences in the public conceptual space constituting the practice of the social sciences. By the nature of the case, such a public theoretical space is one where others have voices very much like the voice of the sufferer. One might consider that the only way in which one might become a part of the practice of theorizing in the social sciences is to enter such a conceptual domain. This might bring out the quagmire/predicament of the politics of theorizing about suffering. Either suffering is private and there can be no theorizing (as something which involves more than one voice) about it or it is public. If it is public, one might consider that it will become incoherent to say that it cannot be understood and spoken about with and by another. If it can be so understood and spoken about by another for instance from the same community (by another dalit perhaps who has the right to speak about other similar dalit experiences of suffering), how can it be argued that non-dalit "others" from outside the community who have similar experiences (in the relevant respects) must not speak/theorize about such an experience?

1.3.3   Gandhi on the Politics of Suffering

One might now consider Gandhi's answer to the question "how should one respond to a politics of suffering?" The first issue is whether Gandhi thought that suffering was private to the sufferer as in an experience that belonged to the realm of the inner life. Could Gandhi bring suffering out into the public realm, that of the political, as it were? On the face of it, it seems fairly apparent that Gandhi could bring suffering, love and even lust, out from the domain of the inner to that of the public realm, i.e. the realm of the political. Yet the politics of suffering in Gandhi took on a very different form from that which it took in the life and work of Ambedkar. There are a number of reasons which can explain these differences and stating these reasons would also bring out the manner in which Gandhi responded to the politics of suffering.

To begin with, Gandhi's understanding of politics had a bearing upon his understanding of the politics of suffering. Gandhi had thought of politics by distinguishing between "power politics" and what he described as "true politics". This distinction had important bearings on his understanding of the politics of suffering. Another important insight which had bearings on Gandhi's understanding of the politics of suffering was his answer to the second question which was raised earlier; that of how one should respond to overriding emotions. This (one might recall) involved a consideration of whether one could adopt some distance from one's own experience of an emotion so as to be able to understand the emotion itself and further to understand the relationship between that emotion and reality. It is to these points that I will turn in this section.

To begin with how Gandhi understood politics itself. One might recall here a speech Gandhi made to the Gandhi Seva Sangh on 21 February 1940;

> We used politics to put our principle into practice. Now after some experience we are renouncing politics. The politics we are renouncing is the politics of acquiring positions of power within the Congress. But this power politics is such a snare that even individuals may have to quit it. (Gandhi 1888–1948, 77: 377–78)

Gandhi went on to explain what he meant by "true politics";

> Politics pervades all our activities. But I am not talking of retirement from politics in this broad sense. I am referring to the politics of the congress and elections and to groupism…I have not forbidden all political activity. I know that in this country all constructive activities are part of politics. In my view that is true politics. Non-violence can have nothing to do with the politics of power. (Ibid., 371)

Gandhi argued that "true politics" had to do with "constructive effort… actual taking over of the Government machinery is but a shadow, an emblem…" (Gandhi 1888–1948, 53: 4). He suggested that such constructive effort could be "performed

independently of any political power" (Gandhi 1888–1948, 68: 123). An engagement with Gandhi's true politics meant that persons who were interested in such
engagements would have to become "fitter instruments of service" (Ibid.);

> That is why I can take the keenest interest in discussing vitamins and leafy vegetables and
> unpolished rice. That is why it has become a matter of absorbing interest to me to find out
> how best to clean our latrines, how best to save our people from the heinous sin of fouling
> Mother Earth every morning. I do not quite see how thinking of these necessary problems
> and finding a solution for them has no political significance and how an examination of the
> financial policy of Government has necessarily a political bearing. (Ibid.)

Gandhi had clearly specified that true politics involved constructive efforts of the
kind elaborated above. This meant that the politics of suffering meant quite different
things to him and to Ambedkar. Much of Ambedkar's response to the politics of
suffering had been built around the idea that only one who was an untouchable could
represent the interests of the untouchables and that such representation was inextricably connected with becoming a separate power group in Indian politics (through
for instance the institution of the separate electorate). Gandhi thought somewhat
differently. For one thing, he thought that though the oppressors had committed the
sin of untouchability their own emotions of guilt and shame could be worked upon
creatively in order "to effect a conversion of the heart" (Nagraj 2015: 46) and grow
into the ability to feel compassion for the suffering which they could not own. For
another, he thought that *savarna* Hindus could respond to and even enter the politics of suffering. This was possible because the "true politics" of suffering was that
which called forth constructive effort. Such effort was also perhaps the only authentic
response that the guilty oppressors could make to their own guilt as it were.

> Untouchability is the sin of the Hindus. They must suffer for it they must purify themselves,
> …Their blind eyes will not be opened by outside interference, however well intentioned or
> generous it may be; for it will not bring home to them the sense of guilt. (Gandhi 1888–1948,
> 27: 321–22)

Taking his *que* from the ancient Indian traditions where the human condition had
been seen to be inextricable from both mortality and a vulnerability to suffering
Gandhi thought that, though they could not experience the *duhkha/* suffering of the
untouchables, the *savarna* Hindus as oppressors (whose predecessors had set up the
pernicious caste system) could make sense of their experience of guilt by gaining
insights into the enormity of their sin. Such a reflection on guilt and an understanding
of its genesis would lead the oppressor to an understanding of the suffering of the
victim (as akin perhaps to that which the oppressor had experienced on account
of racial oppression). More importantly, such compassion could lead the oppressor
to an awareness of his/her own implication in such injustice. Addressing or rather
redressing that sin could then be effected by the oppressor by instituting constitutional safeguards for the victim and perhaps (more importantly) by seeking self-
transformation of both her/himself and of the oppressive community of which he/she
formed a part.

Gandhi had often enough shared his own feelings of guilt and of the somewhat
self-transformative feeling of oneness with the suffering/*duhkha* of the untouchables

(made possible perhaps by the very experience of guilt and shame on account of being implicated in the collective sin of untouchability);

> Though I am touchable by birth past fifty years I have been an untouchable by choice. (cable to William L Shirer, correspondent of the Chicago Tribune, in September 1932 in Gandhi 1888–1948, 57: 106)

One might consider that in these and numerous other such statements, Gandhi could only have meant that the choice he had made was to share in the pain of the untouchables through a self-conscious understanding of his own, all too human *qua* human, vulnerability to suffering; and through an owning of an implication in (and continuity with) an unjust past.

1.4 Concluding Remarks

Having considered both Ambedkar and Gandhi's responses to the three questions framed here, it becomes important to take note of the close affinity between Ambedkar's position and that of modernity. One might reflect on the idea that it is perhaps modernity itself which presented Ambedkar with a different, and apparently more comfortable, set of options to frame answers to these questions. This is because modernity enables the self to think of itself as a different kind of self. One who, as it will turn out (and this will form the subject of Chap. 3 in the book) draws meaning from his/her own individual inwardness and who can therefore choose not to seek continuity with herself/himself as the subject of a painful past. Such a self, as it will turn out, does not also need to *choose to be distant* from the experience of overriding emotions. Quite to the contrary emotions become somewhat essential to the modern self and help that self express her/himself. Chapter 3 of this book will also bring out the importance of such expressivism as an aspect in the making of modern identity.

It might then seem apparent that on the modern account, the self does not need to seek comfort from aspects of the multifaceted past, which might help to mitigate the pain of the experience of injustice and suffering. This is perhaps because the modern self can choose to write history and choose a measure to write such a history. Post the indictment of history, the notion of Justice as fairness in the distribution of benefits and burdens in society, with the Constitution of a Nation as the text, can become part of the mechanism (in the present) to make good the injustice of the past.

Chapter 5 of the present book will make some effort to articulate Gandhi and Ambedkar's alternative insights on what could be meant by the term "justice". It remains then the task of Chap. 4 to bring out the details of that which had so happened in the debate between Gandhi and Ambedkar. In this context, Sect. 4.1.2 of Chapter 4 will unpack Ambedkar's Indictment of Gandhi's response to the *duhkha* or suffering of the untouchables' of India, made across three texts; *Mr Gandhi and the Emancipation of Untouchables* (1942); *Ranade Gandhi and Jinnah* (1943) and

What Congress and Gandhi have done to the Untouchables (1945).[4] In a search for truth without measure, Chap. 4 will also philosophically unpack Gandhi's arguments about absolute equality in the *Bhagavad Gita* and his response to caste and *Varna*.

The six chapters in this book will seek to bring out, in different ways, the organizing insight of the book that, with Ambedkar;

> …we have not just a new localization of thought, valuation—even feeling, as we shall see—but a new kind of localization. The two world views (those of Ambedkar and Gandhi) are incommensureable. They don't determine similar maps within which we can pick out different places; they determine altogether different notions of place… (Taylor 2001, 187). (the parenthesis are my own addition)

It is this incommensurability and very different conceptual maps (organising the ideas of Gandhi and Ambedkar) that this book will go on to unpack. A note on philosophy would be in order here to emphasize that good philosophy should not perhaps, so much as seek to arbitrate between world views, as seek to show that there are different world views at stake in conflicts that cannot be forgotten.

Notes

i.   While the origin of the idea of the "public" sphere can be traced back to ancient Greece, most current discussions are influenced by Habermas. Habermas' larger political project, his theory of communication, and his scattered comments on media converge on the concept of the public sphere (Peters 1993, 541–542). It is the leading motive throughout his theories: the theory of communicative action, discourse-ethics theory, procedural-discursive democracy theory, civil society and the constitutional state theory.

ii. An ancient Greek word used in Greek political thought, especially that of Plato and Aristotle. Derived from the word *polis* ("city-state"), it has a range of meanings from "the rights of citizens" to a "form of government".

References

Ambedkar, B. R. 2011. *The Buddha and his dhamma.* Eds. and Trans. Aakash Singh Rathore and Ajay Verma. New Delhi: Oxford University Press.
Ambedkar, B.R. 2014. *Dr Babasaheb Ambedkar writings and speeches,* ed. Vasant Moon. 17 Vols. New Delhi: Dr Ambedkar Foundation. Ministry of Social Justice and Empowerment, Government of India.
Ardent, H. 1998. *The human condition.* Chicago, London: University of Chicago Press.

---

[4] The year mentioned within parentheses against the texts represent their original year of publication. These have been mentioned to show the chronology of the books. However, for the purposes of reference, I have resourced these books from the set of 17 volumes entitled *Dr. Babasaheb Ambedkar writings and Speeches,* edited by Vasant Moon, 2014. New Delhi: Dr. Ambedkar Foundation. Ministry of Social Justice and Empowerment. Government of India.

Bhattacharya, K.C. 2011. *Swaraj* in ideas. In *Indian Philosophy in English: From Renaissance to Independence*, eds. Nalini Bhushan and Jay L. Garfield, 103–114. New York: Oxford University Press.

Bhattacharya, S. ed 2008. *The Mahatma and the poet: Letters and debates between Gandhi and Tagore,* 1915–1941, 5th ed. New Delhi: National Book Trust.

Gandhi, M. K. 1888–1948. *Collected works of Mahatma Gandhi.* 98 Vols. https://www.gandhiash ramsevagram.org/gandhi-literature/collected-works-of-mahatma-gandhi-volume-1-to-98.php (accessed May 2021).

Guru, Gopal & Sarukkai, S. (eds) 2012a. *The cracked mirror: An Indian debate on experience and theory.* New Delhi: Oxford University Press.

Guru, Gopal & Sarukkai, S. 2012b. Introduction. In *The cracked mirror: An Indian debate on experience and theory.* eds. Gopal Guru and Sundar Sarukkai, 3–8. New Delhi: Oxford University Press.

Guru, Gopal. 2012a. Egalitarianism and the Social Sciences in India. In *The cracked mirror: An Indian debate on experience and theory.* eds. Gopal Guru and Sundar Sarukkai, 9–28. New Delhi: Oxford University Press.

Guru, Gopal. 2012b. Experience and the ethics of theory. In *The cracked mirror: An Indian debate on experience and theory.* eds. Gopal Guru and Sundar Sarukkai, 107–27. New Delhi: Oxford University Press.

MacIntyre, A. 1988. *Whose justice? which rationality?* Notre Dame, Indiana: University of Notre Dame Press.

Nagraj, D. R. 2015. *The flaming feet and other essays: The Dalit Movement in India.* Ed. Prithvi Datta Chandra Shobhi. Ranikhet: Permanent Black.

Nandy, A. 2009. *Exile at home.* New Delhi: Oxford University Press.

Nandy, A. 2015. Foreword to *The flaming feet and other essays: The Dalit Movement in India.* by D. R. Nagraj. Ed. Prithvi Datta Chandra Shobhi. Ranikhet: Permanent Black.

Peters, John Durham. 1993. Distrust of representation: Habermas on the public sphere. *Media, Culture & Society.* 15 (4): 541–571.

Puri, Bindu. 2015. *The Gandhi Tagore debate: On matters of truth and untruth.* Sophia: Studies in Cross-cultural Philosophy of Traditions and Cultures, vol. 9. New Delhi: Springer.

Rathore, Aakash Singh and Ajay Verma, eds. 2011. Introduction. *The Buddha and his dhamma. A critical Edition.* ix–xxiv. New Delhi: Oxford University Press.

Sarukkai, S. 2012a. Experience and theory: From Habermas to Gopal Guru. In *The cracked mirror: An Indian debate on experience and theory.* eds. Gopal Guru and Sundar Sarukkai, 29–45. New Delhi: Oxford University Press.

Sarukkai, S. 2012b. Ethics of theorizing. In *The cracked mirror: An Indian debate on experience and theory.* eds. Gopal Guru and Sundar Sarukkai, 128–56. New Delhi: Oxford University Press.

Shobhi, Prithvi Datta Chandra. 2015. Introduction to *The flaming feet and other essays: The Dalit Movement in India.* by D. R. Nagraj. Ed. Prithvi Datta Chandra Shobhi. Ranikhet: Permanent Black.

Tagore, R. 2008. *The English writings of Rabindranath Tagore,* vol. 3. Ed. S.K. Das. New Delhi: Sahitya Akademi.

Tagore, Rabindranath 2012. *The home and the world.* In *Rabindranath Tagore Omnibus,* vol. 3, 205–425. New Delhi: Rupa Publications India Pvt. Ltd.

Taylor, C. 2001. *Sources of the Self: The Making of the Modern Identity.* Cambridge: Harvard University Press.

Vajpeyi, A. 2013. *Righteous republic: The political foundations of modern India.* Harvard: Harvard University Press.

Chapter 2
Memory, History and *Itihaas:* Ambedkar and Gandhi

Abstract This chapter will move away from the more apparent differences between Ambedkar and Gandhi to examine the differences between their conceptions of memory, history and *itihaas*. While the modern discipline of history involves "measure" and a third-party judgement of the past; *Itihaas* or it so happened, is a retelling of what happened in the past without any attempt at a third party adjudication by measure. The chapter will argue that Ambedkar's self-understanding was "present-centred" and that he saw the past as history and made forays into it by writing two histories—that of the *Shudra*s and of the untouchables. For the old-world Gandhi however there was no writing of history only the telling of an *itihaas* of a people/nation.

Keywords History/*itihaas* · Third party · Modern identity · Memory · Alternative pasts · *Swabhava*/own most orientation · Specific · Ravidas · Kinship · *Satya*/truth · Amnesia

There has been much said about the debate between **Bhimrao Ramji Ambedkar** (1891–1956) and **Mohandas Karamchand Gandhi** (1869–1948)[i]. Gandhi's position on the issues that divided the two has come in for criticism both within and outside of the dalit [ii] movement. Even for scholars who admire Gandhi, his hesitation in rejecting the Hindu past/caste, holding on to an idealized version of *varna* and position against separate electorates has been difficult to support. It is surely telling that even so sympathetic an account, as that offered by Kolge (2018, 102), characterizes Gandhi's approach to untouchability as strategic and containing the "occasional tactic".

The Ambedkar–Gandhi debate is perhaps the most important debate in the intellectual history of India with consequences that continue to reverberate into the contemporary political social and religious life of India. One reason why the debate is as important as it is, is perhaps because it was a conflict between two good men both of whom were equally committed to correcting the wrongs of the past. D. R. Nagaraj brings out the "irony of history" that "Gandhi and Ambedkar confronted each other bitterly on the question of Dalits" (Nagaraj [1993] 2015, 77–78). He asks whether "…Gandhi and Ambedkar" were "really different in their perceptions of the Dalit Problem?" (Ibid, 78). Nagaraj argues "…both of them had basically perceived this as a problem of value" (Ibid, 78). Perhaps in their own way each of them was aware of the other's goodness and commitment to resolving the problem of untouchability. While Ambedkar was bitterly critical of Gandhi one cannot forget that it was Ambedkar who had initially appreciated that it was Gandhi who had first brought up the issue of untouchability in Indian politics. Gandhi, on his part, continued to appreciate, Ambedkar's tremendous and single-minded devotion to the same cause. It is interesting in this context to look at a letter that Gandhi wrote to Ambedkar (fairly late in the debate) on 6th August 1944:

> I know to my cost that you and I hold different views on this very important question. And I know, too, that on broad politics of the country we see things from different angles. I would love to find a meeting ground between us on both the questions. I know your great ability and I would love to own you as a colleague and co-worker. But I must admit my failure to come nearer to you. If you can show me a way to a common meeting ground between us I would like to see it. Meanwhile, I must reconcile myself to the present unfortunate difference. (Gandhi 1888–1948, 84: 272)[1]

The debate is also important because of the importance of the issues it raised about identity, equality, community, and justice. In this chapter, I want to bring out what it is that makes this debate so crucial to the contemporary intellectual, political, religious and social life of India long after the protagonists have departed this land, and indeed the world.

Attempting to explain why this debate is as important as it is will take me far afield from the immediate issues that divided Gandhi and Ambedkar. It will also involve much more than a purely historical analysis[iii] of, when and how, Gandhi's positions evolved, and how they changed over time. The discussion of this debate will move far afield from a meticulous account of events, dates, and politics. In fact, the discussion will move to the making of the modern self in the western world (through philosophical developments between the seventeenth and mid twentieth centuries) to show how that self-understanding came to influence the notion of the self in the thought of Babasaheb Ambedkar. It is surely befitting that modern identity initially appeared, at its best, in dalit consciousness and in the person of Dr. Babasaheb Ambedkar. Once it arrived it was the modern self who led the debates in the constituent assembly as the old-world Indian was reborn as the citizen of a liberal contractarian democracy. This chapter (and book) will argue that the Ambedkar–Gandhi debate was the space in which one can locate the forging of modern identity as it came to be in its confrontations with more traditional notions of the self which had hitherto dominated the mind of India.

---

[1] Gandhi 1888–1948, refers to the *Collected Works of Mahatma Gandhi.* The volume concerned and the page numbers from which citations from Gandhi are drawn have been mentioned within parentheses. These have been mentioned to indicate the exact location of the quotation in the electronic edition of the *Collected Works of Mahatma Gandhi.* However, for the purposes of reference, it may be noted that I have resourced these volumes from the *Collected Works of Mahatma Gandhi:* Volumes 1 to 98. New Delhi: Publications Division Government of India, 1999. Accessed online in May 2021 at https://www.gandhiashramsevagram.org/gandhiliterature/collected-works-of-mah atma-gandhi-volume-1-to-98.php.

Both Gandhi and Ambedkar had been educated in the West which initiated their conceptual and practical engagements with western modernity. However, they went on to develop very different approaches in their responses to modernity, and to its liberal contractarian compulsions to nation building. Many have argued that the nationalist movement was the site of the contestations for modernity between Gandhi and Ambedkar. On one view, while Gandhi thought that modernity could flourish within the limits of the Hindu society, Ambedkar thought that Indian society, in its present condition, would resist the principle of modernity (Verma 2020). Nagaraj looks for "… the root of confrontation between Gandhi and Ambedkar" (Nagaraj [1993] 2015, 78). He locates this in the fact that

> Gandhi represents the traditional Indian mode of tackling the problem of untouchability…the self and the other are indivisible in that mode of perception…. Ambedkar represents the modern Western mode and is closer to militant socialist methods of the Western variety. (Ibid., 78)

Perhaps the positions of Gandhi and Ambedkar were complicated and neither of their responses to the call of nationalism could be reduced to the status of a mere reproduction of western modernity. However, it is also true that it was only in the person of Ambedkar that modern Indian identity came to be. This was an identity that was not only alien to Gandhi but one that he could not and did not aspire for/towards.

It is important to recall that the debate on modernity occupied the minds of (not only these two thinkers but) all Indian intellectuals in the early twentieth century. In fact, the issue of what might encompass the conception of "modernity" could be seen to have directed many of the contestations in the Indian Renaissance[iv]. Gandhi rejected modernity and its central notions and his epistemological strength derived from the manner in which he used reason to critically interrogate and reform tradition. For Ambedkar, however, modernity was the larger project of emancipation through democratic means and a rewritten egalitarian religion.

2.1 Two Good Men: On History and Memory

It is important to locate the ideas which underlay the conflicts between Gandhi and Ambedkar. On the face of it these were conflicts about separate electorates, the status of the ideal village in Gandhi's writing, the approach to be taken for the removal of untouchability or Gandhi's defence of an idealized version of *varna.* This section will move away from these differences to examine insights from Gandhi and Ambedkar on history and *itihaas.* Such insights become important to showing that the opposition between them cannot be understood in terms of a straightforward opposition between the contrary demands of politics and justice simply because both of them were on the same side. They were both interested in securing justice for the depressed classes. Yet this last should not be taken to mean that they were seeking justice in the same way (or even that they meant the same things by the term "securing justice"). The exchanges in this debate are symptomatic of a far deeper conflict, one between, world views. This deeper conflict has to do with the making of modern identity in India and the dismantling of traditional notions of the self and its relation to the past. Perhaps one might say that this debate brought the "the old-world mind of India" (to use K. C. Bhattacharya's term) into head long conflict with modern notions of the self and modern ideas of what life in the world (for that self) involved.

Gandhi had made a well-known (and oft commented) critique of modernity in the 1909 *Hind Swaraj*. In this little book, Gandhi made a distinction between modern civilization and true civilization and he went on to criticize all the apparent aspects/effects of modernity—the legal and medical professions, modern medicine, speed and railways, and political institutions like the Parliament. It is important to note that Gandhi's critique of western modernity was not couched in personal terms of a hatred of the British people or even of colonialism. His reproach of western modernity was directed at its espousal of an isolated life of self-centredness which (in his view) resulted in an emotive, religious and moral vacuum in the inner life of the modern self. Gandhi argued that such a notion of the self (at the heart of modern life and its institutions) had important consequences on life in the community, on nature and on individuals (Parekh 1989: 38). Having diagnosed the deep malaise at the heart of modernity Gandhi advised Indians and Europeans alike to return to their own ancient civilizations. Ambedkar rejected Gandhi's advice and arguments (as put forth in *Hind Swaraj*) against modern civilization (Ambedkar 2014, 9: 282–283)[2]. For Ambedkar, these were "old and worn out arguments" (Ibid., 283), "[t]he ideas which go to make up Gandhism are just primitive. It is a return to nature, to animal life" (Ibid.).

Ambedkar was certainly right to conclude that Gandhi's critique of modernity was intended to advocate a return to more ancient world views based upon the unity between man and nature. Gandhi was opposed to the self at the heart of modernity and to the way of life that he identified with modern civilization and its technological consequences. The next chapter will discuss some aspects of Charles Taylor's (2001) account of the making of modern identity across two centuries in western philosophical thought. This will serve to bring out the deep variance between the modern self and an alternative Gandhian understanding. One will, however, get preliminary glimpses of that opposition in the discussion between Gandhi and Ambedkar on the differences between history and *itihaas.*

The reader might well wonder why I look so far afield at alternative understandings, of history, *itihaas,* and memory (in Gandhi and Ambedkar) as important to understanding the notion of self and as important to the debate between them. The answer lies in how "experience concerns the ways in which the past is used and lives in the present, while expectation deals with the dreams for tomorrow and the point in

---

[2] Ambedkar 2014, refers to the 17 volumes of *Dr Babasaheb Ambedkar writings and Speeches.* The volume concerned and the page numbers from which citations have been drawn have been mentioned within parentheses. These have been mentioned to indicate the exact location of the quotation in the 17 volumes. However, for the purposes of reference, it may be noted that I have resourced these volumes from Ambedkar, B.R. 2014. *Dr Babasaheb Ambedkar writings and Speeches,* edited by Vasant Moon (set of 17 Volumes). New Delhi: Dr Ambedkar Foundation. Ministry of Social Justice and Empowerment. Government of India.

time after which a new space of experience will come into existence" (Bhagavan 2010, 1). Our self-understanding is a product of how we relate to our own past, how we write and think about it, and how such thinking not only informs our present but also effects who we become in future. I will argue here that Ambedkar's self-understanding was 'present-centred' unlike Gandhi who understood himself in an unbroken continuity (albeit a critical continuity) with the past. Taking a present-centred modern point of view, Ambedkar saw the past (as a modern) from the perspective of the academy as professional history and made forays into it by writing two histories—of the *Shudra*s and of the untouchables. Writing history is not simply retelling a story of what happened in the past. Certainly the fact that history involved a third-party delivery of a judgement on the past (identifying and condemning historical injustice) was not lost on Ambedkar. The histories he wrote were meant to be a measure, to judge and dismiss previous ways of representing the histories of the untouchables and the *Shudra*s, and indeed, to create alternative memories for them. They were meant to create a new past, as it were, from the perspective of the present. Two points come to mind here. The first that Ambedkar understood history very much in line with the academy as a search for measure to mete out justice by taking the position of the third party. Consequently, he understood that in keeping with the formulation of measure (economic, Marxist, subaltern, Dalit, feminist, Dalit feminist, Islamic to name a few) writing history involved framing hypothesis and selecting facts to fit such hypothesis. Gandhi completely rejected history understood in modern terms as a measure of the past and used the alternative term *itihaas*. This last was a composite term *iti* and *haas* and meant 'thus it happened'/it so happened. Happenings by the nature of what they were/are, that is, immeasurable individual singularities could not be re-interpreted/erased as they had already happened in their essentially immeasurable singularity. Hence for Gandhi (unlike Ambedkar) there was no writing of history only the telling of an *itihaas* of a people/nation. For him memory involved remembering (and not adjudicating) such singularities/events dealing with all that which had 'so happened' in one's past. These mental recollections of small events could not be wiped out/over shadowed in their entirety in the light of retrospective historical hypotheses' about that which was of specific interest about them. In the time frame of *itihaas* memories could not be erased to leave a clean slate from the standpoint of the present. Rather it was only the animosities surrounding them that could/ought to be so erased. It was the record of animosity that Gandhi sought to erase. Perhaps, it was this idea of working through the memory of past injuries until they had been completely forgotten—as if they had never happened—that had led Gandhi to reject 'history' in favour of *itihaas*.

It now becomes important to go the length between history and *itihaas* to bring out the differences between how Gandhi and Ambedkar related to representations of the Indian past. The crucial difference between history and *itihaas* comes from the concept of measure. Gandhi's selection of the term *itihaas*/it so happened was meant to relate the happenings of past events in their immeasurable singularity precisely because Gandhi did not accept the modern (to him colonial) concept of third-party justice with the figure of the judge as meting out justice to the parties involved in past happenings/conflicts. The discipline of History is at complete odds with *itihaas*.

History moves around the figure of the modern historian (a figure analogous with that of the juror) who selects a measure, formulates hypothesis and then finds facts to fit in with the hypothesis to mete out justice as a third party/impartial judge of the past. So (as already mentioned) one might have many different kinds of history—Marxist, Classical Indian, economic, feminist, Dalit, Dalit feminist, subaltern, Hindu, Islamic among many others. Despite variations all these schools are doing history and not writing *itihaas*. Significantly the distance in time, only serves to create more distance (than that seen in law courts between the judge and the parties in a conflict) between the historian juror and the parties in the past conflicts that have indeed long since passed. *Itihaas* or it so happened is by contrast a retelling of what happened in the past without any attempt at third-party adjudication by measure.

As is fairly well known, there was an integrity in Gandhi's ideas and everything Gandhi said and did was interconnected. Gandhi's ideas about *itihaas* were no exception and they were connected to the rest of the edifice of his moral, economic and juridical ideas. One might recall that Gandhi had rejected the conception of third-party justice held by the liberals in a set of fairly strong arguments in *Hind Swaraj*. It is surely telling, in contrast, that Ambedkar used the modern figure of the juror to point towards the role of the historian[v]. On Gandhi's view, "(t)he parties alone know who is right We, in our simplicity and ignorance, imagine that a stranger by taking our money, gives us justice" (Gandhi 2010, 59). On this view if anyone other than the parties to a conflict are to be involved at all the involvement can only be of someone very close to the parties concerned. Someone who is in a position to come close to the truth/*satya* in the issues involved in the conflict between them. Gandhi thought about how one might come close to parties in a conflict in order to understand the issues and he came up with the connection between *ahimsa*/love and *satya*. For Gandhi, it was *ahimsa* as love that could lead to the truth about what was at stake in conflicts and therefore it was love/*ahimsa* that could help one come close to understanding issues between the parties in a conflict.

One can perhaps connect Gandhi's distinction between history and *itihaas* with another connection he made—that between developing an *ahimsanat*/non-violent disposition and the ability to forget. Some part of the difficulties with thinking about the past and with history providing the measure was that such a way of thinking about the past commits a people to remembering injuries inflicted in the past. One may recall here how third-party justice keeps meticulous records of judgements (about that which was specific about individual conflicts) as precedents. Memory in fact is an important virtue not only in law courts but in modernity and children in schools learn by rote to commit things to memory. What this comes to mean in the present context, is that memories of past animosities dictate responses made by individuals and collectives to different 'others' in the present. Perhaps Gandhi differentiated between 'history' and *itihaas* only to bring out the connection between *ahimsa*/love force and forgetting the animosities of past hatred. Gandhi's arguments were perhaps meant to draw attention to "the seductive charm of history" (Nagaraj [1993] 2015, 23); and the way in which "she convinces us that a partial view is the total view and drives the passionate to act…" (Ibid.). Quite aptly the chapter in *Hind Swaraj* in which Gandhi made this argument was titled "Passive Resistance" and the Gujarati equivalent was "*satyagraha-atmabal*". Gandhi's argument in this chapter suggested that it would be violent to depart from love and respond to the other on a partial view presented by the measure driven historian. This led him to suggest that the ability to forget was essential to develop the moral disposition to forgive and be non-violent towards 'others' from whom one had disagreed in the past.

The second point which follows easily enough from forgetfulness is that Gandhi rejected the modern way of life in/for which history was written and which played a dominant role in modern self-understanding. Gandhi rejected both the modern form of life "concerned with production and reproduction" (Taylor 2001, 211) and the modern agent/self. Central to the modern way of life is perhaps the principle central to utilitarianism, that of "utility". Gandhi rejected this notion for in his alternative world view the *swabhava*/innermost nature/foundational nature of the human was to own kinship (and not seek utility) with the human and the non-human other. In Gandhi's world view, a sense of unity/family took the place of utility. This followed from his belief that the human being was not inclusionarily transcendent to the rest of creation. To the contrary, the human being was a part of creation only by virtue of the *khaas lakshana*/special virtue of the human species. It is telling that on a Gandhian view the special virtue of humanity which entitled the human a place in the non-human world was the ability to accept a unilateral obligation to own kinship with that non-human world (see Gandhi 1888–1948, 36: 5) there will be occasion to revisit this argument later in this chapter and again in Sect. 5.3 of Chap. 5). It is in such a context that one needs to locate Gandhi's arguments against machinery and even the railways in *Hind Swaraj*. For Gandhi such technology is founded upon a utility driven understanding of the human being's relationship with the world. Consequently, all such technology, based as it is on a non-natural/*aswabhavika* understanding, of the human being's relationship with the non-human other ought to have no place in a properly human life.

The next chapter will speak about the self at the heart of Gandhi's critique of modernity and its difference from Ambedkar's self-understanding. I content myself here with contestations about *itihaas* and history.

2.1.1 *Gandhi on History,* Itihaas, Satya, *and* Swabhava

Unlike Ambedkar, Gandhi rejected history in the sense in which that term is used in the academy and the role it played in western self-understanding. He made a distinction between history and *itihaas*:

> The force of love is the same as the force of the soul or truth. We have evidence of its working at every step. The universe would disappear without the existence of that force. But you ask for historical evidence. It is, therefore, necessary to know what history means. The Gujarati equivalent means: 'It so happened'. If that is the meaning of history, it is possible to give copious evidence. But, if it means the doings of kings and emperors, there can be no evidence of soul-force or passive resistance in such history. You cannot expect silver-ore in a tin-mine. History, as we know it, is a record of the wars of the world, and so there is a

proverb among Englishmen that a nation which has no history, that is, no wars, is a happy nation. How kings played, how they became enemies of one another, and how they murdered one another is found accurately recorded in history, and if this were all that had happened in the world, it would have ended long ago. (Gandhi 2010, 87)

Gandhi's reference to history as the record of wars and feuds is metaphorical and meant to indicate how history selectively appropriates memories in line with a hypothesis-driven application of measure meting out judgements through a third-party adjudication of the past. The immediate context for Gandhi's remarks on History and *itihaas* came from the need to explain (to the reader in *Hind Swaraj*) why *satyagraha*/soul force could not find support from any historical evidence. It is interesting to note, in this context, that Gandhi titled his story of early *satyagraha* in South Africa differently in Gujarati and English. What was *Dakshin Afrikana Satya-grahano Itihaas* (An *Itihaas* of the *Satyagraha* in South Africa) became *Satyagraha in South Africa* in English dropping the English word "history" as non-commensurate with *itihaas*. Etymologically *satyagraha* is a firmness/*agraha* about truth/*satya*. For Gandhi truth can be thought of as both relative and absolute. While as an absolute signified by "Truth or God", Truth is the end of the moral life, as relative, truth is a continuous and progressive striving for the truth (as God) that informs the good life. History in the academy is not interested in Gandhi's *satya qua* "truth or God" and so perhaps it has no record of *satyagraha*.

One might re-iterate that as a discipline History is interested in measure (dates, events, wars) and consequently it brackets out questions of truth/*satya* or indeed of *satyagraha*/truth force. In this it is like the liberal conception of justice which, as largely procedural, also brackets questions of context and truth. The discussion of the difference between Gandhi and Ambedkar's understanding of justice will be taken up in Chap. 5 of this book and one must contend oneself with history and *itihaas* for now. The historian collecting evidence to support measure-directed hypothesis asks questions in line with the selected measure. The historian makes moral and political choices about which measure to select, which questions to ask and which facts to select. There can be alternative measures and consequently alternative histories (marxist, subaltern, dalit, feminist, economic, hindu, islamic to name a few) running parallel to each other depending upon the choices the historian (as third party) has made. Consequently, there are possibilities of creating alternative pasts and alternative memories of that past.

History cannot simply record "it so happened" because as a discipline providing measure through a third-party adjudication of the past, it is interested in what it frames, as specific about the happenings rather than in the individual singularities/happenings in their immeasurable uniqueness. Gandhi made this point in *Hind Swaraj*. He was clear that History is not interested in 'it so happened' because it is not interested in the immeasurability of the individual events just as it is not interested in singularity. In a fairly long passage Gandhi explained why history could not take note of the immeasurable singularity of *satyagraha*/soul force/love force.

Thousands, indeed tens of thousands, depend for their existence on a very active working of this force. Little quarrels of millions of families in their daily life disappear before the exercise of this force. Hundreds of nations live in peace. History does not, and cannot, take note of this fact. History is really a record of every interruption of the even working of the force of love or of the soul. (Gandhi 2010, 86)

The search for specificity is part of the hypothesis-driven third-party adjudication of the past that constitutes the discipline of history. Paul Veyne in *Writing history: Essays in epistemology* (1984) has argued:

History is interested in individualized events...but it is not interested in their individuality; it seeks to understand them–that is, to find among them a kind of generality or, more precisely, of specificity...that is why 'specific' means both 'general' and 'particular'. Such is the seriousness of history: ...it does not deal in individuals but in what is specific about them for the good reason that, as we shall see, there is nothing to say of individual singularity. (Veyne 1984, 56)

Singularity does not lend itself to measure. Gandhi used examples to bring out this inability of history to take note of the immeasurable unique individual singularity:

Two brothers quarrel; one of them repents and reawakens the love that was lying dormant in him; the two again begin to live in peace; nobody takes note of this. But, if the two brothers, through the intervention of solicitors or some other reason, take up arms or go to law...they...would probably go down to history. (Gandhi 2010, 88)

History (in the academy) cannot be interested in the quarrel between two brothers because it is interested in measure and rejects "the happening as the singularity that is immeasurable" (Skaria 2010, 148). If the two brothers take to armed assault, they would create a precedent something that could lend itself to measure in a manner that love cannot. Skaria explains that "...the criterion of historicity is the specific. In any strict accounting, it is this socius (and not the past) that is the object of history in our modern sense" (Ibid.).

Another difference between history and *itihaas* emerges from this last point. As one considers that history is occupied with a hypothesis-driven measure of the past and interested in what is specific about facts from the point of view of such a measure one appreciates that unlike history "...*itihaas* is not an inert field in which evidence can be found; a working or a giving has to produce its meaning" (Ibid., 178).

This brings out an important insight on the difference between the world views in which Gandhi and Ambedkar, so to say, lived and thought. Gandhi thought that *itihaas* called for a giving and working out of what had happened in the past. Unlike history *itihaas* tried to understand all parties in a conflict through the only way in which one could understand, such parties, that is by love. *Itihaas* therefore made room for love force and consequently for repenting and perhaps even for the reawakening of love. This became possible because the notion of *itihaas* was based upon the idea that one can only understand the conflicts of the past (or any conflicts) with love and not with measure, hence the non-juridical "it so happened". As constitutively linked with love, *itihaas* alone made conceptual space for the working out of the conflicts of the past. This was on account of the theoretical underpinning of the term *itihaas* as being without measure.

It can now be appreciated that it was such an understanding of the past, as requiring not measure but a working out, that made it possible for Gandhi to speak of the removal of untouchability in terms of self-purification, penance and sacrifice on the part of the upper castes who were implicated in the sin of untouchability. For Gandhi such sacrifice and repentance was close enough to ordinary human life. Somewhat like the story of two brothers he had spoken about in *Hind Swaraj* who had made amends to each other and begun to live in peace (Gandhi 2010, 88). Looking at these points of difference, one might be encouraged to delve a little deeper into Gandhi and Ambedkar on history and *itihaas.*

It is significant that Gandhi had spoken about the distinction between these terms in Chap. 17 of the *Hind Swaraj* entitled *satyagraha-atmabal*/passive resistance. The context becomes important because it serves to emphasize Gandhi's point that in writing history, the historian *qua* historian enacting the role of the third party in meting out justice by a retrospective use of measure could not really give an account of the life natural to human beings. As might seem obvious in giving a hypothesis-driven account of the past (marxist, subaltern, economic, dalit etc.) there could be no interest in small events which came naturally to human beings. Consequently, the relationship that modern history (no matter what measure it selected) forged between the modern subject and his/her past was in itself strenuous (going against one's nature can be seen to create a strain). Gandhi argued that if one thought of the past simply as 'it so happened' without measure one could in fact give an account of human life which might be truer to human nature or the *swabhava/* own most orientation of being human.

Gandhi had thought about the life that was natural/*swabhavika* as a life in harmony with, what it meant to be human. He explained that this was a life of the search for truth. It is important to recall that the search for truth was a search for complete transparency in what one thought and did and also at the same time a search for God. It may be well to recall that Gandhi had famously argued that truth was the most appropriate designation for God. It may also be well to remember that the only path to truth for Gandhi was a non-violent one and (as there was no difference between means and end sought) the being of non-violence was simultaneously the coming into being of truth.

2.1.2   Itihaas: Swabhava *and Relating to One's Past*

It is in such a context that we can understand Gandhi's point that understanding the past as *itihaas* (rather than as history) is more in harmony with man's innermost nature/*swabhava.* However strange as this connection might sound at present this section will make an attempt to explain what Gandhi meant by making it. The term *swabhava* is a composite of two terms "*swa*" and "*bhava*" and it may be rendered "ownmost orientation" or again foundational nature (the connection of this notion with that of *dharma/dhamma* will be spelt out in Chap. 5). One can understand why Gandhi should have thought that *itihaas* was more natural to man or closer to human orientation/*swabhava* by looking more closely at what Gandhi meant by the *swabhava* of being human.

In *Hind swaraj* (which is a much more important text to an understanding of Gandhi's ideas than one might think), Gandhi had spoken about what was natural to man and had argued that *satyagraha* was *swabhavik*/natural to man. In 1926, Gandhi wrote two essays about what came naturally to a human being and constituted his/her innermost orientation. He argued there, "No word seems more abused today than the word 'natural'…not everything that is natural to the brute is natural to man…it must therefore be, and is, man's nature to know and find God" (Gandhi 1888–1948, 35: 357–58).

While these comments might lead the reader to think that man's nature was to worship God, Gandhi made it clear that it was not a form of God seeking in religious places that he was invoking as man's *swabhava*, "And if it is man's nature to know and find God…his duty is to develop all his Godward faculties to perfection…. Man's nature then is not himsa but *ahimsa*…. And from that experience he evolves the ethics of subduing desire, anger, ignorance, malice and other passions…" (Ibid., 358).

Gandhi argued that since the human being was the silhouette/*pratibimb* (in Gujarati) of God it was human nature to seek God. Since Gandhi understood God as truth and thought that truth was one with non-violence, he argued that man's *swabhava*/ownmost nature was perfectly *ahimsanat*/non-violent. A doctor who read Gandhi's essay on man's non-violent nature (in *Young India*) presented an argument which might seem convincing to many in our times: "…to prevent violence is …positively against man's nature" (Gandhi 1888–1948, 36: 3).

Gandhi countered that argument and went on to explain, what he thought was the *khaas lakshana* or the special virtue of humanity, as a species. In a telling passage Gandhi rejected the modern logic of the human being's "inclusionary transcendence" (Skaria 2010, 164) which separates the human from animal (and equally the civilized races from the savage) and suggested that it is the *swabhava* of being human to own kinship with the most distant others.

> Hitherto one has been taught to believe that a species is recognized and differentiated from the rest by its special marks (*khaas lakshana*). Therefore, it would be wrong, I presume, to say that a horse is animal (*pashu*) first and horse after. He shares something in common (*saamanya…lakshan*) with the other animals, but he dare not shed his horseliness and yet remain an animal. Having lost his special virtue (*khaas lakshana*), he loses also his general (*saamanya*) status. Similarly…I would suggest to the medical friend that man can be classed as animal (*pashu*) only so long as he retains his humanity. (Ibid., 160)

This passage is very important because it spells out clearly Gandhi's rejection of modern self-understanding which (post Kant perhaps) is built around the idea of the inclusionary transcendence of human beings. On the modern view, the human beings are animals but rational animals and the latter confers upon them a special status that has entitled a dominion over the non-human world. The same inclusionary transcendence of the human species, it may be noted, lent itself to the justifying narrative of colonialism. For one could argue that the domination of the savage by the colonizer could be justified in terms of the same idea of inclusionary transcendence. Gandhi lived out a different, perhaps more traditional world view, as he argued that human beings were animals only, in so far as, and *by virtue of* participating in the special virtue/*khaas lakshana* of humanity. Consequently, they were not transcendent to the world that they shared with others rather the special virtue of being human only entitled them to share *samata*/the status of equality with the rest of the cosmos.

The *Khaas lakshana* of being human was spelt out by Gandhi, in his letter on "More animal than human" published in *Young India* on 8th July 1926, with reference to the idea "that *ahimsa* (love) not himsa (hate) rules man…" (Gandhi 1888–1948, 36: 6). For Gandhi, such *ahimsa* meant that man was to own "kinship with not merely the ape but the horse and the sheep, the lion and the leopard, the snake and the scorpion… the difficult *dharma* which rule my life, and I hold ought to rule that of every man and woman, impose this unilateral obligation (*ekpakshi farj*) on us. And it is so imposed because only the human is the image of God" (Ibid., 5). This Gandhian notion of the absolute, and one might re-iterate, one sided absolute obligation, of a human being came from the fact that man was the image of God, and therefore had the special virtue of owning kinship with the rest of creation.

Some of the consequences of this idea (of believing that a human being was a silhouette of God) will be explored in the next chapter in the discussion on the making of modern identity as it played out in the life and work of Gandhi and Ambedkar. However, here it becomes important to note that Gandhi thought of the human being as an animal/a part of the human and non-human world only in virtue of his/her *swabhava* of owning kinship with that world.

A word on how this notion of *swabhava* should have mediated Gandhi's thoughts on the difference between *itihaas* versus history. For Gandhi, the human being only shares the non-human world on a status of *samata*/equality (and not inclusionary transcendence) if the human owns up to the unilateral obligation to recognize the human and non-human other as a kin. To recognize as kin involves the rejection of negotiating otherness through utility and by measure. On a Gandhian view, brothers do not require the law courts to mete out justice through a third party, they need only to understand each other through love. The human being needs to relate to the past along the same lines with *ahimsa*/love and without measure. History does violence to the past and to human *swabhava* by approaching the past with measure. It also remains constitutively involved while framing the measure (whether economic, dalit, subaltern, marxist) with the organizing idea of utility. On both these counts Gandhi rejects history in favour of *itihaas*.

It might also be important to make a different (though related) point, one that derives from the above, and has to do with this debate in a more straightforward way. Given that Gandhi had emphasized that the *swabhava* of man involved a unilateral obligation of kinship with the "other" it followed that (for him) the upper castes had failed their own humanity. It therefore became incumbent on the upper caste self to own up to the sin of destroying kinship with the oppressed human other. The onus of making good this fall from humanity fell on the upper caste self and was a natural enough consequence of Gandhi's understanding of the *swabhava* of being human and of the human being's place in the world.

Having explored the centrality of the notion of *swabhava* in Gandhi, it becomes important to note how much at variance this notion was from Ambedkar's more modern understanding of the human self and his/her place in the universe. Ambedkar was fairly familiar with Gandhi's position and countered the Gandhian rejection of an idea at the heart of modernity namely the human being's inclusionary transcendence from the non-human world. He argued,

> … Gandhism…treats man as an animal and no more. It is true that man shares the, constitution and functions of animals, nutritive, reproductive, etc. But these are not distinctively human functions. The distinctively human function is reason, the purpose of which is to enable man to observe, meditate, cogitate, study and discover the beauties of the universe and enrich his life and control the animal elements in his life. Man thus occupies the highest place in the scheme of animate existence…. (Ambedkar 2014, 9: 283)

On the innermost nature/*swabhava* of the human being Ambedkar could not have been at greater variance with Gandhi for he took an enlightenment route stating that the "distinctively human function is reason" (Ibid.). Further in his mind there was no sense of the distinctive nature of man as constituted by a unilateral obligation of kinship with the non-human world. To the contrary, he argued that,

> …what divides the brute from the animal is culture…. How then can a life of culture be made possible? It is not possible unless there is sufficient leisure…. The problem of all problems which human society has to face is how to provide leisure to every individual…. Machinery and modern civilization are thus indispensable for emancipating man from leading the life of the brute, and for providing him with leisure and making a life of culture possible. The man who condemns machinery and modern civilization simply does not understand their purpose and the ultimate aim which human society must strive to achieve. (Ibid., 284)

This complete variance of world views also becomes apparent from the term Ambedkar had used in his Marathi speeches—*manuski*/human-ness. Zelliot brings out the genealogy of that term in the values of fraternity, liberty, and equality in the European Enlightenment tradition when she observes:

> Ambedkar's adaption of western concepts to the Indian scene is also reflected in the terms he used to justify Untouchable political rights: democracy, fraternity, and liberty. In his Marathi speeches, Ambedkar conveyed the implication of these concepts in a simple word, *manuski*, that was readily understood by the most illiterate Mahar villager. Although *manuski's* literal meaning is "human-ness", it serves to evoke feelings of self-respect and humane attitudes towards one's fellow man. (Zelliot 1972, 78)

Though both *swabhava* and *manuski* emphasize the human concern for "other-ness" they work within very different conceptual frameworks. Gandhi's use of the notion *Swabhava* emphasizes that the ownmost orientation of being human is to accept the unilateral obligation of kinship with the human and non-human world. Ambedkar's *manuski* brings in an alternative world perhaps that of the Kantian 'Kingdom of ends' where every human being (as being self-directed/autonomous by the law of reason) is an end in herself/himself and deserves to be singled out from the non-human universe to receive the respect befitting such an end. This respect/treatment involves the selective recognition of the human being as the bearer of rights rather than an owning of kinship with the non-human other. This contrast points to very different understandings of the self and commensurate differences in understanding the place of the self in the world.

The next section will look at Ambedkar's comments on history so that the differences from Gandhi can become more apparent.

2.2   History and *Itihaas*: Gandhi and Ambedkar

These conclusions are the result of such historical research as I have been able to make.

(Ambedkar 2017, *The Preface*)

Whatever conclusions I have reached have not been through historical studies at all. History has played the least part in my make.

(Gandhi 1888–1948, 54: 260)

These two statements express the vast differences in the perspectives and self-understandings of Gandhi and Ambedkar in that they suggest that Ambedkar and Gandhi located themselves differently *vis-à-vis* the past. Gandhi saw himself in continuity with that which had "so happened". He sought *satya/* truth and this seeking of truth was not passive. It demanded a present-centred, retrospective working through the happenings in the past.

At sharp variance from such an understanding Ambedkar located himself in the present as a third party engaged in rewriting the facts of history by selecting measure and framing hypothesis to ask retrospective questions of an unjust past. However, Ambedkar's taking the position of the third party (as I will bring out in Chap. 5) was not quite that of Adam Smith's impartial spectator taking what Nagel calls a "view from nowhere" (Nagel 1986, 70). The questions which he raised were raised from a present-centred perspective yet posed about the past which it should be noted *could never have been* raised in the past. An important consequence of Ambedkar's choice of writing history to establish his relationship with the past was that since history was about third-party justice and measure, it was interested in the *socius*[vi] (and not immeasurable individual singularities). The historian as the third-party pronounced, as it were, a judgement on the sins of the past. As it was the *socius* and no longer the individual who could be made responsible for those sins they could not be atoned for by individuals. The sins of the *socius* could only be made good by contracts between citizens negotiated in the spheres of the political and the legal. History then served as the measure to adjudicate an individual (or community's) relationship with the past.

It was here that Ambedkar differed most sharply from Gandhi. He believed that the now modern victim could make a choice to own/or reject different strands of his/her own memory of the past. The self could in fact choose to accept the veracity of memories of humiliation and assume a selective wilful forgetfulness by rejecting the very location of the victim within the religious society from which such humiliation originated.

History (and not *itihaas*) could lend itself to such a selective rewriting. This was because history involved the modern figure of the historian as a third party and the modern historian/juror could make choices about the questions he/she raised. These were questions related to measure. Such measure helped to set what was specific about the individual singular happenings of the past. It was in the nature of the questioning modern historian that his/her questions could be redirected towards different facts and alternative narratives. This followed from the historian's selection of the answer to the prior question "what was specific about these happenings?" Alternatively, "what was to be the measure to evaluate the past?" As part of the story of the modern subject, history was based in modern life where changes in sets of questions and answers were not seen in terms of a loss in self-understanding. There was also the question of the place of the self in the universe. The modern subject saw himself/herself as both within the order of the non-human world and as transcendent to its concerns. It seemed natural that the human self should negotiate his/her relationship with the human and non-human world primarily in terms of utility.

One can make sense of Ambedkar's move to selectively forget parts of the past (and re-create memory) better only if we contrast it with the *itihaas*-centred religious world view that he was countering. The central issue here is that notwithstanding, reductive evolutionary accounts of religion, to the religious person there is no possibility of making such a choice to forget the relationship with his/her religious tradition. Scruton reminds us that religion involves "a network of relations that are neither contractual nor negotiated" (Scruton 2014, 14). One might see Gandhi's arguments against history here as an expression of the understanding of religious life as involving "relations of belonging" to a past where there is no possibility of making the choice to reject the belonging without a corresponding loss to one's sense of self. The only choice for the believer might lie in choosing to forget the animosity generated by past injuries (as preparatory to forgiving) after he/she confronts and works through the sin committed in the religious past.

On such a view the oppressor and the victim could (either or both) choose to work through the past. From the point of view of the oppressor such a working through had to involve making amends by taking responsibility for his/her sin and making a commitment to atone for the sins of the past. The alternity of this idea of working through the past might appear if one considers that if wounds are not to be left to fester one needs to move "from a politics of rage towards a politics of affirmation" (Shobhi 2015, 4) One might note that choosing to rewrite the past/wiping "the slate clean" (Ibid., xv) instead of working through it could be a complicated exercise. For one, there could be denigration of one's own cultural heritage. For another, in a community-based society anonymity might not come easily since most of the members might not have chosen to become "fragmented into atomized individuals" (Ibid.). Gandhi appeared to have thought that a working through the past required a "widening of emotional concern" (Nagaraj [1993] 2015, 65). Such a widening of concern as a mode of working out the past by its very nature required "a dual identification with both parties of the conflict" (Ibid., 65–66). This led Gandhi to a "subtext of self-purification in the target community of his action" (Ibid., 67).

Another reason that might perhaps have made it imperative for Gandhi to work through the past rather than choose to erase it by a complete rejection of ritual/text could have come from his own primarily religious world view. In such a world view the human and the divine communicated through the realm of the sacred. The past as the repository of the sacred happenings—rituals, texts, ways of life—could not be erased in its entirety without dismantling the self-understanding of the subject and its place in the cosmos:

That indeed seems to be a feature of the sacred in all religions. Sacred objects, words, animals, ceremonies, places, all seem to stand at the horizon of our world, looking out to that which is not of this world, because it belongs to the sphere of the divine, and looking also *into* our world, so as to meet us face to face. Through sacred things we can influence and be influenced by the transcendental. If there is to be a real presence of the divine in this world, it must be in the form of some sacred event, moment, place, or encounter: so at least we humans have believed. (Scruton 2014, 15)

A consideration of the relationship between the more traditional notion of self and the realm of the sacred, might help one make better sense, of Gandhi's hesitation with the complete rejection (rather than reform) of the sacred oppressive past. One might then be better able to understand Gandhi's alternative advocacy of the religious duty to reform religion by critically interrogating sacred text and ritual in the light of reason and morality.

2.2.1 Ambedkar: Rewriting History and Creating an Alternative Memory

It becomes intellectually fascinating to philosophically unpack Ambedkar on history if only for the complete shift it involves in the unmaking of the old-world Indian mind and construction of the modern Indian subject. Ambedkar wrote two histories in close succession *Who were the shudras?* in 1946, and *The untouchables* in 1948. In the preface to both these histories he spoke about history and the historian's task and these insights serve to bring out his complete variance from Gandhi.

However, before moving to those two important histories it is important to take note of Ambedkar's remarks on the past in a lecture that came much earlier and indeed that never came to pass/be delivered—*Annihilation of Caste.* This lecture marks Ambedkar's modern (perhaps Lockean) moment of erasure and can be taken as an important stage in the making of modern self in the intellectual life of India. Quoting Dewey (in the text of this lecture) Ambedkar declared that the present "is what life is in leaving the past behind it. The study of the past will not help us to understand the present" (Ambedkar 2014, 1: 79). This moment of erasure developed and took its course with the two histories that Ambedkar went on to write. Ambedkar not only left behind the past as an *itihaas*/'it so happened' but courageously rewrote its history on a *tabula rasa* of a Lockean kind by rejecting the distinction between, the sacred and the profane, in an enacting of the third-party measure that constituted history. This search was directed by the questions posed by Ambedkar taking on the persona of the modern historian. As the third-party framing the measure, it was natural to substantially alter the questions that had been asked of the past by, as he put it, Brahmin scholars. Ambedkar reframed the questions and tried to interpret the "missing links" in the answers by imagination. Such a selection of questions and consequent discrimination between facts selected as relevant and irrelevant to the answers would not have been possible for the old-world Indian mind which looked for individual singularities in their unique immeasurability in the 'it so happened' of *itihaas*.

In *Who were the shudras?* Ambedkar posed some of these new questions:

> The questions are: why did the Purusha Sukta not recognize the unity of the five tribes and give a mythic explanation of their origin? Why instead did it recognize the communal divisions within the tribes? Why did the *Purusha Sukta* regard communalism more important than nationalism? (Ambedkar 2014, 7: 31)

With an absolutely awe-inspiring scholarship and great attention to texts Ambedkar quoted select passages from (among others) the *Rig, Atharva* and *Yajur* Vedas, the Upanishads, *Manu smriti*, and *Dharma sutras*. Using these to answer his questions, he argued that the *Shudras* were Aryans and that the "*shudras* belonged to the Kshatriya class" (Ibid., 41). Ambedkar concluded with the observation that it "is not that the varna system did not exist, but that there were only three varnas and that the *shudras* were not regarded as a fourth and a separate varna" (Ibid., 140). He deduced from a hypothesis-driven third-party measure of facts/events in history that the status of the *Shudras* came down because of conflicts with the Brahmins who refused to perform the *upanayana*[vii] ceremony of the same. It was this that led to their final social degradation. In 1948, Ambedkar went on to write another history—that of the untouchables. Here, he argued that the untouchables were the broken men who had been degraded because they were despised by the Brahmins for being Buddhists and continuing to eat beef long after other castes had stopped.

This repeated writing of history was a mindful project and in the preface to these histories Ambedkar wrote about the characteristic task of history in the academy and the role of the historian. These remarks provide insights into the theoretical distance between Gandhi and Ambedkar.

> The present attempt to explain the origin of untouchability is not the same as writing history from texts with certainty. It is a case of re-constructing history where there are no texts, and if there are, they have no direct bearing to the question. In such circumstances what one has to do is to strive to divine what the texts conceal or suggest without being even quite certain of having found the truth. The task is one of gathering survivals of the past, placing them together and making them tell the story of their birth. The task is analogous to that of the archeologist who constructs a city from broken stones or of the paleontologist who conceives an extinct animal from scattered bones and teeth or of a painter who reads the lines of the horizon and the smallest vestiges on the slopes of the hill to make up a scene. In this sense the book is a work of art even more than of history. (Ambedkar 2014, 7: 244)

This of course seems to be a modern reading of art and would make little sense of premodern painters or indeed of postmodern painters and sculptors where the work of art bears little resemblance to the slopes that make up the 'scene', as it were. Ambedkar goes on to write in the same passage:

> The origin of untouchability lies buried in a dead past which nobody knows. To make it alive is like an attempt to reclaim to history a city which has been dead since ages past and present it as it was in its original condition. It cannot but be that imagination and hypothesis should play a large part in such a work. But that in itself cannot be a ground for the condemnation of the thesis. For without trained imagination no scientific inquiry can be fruitful and hypothesis is the very soul of science. (Ibid., 244)

Ambedkar makes a telling comparison in this "Preface" between history and archeology, on the one hand, and paleontology, on the other. This is significant since the last two are 'scientific' hypothesis-driven studies of the past which seek to reconstruct it from a present-centred perspective and thus as very different from *itihaas* or 'thus it so happened'. Perhaps in the framework of modernity Gandhi's 'thus it so happened' could share space with 'once upon a time' an ancient relic which has little or no conceptual space in modernity. The fairy tales have all but disappeared. Feminists make a retrospective third-party adjudication and retrospective rejection of these ancient relics from a modern present-centred measure. From within this measure such stories can be and indeed are retrospectively denounced as written from a male-centred perspective.

The scientific hypothesis-driven history Ambedkar speaks about lends itself to parallel accounts of the past depending on what sort of measure the historian selects (economic, marxist, subaltern, feminist among many others) what hypothesis he/she frames and what facts he/she collects to fit the dominant narrative as it were. Ambedkar argues that the historian treats all literature as vulgar and does away with the sacred by dismantling the distinction between the profane and the sacred. He argues,

> ...in my research I have been guided by the best tradition of the historian who treats all literature as vulgar—I am using the word in its original sense of belonging to the people—to be examined and tested by accepted rules of evidence without recognizing any distinction between the sacred and the profane and with the sole object of finding the truth. If in following this tradition I am found wanting in respect and reverence for the sacred literature of the Hindus my duty as a scholar must serve as my excuse. Second, respect and reverence for the sacred literature cannot be made to order. They are the results of social factors…. (Ambedkar 2014, 7: 16)

In the best tradition of liberal philosophy Ambedkar asks the historian to be impartial (as a juror) and not swayed as a Brahmin would to interpret facts so as to support his own authority. Nor again give in to the bias natural to a non-Brahmin who might "go to the other extreme and treat the whole literature as a collection of fables and fictions fit to be thrown on a dung heap not worthy of serious study" (Ibid., 17). Ambedkar emphasizes that the historian must be impartial as he/she frames hypothesis and takes on the role of the third party meting out justice by measure.

> As has been well said, an historian ought to be exact, sincere, and impartial; free from passion, unbiased by interest, fear, resentment or affection; and faithful to the truth, which is the mother of history, the preserver of great actions, the enemy of oblivion, the witness of the past, the director of the future. In short, he must have an open mind, though it may not be an empty mind, and readiness to examine all evidence even though it be spurious. (Ibid., 17)

This language of measure, hypothesis and evidence in connection with truth as the object of the historian's quest must in itself raise the question 'what if Ambedkar was interested in the same truth that Gandhi was pursuing in *itihaas*?'. In other words, one could ask 'was there any difference between the truth marshaled as evidence in history's exercise of meting out third-party justice and Gandhi's *satya* driven *itihaas*?'. I will go into that question in the next section as it deserves a more detailed discussion. Ambedkar's understanding of history with his Lockean moment of erasure, his Kantian deference to reason on the Newtonian model of framing and testing hypothesis and Cartesian doubt of all that does not stand to up to evidence puts Ambedkar among the best of Indian enlightenment thinkers. Though he himself declared, in his address to the 'All India Radio' on 3rd October 1954, New Delhi:

> Let no one, however, say that I have borrowed my philosophy from the French Revolution. I have not. My philosophy has roots in religion and not in political science. I have derived them from the teachings of my master, The Buddha.

Perhaps a consideration of Ambedkar's writing points more towards a rewriting of Buddhism in line with enlightenment values rather than towards a re-interpretation of the latter through Buddhist spirituality.

Here we can locate the proud birth of the modern Indian and the fruition of the process of the making of modern identity in India. Yet this also brings out why two great men committed to the same cause could not agree. They were speaking from within an incommensurable set of conceptual frameworks where history, the past, memory, truth and self-understanding meant very different things. This chapter is not about locating the appropriateness of any one of these approaches but rather about creating a clarity. A conceptual opening in which one can witness more clearly what K. C Bhattacharya (2011) described as the lapse of the "old-world Indian mind" (K. C Bhattacharya 2011, 104) and the birth of the modern subject in India.

To my mind it is surely important to note here Ambedkar's Lockean moment of erasure of the past and the effort, as he said, "to reclaim to history a city which has been dead since ages past and present it as it was in its original condition" (Ambedkar 2014, 7: 244). It is important to note that in this moment Ambedkar is simultaneously constructing a relationship with the radical bhakti saint Ravidas (c. 1450-) who is one of the saints to whom he dedicates his history *The untouchables*. In fact, the imagery of writing the history of the origin of untouchability by reclaiming to history a city long dead is reminiscent of Ravidas' song *Begampura* or the sorrowless city.[viii] Ambedkar creates an alternative memory of the origin of untouchability from a present-centred perspective and as he does so he gives to the untouchables a brave Buddhist past. As he re-constructs the city of the past, Ambedkar lays the corner stone of Ravidas' sorrowless city of the future. Ambedkar used history as a measure meting out justice as a third party and condemning the demeaning Hindu past. Thereafter there was nothing left as it were but to re-create memories of an alternative past to build an equality driven Buddhist city of/in that past. This city became the foundation for the modern sorrowless city of the future, which Ambedkar later gave substance to, in the Indian constitution.

It is important to recall Ravidas' *Begumpura* if only because Ambedkar dedicates his history of untouchability to him (along with Nandnar and Chokhamela) and invokes the image of reclaiming through history the city long dead. The *Begumpura* poem is striking in its search for a city of the future without caste distinctions. Even though Ravidas' bhakti was radical there was acquiescence in, an acceptance of the subaltern status (along with other saints). However, his poem *Begumpura* was different:

The regal realm with a sorrowless name
They call it Begumpura, a place with no pain,
No taxes or cares, nor own property there,
No wrongdoing, worry, terror or torture
Oh my brother, I've come to take it as my own,
My distant home, where everything is right,
That imperial kingdom is rich and secure,
Where none are third or second-all are one,
.......They do this or that, they walk where they wish....

(Hawley 1988, 25).

2.2.2   History as a Search for Truth; Itihaas as Making Space for Satyagraha-Gandhi and Ambedkar

Having discussed history and *itihaas* there remain perhaps some questions about truth. Gandhi spoke of *itihaas* and *satya* when he argued that *satyagraha* could not find a place in measure-directed history. Of *satyagraha* Gandhi said that it was "soul-force or truth-force" (Gandhi 2010, 86) (one could note in passing here Aishwary Kumar's (Kumar 2015, 12) emphasis on Gandhi's use of force). Further since *ahimsa* as non-violence could best be understood as a love of/kinship with the most distant 'other' Gandhi clarified that "(T)he force of love is the same as the force of the soul or truth" (Ibid., 87). He was clear that *satyagraha* or "Soul-force, being natural, is not noted in history" (Gandhi 2010, 88). Gandhi was drawing attention to the fact that love force does not admit of measure, just as, love itself is immeasurable and does not figure (for that reason) in history. *Itihaas* (unlike history) as 'it so happened' made room for love and the non-violent search for *satya/*truth.

It becomes necessary to take a detour here to look at the sense in which Ambedkar (as a modern and a liberal) brackets truth out from the search for measure to write an alternative history for the untouchables. Ambedkar is avowedly interested in putting together the past but he thinks that imaginative "hypothesis" (Ambedkar 2014, 7: 244) which is the "soul of science" (Ibid.) can help to find out the facts which are needed to write the history of the *Shudras* and later of the untouchables. However, such an effort (Ambedkar is clear) needs to bracket away the realm of the religious and the moral as the search calls for an impartiality with which liberals are familiar from the modern figure of the scientist as he selects empirical facts and does science. Such a bracketing of truth in the search for facts while writing history is not difficult to reconcile with the rest of the liberal project. Witness here how Raz writes on the sidelining of truth from issues of procedural propriety in deciding questions of justice. Raz has raised difficulties with Rawls' agnosticism with respect to the truth of his conception of justice (Raz 1990, 7). He has argued that Rawls is only interested in a "... consensus of opinion" (Ibid., 9) and not in the truth of his doctrine. Truth perhaps is not relevant to the public liberal space of the law court while procedure is.

There are then powerful differences between Gandhi's quest for *satya* in *itihaas* which, as he notes in *Hind Swaraj*, provides "copious evidence" (Gandhi 2010, 87) of *satyagraha* and the third-party justice Ambedkar sought in writing history. A word on what Gandhi meant by *satya* might serve to bring out the differences between Gandhi and Ambedkar on what they each meant by truth and what sort of consequences these differences brought to their conception of the self and its relationship with the past.

Gandhi spoke of the good human life as a life spent in the performance of what he called cardinal/casual virtues (the *yamas* and *niyamas* which were the central moral notions in traditional schools of Indian philosophy) in which the predominant place was occupied by truth. It may be recalled that *satya*/truth was also one of the *yamas* to which Gandhi referred frequently. Gandhi had a dual understanding of "truth":

> For me truth is the sovereign principle, which includes numerous other principles. This truth is not only truthfulness in word, but truthfulness in thought also, and not only the relative truth of our conception, but the Absolute Truth, the Eternal Principle, that is God. (Prabhu and Rao 1967, 42)

As an Absolute Gandhi's truth referred to the proper end of individual moral life. This conjured the image of an Aristotelian *telos* or end at which moral life ought to be directed. Without such a goal or 'end' it might be said that this life would be episodic and perhaps lacking the unity/direction which helps to make sense of an individual good life. Gandhi also spoke of truth in another sense as one of the "cardinal… virtues" (Gandhi 1888–1948, 33: 448). In the second sense truth/moral truth informed the aspirant's quest for Absolute truth or God as the highest end/goal of the good human life.

One might say that the central Gandhian insight into morality was that truthfulness as a virtue of character was not only the means to, but constitutive of, truth/God as the goal of moral life. That Gandhi indeed used truth in this dual sense would become clear when we consider that not only did he constantly refer to truth as a *yama*/virtue or disposition of character but that in 1921 he famously reframed the co-relation between God and Truth. Changing from "God is Truth" to "Truth is God": "You will see the fine distinction between the two statements, viz. that God is truth and Truth is God. And I came to the conclusion after a continuous and relentless search after Truth which began nearly fifty years ago" (Prabhu and Rao 1967, 51).

Gandhi thought that truth was the best name for God. He was clearly using "Truth or God" in the unambiguous sense of a transcendent object which gave a sense of direction and unity to individual moral life. This also becomes clear by his use of both 'perfection' and 'certainty' in connection with Truth/God. It might be useful to recall Iris Murdoch's argument (Murdoch 1971, Chap. 2) that without such a transcendent object individual moral endeavour would be fragmentary and plagued by the fragility and transience of ordinary human existence and its concerns.

> I think it is wrong to expect certainties in this world, where all else but God that is Truth is an uncertainty. All that appears and happens about is uncertain, transient. But…one would be blessed if one could catch a glimpse of that certainty and hitch one's wagon to it. The quest for Truth is the *summum bonum* of life. (Prabhu and Rao 1967, 44)

Ambedkar, like Gandhi, looks for truth in history. However, this was perhaps a quest for truth as a transparency in what one thinks, writes, and does. In writing history Ambedkar sought truth as fact/evidence to reveal the terrible fabrications in the sacred books of the Hindus which purportedly explained the origin of untouchability with a story of the cosmos. He argued, "…that what goes by the name of Sacred Books contains fabrications which are political in their motive, partisan in their composition and fraudulent in their purpose" (Ambedkar 2014, 7: 14).

Ambedkar thought that to seek truth as evidence the historian *qua* juror needed to be a stickler for procedural veracity/truthfulness best understood in terms of the impartiality of the liberal judge. He explained this procedural veracity as an absence of bias while recording facts in the context of writing history.

> I am aware that this difference in the attitude of a Brahmin scholar and a non-Brahmin scholar towards this sacred literature –literature which is the main source of the material for the study of the problems of the social history of the Hindus–the former with the attitude of the uncritical recommendation and the latter with his attitude of unsparing condemnation is most harmful to historical research. (Ibid., 17)

A historian has to be "exact, sincere, and impartial" (Ibid.) and keep in mind "no other consideration except that of pure history" (Ibid., 18). Two years later while writing his second history Ambedkar throws more light on this impartial truth seeking and meting out of third-party justice through history when he takes up Goethe's suggestion that:

> The historian's duty is to separate the true from the false, the certain from the uncertain…Every investigator must before all things look upon himself as one who is summoned to serve on a jury. He has only to consider how far the statement of the case is complete and clearly set forth the evidence. (as quoted in Ambedkar 2014, 7: 242–243)

Ambedkar moves on to those cases where empirical evidence may fail the historian/juror and notes that "…Goethe does not tell what the historian is to do when he comes across a missing link, where no direct evidence of connected relations between important events is available" (Ibid., 243). It is significant to note that the manner in which Ambedkar thinks about truth becomes most apparent from the terms that he uses for describing the search for truth. Pertinent here are terms like evidence, third-party justice, and the scientific-criminologist method which Ambedkar employs to argue about imaginative hypothesis and evidence to find truth in history. Ambedkar explains that when a student of history finds "missing links" (Ibid.) in the evidence,

> The question is: what is a student of history to do? Is he to cry halt and stop his work until the link is discovered? I think not. I believe that in such cases it is permissible for him to use his imagination and intuition to bridge the gap left in the chain of facts by links not yet discovered and to propound a working hypothesis suggesting how facts might have been inter-connected. (Ibid.)

Ambedkar is clear that this use of imagination is akin to the modern paradigm provided by scientific research and therefore does no violence to "the canons of historical research" (Ibid.). He urges the historian *qua* third party to concentrate on setting up hypothesis where there is no "direct evidence" (Ibid.) and thereafter evaluate "whether the thesis is possible and if so, does it fit in with facts better" (Ibid.) than any other explanation. He, in fact, goes on to make a comparison between science and literature quoting Maxim Gorky:

> Science and literature have much in common: In both observation, comparison and study are of fundamental importance; the artist like the scientist, needs both imagination and intuition. Imagination and intuition bridge the gaps in the chain of facts by its as yet undiscovered links and permit the scientist to create hypothesis and theories…. (as quoted in Ambedkar 2014, 7: 244).

What is at stake in the debate between Ambedkar and Gandhi is much more than confrontations over an approach to the eradication of untouchability, issues of the role of the village in free India and an idealized version of *varna*. Indeed, it is an enlightenment ushered modernity that is at the heart of these conflicts. The conflict plays out at perhaps its best when we examine their ideas on history and *itihaas*, on truth and *satya*. Ambedkar is self-consciously following a method characterized by an enlightenment driven (and directed) rational clarity and employing the model of the third-party meting out justice while he writes history: "The thesis in great part is based on facts and inferences from facts. And where it is not based on facts or inferences from facts, it is based on circumstantial evidence of presumptive character resting on considerable degree of probability" (Ibid., 245).

Such a search for truth modelled along the lines of post-enlightenment scientific models of reasoning seems to have become entirely about a truth understood in cognitive terms. Ambedkar builds the analogy of the modern figure of the juror who brackets out from consideration everything, apart from circumstantial empirical evidence, in pronouncing a third-party judgement. While Gandhi thought of truth as both a moral and a religious notion it does not seem to be correct to say that he was not interested in truth understood cognitively. One must consider that he spent most of his life trying to attain clarity about how things really were and aligning them to how they ought to be. For Gandhi truth was both a truth telling/coming close to God and attaining clarity about how things really were in the world as a matter of fact. The distance between Gandhi and Ambedkar was one of traversing the distance between truth understood in purely cognitive terms and an understanding of truth without measure as both a cognitive and as a moral/religious notion.

One might ask why it should matter to this debate that Gandhi and Ambedkar should have thought of truth in different ways? Of course, it matters or should matter to the differences between these two good men that they thought of themselves as seeking different things in the quest for truth. Also, that this led them to think of the story of man/history differently. Finally, that what they thought they were seeking as truth (and how they were seeking it) should have led them to think of the self/subject in totally different ways. It were these incommensurable conflicts that one might read as confrontations between the old-world Indian mind and the modern subject that could hold the key to unpacking the debate between them. I have deliberately refrained here from looking at God and will look at this in the next chapter where I speak of the notion of self-identity.

2.3 Memory: D. R. Nagaraj in Conversation with Babasaheb Ambedkar

This chapter has looked at the importance of the distinction between history and *itihaas*. The third term in this triad is memory. History makes no room for the immeasurable and singular narratives that constitute memory. This section looks at the importance of memory to the conflicts between Gandhi and Ambedkar and consequently to the self-definition of the contemporary Dalit movement. In this context it draws some insights from *The flaming feet*, a set of influential essays by D. R. Nagaraj. Nagaraj (1984–1998) was a political commentator and cultural critic. Like Gandhi, Nagaraj was not a dalit by birth but by adoption. He was an active participant of the *Dalit Bandaya* movement in Karnataka.

In this section, I want to develop some of the things that Nagaraj said (across his set of essays) about memory. He had argued that the "firm riveting of the Dalit movement to the present" (Nagaraj [1993] 2015, 33) was on account of a "wilful amnesia" (Ibid.) regarding the past. This in itself put a strain on the post-Ambedkarite Dalit movement to "act as an instrument to promote and safeguard the interests of select groups" (Ibid.). This in turn meant that the movement could largely reflect "only the aspirations of city-based groups" (Ibid.). With good reason of course as these groups were better trained and therefore more able to assume and enact modern roles like those of the scientist, juror and historian. A second and related theme of the movement, as it developed under the leadership of Babasaheb, was "the problem of defining alternative cultural values not only for an individual Dalit but for the entire movement" (Ibid.). Nagaraj argues that the state of amnesia wilfully adopted by the movement by itself promoted a state of stupor which discouraged the strenuous exercise of constituting a new culture. He argues:

> Dr. Ambedkar could never tolerate this cultural inertia, and his entire life can be summed up as a relentless battle against such a mental state, although this landed him in many problems while defining the relationship between a movement and the structure of it's memories. This was one of the areas where Dr Ambedkar clashed bitterly with Gandhi. (Ibid.)

As has been oft noted, Gandhi approached the problem of untouchability, not exclusively, but as predominantly a religious problem—a problem of the collective Hindu self. Ambedkar had participated in what might be best described as the religious route so to say. In the early 1920s, he had engaged in 'Sanskritization' in which members of the untouchable communities imitated high-caste wedding rituals. However, he distanced himself from all such efforts by the 1930s. He went on to play an important role in some temple entry *satyagrahas*, in 1927 at Amraoti, in 1929 at Pune, and between 1930 and 1935 at Nasik, in fruitless efforts to enter the Kala Ram temple. However, in 1935 he stepped away from this approach too and there came the Yeola declaration that he would not die a Hindu. Thereafter for him the Dalit movement itself took on the form of "an attempt to build the cultural politics of disidentification vis-a-vis Hindu society and Gandhian modes of reasoning and feeling…" (Ibid., 69). There was a complete rejection of a shared Hindu self and he realized that it was imperative to write history (meting out justice as a third party) and build memories. The Dalit movement needed to build an alternative past.

Following Nagaraj there are a few points about Ambedkar's rewriting of history (discussed in the previous sections) and consequent erasure of memory that I want to emphasize here. The first has to do with the wiping out of cultural memory. The disidentification with the Hindu past in Ambedkar's modern moment of writing history had to involve measure, judgement and consequently a *disowning* of previous models of representing the past now judged as oppressive. Such an erasure and process of disengagement with the past could only proceed by dismantling the sphere of the spiritual-religio the "world of Gods and Goddesses" of the oppressed (Ashis Nandy in the foreword to Nagaraj [1993] 2015, v). At one go there was an absolute loss of cultural memory and a consequent erasure of the religio-spiritual life of the dalit self. For one thing, such a banishment of the Gods and Goddesses meant that even the restricted freedom of movement (of the deities from temples to dalit homes and sometimes from dalit homes to temples) was henceforth disallowed. As Nagaraj has argued, this was more than a disengagement, it was an absolute loss of the religious/spiritual past. This was also a loss that would be felt in the huts in the *Shudra* quarters as the Gods and goddesses had enjoyed a mobility that was denied to individuals.

> Actually, these Goddesses have a charming way of appearing both at conservative temples and at *shudra* hut-temples. Many a time the deity who is worshipped with the grandeur of Sanskrit verses and complicated rituals is originally a *shudra* Goddess. (Nagaraj [1993] 2015, 179)

The second point I seek to make about memory is related to this first. The erasure of cultural memory was felt in the self-representation of the dalit self. The multidimensional self was replaced by the re-constructed and now "two dimensional" modern dalit self-constituted by "only humiliation and pain" (Ibid., 162). The "bonsai like compression ..." (Ibid., 214) of the past Hindu tradition was reflected in the dalit self. The "dualist reading" of the Indian culture as a "binary opposition between the cultures of dalit-bahujans and Dwijas" (Ibid., 175) and the disowning of the dalit-bahujan past was reflected in the, now, one-dimensional self.

The third point is that this forgetting of the past involved a "self-minoritization" and also a related "self-closure". Ambedkar's modern moment of Lockean erasure also wiped out the memories of connection/sharing with the artisanal communities. The dalit past was previously a shared past and it is this shared past that reverberates perhaps in the philosophical *dohas*/stanzas of the weaver saint Kabir. The common memories of shared protests (of the dalit and artisanal communities in India) had to be erased along with the Hindu past of the dalits

> Ambedkar's was a great imaginative act of negotiating with the process of colonial modernist history. It was an act of bargaining with history itself. He had to break the organic unity of Dalits and Dastakars, for in the modernizing-colonizing combine the latter had no future. (Ibid., 119)

Perhaps this rejection was entailed by the coming to age of the modern self in Ambedkar's scientific and technological project of modernity. It was almost a logical outcome of this project and it was perhaps the conflict with Gandhi that led Ambedkar to so completely break away from traditional artisanal communities. However, this rejection of the common heritage with such communities led him to overlook the alliances between modernity, industrialization, capitalism and upper-caste society. This was something that the dalit movement under Ambedkar's leadership (and after him) failed to appreciate as the direct consequence of embracing the self and world view of modernity.

Modernity, the modern self, dalit self-minoritization and erasure of the past left the Dalit movement as a seething "politics of rage" (Ashis Nandy in the foreword to Nagaraj [1993] 2015, xv). While such an Ambedkarite politics of disidentification and rage was both a well-deserved and fitting response to the oppressive Hindu society there were limitations to its adequacy to meet the challenges posed by living together in the same space. There were (and still are) challenges to solving the problem of untouchability which might involve something more than affirmative action—legal and institutional reform and reservation. At some level in conflicts where the parties live close to each other both parties to the conflict need to have a change of heart. This was the move that Gandhi proposed in his debate with Ambedkar. Gandhi tried to widen "the circle of emotional concern" (Nagaraj [1993] 2015, 61) by identifying with both the parties to this and indeed every other conflict.

However, this widening of the circle of emotional concern and Gandhi's attempt at dual identification with both parties can also be seen as an act of bad faith. It is important to look at this connection at Arundhati Roy who argues that such dual identification gave evidence of Gandhi's inauthenticity and duplicity: "The man who raged against machines was kept afloat by industrialists" (Roy 2019, 65). Or again of Gandhi's mediations in the Ahmedabad mill workers strikes Roy argues; "While workers could not strike for fair wages, it was perfectly correct for Gandhi to be generously supported by the industrialists" (Ibid., 83).

It seems important to digress a little to speak here of how exactly Gandhi put the support received from industrialists (whom he opposed) to use. Having taken and diligently practised the vows of voluntary poverty, non-possession and non-stealing (holding on to more than one needs); there was no personal use to which Gandhi put/or indeed could put any aid that he ever received. It seems rather an act of bad faith to read all attempts to identify with both parties to a conflict as a conflict of interest. In the case of untouchability Gandhi simultaneously identified with the untouchables (as a self-styled adopted son) and at the same time asked for self-purification from his kin- the upper-caste oppressors. Perhaps, this was less utopian a moment than Ambedkar's modern moment of erasure. For Gandhi had perhaps a better understanding of the nature of the enmity between the *dwijas* and the dalits in Indian society. Here the enemy was "intimate": "The concept of intimate enmity denotes states of interdependence at many levels—emotional, intellectual, and material states—between different groups and communities" (Nagaraj [1993] 2015, 61).

It is the concept "of the stranger that is central to the problem of the widening of emotional concern" (Ibid., 63) and to understanding the nature of the kind of enmity that is involved in the caste conflicts in Indian society. There is a vast difference between the manner in which the premodern and post-enlightenment societies deal with the stranger and the strange. It is this difference that becomes one of the starting points for differences in the approach that Gandhi and Ambedkar take to the problem of untouchability.

Ambedkar emphasizes that the *dwijas* and the untouchables are strangers to each other. In premodern societies, the stranger was defined as "the man who comes today and stays tomorrow" (Ibid., 63). Perhaps he was the man who was made at home by the householders. However, in the post-enlightenment world the nation state does not want/care to make the stranger at home. At best the state *takes care* of the stranger by *permitting* him to become a citizen and consequently a bearer of rights. In more recent times the stranger is the immigrant—the person without a nation whom no one makes at home. In the best case it is rights that represent the modern strategy of taking care of the stranger, provided he/she is an immigrant, worth a welcome.

Quite literally in another world, for Gandhi, the past was still shared; the untouchables were the 'other' they were strangers but strangers could be made at home. The *swabhava* of being human called upon the *dwijas* to own kinship with these intimate 'others' by owning up to the unilateral obligation such kinship involved. However, in modernity the only way to respond to the stranger was by *permitting* him to become a citizen and consequently a bearer of rights. The Ambedkar and Gandhian approach to untouchability involved a conflict between incommensurable world views. Here there was the traditional world view posed *vis-a-vis* the world view propounded by the post-enlightenment modernity. Both the protagonists poised against each other (on either side of the debate) were good men; only they belonged to parallel worlds, perhaps, of a Leibnizian[ix] kind.

There is one last point that one might make about memory in connection with this debate. In that, it is significant to note that in his very insistence on creating an alternative memory Ambedkar "gave up modern forms of reasoning" (Ibid., 162). He affirmed the need to re-construct a new memory and in that re-construction he departed from modernity's fascination with a memory-less past and present. However, perhaps Ambedkar did not quite abandon modernity, in and by, this act of re-constructing memory after all. He still remained a modern in so far as he participated in writing history rather than following events in *itihaas*:

> …this is one of the most moving chapters of Indian history since it involves denying a real memory as well as the near academic venture of creating a new past: the conversion to Buddhism was an act to make this memory a living reality. (Ibid.)

The next chapter will look at Ambedkar's conversion as an act by which he confirmed his re-created past. Ambedkar simultaneously employed that act of confirmation to create the enlightenment-directed new Buddhist community of the future. The next chapter will discuss these and other issues as it examines Gandhi and Ambedkar on the self, community and God.

Notes

i.   An account of some important comments has been given in the Introduction to the book.

ii.   Ambedkar himself rarely used the term *Dalit.* The term comes from the
       Sanskrit *dal*—literally "split"/"broken open". It came to represent the condi-
       tion of being "ground down". By the 1970s, however, the term was divested of
       its negative connotation and adopted as a self-description by ancient India's
       erstwhile "untouchable" groups.
iii.   I will question, with Gandhi, the unchallenged hegemony of "history" as it
       regulates individual and collective relationship to the past in modernity.
iv.   Recall Sri Aurobindo's (1997) paper on the "Indian Renaissance", K.C Bhat-
       tacharya's (2011) lecture on "Swaraj in Ideas" and Gandhi's (2013) *Hind
       Swaraj.*
v.   See page 42 in this chapter.
vi.   It comes from the Latin meaning "comrade, friend, ally" (*socialis* in its adjec-
       tival form). The word has been used to describe a bond or interaction between
       parties that are friendly, or at least civil; it has given rise to the word society
       and refers also to social body.
vii.   Literally means "the act of leading to or enlightenment or near the eye (or
       eyesight/vision/third eye/pineal gland)"; it is a ceremony in which a *guru*
       (teacher) accepts and draws a child towards knowledge and initiates his/her
       second birth, that is, the birth of the young mind and spirit.
viii. It is interesting to note here that other bhakti saints also sang of cities which
       were havens of freedom. Tukaram sang of "Pandharpur" where all were equal.
       Kabir the weaver saint sang of "Premnagar" a city of love.
ix.   Gottfried Wilhelm (von)Leibniz (1646–1716) had thought that there were
       infinitely many possible worlds, each with different physics, subject to the
       organizing principle that all the laws of nature should together not imply a
       contradiction. Leibniz was clear that even an omnipotent God would not be
       able to actualize contradictions. A "possible system of physical laws" would
       then be one criterion by which God had chosen the actual world. Since above
       all God had an innate goodness, he would also have seen fit to make the best
       possible world.

References

Ambedkar, B. R. 2014. *Dr Babasaheb Ambedkar writings and Speeches,* ed. Vasant Moon (set of 17
    Volumes). New Delhi: Dr Ambedkar Foundation. Ministry of Social Justice and Empowerment.
    Government of India.
Ambedkar, B. R. 2017. *The untouchables: Who were They and Why They Became Untouchables?*
    New Delhi: Samyak Prakashan.
Aurobindo, S. 1997. Renaissance in India. In *The Complete Works of Sri Aurobindo,* 37 vols.
    Pondicherry: Sri Aurobindo Ashram Trust.
Bhagavan, M., ed. 2010. *Heterotopias: Nationalism and the Possibility of History in South Asia.*
    New Delhi: Oxford University Press.

Bhattacharya, K. C. 2011. Swaraj in ideas. In *Indian Philosophy in English: From Renaissance to Independence*. eds. Nalini Bhushan and Jay L. Garfield, pp. 103–114. New York: Oxford University Press.

Gandhi, M. K. 1888–1948. *Collected Works of Mahatma Gandhi*: Volumes 1 to 98. New Delhi: Publications Division Government of India, 1999. Accessed online in May 2021. https://www.gandhiashramsevagram.org/gandhi-literature/collected-works-of-mahatma-gandhi-volume-1-to-98.php.

Gandhi, M. K. 2010. *Hind swaraj and other writings*, ed. Anthony Parel. New York: Cambridge University Press.

Hawley, J. S. (ed.) 1988. *Songs of the Saints of India*, trans. by Mark Juergensmeyer. New Delhi: Oxford University Press.

Kolge, N. 2018. *Gandhi Against Caste*. Delhi: Oxford University Press.

Murdoch, I. 1971. *The Sovereignty of God*. New York: Routledge.

Nagaraj, D. R. [1993] 2015. *The Flaming Feet and Other Essays: The Dalit Movement in India*, 2nd ed, ed. Prithvi Datta Chandra Shobhi. 5th impression. Ranikhet: Permanent Black.

Parekh, B. 1989. *Colonialism, Tradition and Reform: An Analysis of Gandhi's Political Discourse*. New Delhi: Sage Publications.

Prabhu, R. K., and U. R. Rao. 1967. *The Mind of Mahatma Gandhi*. Ahmedabad: Navajivan Publishing House.

Raz, J. 1990. Facing diversity: The case of epistemic abstinence. *Philosophy & Public Affair (wiley)* 19 (1): 3–46.

Roy, A. 2019. *The Doctor and the Saint: The Ambedkar-Gandhi Debate: Caste, Race and Annihilation of Caste*. New Delhi: Penguin Books.

Scruton, R. 2014. *The Soul of the World*. New Jersey: Princeton University Press.

Shobhi, P. D. C. 2015. Introduction: *Khadgavali Kavya*". In *The Flaming Feet and Other Essays: The Dalit movement in India*, 2nd ed, ed. Prithvi Datta Chandra Shobhi. 5th impression. Ranikhet: Permanent Black.

Skaria, A. 2010. The Strange Violence of *satyagraha*: Gandhi, *itihaas*, and History. In *Heterotopias: Nationalism and the Possibility of History in South Asia*, ed. Manu Bhagavan, 142–185. New Delhi: Oxford University Press.

Taylor, C. 2001. *Source of the Self: The Making of the Modern Identity*. Cambridge: Harvard University Press.

Verma, V. 2020. Modernity, Colonial Injustice and Individual Responsibility: A Study of Gandhi and Ambedkar. In *Gandhi and the Contemporary World*, ed. Sanjeev Kumar, 113–128. London: Routledge.

Veyne, P. 1984. *Writing history: Essays in Epistemology*. Middletown: Wesleyan University Press.

Zelliot, E. 1972. Gandhi and Ambedkar—A study in leadership. In *The Untouchables in Contemporary India*, ed. J. M. Mahar, 69–96. Tucson: University of Arizona Press.

Chapter 3
Ambedkar and Gandhi: Self, Community and God

Abstract This chapter argues that the differences between Ambedkar and Gandhi emerged from their incommensurable conceptions of the self and the relationship between the self and the world. The chapter will make philosophical use of Charles Taylor's exposition of the making of modern identity in the West to bring out the three aspects of the making of self-identity which become central to modern self-understanding. It will suggest that it was not exchanges over *varna* or separate electorates but the ***coming of age of modern identity*** that led Ambedkar into a difficult debate with Gandhi. In this context, this chapter will examine the notions on self, community and God in Ambedkar and Gandhi.

Keywords Self · Modern Identity · Charles Taylor · *Bhagavad Gita* · Enlightenment/*Aufklarung* · Background moral frameworks · Strong evaluation · Idea of the good · Constitutive Good · Religion · *Dhamma* · *Navayana*/"new vehicle" · God

The first chapter had argued that the differences between Bhimrao Ramji Ambedkar (1891–1956) and Mohandas Karamchand Gandhi (1869–1948), two of the most important non-Western thinkers of our times, emerged from their very different conceptions of the self and of the relationship between that self and its past. This book is not as much interested in relating the story of the confrontations between Gandhi and Ambedkar as it is in bringing out the divergences of presuppositions and world views that underlay those confrontations. The chapter will argue that the differences between Ambedkar and Gandhi emerged from their incommensurable conceptions of the self and his/her relationship to the world. One need only consider (the arguments of the last chapter) that while Gandhi saw the self in continuity with India's *itihaas* Ambedkar dedicated himself to the making of the radically disengaged modern Indian self.

However, there seemed to be some difficulties with the central argument of the last Chapter. It appeared that while the first chapter had made arguments in support of the point that Ambedkar initiates and (in some aspects) completes, the making of modern Indian identity his self-conscious re-construction of an alternative memory for/of dalits [i] seem to signify a breakdown of that very identity. It is significant to note that the making of modern identity post the seventeenth century (in the Western

© Springer Science+Business Media Singapore 2022   55
B. Puri, *The Ambedkar–Gandhi Debate*,
https://doi.org/10.1007/978-981-16-8686-3_3

world) certainly showed no such nostalgia for the past. The coming to be of the
modern subject was the coming to be of a self who was constituted by an individualistic independence which was reflected in a sense of comfort with a memory-less
past. The question faced by many commentators on the Ambedkar–Gandhi debate
is whether a hankering for an alternative past reconciles Ambedkar with Gandhi and
indeed with more traditional world views. If one considers Ambedkar's engagement
with writing history to confer a Buddhist past to the dalits in continuity with, the much
later confirmation of that history by a public act of (what seemed to be an almost
retrospective) conversion, one might read this hankering for an alternative history as
a lapse in the making of modern identity. Commentators on the debate have indeed
read it as such, and have argued, that the debate with Gandhi transformed Ambedkar
and led him to recognize the importance of Religion and of the religious community
to individual identity. Such recognition (one might say) sits uneasily with the modern
subject for whom a public ceremony of conversion, would in itself, be inauthentic
given that liberal public space has no room for such religiosity.

Giving voice to such readings Lal (2020) has argued that Ambedkar was an
intensely religious man. Though Ambedkar was distrustful of the concept of a
personal God and of any account of personal revelation, he was convinced of the
necessity of religion in human life. Lal has argued that Religion (for Ambedkar)
could bind people into a religious community with solidarity, love and compassion (Lal 2020). In a similar strain, Ananya Vajpeyi argues that "…in the final
analysis he (Ambedkar) wanted the Untouchables to reconstitute themselves as a
religious community in a more traditional sense of religion" (Vajpeyi 2013, 222).
This according to Vajpeyi, drove Ambedkar to conversion, and brought him "paradoxically" closer to Gandhi (Ibid.). Conjuring the metaphor of enlightenment as
spiritual salvation Vajpeyi argues that "(i)In recasting the untouchables as Buddhists
Ambedkar was conceding that tradition remained the ferment that would slowly
flood with light" (Ibid., 242). Again perhaps Gandhi's most bitter critic Arundhati
Roy writes of Ambedkar's conversion;

> It was his most radical act. It marked his departure from Western Liberalism and its purely
> materialistic vision of a society based on 'rights', a vision whose origin coincided with the
> rise of modern capitalism. (Roy 2014, 139–140)

In the first chapter I had, in a sense rejected, any/all such readings by arguing that
there was no anomaly in Ambedkar's relationship with liberal Western modernity.
Ambedkar's act of writing history was in itself a modern act *par excellence*. Taking
this point a little further, this chapter is going to initiate a discussion on self, community and God in Gandhi and Ambedkar. Towards this end, this chapter will discuss
the powerful alternity of their approaches to agency and self as preparatory to the
discussion of their very different approaches to the eradication of untouchability in
Chap. 4.

The present chapter will argue that Gandhi's differences from Ambedkar were far
from being merely strategic (Kolge 2017, 102) or worse still acts of bad faith emerging
from what Roy describes as "brutal, institutionalized injustice" (Roy 2014, 43). The
differences between Gandhi and Ambedkar cannot be confined to Empire, caste and

Franchise. Rather such differences emerged from more fundamental divergences about the notions of the self (who was enacting the role of oppressor or victim) and from very different notions of the religious community in which such roles were being enacted. The appropriate understanding of the differences between Gandhi and Ambedkar (and the location of these differences in powerfully alternative notions of the self, Religion, God and community) might reveal that neither Ambedkar nor Gandhi could retrospectively be judged to be right or alternatively that both could be right and wrong at the very same time. Or one might simply say that all such questions are literally nonsensical and can admit of no answers. Just as the following is perhaps a nonsensical question: 'Which is the **best** world to live in, the one in which our ancestors revered tradition, or, the one in which we live now or perhaps the one coming in the future where families might indeed be given up as coercive?'—(Where 'best' is taken to be a normative term and not simply in the sense of 'best'/most useful/appropriate for me).

Good philosophy cannot answer such questions or arbitrate which self-understanding or conception of Religion/God is normatively superior. The most that it can do is clear up the conceptual space and bring out what is really at stake in these questions and that is about the amount of clarity which such themes can take.

This chapter will explore this theme across four sections and a conclusion. The first section 'The making of modern identity' will bring out the importance of the self and of agency to the debate between Gandhi and Ambedkar. In this context, it will (across subsections) discuss the development of modern identity in the Western world in line with Charles Taylor's philosophical account of the same. The second section 'Gandhi on the *Bhagavad Gita*: Putting together a Gandhian conception of the self' will attempt to put together a Gandhian conception of the self will attempt to put together a Gandhian conception of the self in line with his several comments on the *Bhagavad Gita*.[ii] It will also bring out the relationship between that self and the traditional religious community. The Third Section 'Ambedkar: On self Religion and God' will explore (across three sub sections) Ambedkar's more modern conception of the self and his attempt to re-write Buddhism as a "new religion" (Ambedkar 2014, 17 Part 2: 104)[1]. for a "new world" (Ibid., 105) along the lines framed by the enlightenment values, i.e. liberty equality and fraternity. The conclusion will suggest that Ambedkar's religious turn did not signify a move towards tradition and away from modernity. Rather, somewhat like his writing of history, Ambedkar's re-writing of Buddhism was a modern act and signified the coming of age of the modern Indian subject.

---

[1] Ambedkar 2014 refers to the 17 volumes of *Dr Babasaheb Ambedkar writings and Speeches*. The volume concerned and the page numbers from which citations have been drawn have been mentioned within parentheses. These have been mentioned to indicate the exact location of the quotation in the 17 volumes. However, for the purposes of reference, it may be noted that I have resourced these volumes from Ambedkar, B.R. 2014. *Dr Babasaheb Ambedkar writings and Speeches*, edited by Vasant Moon (set of 17 Volumes). New Delhi: Dr Ambedkar Foundation. Ministry of Social Justice and Empowerment. Government of India.

3.1 The Making of Modern Identity

3.1.1 Gandhi and Ambedkar: On Self and Agency

The notion of the self enters the Ambedkar–Gandhi debate most directly through arguments about agency that came up over the issue of the appropriate method to remove untouchability (there will be some occasion to visit arguments over the removal of untouchability in more detail in the next chapter). There is no doubt that both Gandhi and Ambedkar were committed to the removal of untouchability. However, while Gandhi spoke of self-purification and atonement by upper castes, Ambedkar argued that the depressed classes must assume agency for reform. This issue came to its most dramatic head on the occasion of the arguments over separate electorates at the Second Round Table Conference in London in 1932 with Gandhi claiming to represent the depressed classes in his own person. However, this was not the start of the matter nor of course the end of it. The *itihaas* of the anti-untouchability and anticaste movements involved many brave reformers before the debate between Gandhi and Ambedkar took centre stage on the issue.

One might look back at past ages and remember that in South India in the mid-twelfth century, there were challenges to caste from the revolt of the Veerashaivas led by Basava. From the fourteenth century onwards, the anticaste protests were expressed in the songs of the bhakti saints—Cokhamela, Ravidas (whose poem I had occasion to refer to in the last chapter), Kabir, Tukaram, Mira and Janabai. The nineteenth and early twentieth centuries saw a host of reformers. There were Jyotiba Phule and his *Satyashodhak Samaj* and Pandita Ramabai in Western India. In 1828, Raja Ram Mohan Roy founded the *Brahmo Samaj*. In 1875, Swami Dayananda Saraswati founded the *Arya Samaj*, and in 1897, Swami Vivekananda established the *Ramakrishna Mission*. Swami Achhutanand Harihar, who led the Adi Hindu movement, started the *Bharatiya Achhut Mahasabha* (Parliament of Indian Untouchables), and edited *Achhut*, the first dalit journal. In Malabar and Travancore, caste was challenged by Ayyankali and Sree Narayana Guru. Iyothee Thass and his *Sakya* Buddhists challenged Brahmin supremacy in the Tamil world. Ambedkar's contemporaries in the anticaste tradition included Jogendranath Mandal of Bengal, E. V. Ramasamy Naicker (also known as "Periyar") in the Madras Presidency and Babu Mangoo Ram, who founded the *Ad Dharm* movement in Punjab.

It is important to note that though there have been many figures in the struggle against caste there is no doubt that the movement for the abolition of untouchability gathered its final momentum in the efforts of Babasaheb and Gandhi. It is not only that the movement gained more prominence in national politics (which of course happened) once it became the subject of contestation between Gandhi and Ambedkar but rather that the nature of the issues brought up in the movement underwent a conceptual change. The contestations between Gandhi and Ambedkar brought out the two world views (one traditional and the other inspired by Western modernity) fighting for space at the heart of the antiuntouchability campaign. The progressive change in emphasis (in the movement against untouchability) from temple entry to civic rights did not only mean that Gandhi had lost political ground to Ambedkar. It signified something much more important than that. Gandhi had lost philosophical ground to Babasaheb. This loss of ground was far more crucial than a merely political loss. Rather it was symptomatic of the arrival of the modern subject in the dalit movement who rejected temple entry and the *atman*-driven self at the heart of Gandhian politics. There is no doubt that it was Ambedkar who set the conceptual terms for the victory when the constituent Assembly of Independent India passed a provision legally abolishing untouchability on 29 November 1948, nine months after the death of Gandhi.

In the next subsection, I want to look a little more closely at the making of modern identity with a view to extricate, as it were, the genealogies of the sources of the Self in the intellectual history of the modern West. Such an archaeologico-philosophical exercise will serve to bring out the way in which the conflict between Gandhi and Ambedkar reflected the philosophical issues involved in the coming of age of the modern subject in the Western part of the world. This subsection will make (somewhat copious) philosophical use of Charles Taylor's exposition of the making of modern identity in the West to bring out the aspects that become central to such a modern self-understanding. I will argue that these aspects and modern self-understanding itself, came of age in India, (in the writing and) under the leadership of, B. R. Ambedkar. It was not exchanges over *varna* or separate electorates but this coming to age of modern identity that led Ambedkar into a difficult debate with M. K. Gandhi.

3.1.2   Charles Taylor and the Making of Modern Identity

Taylor raises a question about the sources of the modern self and clarifies that this is a question of diachronic causation. What this means is that when one asks about the coming to be of "modern identity" one also raises questions about the set of precipitating conditions. This latter, of course, takes us into a statement of some of the features peculiar to Western civilization in the early modern period. The point is that we cannot see these two things—modern self-understanding and the set of practices that the (post eighteenth century) Western self-engaged in—in isolation from each other. It is in taking the answers to these (inter-related) questions together that one can perhaps explain the sources of the appeal of modern identity for people across the world (and across colonial and post-colonial India) who were increasingly drawn to think about themselves as modern subjects.

Clearly, modern understandings of the self, of the human predicament in the world and of moral ideals, are powerfully linked to a specific set of precipitating conditions. They are in fact linked to more modern capitalist economy, democratic governance, technology-driven science, the modern emphasis on disciplinary movement and to the several practices and institutions associated with these. One might think here of Gandhi's insight into these connections as evidenced by his often quoted critique of modern civilization. Gandhi insightfully located the moral lacunae at the heart of modernity and linked its indifference to the good human life with its (modern) institutions and with ideas of democratic and economic governance (note Gandhi's critique of Parliament in *Hind Swaraj* (2010)). Charles Taylor has brought out three broad aspects by which one might distinguish modern identity from older and more traditional self-understandings. Attempting to unpack these will take us through defining moments in the history of Western philosophy—from Plato through Descartes, Locke and Kant—to explore the sources for the making of modern identity.

It might seem strange to the reader that I should choose to go from an account of the differences between Ambedkar and Gandhi on history and *itihaas* to Taylor's account of the making of modern identity which takes me through defining moments in the coming of the enlightenment/*Aufklarung* in the Western world. However if one reflects upon the influence of the notion of agency on the disagreements between Ambedkar and Gandhi, one might appreciate that it becomes important to philosophically unpack the genealogies and aspects of their very different ideas of the self and consequently of the relationship between the self and the community. This last will involve a discussion of the central features of the modern understanding of the self, if only to help better understand Ambedkar's impatience with Gandhi's approach to untouchability. As a correlative to this, Taylor's account could also help to bring about a better understanding of Ambedkar's position on the religious community and his reformulated socially engaged modern Buddhism "new vehicle" or *Navayana* as he called it (on the eve of his conversion to Buddhism) in 1956.

Taylor identifies three facets of modern identity;

> …first, modern inwardness, the sense of ourselves as beings with inner depths, and the connected notion that we are 'selves'; second, the affirmation of ordinary life which develops from the early modern period, third, the expressivist notion of nature as an inner moral source. (Taylor 2001, X)

The first Taylor traces from Augustine, through Descartes and Locke to the present day. It is with this inwardness and the obsessive individualism of the modern age that I seek to begin, and with which, I am predominantly concerned. It does not detract from this discussion that (as moderns) we might not be conscious that our identity has anything at all to do with western philosophy and its central ideas such as the Cartesian dualism of mind and body. As Taylor says "the ideals and interdicts of this identity—what it causes in relief and what it castes in shadow-shape our philosophical thought, our epistemology and our philosophy of language, largely without our awareness." (Ibid., 9).

Before moving on to discuss the first aspect of modern identity, the sense of inwardness, it is important to look at an idea powerfully connected with the inwardness of the modern self. This is the idea of the good and what it has come to mean to the modern agent. A discussion of the idea of the good is merited (at this initial point) because notions of the Self and the good are intimately interconnected. In fact, one cannot get into any discussion of how modern self-identity came to be so powerfully inward looking without saying something about a corresponding change/evolution in the idea of the good. As might seem obvious at the start one needs to clarify what the term 'the good' means. As Taylor explains, it means, "anything considered valuable, worthy, admirable, of whatever kind of category." (Ibid., 92) A consideration of this idea reveals that the idea of the good evolved and underwent changes, from the ancient to the modern world. The ancients had insightfully distinguished life goods (what Aristotle called external goods) from a notion of the constitutive good. It is significant to note that the ancient world took the latter to be good in a fuller sense than external goods (which included money, fame even friendship/*philia*). In that, a constitutive good was not a means to an end but rather always "something the love of which empowers us to do and be good" (Ibid., 93) One might recall that when Gandhi spoke of "Truth or God", he was invoking the notion of a constitutive good (or God). It might help to explain this difference, between external goods and a constitutive good by recalling the Platonic form of the good as the object of an empowering love and indeed as being the source of the good. Somewhat in sharp contrast to this Platonic form of the good (represented, one might recall, by the sun in the cave analogy of the *Republic*) the modern agent regards herself/himself as the source of the idea of right. Murdoch makes much of this shift in modern moral philosophy from the good to the right:

> It is significant that the idea of goodness (and of virtue)has been largely superseded in Western moral philosophy by the idea of rightness,supported perhaps by some conception of sincerity.This is to some extent a natural outcome of the disappearance of a permanent background to human activity:a permanent background,whether provided by God, by Reason,….or by the Self. (Murdoch 1970, 52)

One might say that the modern subject has altogether discarded making what Taylor calls "strong evaluation" (Taylor 2001, 4) and the related idea of a constitutive good which makes all such evaluation possible. Taylor has argued that the modern agent has also rejected the idea of a constitutive good as the source of love which inspires and moves, as it were, the subject to lead a good human life. Of course with these dismissals, the modern agent has also rejected the important idea of owing allegiance to a partially or comprehensively (to use Rawls' term) articulated "background picture" (Ibid., 8) lying behind one's moral and spiritual intuitions.

One might also say, paradoxically enough, that the only constitutive good which might be accepted (though not acknowledged as such) by the modern subject is precisely the ability to be disengaged from all those notions that have traditionally been taken as constitutive goods. Notice the "courageous disengagement" (Ibid., 94) and lucidity of Ambedkar's complete rejection of the background picture of a Hindu *rta*/cosmic order. With this disengagement, the love empowered by/for the constitutive good/God has also been completely rejected by Ambedkar as by the modern self. It has, in fact, been replaced by respect (notice, in Kant for instance, the idea of the holy will inspired by reverence for the moral law) and empowered by a modern humanism. This is an important shift, and as we shall see, it somewhat serves to set the divide between Gandhi and Ambedkar.

The nature of the cosmic moral order of the universe (what the ancient Indian tradition designated as *rta*) in all its different articulations, across various languages, has all but faded away, both from modern Western moral philosophy and from the popular culture of modernity. As Iris Murdoch has put it, modern Western moral philosophy has tended to focus on what it is right to do rather than on what it is good to be, on defining the content of obligation, rather than the nature of the good life (see Murdoch 1970, ch. 2). This shift has led to a corresponding change in the understanding of the nature and role of morality. It has led to the rejection of the authority of moral claims that draw their weight from ontological accounts such as those which might speak of human beings as creatures of God. To see what change the shift from the good to the right has brought about one might consider Ambedkar's account of *Dhamma vis a vis* Gandhi's account of the human being as a silhouette/*pratibimb* of God (which was referred to, in passing, in Chap. 2). It is only against such a background ontology (as I had argued in Chap. 2) that it can become imperative for human beings (on a Gandhian view at least) to live up to the unilateral obligation of owning kinship with the most distant human and non-human other.

Modern naturalist consciousness has done away with all such, and indeed any "given ontology of the Human" (Taylor 2001, 5), as irrelevant to morality. This needs to be understood against earlier/ancient cultures, such as the one inhabited by the old-world Gandhi, where "some framework stands unquestioned which helps define the demands by which" (Ibid., 16) individual members of communities "judge their lives and measure, as it were their fullness or emptiness" (Ibid.). Taylor explains what it might have meant to have lived against such frameworks which have been rejected by modern naturalist consciousness. These are fossils from an ancient age as it were;

> To think, feel, judge within such a framework is to function with the sense that some mode of life, or mode of feeling is incomparably higher than others which are more readily available to us… (Ibid., 20)

What is important about such frameworks is that they are connected with the idea of a constitutive good/God which inspires strong evaluations. The most significant thing about such moral evaluations is that they are to be made independently of individual desires, needs (even of organising ideals; such as Rawls' notion of justice as the first virtue of social institutions) and the human universe. The philosophically operative term here is 'independently' of;

> …the fact that these ends or goods stand independently of our desires, inclinations, or choices, that they represent standards by which these desires and choices are judged. (Ibid.)

The difficulty is that (partially or comprehensively articulated) background frameworks sit uneasily with the autonomous nature of the modern subject. Part of the reason (why they sit uneasily and have to be discarded by the modern subject) is because these frameworks/ontological accounts have often been put to unjust use. It is significant to note that some part of the explanation of why modern subjects distrust articulation of such frameworks comes from the "sinister purposes" (Ibid., 97) to which such explanations have often been put. One might refer (for instance) to the manner in which commentators used interpretations of the *Purusa Sukta* hymn of the *Veda* to justify unjust restrictions on allegedly lesser beings. That said, it is also important to recognize and accept that the rejection of background moral frameworks (cast in some given ontology of the human) has also been on account of the "epistemological cloud" (Ibid., 5) under which such accounts find themselves in a world driven by modern natural science and empiricist epistemology. It is interesting to note that moderns reject such frameworks (of cosmic order, of God as a creator bequeathing his commandments) as the source of moral value and are universalists about the respect for life. However, though such universalism leads them to draw the boundaries around the human race, this, often enough leaves out the non-human world. Perhaps this is a natural enough consequence of what Weber called the "disenchantment" of nature and the rejection of the sense of the cosmos as a meaningful order. The goods[iii] (if we can call them that) that modern philosophers celebrate are "human-centered: freedom, active benevolence, universal rights" (Ibid., 102).

It is important to make the point that modern liberal philosophers who might accept these human centred goods must yet remain hesitant **even about using them** to formulate a fully articulated background picture constituted entirely by such goods. This is because liberalism demands an equidistance from any/all particular moral framework(s) given that in a plural democratic society there are many moral frameworks competing for public space. One might ask whether it is best to keep silent (like most modern liberal philosophers) about the possible frameworks (even where these are acceptable human centred ones), behind our moral choices. Despite the fact that, such a silence seems to be imperative given the liberal commitment to plurality in our times, both Taylor and Murdoch (among others) have argued at length that any "naturalist reduction which would exclude frameworks altogether from consideration cannot be carried through…" (Ibid., 23). Philosophers like Taylor, MacIntyre and Murdoch (among others) have argued that silence about frameworks of the good impoverishes human moral life. The difficulties of doing without background frameworks (articulating one's idea of the good) become apparent when one reflects on the necessity of keeping moral motivation a going concern in human life. The point is perhaps that getting motivation off the ground and making moral choices often requires making an appeal to some substantive background moral frameworks; and whether such frameworks be, transcendent to or embedded in the human world, one needs to be able to refer to them all the same while making such choices. In this context, it is important to recall Ambedkar's insights on the necessity to associate the notion of the "sacred" with that of morality so that morality could become "sacred and universal"[iv] (Ambekar 2011, 173). Taylor's remark about why it is impossible to "to conceive a person or even a culture which might so understand his predicament as to do altogether without frameworks…" (Taylor 2001, 26) might also, of course, bring to mind Ambedkar's re-writing of Buddhism along enlightenment lines perhaps to provide just such a framework. In this context it is significant to note Kumar's emphasis on Ambedkar's "struggle for an ethical and political religion" (Kumar 2015, 10).

Having said that it remains to be determined if Ambedkar's conversion to Buddhism (in 1956) and his reformulated "political religion" (Ibid.) new vehicle/*Navayana* could be considered as an effort to re-construct such an unques-tioned background framework? One can perhaps even ask if Ambedkar was inter-ested at all in providing such a background framework containing answers to moral questions independently of human desires and in accordance with a (partial or comprehensive) account of a constitutive good? An important aspect to having such a background framework (on Taylor's account of it) was to be able to access a standard to make strong evaluations independently of human desires/needs. If Ambedkar's *Navayana* did serve to provide a background framework the question still remains whether he had intended to use this framework for "theologizing his political views"[v] (Rathore and Verma 2011, xi) or as a religious framework in the more traditional (and conventional) sense of the term? One might find an answer to this question if one spells out some of the reasons why there should be difficulties in doing away with (what Rawls terms) "comprehensive"[vi] (Rawls 2005, 13) theories of the good, background frameworks and the notion of the constitutive good/God. This last could seem to throw some light upon Ambedkar's need to re-think Buddhism and create a new kind of religious community.

Taylor answers an apparent version (I say apparent because as I will argue later Ambedkar was not looking for a framework that could be taken as "religious" in the conventional/ordinary sense of the term) of the question posed by Ambedkar's conversion by bringing up insights about the close connection between having a background framework and the notion of self-identity:

> …the question is often spontaneously phrased by people… who am I? But this cannot necessarily be answered by giving name and geneology. What does answer this question for us is an understanding of what is of crucial importance for us. To know who I am is a species of knowing where I stand…. My identity is defined by the commitments and identifications which provide the frame or horizon within which I can try to determine from case to case what is good, or valuable, or what ought to be done, or what I endorse or oppose.In other words it is the horizon within which I am capable of taking a stand. (Taylor 2001, 27)

I would like to go back to the point that—Taylor's answer to the question "who am I?"—positing a connection between having a sense of oneself and having a background framework might not quite explain Ambedkar's move to re-interpret Buddhism. Taylor's question (or indeed answer) might also not help to situate Ambedkar's conversion to Buddhism because it is possible to argue (and I will go on to argue) that Ambedkar's conversion was not an act of accepting the comprehensive Buddhist account of the good as an account that provided (the moral aspirant with) a standard for moral evaluation independent of human desire and need. Taylor has argued that there is a "connection between identity and a kind of orientation. To know who you are is to be oriented in moral space, a space in which questions arise about what is good or bad, what is worth doing and what not…" (Ibid., 28). There is a close parallel with spatial orientation here (a connection which Taylor explic-itly makes) which specifically connects with some issues at stake in the Gandhi and Ambedkar debate (think for example of sacred temple space and its exclusions). I would suggest (in this and the next chapter) that Ambedkar's conversion was not related to any interest in **reclaiming** a framework understood as an orientation to the good or a space in which answers about the good were located. Quite to the contrary his conversion was prompted by an interest in **re-writing** a framework which would account for notions of what it might be right to do along the lines dictated by the familiar enlightenment values. The significant point to note about the enlightenment was that individuals were free to answer questions about the good in their own ways and did not need to be oriented in moral space by any *a priori* notion of the constitutive good. Ambedkar's *Navayana* was (in his own words) a "new religion" (Ambedkar 2014, 17 Part 2: 104) for a "new world" (Ibid., 105) which was built around a commitment to enlightenment liberty, and which therefore, could not retain any commitment to the traditional Buddhist notion of a constitutive good spelt out, for instance, in Buddha's Four Noble Truths.

This also becomes evident from the fact that, in the very process of making a selection between different religions as possible candidates (religions) for conversion, Ambedkar had already done away with the need to have a religious background framework. One might consider that the process of **selecting** a religion involves placing oneself outside all religions, which are candidates for selection, and suggests a turn inwards (into the self) where order (and the basis of making that choice between religions) is created/found within the self rather than sought outside in a transcendental realm. I would see such rejection of all background frameworks as the critical and modern moment in Ambedkar's life. It is a moment that goes back in the history of Western philosophy to Locke's famous rejection of all innate ideas. It was perhaps this rejection of a cruel religio-moral order and significantly of all such orders thus located outside of the individual that one can see dramatically reflected in Ambedkar's move to publicly burn the *Manu Smriti* in December 1927. This was not only because with Ambedkar "an encounter with sacrilege was always round the corner" (Kumar 2015, 5) but because Ambedkar sought to demolish the unjust ancient only to rebuild anew on the more secure foundations of experience and sensation legitimated, by and in, the individual.

Speaking of rupture it seems important to look at a more contemporary reading that looks at this rupture in a slightly different time and conceptual space. Kumar (2015) traces this moment of rupture to 1936 and to Ambedkar's *Annihilation of Caste* arguing that:

> This freedom to believe,which underwrites the right to a just religion,not only exceeds the organized,hierarchical,and ecclesiastical limits on faith,it exceeds even the practice of mysticism that had lent lower caste protest in the precolonial period its emancipatory charge.It is in this rupture from premodern genealogies of emancipatory mysticism and Humanistic pieties of modern nationalism alike that Ambedkar would emerge as the thinker of the theologico-political in its classical and insurrectionary sense. (Kumar 2015, 9)

Kumar explains that by "the classical and insurrectionary" (Ibid.) he has "in mind a tradition of grappling with the inextricable relationship between force and justice, a tradition whose lineage Ambedkar would himself trace to the Rousseauist strand within modern revolutionary thought" (Ibid.).

While I agree with Kumar that there is a rupture from the premodern in Ambedkar if I had to speak of a moment which best represents that rupture, I would locate it much earlier in 1927, in Ambedkar's public burning of the *Manu Smriti*. However, and more importantly, while Kumar speaks of the rupture from the genealogies of emancipatory mysticism, I would (and will) argue that Ambedkar's burning of the *Manu Smriti* represents a rupture not only from the unjust religious tradition but also from what has ordinarily been understood as "religion" itself. For what has been built anew is not religion (can religion be built anew?) but *dhamma*. Ambedkar had himself explained the difference (of which more will be said a little later in this chapter) between the two. The second point important to make here is perhaps that while Kumar seeks to trace this rupture to the tradition of grappling with "the inextricable relationship between force and justice" (Ibid.). I will argue (in what follows) that it needs to be traced to something more fundamental. While the relationship between power and force is in a sense outside the self/external to the self; Ambedkar's rupture had to do with something at once more basic and fundamental. It had to do with his re-thinking and rejection of premodern notions of the self, self-understanding and the relationship between the self and the world. Ambedkar's moment of rupture is best related to the genealogies of the self that defined modernity and can be traced back to the notions of the 'self' in the writing of the European philosophers in the post seventeenth century.

Keeping this in mind then there are two additional points that need to be made. The first that Ambedkar was perhaps not looking for a background comprehensive moral framework at all. For instance, one that provided a standard for making strong evaluations independently of human desires and need; an ancillary point is that Ambedkar was not looking for an orientation in a moral space that came from an unquestioned commitment to the idea of a constitutive good. The second point is related to the idea that there is a connection between having such a background picture and the sense of individual identity. Unlike the ancients (indeed unlike Gandhi) and in the modern way Ambedkar felt no need to embrace a connection between a felt allegiance to a background framework and individual identity. It was hardly surprising then that he had very soon distanced himself from the dalit move to reclaim sacred space or the temple entry movement, which for Gandhi at least, was very important to the movement to dismantle untouchability.

Another important aspect to this move to free individual identity from dependence upon comprehensive background moral frameworks was that Ambedkar perhaps felt close to the appeal of another modern argument. It is important to note that a critical aspect to becoming enabled to erase one's allegiance to background moral frameworks which set standards for human beings independently of their will/need was that this erasure could be felt as freedom by the modern individual. There was a strong appeal in the liberation felt by the modern subject in breaking free of allegiance to any such standards (in this case of course to unjust standards). One might consider that "the modern notion of freedom which develops in the seventeenth century portrays this as the independence of the subject." (Taylor 2001, 82).

One might consider yet another factor which might have drawn Ambedkar towards the rejection of ideas of the good and ancient moral frameworks such as the idea of *rta* or that set by the place of ignorance/*avijja* in the Buddha's Four Noble Truths as traditionally understood. This appeal might be best put as the second aspect of Taylor's three features of modern self-identity. As Taylor argues, "the affirmation of ordinary life, while necessarily denouncing certain distinctions, itself amounts to one; else it has no meaning at all…" (Ibid., 23). Perhaps Ambedkar felt this appeal strongly and felt drawn to the affirmation of the concerns of ordinary life. This is what might have lead him to re-write Buddhism as socially engaged and as resting upon the affirmation of ordinary life in the political/civic community. Such a *Navayana* would (in his view) answer questions about identity with reference to the concerns of everyday life. More importantly the *Navayana* would place forth a conception of *Nibbana/*salvation understood in terms closer to the *Aufklarung/* Enlightenment than in spiritual terms. It is significant to note that Ambedkar's new Buddhism was about an affirmation of ordinary life in society as a life governed by the ideals of fraternity, equality and liberty.

The question still remains whether Ambedkar's conversion was an expression of his adoption of the comprehensive background moral framework constituted by traditional Buddhism. The important characteristic of such a framework would be that it could make space for strong moral evaluations **independent of** individual desire and need. Perhaps it is better to ask whether the *Navayana* shared in the idea of the constitutive good represented by the religious framework of traditional Buddhism. The difficulty with answering this second question in the affirmative comes from the fact that Ambedkar's re-thinking of Buddhism, self-consciously distanced itself, from Buddhist metaphysics selectively reporting only chosen events from Buddha's life. More importantly, the *Navayana* distanced itself from beliefs that exerted a defining influence on Buddhist ethics as evidenced by Ambedkar's radical re-interpretation of the Four Noble Truths on which Buddhist philosophy and ethics traditionally rests. Such selective readings and re-interpretations lead some scholars to suggest that Ambedkar's *The buddha and his dhamma* was not a religious but a political re-writing of Buddhism (Verma and Rathore 2011, x–xi). Whether or not this is true (and whatever be the merits of the case) it is clear that Ambedkar's *The buddha and his dhamma* remained caught up between a rejection of the traditional reading of central Buddhist beliefs and the espousal of enlightenment driven values. *The buddha and his dhamma* failed to embrace the Buddhist ontology of the human or set up a substantive discussion on the idea of the good human life (or indeed *Nibbana*) understood independently of, and apart from, life in the civic community.

In this context it is important to remember that this is a version of what is a more general difficulty with modern naturalist moral consciousness. The fact that inescapable moral frameworks do not find any articulation in modernity simply because of the pluralism that characterizes the times in which we live and which makes it difficult to find a fully articulated framework with which every group (indeed even the same individual at different times in his/her life) would agree. Under the influence of a naturalist temper, modern moral philosophy is built along external and non-culture specific terms. The naturalist temper and its epistemological assumptions become the basis of moral theories (such as utilitarianism) which attempt to do altogether without background qualitative distinctions in order to be acceptable to people with diverse commitments.

While this last point has been the subject of much discussion (Taylor 1989; MacIntyre 1988; Murdoch 1970), I am interested in making the much simpler point that rejecting background frameworks of any kind is straightforwardly linked to the modern self-understanding. It is not surprising to note in this context that in the modern West self-understanding/identity has come to be about rights rather than about background moral frameworks connected with the idea of a constitutive good. A right is a legal privilege which, in Lockean terms, is inalienable and cannot be wavered. Taylor has argued that modern moral thinking comes to have three axes— our respect for and obligations towards others, our understanding of what makes a full human life and the notion of individual dignity. All of these axes are connected to the modern notion of respect for human beings; a respect that can only be unpacked in terms of rights.

Interestingly, Gandhi also understood the importance of rights to the human person and *satyagraha* was conceived as a method of securing rights through voluntary acceptance of suffering in one's own person. However, this last point (about self-imposed suffering for the sake of securing/earning rights) made for all the difference between Gandhi and modern self-understanding where rights like property (once it was acquired) belonged to man *qua* man. Gandhi had thought seriously about rights and had presided over the formulation of a charter of economic and social rights for all Indians as early as 1932. However, at the same time he had also argued against the idea of unconditional human rights (accruing to man *qua* man) while responding to the drafting committee for the universal declaration of human rights (this last point will be discussed at greater length in Chap. 5 of this book). Gandhi's position on rights put him at some distance from modern self-understanding and from Ambedkar. However, the fact that Gandhi had indeed formulated a charter of economic and social rights for all Indians (while resisting a re-iteration of the Western liberal discourse about rights) should indicate that one cannot read Gandhi as obdurately resisting modernity. The clue to read Gandhi perhaps could come from a lesser read essay, K. C. Bhattacharya's "*Swaraj* in ideas",[vii] which argues that Indians need to respond to modernity from within the old-world mind of India; that is quite in their own terms.

In liberal philosophy a right is seen as "a quasi possession of the agent to whom it is attributed" (Taylor 2001, 11). While Ambedkar endorsed such an understanding he seemed to have argued that rights involved more than simply making legal provisions. In the essay titled, *Ranade, Gandhi and Jinnah,* Ambedkar had emphasized that "rights are protected not by law but by the social and moral conscience of society" (Ambedkar 2014, 1: 222). As Sect. 3.3 of this chapter will attempt to argue, Ambedkar brought in a re-written Buddhism in support of a constitutional morality safeguarding individual rights. Yet having said that, there remained a world of difference between the positions of Gandhi and Ambedkar in that Gandhi rejected the idea of rights understood as unconditional and inalienable possessions of man *qua* man. In this connection, he spoke of the right usurper[viii] as the person who claimed human rights without having done his/her own duties to significant human and non-human others and indeed to the cosmos. As mentioned above in Gandhi's view, rights were not due to man *qua* rational animal. Rather they were conditional upon the individual concerned having fulfilled his/her duties to human and non-human others. The rejection of the idea that rights are inalienable possessions of man *qua* man (an idea somewhat central to modern self-understanding) brought Gandhi into straight-forward conflict with modern self-understanding. This perhaps makes it important to explicate what, or rather who, is the modern agent/self?

3.1.3 Charles Taylor: The History of Western Philosophy and the Inwardness of Modern Identity

As noted earlier the first aspect of the modern subject/self is the powerful inwardness which seems to be characteristic of "the world of modern, western people" (Taylor 2001, 111). We can best unpack this inward looking modern self-understanding if we locate it in the intellectual history of modern Western philosophy, where it was a long time in the making, as it were. It is perhaps in the early modern figure of John Locke that we find the distinctive idea that human identity is inseparable from inwardness, i.e. from an essentially inward looking self-awareness/consciousness. The Lockean insight is what inspires moderns to reject the idea of human life as an *a priori* unity. Significantly, it is post Locke that individual identity is seen to be about self-consciousness and not about attachment to moral frameworks or communities of belonging.

One might relate this point to the suggestion (made in the last section) that Ambedkar had rejected the notion of a connection between individual identity and an attachment to moral frameworks with the associated idea of a constitutive good/God. The Lockean understanding of the self evolves into contemporary accounts such as that of Parfit's, who (much later) argues that human identity does not have to be defined in terms of a whole life. One can in fact (on such essentially modern accounts) choose to reject one's childhood and become quite a different person in one's mature years without any loss to one's self-awareness/identity (Parfit 1984, Chap. 10–13). Taylor calls this the making of the "punctual" (Taylor 2001, 49) self. The modern self is "punctual because the self is defined in abstraction from any constitutive concerns …It's only constitutive property is self-awareness. This is the self that Hume set out to find…" (Taylor 2001, 49). On this view the self can, without loss, give up parts of his/her life as "unredeemable" (Ibid., 51). One might see the bearing of this modern self-understanding on the conflicts between Gandhi and Ambedkar. For Ambedkar the Hindu temples could be forgotten, Hindu Gods banished out of the dalit huts and the history of the dalits as Hindus erased (along with the unjust Hindu scriptures) as unredeemable without any loss of/to self-identity.

For Gandhi however though a great sin had been incurred by the Hindu self, such an erasure of a past (albeit an unjust past) could cause a disorientation in self-identity, as much as, in moral space. Gandhi argued that tradition could not be erased but had to be re-interpreted (somewhat critically) so that the religion could be reformed without loss of/in (what ancient world views regard as) the *a priori* unity/continuity of the self. It was probably arguments such as these that had driven Gandhi to posit an idealized version of *varna*. One might note that Gandhi had often argued that it was on the basis of qualities and not birth that individuals belonged to *varnas* and that one and the same individual belonged to all the four *varnas* according as he/she manifested these qualities at different times. One might appreciate that this apparently unrecognizable version of *varna* which, in fact, appeared useless to both his contemporaries and his commentators, was nonetheless very important to a Gandhian understanding of self-identity. An idealized and re-interpreted conception of *varna* made space for a reform of the background framework. It thereby also made space to keep the continuity of the unified self a going concern in one's own self-understanding and *itihaas*. Reform of tradition and the idealized reading of *varna* could come to mean that individual identity need not rest on a congenital split and erasure that rejecting the past would necessarily involve. In order to understand the attractions of this notion of reform *vis a vis* Ambedkar's interest in erasure, one needs only to reflect on all that is involved in background frameworks; a given ontology of the human, a sense of the relationship between the human and the divine, a given understanding of the community and of the good. This last is of course bound up with language and different languages articulate the good in different ways. However, there is a lot more at stake here than words;

> A sense of the good finds expression not only in linguistic descriptions but also in other speech acts… of prayer …goes beyond the bounds of language…The gesture of ritual, its music, its display of visual symbols, all enact in their own fashion our relation to God… (Ibid., 91).

A telling passage from Gandhi's *Discourses on the Gita* comes to mind here;

> If we also pronounce the words correctly, we shall approach God with water in a vessel as clean as possible. We shall have placed a *bel* leaf in the water with utmost attention to cleanliness, and filled the vessel with water from the purest source. Such things are meaningless in themselves; but they lend grace where there is faith. A man of faith will make his gift as artistic as he can. Today's craftsmanship is lifeless and no craftsmanship at all… we should not, thus, let our recitation of the *Gita* become dry at any time. (Gandhi 1888–1948, 37: 350)[2]

It becomes important to note here that the modern split of the unified self (seen in ancient world views as being essentially in continuity with his/her own *itihaas*) does not quite dissipate the modern subject. This is because the making of modern identity involves the shift of control to the individual mind over what happens to transpire in the world of matter. To understand this, one needs to move away from Locke to Descartes whose dualism of mind and matter greatly influenced modern self-understanding. One of the elements in the inwardness associated with modern

---

[2] Gandhi 1888–1948, refers to the *Collected Works of Mahatma Gandhi*. The volume concerned and the page numbers from which citations from Gandhi are drawn have been mentioned within parentheses. These have been mentioned to indicate the exact location of the quotation in the electronic edition of the *Collected Works of Mahatma Gandhi*. However, for the purposes of reference, it may be noted that I have resourced these volumes from the Collected Works of Mahatma Gandhi: Volumes 1 to 98. New Delhi: Publications Division Government of India, 1999. Accessed online in May 2021 at https://www.gandhiashramsevagram.org/gandhi-literature/collected-works-of-mah atma-gandhi-volume-1-to-98.php

identity is the idea of control of mind over matter. This, is no small measure, comes from Descartes' dualism. While Plato's ethics of reason and reflection involved a turn inwards (and in that it gained over Homeric action and glory); the rational order had still to be discovered outside of man by an ascent to the forms and towards the transcendental idea of the good. Perhaps before Descartes, it was Augustine (among the ancients) who took the turn inwards in the history of Western philosophy. However, Augustine introduced "an inwardness of radical reflexivity" (Taylor 2001, 131) only to take the self towards God. It is significant to take note of Augustine's insights on inwardness and memory, if only, to see the difference from Ambedkar's dismantling and remaking of memory. For Augustine the self finds God at the end of the turn inwards and move towards memory/remembering. The Augustinian inward turning soul is in fact said to remember God at the end of memory. How telling might it be to consider here that Ambedkar not only found it possible to erase the Hindu God/Gods who came at the end of the collective/individual dalit memory; but also found it possible to rebuild upon that very erasure a re-interpreted Buddhist framework and a new past.

Tracing inwardness through modern Western philosophy one can see how it became possible for Ambedkar to turn the moment at the end of memory around from God (as in Augustine) to man. It is a figure far removed in time and place that can show how Ambedkar was in fact able to do this with great courage. This figure was that of Rene Descartes and Ambedkar's was a courage born of ease with the idea that memory can indeed be so turned around. It was with Descartes, unlike Plato and Augustine, that moral sources were no longer outside the human being but came to be internalized within the human. In fact the disenchantment of the universe can be seen to have been initiated with Descartes radical separation of mind from the universe of matter. Another important aspect of modern self-understanding also comes from this separation and that is the anthropocentricism of modern self-understanding. Post-Cartesian dualism, the human being and ordinary human life come to be at the centre of the universe. It was the independence of mind from matter which facilitated modern anthropocentricism and the control of matter by mind. With Descartes rationality came to be understood as a capacity/power of the mind to construct order. Subsequently (and consequently), it became possible for the human being to reject all ancient conceptions of order. One might say that post Descartes, the human being has the power to give herself the certainty she needs and everything else flows from there.

To see how far Gandhi was from Cartesian dualism one need only think of his need for certainty from God/Truth and his references to a Socratic 'inner voice'/voice of God at difficult times in his life and politics. Having put man at the centre of things Western philosophy (as noted at the start of this section) saw the source of the good human life in the inwardness of the self. The good life came, more and more, to be located in the agent's sense of her own dignity as a rational being. While one might say that this last idea was fully developed with Kant's categorical imperative it was certainly initiated by Descartes.

As Taylor speaks about the shift inwards, (something we now take for granted), he points out that it is with Descartes that "...rationality is no longer defined substantively, in terms of the order of being, but rather procedurally, in terms of the standards by which we construct orders in science and life" (Ibid., 156). With the inwardness there is also a notion of self-sufficiency and an ideal of the human agent "who is able to remake himself by methodical and disciplined action" (Ibid., 159). This is increasingly reflected in the bureaucratic and military administration, in forms of democratic governance in the modern world, and in this context, in the citizen of Ambedkar's Constitution of India.

One might now go back to Locke moving (beyond Locke's inwardness) to his epistemological concerns. While one might consider that an inward looking self-understanding leads to a radical disengagement from the world outside of the mind; one ought also to note that it was Locke's picture of knowledge which initiated the rejection of all innate ideas. With this conceptual move, Locke had gone on to reject tradition and bring epistemological control within the individual human subject. It is important to re-iterate and note that it was the rejection of innate ideas that brought epistemological control to the human being. One might find a philosophical parallel, centuries later, in Ambedkar's move to reject tradition;

> In rejecting innateness, Locke is also giving vent to his profoundly anti-teleological view of human nature, of both knowledge and morality. The motives for this... have much to do with winning a certain kind of control. (Ibid., 164–65)

The critical moment in knowledge (for Locke) is that of rejecting any view that thinks of human beings as "naturally tending to or attuned to the truth" (Ibid., 165) that they simply accept. Think here of Gandhi's notion of individual human life as moving non-violently towards the truth or God. In sharp contrast, for the modern subject it is only after demolishing structures (like Gandhi's) where truth is to be sought in the order of the cosmos (and outside the human being) that human knowledge can be rebuilt on surer foundations, that is, upon individual experience and sensation. It is surely significant that Ambedkar took this Lockean turn towards experience as conferring truth. In effecting this turn, Ambedkar also wrestled authority/control from tradition and custom to restore independence and responsibility to the individual. Locke's epistemology and his reification of human psychology played an important role in the enlightenment and in the making of modern identity. Ambedkar is comfortable with a self-understanding built around the sense of individual control, over what is to count as knowledge (indeed about what is to constitute religion and which religion one should select), which Gandhi is simply unable to share.

The inwardness of modern (and what was initially) Western self-understanding is accompanied by two parallel movements—disengagement and control. To elaborate these ideas, it is important to see that there is a move within the modern subject towards a radical disengagement with the cosmos and towards an inwardness and self-sufficiency which can only be understood against the history of modern Western philosophy;

> The crucial capacity for the great ancient moralists was that of seeing the order....By contrast, the modern ideal of disengagement requires a reflexive stance. We have to turn inward and

become aware of our own activity and the processes which form us. We have to take charge of
our own representation of the world which otherwise goes on without order and consequently
without science;... Disengagement demands that we stop simply living in the body within
our traditions or habits and by making them objects for us, subject them to radical scrutiny
and remaking (Ibid., 175)

It is important to consider how this turn inwards (first in Augustine and then in
Locke and Descartes) lent itself to an objectification of the self. Modernity (witness
here the ideas of both Locke and Descartes) pushed disengagement and what Nagel
calls "the view from nowhere" (Nagel 1986, 70) to a point where the person could
separate herself not only from the material world but also from herself. Since modernity confers the centre stage to the first-person perspective and takes a radically
subjective stance the modern subject looks upon herself quite as an object. It is a one
of the "great paradoxes of modern philosophy" (Taylor 2001, 175) that taking the
turn inwards so to speak;

…calls on me to be aware of *my* activity of thinking or *my* processes of habituation, so as to
disengage from them and objectify them…. (Ibid.)

Once we (as modern subjects) are able to thus disengage from ourselves and
consequently to think of ourselves in a third-person perspective, the self is no longer
the source of the spiritual life or the foundation of the ontology of the human. Quite
to the contrary:

…we come to think we 'have' selves as we have heads. (Ibid., 177)

What this comes to mean is that for the disengaged moderns the search for the self
is no longer felt and understood as a search for a given ontology of the human but is
rather seen as a search to come to terms with oneself. Such a coming to terms with
oneself involves looking at oneself from an introspective, rational and disinterested
stance. With Montaigne this becomes a theme of modern culture. The search for
identity is no longer felt in terms of a quest for belonging to a community or for a
repository of answers to questions posed by moral choices. It is a search now for what
I (the individual) am, what I want and what I will to be for myself. Taylor describes
this as a "three-sided individualism" which is "central to modern identity" (Ibid.,
185). The self which is seeking to come to terms with itself ('it' is appropriate as the
self has been transformed into an object) is seeking self-responsible independence,
recognized particularity and the individualism of personal commitment.

Taylor traces the individualism of personal commitment to the Stoic notion of
the will in its capacity to give/withhold consent. Epictetus's *prohairesis*[ix] becomes
a central moral power in modernity and this goes back to the original stoic writers
who thought of the individual as a solitary wonderer whose consent founded political authority. This last aspect of the inwardness essential to the modern self has
had the most important consequences—on the making of modern identity—and on
Ambedkar's debate with Gandhi. It "yields a picture of the sovereign agent who
is by nature not bound to any authority. The condition of being under authority is
something which has to be re-created." (Ibid., 194) It is important here to take note
of the influence of Locke, Descartes and Montaigne in the political atomism that

arose (after the seventeenth century) in the western part of the world. This atomism finds echoes in the social contract theories of Grotius, Pufendorf, Locke and others. In earlier theories, the issue of consent had been put in terms of a people establishing a government by consent in the form of contract. It is important to note that in such theories, the existence of the community itself had not been questioned but rather taken entirely for granted. However with the framing of the sovereign nature of individual identity as a coming to terms with oneself and with the particularity of individual commitment there was a questioning of the membership of the community. One might recall Ambedkar's speeches in the Constituent Assembly of India in which he raised the issue of the fulfilment of the demands made by the dalits as a prerequisite to their acceptance of membership of the imagined community of the nation in the making. Ambedkar's speeches and demands need perhaps to be understood in the context of changes in Anglo American philosophy just after the seventeenth century. It was in the post seventeenth century Anglo American philosophy that a different set of questions started to make sense. These included questions such as 'Where does the authority of the community over its members come from?'

This last question could perhaps be seen to have exerted a significant influence on the debate between Gandhi and Ambedkar especially around the issues that surrounded the Poona Pact in 1932. One could perhaps even say that the debate between Gandhi and Ambedkar really took off the ground once Ambedkar confronted Gandhi, with what was essentially, a political atomism, bequeathed by post seventeenth-century Western philosophy. It is almost as if some part of Taylor's arguments about the making of modern identity are relevant to the political atomism in India in the 1930's. Such political atomism was a part of the making of modern Indian identity and involved in the debate about separate electorates between Gandhi and Ambedkar;

> The new theories add to the traditional contract founding government a second one, which precedes it: a contract of association…now the theory starts from the individual on his own.Membership of a community with common power of decision is now something which needs to be explained by the individual's prior consent…. (Ibid., 193)

The inwardness of modern identity leaves the agent to discover purposes, commitments and order on his/her own which are then to be applied to political society. Such is the sovereign and modern agent who is not under any authority—whether of the religious or of the given political community. It is significant to note that it is characteristic of modern identity that the modern subject lends his/her consent to membership of political society (and as I will argue, membership of the religious community) only as understood instrumentally—as an instrument to attain ends of individuals and then ends of groups (dalits?). It is just such a political atomism that gets inbuilt into the idea of the individual ownership of rights which Gandhi resisted. What Gandhi was resisting was the idea that individual's own basic immunities—such as liberty—on the model of their ownership of property (one might consider that Gandhi thought of proprietors as **trustees** and not **owners** of property). One might get some insight into Gandhi's difficulty with this idea of ownership if one were to reflect upon the point that the modern idea of ownership of rights reflects the radical stance of disengagement from (and objectification of) one's own self.

It is important to make one last point about inwardness if only to evidence just how deeply entrenched individualism is in/to modern identity. Modernity does away with the *ontic logos* and the idea that thought and valuation is out there in the cosmos and divine order of things. There is a shift of localization, so to speak, the valuation of the external world is literally in the mind. Modernity has moved conceptually far away as it were from Plato's theory of knowledge according to which, one might recall, actual knowledge relates to the object outside of the self. According to both Plato and Aristotle, true knowledge and true valuation is not located in the knowing mind but only comes about when that mind connects itself to how things are ontically. One might think here of the *Advaita Vedantic* theory of perception where the *antah karana*[x] literally flows out to take the shape of the external object in order for perception to take place. In the world view of the ancients, there is no idea of the representational construal in the individual mind which later comes to be important in the theories of Locke, Descartes and Liebnitz and which was taken up by the empiricists (note the movement from Platonic ideas/forms to Cartesian ideas). With modern identity—one might say—the shift from the world view of the ancients was essentially complete—all order, all control and all valuation was located in the individual mind.

In this context, one could suggest perhaps that Ambedkar's writing of history to create a new past stands very much in the course of modern identity. Just as it is important to see that Gandhi's truth (or God) was ontically located and it was on account of this that he thought of the past as *itihaas*/it so happened and not 'history'. Gandhi and Ambedkar's world views were not only different they were conceptually incommensurable. I will take Taylor's argument in a very different context, from that in which it had been made, to say of these world views that;

> t(T)hey don't determine similar maps within which we can pick out different places; they determine altogether different notions of place. For the modern disengaged subject, thought and valuation are in the mind in a new and stronger sense,because minds are now the exclusive locus of such realities… (Ibid., 187)

3.1.4 The Making of Modern Identity and the Emphasis on Ordinary Life: Gandhi and Ambedkar

Enough has been said of the first strand of modern identity and the move inwards. The second aspect of the making of modern identity (which Taylor speaks about) is what has been called the affirmation of ordinary life. Ordinary life means just what it conjures, the nature of things we need to continue and renew life, production and reproduction. These are things related to (what one might call) the infrastructural requirements for living a life of goodness. In ancient world views, these were just so, merely infrastructural, and indeed ancillary to the living out of the properly human life. Gandhi tried to keep the demands of ordinary life in their place (as merely ancillary) by taking the vows of non-possession and celibacy. Gandhi's vows were quite in keeping with traditional ancient world views and they bring to mind the stoic relegation of the fulfillment of vital and sexual needs to the status of *adiaphora* things that require detachment as ultimately these are things that are indifferent. Indeed in *Gandhi and the Stoics*, Sorabji (2012) brings out the parallels between the relegation of the goods necessary for ordinary life, to the sphere of the inessential, in Gandhi and in the Stoics. I will make some philosophical use of this idea of keeping the requirements of ordinary life in perspective in the next section when I attempt to make sense of Gandhi's notion of the self. In this context, it is important to note that the affirmation of, and emphasis on, ordinary life is a strong aspect in the making of modern identity.

It is this affirmation of ordinary life that leads to the shift from the hierarchies in ancient society where ways of contemplation and honour were exalted at the expense of trade, commerce and labour. The emphasis on the needs of ordinary life is a great leveller in that everyone can relate to them in precisely the same way thereby making old hierarchies seem fundamentally misguided:

> The centre of the good life now lies in something which everyone can have a part in, rather than in ranges of activity which only a leisured few can do justice to. (Taylor 2001, 214)

The Baconian revolution in science had reversed the hierarchies of according highest status to contemplation (recall Aristotle's exaltation of the life of contemplation) by arguing that traditional sciences have fallen short in that they have failed to concern themselves with function and operation. In early modern thinkers, the end or goal of science was increasingly seen as relieving the condition of man. As a corollary to this new understanding of the end of science, there came to be a related emphasis on commerce and on labour both of which were great levellers in their different ways. The former defined the bourgeois ethics that played an important role in liberal society and the revolutions of the eighteenth century. The emphasis on labour in bourgeois ethics which played an important role in liberal society might seem close enough to Gandhi's inclusion of (Timothy Bondaref's notion of) bread labour as a *niyama*/virtue as well as his recommendation of *charkha*/spinning as mandatory for all Indians. In his several comments on the *Gita*, Gandhi had argued that working with one's hands is the *yajna*/sacrifice for Indians in the present *yuga*/time, i.e. the *yugadharma*/*dharma* prevalent in a specific time. Yet it might seem apparent on some reflection that Gandhi's insistence on bread labour may not quite amount to the modern affirmation of the role of commerce in human life or indeed affirmation of ordinary life itself. Gandhi had famously critiqued large-scale industrialization and distanced himself from mainstream trade and commerce by a contrary emphasis on crafts and small-scale production in the village. In this he found no re-iteration from Ambedkar, who on the contrary, distanced himself from village crafts (perhaps) on account of his all too understandable hostility to the village itself.

One might appreciate that Gandhi's emphasis on bread labour was not yet an endorsement of the modern affirmation of ordinary life by going back to unpack Taylor's account of the second aspect of the making of modern identity. Taylor traces this- the importance of ordinary life to the inward looking individualistic modern self- to sources seemingly very far removed from it. Surprisingly enough, he traces this importance to a theological point of origin. Taylor argues, in fact, that the ground for this coalescing of inwardness and pre-occupation with the concerns of everyday life was laid by Christian spirituality and the reformation. Taylor views the three centuries of the success of the protestant movements as doing away with the role of mediation, dependence on the church and special status of monastic orders as making space for "one's wholehearted" (Ibid., 217) personal commitment to religion and to God. In his view an ancillary role was played by philosophy with Locke's deism making space for a new emphasis on the importance of meeting one's basic needs and for the common good of man;

> This then is what God calls us to; to act strenuously, and also efficously, to meet our needs, but with an eye also to the common good. (Ibid., 239)

Locke's deism and the theory of moral sentiments in Shaftesbury and Hutcheson prepared the grounds for the radical secular and essentially unbelieving enlightenment where there was no role for providence or the religious order and ethics was seen in terms of utility. Through the utilitarianism of Bentham and Mill, the world gradually appeared as a neutral space where individuals sought to produce the greatest good and avoid pain. It is significant (in the present context) that the avoidance of pain and suffering as an important aspect of the emphasis of ordinary life in modern identity; coalesces in some part, with the Buddhist emphasis on the *Arya satya*/Four Noble Truths, regarding suffering and the removal thereof at least in the re-interpreted Ambedkarian version. As Taylor reminds us the three goods central to the outlook of radical enlightenment are, self-responsible reason, the idea that the ordinary fulfilments human beings seek are worthy of being pursued; and the ideal of universal and impartial benevolence (Ibid., 322). Gandhi's notion of bread labour as a *yajna*/sacrifice clearly could not lend itself to considerations of utility and the concerns of maximizing pleasure in the living out of the concerns of ordinary life.

Moving on now to the third aspect of the making of modern identity (in Charles Taylor's account of the same)—the expressivist notion of nature as an inner moral source. The "…idea of nature as an intrinsic source goes along with an expressive view of human life" (Ibid., 374). Taylor brings out this important aspect of modern identity by arguing that the "originality of vocation" (Ibid., 376) of individuals and nations comes from this third feature of modern identity. One which creates a constitutional tension in modern identity-between an enlightenment driven need for disengagement and a somewhat contrary need for expressive self-articulation. Both (as might seem obvious) seem inescapably related to modern identity, but both are also in constitutional tension within the individual modern subject. It is this tension perhaps that makes for the quintessentially modern moral predicament. Taylor explains this constitutional tension by taking us back through the German *sturm und drang* movement, Romanticism in Germany and England and through these influences to Herder, Goethe, Rousseau and Hegel. Taylor traces this influence in poetry (Shelling, Wordsworth) in French and English literature and in art. This strand in the making of modern identity comes from the idea that nature (and not only individual reason) is a source of inspiration in/for man. There is no doubt that (though a lot more was involved in it) Romanticism was most certainly a revolt against the classical stress on rationalism, tradition and formal harmony. The Romantics countered these by an emphasis on the rights of the individual and on individual imagination and feeling. Unlike Lockean Deism, which spoke of fulfilling the concerns of ordinary life in accordance with the divine plan, there was an important shift in the romantics. These writers argued that it is individual impulses which bring out the importance of personal fulfilment and they emphasized the harmony of individual fulfilment with the fulfilment of "others". In the Romantics, it is not God but the voice of nature within the human being which drives individual fulfilment. What is very important to note in the present context, is that post the Romantics, there gradually comes to be an important connection between a moral stance to the world and individual self-expression;

> To have a proper moral stance towards the natural order is to have access to one's inner voice. (Ibid., 370)

Significantly, it was the voice of nature (neither practical rationality nor God's divine plan) that emerged as the source of good and innocent desire and as the voice within. Post the Romantics, there was an emphasis put on feeling and on the idea that there was a value in sentiments for the sake of the sentiments in themselves. As Taylor puts it, what came to be important was;

> …a certain way of experiencing our lives, our ordinary desires and fulfilments and the larger natural order in which we are set. (Ibid., 272)

One might think that there was nothing new in this move and that this move might have been in the lineage of the Aristotelian idea that sentiments were of value because of their impulse to move human beings towards a certain mode of life. However, the move to sentiments in the romantics made perhaps for quite a different impulse. Post the romantics individual feelings became important to the human and essentially underived notion of the good. Importantly, traditional modes of life and of ethical concern could now be re-defined by sentiments towards a fusion of the sensual and the spiritual. What is significant, especially from the point of view of the discussion on the Ambedkar–Gandhi debate, is that post the Romantics, individual expression is understood as that which "helps to define what is to be realized" (Ibid., 375). It is only by articulation and by expression that the individual can give a direction to his/her life. This last should help to situate Ambedkar's need to re-write Buddhism. This was a modern move, a move to express values for oneself and by oneself. Significantly it served to define what Ambedkar sought to realize—a social order defined by liberty, equality and fraternity.

Taylor argues that it was expressivism that gave some depth to and became the basis for an enhanced and better defined individualism. In the late eighteenth century expressivism got involved with the emphasis on originality and uniqueness which became somewhat critical to modern self-understanding. While the stress on difference is not altogether new in the history of philosophy, what is new, is the idea that human beings need to express themselves and live in tune with their individual uniqueness. The newness of this last awareness comes to appear for the first time in

Indian self-consciousness in Ambedkar's writing of the text for the new Buddhism. Ambedkar's expressive individualism became a very important part of modern Indian self-understanding (and thence of Modern Indian dalit self-understanding) and led, among other things, to creative imagination in art, poetry and music. On another and perhaps different note, it also led to arguments about the importance of 'the right to speak' for oneself as a group and as an individual in Ambedkar and (after him) in modern dalit scholars (this will be the subject of some discussion in the conclusion to the book).

Taylor brings out the tension between this modern emphasis on expressivism and the disengagement which involves a division between nature and reason in enlightenment modernity. He argues that there is some need for reconciliation between the insights of Spinoza and Kant which gets initiated and emerges in Kant's engagement with aesthetic sensibility in the third critique. Taylor argues that the 1790s emphasis that "autonomy must be reconciled with unity with nature" (Ibid., 382) drove thinkers who "emerged out of the expressivist stream…" and "strove to unite radical autonomy and expressive unity…" (Ibid., 384). The expressivist philosopher (who thought of nature as a resource) developed a theory of history where human beings moved from a stage where there was a primitive unity of reason and desire, through a conflict-driven division, to a third stage where reason and expressivist freedom/autonomy were reconciled. The picture of the self that emerges post the expressivist revolution is one of self-discovery "only open to a mode of exploration which involves the first-person stance" (Ibid., 389). This expressivist power transforms the notion of self-identity in modernity and intensifies its inwardness. It is also important to note, with Taylor, that whatever be the differences there is a conceptual link between later philosophers doing phenomenology with/and the "philosophical overturnings" (Ibid., 461) from Wittgenstein to Schopenhauer, Heidegger to Dilthey who "stand close to facets of modernist consciousness in their rejection of the hegemony of disengaged reason and mechanism" (Ibid.). As Taylor puts it;

> This comes from the retrieval of the lived experience or creative activity underlying our awareness of the world, which had been occluded or denatured by the regnant mechanistic construal. The retrival is felt as a liberation, because the experience can become more vivid and the activity unhampered through being recognized, and alternatives open up our stance towards the world which were quite hidden before. (Ibid., 460)

Taylor has identified the inner conflict in the modern subject- one between the tendency to radically individual (essentially disengaged) rational control and the power of expressive self-articulation involving lived experience- which both "complicates and enriches the modern moral predicament" (Ibid., 390). I will argue that this tension unfolds itself in the making of modern Indian identity in the figure of Babasaheb Ambedkar. The constitutional tension which (as Taylor argued) made for the modern moral predicament is that which plays out as the tension between the demands of disengaged reason and the need for expressive self-articulation (in harmony with others) in Ambedkar. It is the inner unfolding of such a tension that led him perhaps to write *The Buddha and his Dhamma* (Ambedkar 2011). Such considerations might lead to the insight that this text might not quite signify that Ambedkar took a Gandhian turn to recognize the importance of religious belonging. Quite to the contrary, it might have marked the coming to be of modern Indian identity with its characteristic and defining predicaments. As such modern identity came of age in India in the person of Babasaheb, the demands of disengaged reason played out the conflict with the urgent need for expressive self-articulation as a *Navayana* or rationally re-written yet socially engaged Buddhism. It was not that Ambedkar recognized the demands of religion over disengaged reason facing a disenchanted cosmos. Rather he gave vent to the need for self-expression which he recognized had to be both rational and in harmony with others. It is surely telling that Ambedkar read such harmony (with others) as enlightenment fraternity rather than as a Gandhian kinship between the human and non-human world. Ambedkar was perhaps responding to insights born from the post Romantic emphasis on lived experience in writing a *Navayana*/a new religion. Perhaps then Ambedkar's new religion was born at the moment of tension which marked the birth of modern identity in the Indian subject and in the dalit movement.

3.2 Gandhi on the *Bhagavad Gita*: Putting Together a Gandhian Conception of the Self

3.2.1 *The* Bhagavad Gita *and Gandhi's Conception of the Self*

Moving away from that modern self and from the birth of modern identity in India, this section will bring out somewhat contrary insights from Gandhi. These insights on the nature of self-identity from the old-world Gandhi are primarily drawn from his several comments on the *Bhagavad Gita*.[xi] Before moving on to Gandhi's more traditional notion of the self, it is important to reflect a little upon the choice of the *Gita* from Gandhi's somewhat copious writings to bring out his insights on the nature of self-identity.

The first reason for selecting Gandhi's several comments on the *Gita* to serve as the primary conceptual resource for his ideas about the nature of the self comes from the significance of Gandhi's choosing to write extensive comments on a central religious text. It would be proper to note here that Gandhi's comments on the *Gita* were fairly extensive and that these writings exclusively devoted to the *Gita* cover nearly a thousand pages of his collected works.[xii] It becomes important to note here that the *Gita* is not only a central text for the Hindus, but it is powerfully concerned with the Hindu conception of the good human life. It is surely significant that Gandhi had recognized the importance of the *Gita* to the Hindu religious tradition and chosen to write comments on it. This assumes more significance in the light of the well-established tradition in Hinduism of writing *bhasya*/commentaries on canonical texts as a form of establishing continuity with the tradition while paradoxically establishing the foundation for a new philosophical system. Gandhi perhaps saw his own move to re-interpret the *Gita* as a re-interpretation of tradition which could make room for reform while retaining the self's continuity with philosophical Hinduism. In the preface to the *Anasaktiyoga* he says:

> On examining the history of languages we notice that the meaning of important words has changed or expanded. This is true of the Gita. The author has himself extended the meanings of some of the current words. We are able to discover this even on a superficial examination... Thus the author of the Gita, by extending meanings of words, has taught us to imitate him..... (Gandhi 1888–1948, 46: 173–4)

In his writing on the *Gita,* Gandhi made comments about the self and about the nature of the good human life. These appeared to have been a part of a self-conscious articulation of a background moral framework for the old world Indian self (on the brink of modernity) who sought for an orientation in moral space. It is such reflections that make it important to look at Gandhi's comments on the *Gita* in the present context and indeed in the present section.

Gandhi's comments on the *Bhagavad Gita* become important on account of a few additional reasons. The first additional reason (which derives from the previous point) is that the background moral framework for the individual self that Gandhi unpacks in these comments is a self-consciously religious framework; which speaks of the relationship between God and the self. The acceptance of the place of God in relation to the self puts Gandhi's self-understanding at some conceptual distance from modern self-identity and from Ambedkar. Since this section examines Gandhi's notion of the self (in relation to his debate with Ambedkar), it becomes important to examine the relationship between the self and God in Gandhi in the context of his comments on the *Gita*. The second additional reason to look at Gandhi's comments on the *Gita* is that it is in his writing on the *Gita* that Gandhi makes a significant argument about the duty of the devout to re-interpret religious texts in line with faith and reason. In this context one may note of a few passages from the *Anasaktiyoga*;

> Because a poet puts a particular truth before the world, it does not necessarily follow that he has known or worked out all its great consequences, or having done so, he is able to express them fully... A poet's meaning is limitless. Like man, the meaning of great writings suffers evolution. ...It is possible that, in the age prior to that of the Gita, offerings of animals in sacrifices was permissible. But there is not a trace of it in the sacrifice in the Gita sense. In the Gita continuous concentration on God is the King of sacrifices. The third chapter seems to show that sacrifice chiefly means bodily labour for service... similarly has the meaning of the word *sannyasa* undergone, in the Gita, a transformation. The *sannyasa* of the Gita will not tolerate a complete cessation of all activity. The *sannyasa* of the Gita is all work and yet no work. Thus the author of the Gita, by extending meanings of words, has taught us to imitate him... The Gita is not an aphoristic work; it is a great religious poem... With every age the important words will carry new and expanded meanings. But its central teaching will never vary. The seeker is at liberty to extract from this treasure any meaning he likes so as to enable him to enforce in his life the central teaching. (Ibid., 173–175)

To encourage the devout to re-interpret the *Gita* and extract new and expanded meanings (Ibid., 175) in line with reason and morality, Gandhi goes on to argue that the *Gita* does not contain a set of universal categorical moral rules. His arguments here and elsewhere seem to indicate that it is difficult to conceive of morality as a set of uncompromising general rules as sensitivity to the context (one might find oneself in) matters when making moral decisions. The sense here is that once one has imbibed the central meaning of a/any religious text one can live by that meaning only by re-interpreting what it implies in the context of one's own specific situation. It is significant that on a Gandhian understanding, re-interpretation of religious texts becomes a religious duty because the devotee can only live by the meaning of a text by applying it anew to changes in his/her context. Such re-thinking involves the need to respond to the text from within a good human life. Gandhi re-iterated the need for re-interpretation often enough;

> Nor is the Gita a collection of do's and I's. What is lawful for one may be unlawful for another. What may be permissible at one time, or in one place, may not be so at another time, and in another place. Desire for fruit is the only universal prohibition. Desirelessness is obligatory. (Ibid., 175)

This Gandhian emphasis on the religious *qua* religious duty of re-interpretation of religious texts, in keeping with the change in time, has important implications for Gandhi's contestations with Ambedkar. The first thing to note is that these contestations related to matters regarding the relationship between the individual and the religious community and the freedom of the modern self to move away from this relationship and the community. Given such a context, Gandhi's emphasis on the religious duty of the re-interpretation of sacred texts (and religio-moral rules) becomes very important. Such a Gandhian emphasis on re-interpretation rather than rejection could in fact explain Gandhi's own rejection of the modern denial of the *a priori* unity of the self and the freedom to discard parts of the past as irredeemable without any loss to self-identity.

It is significant to note in this context that in Gandhi's understanding, it was not possible for the self to give up any part of his/her past/*itihaas* as irredeemable without a corresponding loss in his/her sense of self-identity. I will argue (in the next chapter) that it was in order to avoid such a loss to the self's sense of self and in order to maintain the *a priori* unity of the self that Gandhi defended an idealized version of *varna*. However, this should not be taken to mean that Gandhi summarily rejected the enlightenment values which inspired modern humanism and modern self-understanding. Some part of the importance of Gandhi's comments on the *Gita* derives from the fact that he sought to reconcile an enlightenment driven emphasis on 'reason', which he re-thought as a tradition-constituted and tradition-constitutive concept (the difference between Gandhi's understanding and the liberal understanding, of the terms 'reason' and 'justice'; will be further brought out in Chap. 5 of this book), with the importance of religio-moral belonging. It would be significant to note here that Gandhi's reconciliation was sought through an emphasis on the *niyama*/casual virtue of *swadeshi*/literally 'of one's own country' (which formed a part of an expanded list of *niyamas*/virtues).[xiii] In Gandhi's understanding of it, following the virtue of *swadeshi* meant making a commitment to one's more immediate environment and in the matter of religion this came to mean the duty to reform (rather than reject) the religion of one's ancestors. Such *swadeshi* was not to be taken as a re-iteration of traditional text and ritual. Rather in Gandhi *swadeshi* was understood in terms of the duty of the devout to remain true to the spirit, and not the letter, of the religion of one's ancestors in the times in which one lived. This involved the effort to re-interpret religious texts in line with reason and morality. This duty of re-interpretation in line with (a tradition-constituted and tradition constitutive notion of) reason and morality served to reconcile the more contemporary enlightenment values with the traditional religious community of one's forefathers. While Gandhi shared the enlightenment emphasis on liberty and equality [which as Kumar explains are in a "founding" tension in modern political thought (Kumar 2015, 24)] he seemed to have done this without disrupting that self's unbroken and *a priori* unity with its own past.

The last reason for selecting the *Bhagavad Gita* as a primary resource for Gandhi's understanding of the self derives (somewhat paradoxically) from Ambedkar's denunciation of this text. It may be recalled that there was a dissonance between Ambedkar's early references (in the 1920's) to the *Gita* and later rejection of that text:

> The Bhagavat Gita is not a gospel and it can therefore have no message and it is futile to search for one…What the Bhagvat Gita does is to defend certain dogmas of religion on philosophic grounds…It uses philosophy to defend religion. (Ambedkar 2014, 3: 361)

One can see the same denunciation in commentators like Kumar who make much the same point re-iterating that:

> …his (Gandhi's) attraction to its world of transcendent truth and meaning… was a question of limits, a question of faithfulness to the laws of genre, a fidelity to the law as such. (Kumar 2015, 77)

Such contrary readings make the *Bhagavad Gita* important to the philosophical divergences between Gandhi and Ambedkar. It becomes important to ask what were Ambedkar's problems with the *Bhagavad Gita* if only to see how Gandhi's several comments on the *Gita* might have had a bearing on such problems. It is interesting to note here that while Ambedkar had referred to commentaries on the *Gita* by Gandhi's contemporaries; he made no philosophical use of Gandhi's rather prolific comments. The first difficulty Ambedkar raises with the *Gita* is that the *Gita* justifies war and that it does so by undermining the empirical body "…it is a mistake to think that the body and soul are one…when death occurs it is the body that dies…" (Ambedkar 2014, 3: 361). Kumar argues that;

> What he (Ambedkar) finds so condemnable in the *Gita*, in other words, is the denial of finitude, which is so improper to any classical ethics, of civility, liberty and government, let alone virtuous sacrifice. (Kumar 2015, 155).

It is this insight perhaps that led to Ambedkar's pre-occupation with "the materiality of life" (Ibid., 156) in *The buddha and his dhamma*. Kumar takes this argument further to argue that for Ambedkar perhaps Gandhi's comments on the *Gita* are a denial of the "demands of a materialist and revolutionary democracy." (Ibid.) It is important to consider whether Gandhi's notion of the self (as re-constructed here from his commentaries on the *Gita*) does indeed undermine the demands of democracy and civility by undermining the ultimacy of the material body. One might argue that Gandhi's devaluation of the claims of the body and of egoistic self-interest, associated with that body, might make for respect for the interest of the conflicting "other" posing a threat to one's body and self-interest. The chief obstacle posed by Gandhi to what Kumar terms the path of 'revolutionary democracy' (Ibid.) could emerge from Gandhi's move to undermine an obsessive modern individualism by putting the demands of the empirical body in some perspective.

As Kumar has recounted the second difficulty with the *Gita* which Ambedkar points out in his unfinished essays; is that the *Gita* re-affirms "the relation-ship between the power of religious institutions… and… theologico-political discourses on action and sacrifice of which the *Gita* had become a galvanizing instance(?)."(Ibid.,151) As Ambedkar argued the *Gita* defends rather than under-mines pernicious "dogmas" (Ambedkar 2014, 3: 361);

> Another dogma to which the Bhagavat Gita comes forward to offer a philosophic defense is Chaturvarnya…It offers a philosophic basis to the theory of Chaturvarnya….The third dogma for which the Bhagvat Gita offers a philosophic defence is the Karma marga. By Karma marga the Bhagavat Gita means the performance of observances ,such as *Yajna*s as a way to salvation… (Ibid., 361–362)

The difficulty however was not only with the nature of these doctrines/dogmas but as, Kumar puts it, with the *Gita* itself because;

"A whole matrix of disciplinary obligations (*kshatriyadharma, maryada dharma, rajadharma*) comes to be founded on one sovereign truth: the groundlessness of the divine" (Kumar 2015, 155). Kumar suggests that it was in the light of these classical problems such as "the relationship between state and religion" (Ibid., 151) that "nationalist readings of the Gita began to look specially unfaithful to Ambedkar." (Ibid.) One might easily see that for Ambedkar the *Gita* could present difficulties on two different counts. For one, the concept of *maryada* is in itself that of limits to freedom. Such limits sit uneasily with modern notions of self-identity. However equally unsettling to Ambedkar and modern notions of the self is the idea of God as groundless.

One might raise a point in defence of Gandhi at this juncture. One could argue perhaps that Gandhi's several comments on the *Gita* spoke to the most important of Ambedkar's arguments even though these came later and remained unpublished (I will discuss how Gandhi's *Discourses on the Gita* and Ambedkar's *Annihilation of Caste* present an ideational site for a philosophical encounter in Chap. 4 of this book). For instance, one could argue that the idea that the *Gita* recommends (by it's own example of re-interpreting ancient terms such as *sannyasa* and *karma*) it's own re-interpretation in line with changes in time and evolving social morality, dissolves the notion, that Gandhi had an orthodox notion of *maryada dharma*. This last point is perhaps born out by Gandhi's repeated emphasis on re-reading the *yajna*/sacrifice of the *Bhagavad Gita* as service/*sewa* of those most distant from oneself. In making such a re-reading of *yajna* as *sewa* Gandhi perhaps moved decisively away from the complicity between sacrifice and the theologico-political ends, to which *yajna* might have been put, as a category in nationalist discourse.

3.2.2 Gandhi: Self, Community and God

Once applied to the religion of one's ancestors, the Gandhian emphasis on the *niyama*/virtue of *swadeshi* understood as a primary commitment to one's more immediate environment, created an obligation to re-interpret one's traditional religious texts and choose to reform such texts rather than reject the religious community (of one's own past/ancestors) as irredeemable. As noted above such an emphasis on reform rather than erasure made it possible for Gandhi to maintain the *a priori* unity of the self even when confronted with an essentially unjust religio-socio community. One might note that there could be philosophical implications of re-interpretation/reform *versus* erasure some of which will be explored in the chapter which follows this one.

However, speaking of the reform of religious texts, could and did, generate opposition. Some part of such opposition could be conceptual and consequently more damaging than the simply unthinking insistence from the orthodox. The latter it would seem, could be easily dismissed, as merely pedantic. However, there could be more serious opposition. One could for instance argue, that if a religious text is really 'a revelation from God, spoken by the Eternal', it is difficult to speak of a religious duty of re-interpretation. For one might well ask of the text "how can it exist in time, as a mere text among others, to be interpreted…?" (Scruton 2014, 22).

One might be able to shed some light on Gandhi's position if one considers Scruton's insight into the retreat of the sacred from the text once one considers it as fixed on some object/meaning. As Scruton argues;

> …when a faith-community settles on some particular object, or rite, or words as sacred, it *loses* the presence of the thing in question, which retreats into the eternal as did the God of Moses and Abraham when his temple was destroyed… (Ibid.)

The point is that once creative interpretation is forbidden the text ceases "to be a record of God's presence among us, and becomes the proof of his absence-the trace left behind as he departed forever from our midst." (Ibid., 22–23).

Gandhi appeared to have shared such philosophical insights into the connection between God's presence in the devotee's world and critical discourse with one's own religious tradition. He therefore insisted that the self had a duty to the re-interpret the religious text;

> So many things were interpolated into the Shastras in the course of time, but we have gone on believing that everything in them is divinely inspired. By doing this, we make ourselves mere pedants. (Gandhi 1888–1948, 37: 101)

Perhaps Gandhi thought that to speak to the sense of the sacred in the text is really to "confront God as he is, not confined in this or that moment or this or that corner of the world" (Scruton 2014, 23).

Before moving on to a discussion of Gandhi's conception of the self it is important to note that most commentators have almost entirely side-stepped the *Bhagavad Gita* in putting together Gandhi's conception of the self. Note here, for example, Kumar (2015) on Gandhi's "idea of spirit-indeed, of the soul," (Kumar 2015, 80);

> Gandhi would come to conjure the image and metaphor of spirit prolifically, first in South
> Africa… and subsequently in India… But unlike the concept of force, he never got down to
> elaborating on it. (Ibid., 84)

This statement evidences the complete disregard (in/by the academia) of Gandhi's
several comments on the *Gita* where he had spoken about the nature of the soul/*atman*
in some detail. Perhaps such disregard is due to the fact that Gandhi's notion of the
spirit/soul involves a consideration of quite a different dualism from that of the
Cartesian kind. Gandhi had (very early on) distanced himself from those who "seem
to be nutured in modern traditions-who seem to be filled with the writing of modern
writers…" (Gandhi 1888–1948, 22: 250). In his comments on the *Bhagavad Gita*,
Gandhi speaks of the self as having two distinct aspects a soul/*atman* and an empirical
body. This Gandhian dualism is one that appears to be in continuity with the Indian
philosophical tradition:

> The atman and the body are separate things. (Gandhi 1888–1948, 37: 97)

Accepting that these two entities are different from each other Gandhi explains
that difference by pointing to the fact that while the body is perishable the;

> …atman was never born and will never die; …The atman is unborn, eternal and ancient.
> (Ibid., 92)

Again contrary to Descartes' mind and body dualism that set the philosophical
foundation for modern identity, Gandhi did not think that the *atman* and mind–
body continuum are independent and set over against each other. Rather, drawing
from the schools of Indian philosophy, Gandhi accepted that it was the *atman*/soul
rather than the mind (which one might note in traditional accounts, for instance
that of Patanjali, along with the ego/*ahamkara*, was a part of the body/empirical
outfit) that ought to rule the psycho physical organism. Gandhi had argued that
"…the body, if it sought to drive the atman, would never succeed." (Ibid., 91) This
led him to think of self-rule/*swaraj* as a state of moral equipoise with the soul in
control of the empirical body, mind and ego. Such an understanding drew inspiration
perhaps from the discussions of the *sthitaprajna*/person of resolute intellect of/in the
Bhagavad Gita. Stepping away from metaphysical positions Gandhi explained, to
the lay listeners, in his discourses what such self-rule could mean for the individual
self and for individual moral life;

> 'subduing the atman by the atman' means overcoming the baser, the demoniac impulses in
> the mind through the atman, that is through the Godward impulses. (Ibid., 166)

This reference to the rule of the mind–body unit by the *atman* connects Gandhi's
conception of *swaraj* as self-rule with the state of moral equipoise associated with
the *sthitaprajna*/person of resolute intellect of the *Bhagavad Gita*. It also becomes
very important to recall here that Gandhi had spoken of India's freedom as *swaraj*
(etymologically a composite of two words *swa*-self and *raj*-rule) rather than as independence. Placing himself in continuity with the idea of true freedom understood as
spiritual freedom/*moksha* (in the Indian philosophical tradition) and not the *Aufklang*

of the enlightenment Gandhi had argued that political freedom must rest on individual self-rule. He had argued, in fact, that the political freedom that an individual/collective might attain (at any point of time) would only be in exact proportion to the self-rule that the individual's that made up the collective could actualize within (the self) at that point of time. In his discourses on the *Gita* Gandhi makes this connection fairly explicit;

> If, however we regain the sovereignty which is rightfully ours, then we would be able to subdue the mind, the intellect and the senses whom at present we have accepted as our masters, as in our country we have accepted foreignors as our masters and believe that we get the food we eat because of them. (Ibid.)

This might lead us to think that in speaking of self-rule as essentially the rule of the self by the self Gandhi was endorsing a conception of moral autonomy quite in line with the inwardness of modernity. One might think, for instance, that the Gandhian idea of self-rule is in the conceptual lineage of philosophers like Kant who think that autonomy derives from an inner reflexivity resting ultimately upon individual reason and its dominion over the world of matter. However there is a difference between the self-ruled Gandhian person and the morally autonomous Kantian. This difference is, of course, conceptual. In as much as, Gandhi is looking at *swaraj* as the rule of the soul/*atman* (or of man's Godward impulses) over the psycho physical organism/self. This is different from the Kantian notion of moral autonomy where it is reason (disengaged from even the noblest of inclinations) whose rule over the individual self/will becomes the initiating moment of self-knowledge and freedom of the will. This difference (and the implications of such difference) becomes even clearer, when one considers, the relationship of the Gandhian self-ruled person with the material world. Gandhi, it may be recalled, argues that the foundational nature of the human being is to own kinship with the human and the non-human world[xiv] (Gandhi 1888–1948, 36: 5). It is here perhaps that Gandhi's adoption of the background religio-moral framework of the *Bhagavad Gita* drawing in some part from the non-dualist metaphysics of the *Advaita Vedanta* comes out most clearly.

Once again drawing from his commentary on the *Gita*, one can see that Gandhi's dualism of soul and body is far removed from the Cartesian division between mind and body. The latter, it may be recalled, puts the rational individual at the centre of the universe and sets up the dominion of mind over matter. Naturally enough the universe becomes purely instrumental to the purposes of the mind. Gandhi's notion of the rule of the individual's empirical body–mind continuum by its soul makes it possible to argue for the oneness of all souls;

> It is not easy to see all creatures in ourselves. The key …is, that we should see others in oneself by seeing them and oneself in God… what distinction then, can there be between a Brahman, a *chandal* and a Sudra? (Gandhi 1888–1948, 37: 229)

This Gandhian universalism has seemed suspect to Gandhi's critics with Kumar arguing for an essentially bad faith which makes the "pretense of merging with—without converting its own principles…" (Kumar 2015, 85). The Gandhian conception of the individual self as a soul–body–mind continuum ruled by the soul/higher moral impulses became the basis for the oneness of the individual soul with other souls on the one hand and with the universe as imbued with God/divine soul on the other. One might also take note here of the conceptual distance between the inwardness of the self-seeking to overcome the ego-driven demands of the empirical mind–body by the rule of the higher moral impulses- from (in sharp contrast) the reflexivity that transforms the modern self to look upon itself as an object. The first, one might think, is a state of being best described as an attempt to come to a realization of oneness with human and non-human others. Indeed one might think of it as an experience of progressive non-difference between the individual and the universe as it were. The second—the inwardness of the modern self—is a reflexivity that turns the individual to look upon itself as an object distinct from every human and non-human other. It is as such a unique being, one might note, that the modern self becomes the source of all value for itself.

At this point, it becomes important to take up an important contemporary critique of this idea of "the "spirit" itself, which Gandhi often used interchangeably with more classical terms, such as feeling (*bhaav*), sacrifice (*yajna*), soul (*hriday*)…" (Ibid., 89).

Kumar couches the critique in terms of questions: "Why did Gandhi speak so frequently of spirit? What conceptual and rhetorical work did such a capacious figure do for him? Where did its force- …come from?" (Ibid.)

It turns out that what Gandhi spoke of as "soul force" Kumar describes as Gandhi's "spiritualization of resistance" (Ibid.). This last which I would choose to, describe as the *agraha* or insistence on truth (rather than force), made the transformation of the Gandhian self possible in *swaraj* or self-rule. However for Kumar, as it turns out, this moral self-mastery, though it took on the fervour of religiosity, was rather an insidious and exacting affair;

> But the question was, did this exemplary principle of self-dissolution, the assimilation of one's own self into the transcendent being-a sacrifice that alone secreted the possibility of freedom—become proper to *satyagraha* precisely by remaining mystical, its epistemology and practice restricted to the innermost rationales and reasons of the masterly human (and God) alone? In this demand for the dissolution of the subject in the interest of equality, did a certain inequality, a transcendentalism of limits, insinuate itself at the heart of Gandhi's spiritual experiments? (Ibid., 90)

Kumar sees this insinuation of inequality in Gandhi's dualism (of the soul–body) with its close association to *agraha*/firmness/insistence and *yajna*/sacrifice as essentially pernicious and in bad faith;

> It is precisely the imposition of limits on the unequal's faculties, in other words, that enables *satyagraha*'s immeasurable reverence towards the unequal's existence, so that measure, limit (*maryada*) as such, can be imparted the force of a spiritual and disciplinary obligation (*maryada dharma*) whose fulfilment is the duty both of the *satyagrahi* and unequal. (Ibid.)

Kumar argues that Gandhi's religious universalism "attaching the essence of the untouchable existence to the figure of God himself." (Ibid.) in the neologism *harijan* (a name he chose in 1931) was a "trivialization, even forgetting of conflict and exclusion." (Ibid., 85).

To go back to Kumar's question-what possible conceptual and rhetorical work did such a capacious figure of soul/spirit do for Gandhi? Kumar thought that the answer lay in the fact that it was the figure of the soul which made room for an insidious soul–force (what Kumar calls *atmabal*). It was also this concept of the soul that made for the "spiritual sanctity" (Ibid., 79) and "invincible moral and political legitimacy" (Ibid., 73) of the state and of the "hierarchical four-fold caste system" (Ibid., 76). This *atmabal* often couched as "ambiguous compassion always tempered by a retributive form of rationality, laid the groundwork for Gandhi's moral ontology, or what he might have called the fullness of force, one that aligned *satyagraha* with the sacrificial faith of a very modern sort" (Ibid., 88). A "theologico politico" sort of sacrificial faith that became inextricable from "classical discourses of rule, ability and obedience" (Ibid.)

For Kumar, Gandhi's dualism of soul–body with the metaphor of self-mastery using *bal*/force and sacrifice was "spiritual violence" (Ibid., 68) and an exercise of force which "in the name of" (Ibid., 82) *swaraj* or self-rule offered a "brilliantly oriented theory of freedom as obligation to the law… that would both resist and collude with the most dogmatic injunctions of classical religion." (Ibid.)

It remains however to be determined, if the *agraha*/insistence/firmness that Gandhi associated with the soul/spirit, was nothing but force as such force has perhaps been understood as a "category in the modern political tradition" (Ibid.). Kumar argues that there is nothing to separate Gandhi's *atmabal* coming from the soul from force/*bal* as "a tactical instrument of the more realist obligations of politics" (Ibid., 69). He also argues that Gandhi's association of love with force, in love force which is the soul's force, is "the counterintuitive formulation of force as a symptom, or even extention of love…" this was Gandhi "bringing an unprecedented rigor to reconceptualizing… "force"." (Ibid., 82)

One might well ask, to begin with, whether the connection which Gandhi had made between love and force can be taken to be unprecedented in itself? Surely if the force of love refers to the power to transform **with love** there is no force quite like that of love. One might then say that notwithstanding Kumar (Ibid., 82) the connection has precedents in the *itihaas* or it so happened of humanity. Yet the connection could still be thought of as unprecedented if one were to look at force as a "category in the modern political tradition" (Ibid.). It remains then to ask if the force born of love, wielded by the Gandhian soul/*atman*, is indeed a category akin to that of "force" in the modern political tradition? To be akin to "force" as a modern political category Gandhi's *atmabal* would perhaps have to invoke some element of violence or the threat thereof and more importantly the related idea of compulsion/compelling. Gandhi had himself clarified what he meant by the force/*bal* of love clearly enough. For him the force of love was primarily transformative and only derived its compelling aspects from love's own inherent strength/power to transform (with love, as it were) both the giver and receiver of love. The Gandhian *satyagrahi* eschewed all forms of violence (and Gandhi ruled out even possibilities of humiliating the opponent) so that he/she could evoke the love dormant between the opponent and him/herself in order to transform both him/herself and the opposing other. Note, in this connection, Gandhi's distinction between *satyagraha* and *duragraha*. In his account of *Satyagraha in South Africa* (which was also the English translation of the name of the book containing the account of early days of the practice of *satyagraha*), Gandhi introduced the term *duragraha* or persistence in wrong doing. He cautioned the Indian community to be ever vigilant and "not transgress the limits prescribed by wisdom and appreciation of their own capacity. Satyagraha offered on every occasion… would be corrupted into duragraha." (Gandhi 1888–1948, 34: 171) Gandhi also cautioned that any practice of humiliating the opponent or subjecting him/her to any form of compulsion (or humiliation) would lead to a change in the character of the movement from *satyagraha*/firmness on truth to *duragraha*/wrong doing.

The important question here is—'whether any one can be compelled/forced into being transformed?' One needs to ask perhaps what might be involved in transformation. For one thing, transformation through being met with by love (rather than with anger or hatred) involves coming to see things/issues between people differently or, in Gandhi's words, coming closer to the truth/how things really are between two parties in a conflict. It is the nature of love that it transforms with great ease rather than by compulsion and perhaps it is with the same ease that love calms anger and hate. Once anger is removed and hate dissipates there is also increasing possibility that conflicting parties might overcome suspicion and come closer to seeing things as they really are, independent of how they might appear to be, when seen from within egoistic points of view. Gandhi's love force/soul force/*atmabal* refers then to the soul's power to transform by love and make such clarity of vision possible.

Gandhi cites examples of how love might transform conflicts within the family (between two brothers, between a father and a son in *Hind Swaraj*) as examples of love/soul force and it seems clear from such examples that Gandhi's soul force/*atmabal* has nothing in common with the idea of force as it has been conceived as a modern political category. Gandhi had himself broken from modernity, and this was not a break with modern institutions, as much as it was a conceptual rupture. It is perhaps fitting then to note that he had drawn such an idea of love force as transformative (and as part of the moral ontology of the soul/*atman),* from Patanjali. It is important to emphasize that Gandhi had himself credited Patañjali with this moral discovery:

Ahimsapratishtaya tatsa thirdho veratyaga 'HATE DISSOLVES IN THE PRESENCE OF LOVE' (Patañjali yogadarshanam ii.35). (Gandhi 1888–1948, 48: 327).

Gandhi's argument about love/soul force implied that once self-centred emotions were dissolved by humility and love the self would progressively grow into the ability to 'see' things as they really were outside the patterns of appropriation directed by his/her egoistic concerns. The self could thereby awaken possibilities of transforming both her/himself and the opposing 'other' in any conflict.

Given that Gandhi had thought of the self as an individual *atman*–mind–body within such a background framework it followed that traditional religious texts which had unjustly made distinctions between selves who belonged to different castes were simply misguided. It followed that Gandhi should have argued that such religious texts needed to be denounced as morally wrong/mistaken, contrary to reason and as demanding re-interpretation by the devotee. This led Gandhi to recommend that the self-ruled individual (ruled by the higher moral sensibilities perhaps) who had attained freedom from the demands of the empirical body–mind ought to put aside the text "*shabdabrahman*" (Gandhi 1888–1948, 37: 233) and indeed move "beyond the endless forms of karma and rituals enjoined in the Vedas…" (Ibid.). For Gandhi all such rituals and action would be nothing but an interplay of the several qualities/*gunas* of nature/*prakriti* which effected the individual only in so far as the individual was seen as a body/empirical unit. Once the higher moral impulse/soul was admitted as a master of the mind–body continuum, it was possible to put aside the discriminative practice that emerged from a pre-occupation with the self acting **as if** it were only a body.

The presence of God in his background framework also made it possible for Gandhi to conceive of the relationship between the world of matter/nature and the individual self in non-instrumental terms. Gandhi was at considerable philosophical and conceptual distance from a Cartesian conception of the self where the mind could make use of matter. One might recall in this context that for Gandhi both the universe and the individual were part of the wider divine cosmic order/*rta*.

It might also seem possible to say that the drama and angst caused by the constitutional tension, which Taylor had identified within the modern self, did not quite play out in a Gandhian self-understanding. This (it may be recalled from the last section) was the tension between the demands of rational disengagement and expressivism. The Gandhian self was far removed from the tension between an enlightenment-driven need for disengagement and the somewhat contrary need for expressive self-articulation because the Gandhian self was simply not radically disengaged and inward looking, in the modern way. It is significant that the Gandhian self did not see her/himself as the source of the order he/she was seeking and rather saw her/himself as a part of the wider cosmic order. Since the Gandhian self was not modern (that is not yet disengaged from the external world) the self did not yet exhibit the constitutional tension between the demands of such a disengagement and expressivism (as a need to be in harmony with nature) which (Taylor had argued) afflicted modern identity. This also meant (and this is important) that in a Gandhian understanding of the self, reason could function in harmony with, an expressivism inspired by nature. It was this harmony of human nature with itself, it's seemingly disparate instincts in harmony, that could make room for re-reading religious texts along the lines of a rational faith guided by moral norms. It is significant to note that in a Gandhian understanding reason could function, just as well, alongside faith; as there was no prior commitment (in Gandhi) to a procedural rationality that rested on the individual's radical disengagement from his/her religious (or indeed any other particularities of) context. One could say that there was (in Gandhi) no discontinuity between individual fidelity to reason (as a tradition constitutive and tradition constituted term) and making space for self-expression in religion as such expression had played out within the tradition of one's ancestors. The Gandhian self was free from the modern need to disrupt the narrative and artistic continuity of the essentially unbroken self.

Gandhi's re-iteration (at many places) of the need to re-read religious texts (like the *Gita)* in line with reason is surely significant and needs some reflection. One might realize why this re-iteration is important once one realizes that the modern understanding of reason is purely procedural. In the ancient Western Tradition, in Plato for example, to really know something is to be able to give an account, that is, say/explain why something is so. However, for the moderns, for Locke for example, the requirement to work out the account of why things are so is purely procedural and rests on the laws of rational thinking. Of course there are differences between how moderns formulate the canons of rational thinking. Locke and Descartes (for instance) formulate the canons of rational thinking differently. However, the basic point is that these canons are the only method of getting things right. As Taylor puts it "Rationality is above all a property of thinking, not of the substantive content of thought" (Taylor 2001, 168). This might be the place to point out that such a modern and liberal understanding of rationality is not the only way to understand rationality. MacIntyre argues that there are multiple rationalities just as there are multiple concepts of justice;

> So rationality itself, whether theoretical or practical, is a concept with a history; indeed, since there are a diversity of traditions of enquiry, with histories, there are, so it will turn out, rationalities rather than rationality, just as it will also turn out that there are justices rather than justice. (MacIntyre 1988, 9)

On MacIntyre's understanding, and this I suggest, is the way in which we can understand Gandhi's understanding of the harmonious relationship between faith and reason, there is an understanding of reason wherein "traditions …have embodied rational enquiry as a constitutive part of themselves" (Ibid., 8). That is:

> …the concept of rational justification which is at home in that form of enquiry is essentially historical. To justify is to narrate how the argument has gone so far. (Ibid.)

The important part of MacIntyre's argument is that when it comes to re-interpretation;

> …what justifies the first principles themselves, or rather the whole structure of theory of which they are a part, is the rational superiority of that particular structure to all previous attempts within that particular tradition to formulate such… principles; it is not a matter of those first principles being acceptable to all rational persons whatsoever– (Ibid.)

Reflection on such an argument might make it possible to understand Taylor's point that if one considers the model of the ancients along the lines of Plato and Aristotle the truth that we seek by the exercise of our reason is a "vision of the order of things" (Taylor 2001, 168). Another important difference between accounts of rationality in the ancients and moderns is that the ancients simply did not think of rationality in procedural and thereby disengaged terms. This means that ancient accounts could make room for trust and for guidance from the person with wisdom. Indeed for, what the Indian tradition, calls *sabda pramana*/verbal testimony. One might consider the role of guidance from the man of practical wisdom/*phronesis* to arrive at the truth in an Aristotelian framework. The point I am making here is that Gandhi's references to interpreting religious texts in line with reason (and morality) cannot be understood in terms of the modern and purely procedural understanding of reason. Since Gandhi's understanding of reason is not purely procedural he does not have to insist that reason demands that its own exercise must be contingent on the possibility of the radically independent subject. On a modern liberal understanding of rationality for instance the exercise thereof requires that the subject must disengage her/himself from the particularities of context including in important part his/her religious beliefs and opinions. There is no idea in Gandhi that the exercise of reason involves that the path the subject follows be radically independent and disengaged from the aspirant's sense of belonging to his/her tradition.

This makes room for the exercise of reason, for want of a better term, understood in both procedural and substantive terms in Gandhi. The devotee can in this exercise, quite consistently use reason in the form of a critique, subjecting the religious tradition (within which he/she might indeed locate her/himself) to revision given that truth "claims are being made for doctrines whose formulation is itself time-bound and that the concept of timelessness is itself a concept with a history, one which in certain types of context is not at all the same concept that it is in others" (MacIntyre 1988, 9). As MacIntyre says the mode of justification within an ancient tradition (of which Gandhi was indeed a part) was very different from that of the Enlightenment;

> By contrast from the standpoint of tradition-constituted and tradition-constitutive enquiry, what a particular doctrine claims is always a matter of how precisely it was in fact advanced, of the linguistic particularity of its formulation, of what in that time and place had to be denied, if it was to be asserted, of what was at that time and place presupposed by its assertion and so on. (Ibid.)

However, it is surely significant that Gandhi's reference to reason interrogating religious texts would be oriented towards a truth still seen to be lying outside the subject and in the order of things. This makes for an exercise of reason in Gandhi seen in terms which are not purely procedural. It also makes it possible for him to think of a rational subject who is not necessarily disengaged and hence not necessarily subject to a constitutional tension between the demands of expressivism and such disengagement.

Interestingly, Ambedkar fails to appreciate the powerfully alternate sense of the "tradition-constituted and tradition-constitutive" (Ibid.) mode of the interplay of reason and faith in Gandhi's rational re-interpretation of religious texts. Ambedkar had argued that modernity, as it arrived in India, with its most powerful weapon (reason) failed to challenge the traditional notion of caste and confront the idea of the transgressor in any significant way. Oblivious to the insight that there could be multiple understandings of rationality itself Ambedkar pointed to the absence of any role for an enlightenment driven conception of rational justification in the ancient Indian traditions. He substantiated his argument by pointing out that the Hindus were forbidden or rather trained not to apply reason when it came to following commandments and prescriptions that flowed from the *Vedas* and the *Shastras* since "rationalism as a canon of interpreting the *Vedas* and *Smritis*, is absolutely condemned …and regarded as wicked as atheism" (Ambedkar 2014, 1: 72), therefore, "a Hindu cannot resort to rational thinking" (Ibid.) even as cases of transgressions are selectively allowed and selectively punished.

Showing contrary insights the Gandhian self re-interpreting the *Gita* (both writing and listening to the lectures on the *Gita*) was comfortable with re-interpreting the central terms of the *Gita* such as sacrifice/*yajna* keeping in mind that all these concepts were situated in particular historical contexts and that the tradition had to rework itself from within its own dominant system of meanings with the changes wrought by time and place. Gandhi had argued for instance (as seen above) that *yajna* should be re-interpreted (in the India of the 1930s) as disinterested service of those most distant from oneself rather than as making oblations into a sacred fire. This also led him to think about the *Bhagavad Gita* as a text about equality (this will be brought out in the chapter which follows). The sense of comfort with such radical re-interpretation alongside contrary interpretations came from a self undivided by the Cartesian divide between mind and matter. The absence of such a constitutive dualism kept intact the notion of moral order within and of *rta*/moral order without in the cosmos.

It might be appropriate to end this section with a note about (what was referred to above) Gandhi's re-interpretation of sacrifice/*yajna*. This note seeks to counter the argument made by Kumar (2015) that "sacrifice" (which appears and re-appears in Gandhi's thought from 1907) involves "a certain notion of force through such formulations as "ethics of destruction" and "mastery over passions"." (Kumar 2015, 28). Force (Kumar suggests) "contains a people's right to reinstitute their conceptual, spatial, and cognitive order in which the plurality and incommensurability of everyday experience might be militantly rethought and reclaimed but in which the singularity of each person's existence and finitude might still be generalized through sacrifice toward a just universalism." (Ibid.) Kumar makes the point that both Gandhi and Ambedkar "place the imperative of an interpretative and conceptually transformative *coup de force*-indeed the notion of force (whether the "force of law" or "force of arms," "soul force" or "that of the hand")—at the core of moral relations" (Ibid., 27). As he explains;

> …force is the condensation of the subject's experience and intense will to act, …Force is the moral firmness (*agraha*) that constitutes the inalienable truthfulness of being; it is existence that is irreducibly free, equal and fearless (Ambedkar's *samata*). (Ibid., 29)

Before I close this section, I want to make the more limited point that Gandhi's conception of *yajna*/sacrifice is constituted by the idea of self-restraint which, in its turn, is a restraint of the ego/*ahamkara* and of self-interest in a disinterested service of the other most distant from the self. To describe such a restraint of selfish interests in terms of the exercise of "force" over one's own self might make it difficult to speak of an ethics of altruism (or of benevolence) at all. The only way in which one might be free of selfish interest, on such a view, would be to *force* ourselves to be so. Force involves the sense of compulsion which is seldom associated with a feeling of happiness or even contentment. One need only consider whether in some sense it could be internal to the conception of the good life that an aspirant feels a sense of joy in such a life. Without such a sense one would be committed to a very strange position in/on moral philosophy where it would become conceptually untenable to associate an 'ethics of altruism' with contentment/joy given that such an ethics, and the related notion of restraint of the self by the self, would involve the exercise of a force, akin to, the force of arms or the force of law. Given that for Gandhi (like

Aristotle) happiness was internal to the good human life, and to *swaraj* and *yajna*, it might seem difficult to think of such notions in terms of a *coup de force* and force itself

3.3   Ambedkar: On Self, Religion and God

This chapter has been arguing that the differences between Gandhi and Ambedkar drew from their very different notions of the self who was at the centre of their conflicting approaches to untouchability. Such differences (I have suggested) emerged from their very different locations *vis-a-vis* the philosophical shifts in modernity that had somewhat transformed the understanding of the relationship between the self, God and community. These shifts (as brought out in the first section of this chapter) had radically altered modern self-consciousness and the modern understanding of the human being and his/her place in the world.

Gandhi (as seen in the last section) had thought of the self in continuity with the Indian philosophical tradition, often drawing from the *Bhagavad Gita*, to speak of the self (a continuum of soul body) as an infinitesimal part of a cosmos governed by 'Truth or God'. In a complete departure from Gandhi (and indeed from all accounts that drew from tradition), Babasaheb Ambedkar thought of the self and of the relationship of the self to the rest of the world in terms that were closer to modern self-consciousness. The next two subsections will go on to philosophically unpack these relationships and Ambedkar's alternative self-understanding.

3.3.1   Ambedkar: On the Self and the Community

This section will bring out Ambedkar's alternative understanding of the self and the relationship of that self to the new Buddhist community that he sought to constitute through his *Navayana* Buddhism. It seems somewhat apparent that these two issues are intimately inter-related—as the manner in which one might think of the self would in turn determine the manner in which one might conceive the relationship between that self and the community—of which the self is/chooses to be a part. Ambedkar's understanding of the self seemed to have been very different from that of the old-world Gandhi and consequently perhaps he thought of the relationship between that self and the new Buddhist community very differently from Gandhi who (one might recall) had invoked kinship as the appropriate relationship between members of a community. Since one must begin at the beginning, it becomes important to philosophically unpack (what I would delineate as) the four aspects of Ambedkar's understanding of the self.

The first aspect which is only brought out in passing (and as preparatory to the section which immediately follows this) is that Ambedkar's self was conceived to be at the centre of the world as he shared in a modern and primarily anthropocentric/man-centred understanding of the world. The second more substantial insight concerns Ambedkar's rejection of the existence of the soul/*atman* and alternative understanding of the self as a "human personality" (Ambedkar 2014, 3: 99). Ambedkar had understood this human personality/self along Cartesian lines as a combination of the body and the mind. The third insight (from Ambedkar) is that while he had indeed spoken of the spiritual super-existence of the self, Ambedkar had a very modern understanding of the role of the "spiritual" in individual life. He seemed to have understood the self's spiritual quest in more modern terms as the human being's coming to terms with him/herself. The fourth and last Ambedkarian insight into the nature of the self is one which might seem to follow, naturally enough, from the first three; and which, might be best described by saying that Ambedkar had understood the human being (along lines best brought out by Kant) as an end in himself/herself.

To say a little more about these four points will also serve to unpack the conceptual and philosophical distance between the alternative world views which lay at the opposite ends of the debate between Ambedkar and Gandhi. To begin with Ambedkar's first insight into the nature of the self; as already noted Ambedkar had emphasized a vision in which the human being was at the centre of the universe. He had argued in fact that there had been a transformation of world views (a revolution in religion of which much more will be said in the immediately following section) from the ancient to the modern world which had led, in its turn, to human personality coming to be at the centre of the universe:

> By this revolution God has ceased to be a member of a community… God has ceased to be the Father of man… He has become the creator of the Universe… By this revolution man has ceased to be a blind worshipper of God doing nothing but obeying his commands… It is man who has become the centre of it. (Ibid., 21)

The second important insight was that, in Ambedkar's understanding, the individual human self had no association with an *atman* or soul. Ambedkar made it clear in *The buddha and his dhamma* that he agreed with the Buddha's rejection of the notion of a soul that endures through time;

> He (the Buddha) was an annihilationist so far as soul was concerned. He was not an annihilationist so far as matter was concerned… So interpreted, the Buddha's view is in consonance with science. (Ambedkar 2011, 176)

> The Buddha said that religion based on soul is based on speculation. Nobody has seen the soul or has conversed with the soul. The soul is unknown and unseen. The thing that exists is not the soul but the mind. Mind is different from the soul… A religion based on soul is therefore not worth having… Belief in the existence of soul was also a part of the Brahmanic Religion. In the Brahmanic Religion the soul is called *Atma* or *Atman*. In the Brahmanic religion, *Atman* is the name given to an entity which is held to be abiding separate from the body, but living inside the body, constantly existing from the moment of his birth… Did the Buddha believe in the soul? No. (Ibid., 138–139)

Having rejected the more traditional notion of the self as a *atman*–body continuum, and in sharp contrast to Gandhi, Ambedkar explained the nature of the human self in alternative terms as a combination of physical and mental elements (a body and a mind) which he substantiated along the lines of Buddha's theory as *Nama Rupa*;

> The theory is the result of the application of the Vibhaja test, of sharp, rigorous analysis, of the constituent elements of Sentient being, called Human Personality. Nama-Rupa is a collective name for a Sentient Being. According to the Buddha's analysis, a Sentient Being is a compound thing consisting of certain physical and certain mental elements. They are called *Khandas*....wherever there was rupa or kaya there was consciousness accompanying it. (Ibid., 140–141)

Almost as if he was attributing his own, more modern understanding of the self to the Buddha, and thereby bringing out the alternative (and more modern) insight that the self is a combination of the empirical mind and body Ambedkar wrote of the Buddha's teachings that;

> The first distinguishing feature of his teachings lay in the recognition of the mind as the centre of everything. Mind precedes things, dominates them, creates them. If mind is comprehended, all things are comprehended. Mind is the leader of all its faculties. Mind is the chief of all its faculties… (Ibid., 62).

Ambedkar seemed to have read Buddhism itself along the lines suggested by developments in Western philosophy, more specifically along Cartesian lines, in suggesting that the Buddha had a procedural understanding of rationality giving precedence to the procedures/rules of rational/logical thought.

> There is, however, one test which is available. If there is anything which could be said with confidence it is: He was nothing if not rational, if not logical. Anything therefore which is rational and logical, other things being equal, may be taken to be the word of the Buddha. (Ibid., 185)

It was such a Cartesian dualism, a procedural understanding of rationality and the modern appreciation of mind dominating matter that led Ambedkar to share in the radical individualism of the post enlightenment philosophers. However, there might still be room to ask whether Ambedkar came close enough, to a more traditional understanding of the self, if one were to consider his, apparently contrary, reference to the self/body-mind continuum as having a "spiritual super-existence" (Ambedkar 2014, 3: 95). This last point takes this discussion to the third aspect of Ambedkar's understanding of the self. In Chap. 2 of his posthumously published *The Hindu Social Order*, Ambedkar wrote about the "human person" (Ibid., 95) and his/her spiritual super-existence;

> Why must the individual be the end and not the means of all social purposes? For an answer to this question, it is necessary to realize what we precisely mean when we speak of the human person. (Ibid.)

Quoting the liberal Thomistic French Philosopher Jacques Maritain[xv] Ambedkar explained that the mind–body continuum/self had a "spiritual super-existence";

> When we say that an individual is a person, we do not mean merely that he is an individual, in the sense that an atom, a blade of grass, a fly, or an elephant is an individual. Man is an individual who holds himself in hand by his intelligence and will; he exists not merely in a physical fashion. He has spiritual super-existence through knowledge and love, so that he is, in a way, a universe himself, a microcosm, in which the great universe in its entirety can be encompassed through knowledge… The notion of personality thus involves that of totality

and independence, no matter how poor and crushed a person may be, he is a whole, and as a person subsistent in an independent manner. To say that a man is a person is to say that in the depth of his being he is more a whole than a part and more independent than servile. (Ibid., 95–96)

It is significant that in speaking about the spiritual life of the human self, as the "super-existence" of that self, Ambedkar should have made no reference to a soul/*atman* who strives for self-realization in a wider order outside of itself. Ambedkar had (as already noted) rejected notions of a soul transmigrating from birth to birth and he had re-interpreted Buddha's position on *karma* and transmigration stating that the "cases of misrepresenting are common with regard to karma and rebirth" (Ambedkar 2011, 185). To look more closely at the passage quoted above, it might seem apparent that, what Taylor has described as the three-sided individualism (what I am, what I want and what I will) of modernity, comes to characterize the Indian self for the first time, as it were, in the writing of Ambedkar. However, it still remains that Ambedkar had thought of this individualistic self as more than the body and as a being who was capable of a spiritual life by extending her/himself through "knowledge and love" (Ambedkar 2014, 3: 95). There might then be some room to argue that though he had summarily rejected the notion of the *atman* Ambedkar's reference to "spiritual super-existence" (Ibid.), as noted earlier, might have brought him close enough to Gandhi's notion of the *atman*-driven and more traditional understanding of the self. It is such considerations that have perhaps prompted scholars to argue that Ambedkar's turn to religion brought him closer to Gandhi's more traditional notion of the soul/*atman*.

It becomes very important then to examine this third aspect of Ambedkar's understanding of the self and to ask whether his reference to the "spiritual super-existence" (Ibid.) of the human person ought to be read in more traditional terms as a search for the foundation of the ontology of the human. In this context I would like to go back to the discussion in Sect. 3.1 of this chapter on the inwardness of the self in modernity. As noted there, modernity puts the first-person perspective at the centre of things and takes a radically subjective stance. Subsequent to such a subjective stance the modern subject begins to looks upon 'itself' quite as an object. It is important to recall that I had suggested that once the human being is able to think of her/his own self in a third-person perspective the self is no longer seen to be the source of the spiritual life as a quest for the foundation of the ontology of the human. Quite to the contrary:

…we come to think we 'have' selves as we have heads. (Taylor 2001, 177)

Or perhaps as we have faces, noses, legs and hands. What this comes to mean is that the modern self (which is an object to itself) begins to think of the distinctively human spiritual quest as all too human and as a search to come to terms with itself as an object. Akin perhaps as a quest to come to terms with oneself as a body—fat, thin, ugly—which can be pursued in psycho analytic therapy. An important aspect to such a coming to terms with oneself is that one needs to come to terms with oneself in the presence of other selves with whom one has to be in some kind of relationship. The significant point is that the spiritual is no longer understood as a search for answers about the end/*telos* of individual human life or for a repository of answers to questions posed by moral choices. Such a *telos* might be, and has indeed often has been, seen in more traditional world views as being a part of and belonging to a traditional religious community. After the self takes a radically subjective turn (and becomes an object to itself) the spiritual aspect of human life is seen in powerfully alternative terms as a search for what (the individual) is, what he/she wants and what he/she wills to be. One may re-iterate that Taylor had described this as a "three-sided individualism" which is "central to modern identity" (Ibid., 185).

It is only if we turn to this three-sided individualism of modernity that we can perhaps quite understand Ambedkar's reference to the spiritual aspect of human personality. While Ambedkar certainly speaks of the "spiritual super existence" (Ambedkar 2014, 3: 95) of the self; the term "spiritual" has been understood by him quite differently from how that term had been understood in/by more traditional accounts of the spiritual. These differences accrue from the differences between ancient and modern understandings of the self. The radical inwardness of modernity leads the self to see itself as an object after a process of radical disengagement from itself. An important aspect to the objectification of the self (which Kant expresses perhaps as that which makes the unity of apperception possible) is that the spiritual is no longer a search for the truth of oneself. On the contrary, in modernity, the spiritual comes to be powerfully associated with the self's coming to terms with its own perception of itself in a powerful inner reflexivity where the self **appears to itself** as an object. This is of course very different from traditional world views which did not think of the self as radically disengaged from itself and from everything else.

In traditional world views, the self's spiritual quest could signify and be seen in terms of a striving to complete himself/herself by growing into a relationship with nature and the divine. Alternatively one could see such a relationship, as perhaps Gandhi did, as a move within to unfold layers of self-deception and come to the truth as God who could be reflected within as outside the self. Notice Augustine's spiritual move to find God at the end of memory. Alternatively the spiritual could be sought, like Tagore, in an inter-relationship with the natural world seen to be mediating the relationship between man and God.

In Ambedkar there is a contrary and more modern understanding of "spiritual super-existence" (Ibid.). As already noted he does not think of the spiritual as a search for the truth within. An unfolding perhaps of layers of self-deception till he could come to the foundation of the ontology of the human. To the contrary for Ambedkar, the spiritual has to do (as noted) with taking a radically subjective turn to ascertain the nature of the subject as a bearer of rights, as subject to compelling needs and as a "totality and independence" (Ibid.) or an independent will. On Ambedkar's understanding it is significant that the spiritual super-existence of the human being comes to signify that the human person can indeed take such a radically subjective turn and experience being "a universe in himself" (Ibid.). Consequently, for Ambedkar the human being's spiritual life does not involve him/her in any attempt to identify with the world outside as he/she experiences freedom in being an independent universe to herself/himself.

The spiritual impulse in Ambedkar's modern self perhaps manifests itself as the very disengagement of the disengaged self. Such disengagement [as Nagel put it "the view from nowhere" (Nagel 1986, 70)] is expressed as the rational urge to know the world of matter through reason driven science. At another level the spiritual aspect manifests itself in affirming the value of ordinary life. Such affirmation of the value of living such a life in harmony with others in the community manifests as the need to relate to/love other selves. Ambedkar therefore explains what he calls the "spiritual super-existence" (Ambedkar 2014, 3: 95) as brought about through "knowledge and love" (Ibid.), so that the human being who is "a universe himself, a microcosmos" (Ibid., 95–6), can encompass the great universe in its entirety "through knowledge" (Ibid., 96) and experience a relationship to other selves through "love" (Ibid.).

This puts Ambedkar at the opposite end of the philosophical spectrum, as it were, from ancient world views (we may look here at Gandhi, Plato, Aristotle or the *Gita*) where the turn inwards takes the subject (which is not yet an object to itself) to experience the self (which is not a universe in itself) becoming complete by negotiating a relationship with the universe. That is by negotiating with the human and the non-human and indeed with the transcendental divine world outside of herself/himself.

To bring the debate between them back into focus, one might consider that for Ambedkar like Gandhi, the spiritual aspect of human life involved a turn inwards. Only this was not a turn towards 'Truth or God' (like Gandhi) but the self's subjective turn to look upon itself as an object. On taking this turn the modern subject would find him/herself through the experience of realizing him/herself as an independent universe and as the source of the moral law and of all value. Quoting the liberal Thomistic French philosopher Jacques Maritain; Ambedkar says of this modern self, that such a self would be complete/independent in herself/himself, and would seek to form relationships with other selves so as to be able to live in the civic community. This perhaps was what he sought in the new Buddhist community of the future;

> By love he can give himself completely to those who are to him, as it were, other selves. For this relation no equivalent can be found in the physical world... The value of the person, his dignity and rights, belong to the order of things naturally sacred... (Ibid., 96)

It can be concluded decisively then that in Ambedkar's account of the modern subject there is an affirmation of each of the three aspects in/of the making of modern identity discussed by Charles Taylor—that is, inwardness, pre-occupation with the concerns of ordinary life and the expressivist turn in human nature.

It seems clear enough that for Ambedkar the source of all values (which for him meant the familiar enlightenment liberty, equality and fraternity) lay in the self's very inwardness. A necessary corollary to such an understanding of the self was that there was no necessity to look to God or the transcendental cosmic order outside the self and outside the concerns of ordinary life to locate such values. This turn inwards was taken by the Ambedkarian self in a Kantian direction and it re-affirmed the idea (and this was the fourth and last aspect of Ambedkar's account of the self) that all human beings were ends in themselves and also the related idea that all human beings

were, as such ends, absolutely equal. It seems natural enough for Ambedkar to have
re-affirmed that;

> Fraternity is the name for the disposition of an individual to treat men as the object of
> reverence and love and the desire to be in unity with his fellow beings. This statement is well
> expressed by Paul when he said 'Of one blood are all nations of men…'. Equally well was it
> expressed when the pilgrim fathers on their landing at Plymouth said: 'we are knit together
> as a body in the most sacred covenant of the Lord… by virtue of which we hold ourselves
> tied to all care of each others' good and of the whole'. These sentiments are of the essence
> of fraternity. (Ibid., 97)

One might now consider how Ambedkar conceived the relationship between the
modern self of his making as it were and the new Buddhist community which was also
of his making. For Gandhi of course that relationship would be specified as that of
kinship as (noted earlier in this chapter) Gandhi's notion of the *swabhava*/innermost
orientation of being human imposed the unilateral obligation/*ekpakshi farj* on each
individual to own kinship with the human and non-human other. On a contrary note
Ambedkar's understanding of the self and its spiritual super-existence did not posit
kinship between human persons or between the human and non-human world or even
between the human person and God. As he re-iterates, at many places, for modern's,
God, is no longer a father. It follows that for Ambedkar, at least, the appropriate
relationship between human persons in a community of co-religionists cannot be
thought of as kinship. This is evident enough from his argument that modern humans
do not see themselves as children of the same father/God (or indeed even of different
Gods). Since human beings are no longer children of the same father, the relationship
between them, guided only by the concerns of ordinary life in the civic community
(not family), is best understood as fraternity. This is not a play of words and it makes
all the difference to the differences between Gandhi and Ambedkar.

However, what would one make of the somewhat contrary note struck by
Ambedkar's move to strengthen the foundations of the liberal understanding of
Fraternity by introducing "religious" (it is important to add the *caveat* that we would
be misled if we took Ambedkar's use of the word "religious" in the conventional
sense of that term) arguments which took him to the re-writing of Buddhism. One
may note the connection between such a re-writing and his efforts to re-constitute
the dalits into a religious Buddhist community. The question that is raised by such
a re-constitution is whether Ambedkar (like Gandhi) saw the new Buddhist community along the lines of kinship and the family? This then would overturn the earlier
argument that he had a more modern understanding of the relationship between the
self and the 'other' one indeed guided primarily by the liberal value of fraternity in
the civic community. I would like here to suggest that what is significant about the
Navayana or re-interpreted Buddhism is that Ambedkar (somewhat like Rawls who
came much later in time) attempted to re-interpret Buddhism by introducing only
those elements from a comprehensive Buddhist account of the good that could find
legitimate space in an essentially minimalist, liberal, political public space.

I would like to go philosophically far afield here and digress a little bit to speak
of Rawls (who came much later than Ambedkar and whom I will also bring up in
Chap. 5) and re-visit the distinction between comprehensive and political conceptions

of justice. As a point of order I would draw from Richard Sorabji's observation that it is not necessary that philosophers should have met each other or even been acquainted with each others theories. Sometimes reading things (albeit from vastly different epochs and contexts) in parallel can throw up insights which can help to better understand doctrines far apart in age and inspiration (Sorabji 2012). It is with just such an intent that I bring up Rawls's distinction between a comprehensive general account of the good and a purely political conception of justice;

> In this respect a political conception of justice differs from many moral accounts, for these are widely regarded as general and comprehensive views... By contrast, a political conception tries to elaborate a reasonable conception for the basic structure alone and involves, so far as possible, no wider commitment to any other doctrine. (Rawls 2005, 13)

Rawls had clarified in his second book that he was interested in formulating a reasonable, and more importantly, a purely political conception of justice which could form part of an overlapping consensus between diverse people in a civil society. In this context, Rawls had explained the difference between such a political conception and wider more comprehensive accounts of the good. Perhaps the distinction between a purely political conception of justice and a comprehensive account of the good could be useful to an understanding of Ambedkar's position on religion. This is because what Rawls describes as a comprehensive account of the good signifies precisely the kind of account of religion that Ambedkar was trying to avoid when re-writing Buddhism in *The Buddha and his Dhamma* (2011). Rawls explains the difference between a purely political conception of justice and more comprehensive moral conceptions;

> This contrast will be clearer if we observe that the distinction between a political conception of justice and other moral conceptions is a matter of scope: that is, the range of subjects to which a conception applies and the content a wider range requires. A moral conception is general if it applies to a wide range subjects, and in the limit to all subjects universally. It is comprehensive when it includes what is of value in human life, and ideals of personal character, as well as ideals of friendship and of familial and associational relationships, and much else that is to inform our conduct, and in the limit to our life as a whole. A conception is fully comprehensive if it covers all recognized values and virtues within one rather precisely articulated system; whereas a conception is only partially comprehensive when it comprises a number of, but by no means all, non political values and virtues and is rather loosely articulated. Many religious and philosophical doctrines aspire to be both general and comprehensive. (Rawls 2005, 13)

One might suggest that as a minimalist liberal constitutionalist [Kumar speaks of the "rigor of his constitutional Imagination" (Kumar 2015, 8)], Ambedkar chose to re-write Buddhism to strengthen fraternity in the new Buddhist community of the future so as to make for the stability of the civic (and thereafter political) life of the dalits. Political/civic life in Ambedkar's view, needed to be supported by values coming from within "religious" non-comprehensive accounts of what it might be right to do rather than good to become. Ambedkar thought that such support was required if civic life was to be stable for the right reasons. Once again I will invoke Rawls here as he suggests that if the political conception of justice in a liberal democratic society (which is essentially plural) is to be stable for the right reasons it needs to be supported by an overlapping consensus (formed around purely political values) between rival and comprehensive competing accounts of the good. One might perhaps suggest that Ambedkar wrote the *Navayana* to bring the diverse dalit community together (it may be recalled that even when Hindu this community could be/was divided by rival comprehensive accounts of the good built around regional Gods and Goddesses) in just such a consensus; around minimal moral and political values to facilitate and stabilize the civic/political life of the dalit community. Thereby Ambedkar engaged with the task of setting fraternity in place in/for the new Buddhist community to prepare the ground as it were and make room for other engagements (primarily contractarial) with the Indian nation. Ambedkar had already prospectively imagined that such engagements would necessarily involve political demands (and demands for affirmative action) for the new dalit community of the *Navayana*. Ambedkar's re-writing of Buddhism then appeared to have involved purely social and political values, and hence, his *Navayana* was not even a partially comprehensive account of the good; being concerned, as it was, only with what it was right to do rather than with what it might be good to become. It was not therefore 'religious' in the accepted/conventional sense of the term.

This could suggest that Ambedkar's religious turn which took him towards the new Buddhist community was somewhat philosophically close to Rawls' move in formulating an overlapping consensus (in his second book) to ensure the stability of a purely political conception of justice for a plural democratic society. Ambedkar's move to the New Buddhist community was perhaps intended to build an overlapping consensus on minimal moral and political values (with a special emphasis on fraternity) between dalits who might have had diverse commitments to various, sometimes regional/local, Gods, Goddesses and sects (from within a plural Hindu array of such divinities and sects); as a precursor to ensuring the stability of justice and rights (for the dalits who were part of that new community) in an essentially plural democratic society. He therefore attempted to lay down the foundation for such fraternity between the converted dalits as a prerequisite for the demands for justice/rights—for the dalit community. Note in this context Kumar's observation that "the moral logic at work in *Annihilation of Caste"* was "(t)To affirm religion not for its own sake but to affirm it in order to make what was just strong and what was strong just; to acquire a 'means of defense' for the weak without lapsing into hostility and militarianism…" (Ibid., 10).

This point might become more apparent when one considers, in somewhat more detail, how Ambedkar thought about (what was meant by) 'Religion' which will form the subject of the next subsection.

In this connection, it is significant to note that in drawing upon arguments for fraternity from within the non-comprehensive account of what it might be right to do in his *Navayana* or re-interpreted Buddhism, Ambedkar did not quite give up his commitment to minimalist liberal democracy or the "rigor of his constitutional imagination" (Ibid., 8). One might note that though he often argued that it is through religion that fraternity can become available he also cautioned that it is also religion (as a comprehensive and general account of the good) that could prohibit one from developing *maitri*/friendship. In giving a historical explanation for the absence of fraternity in the subcontinent, for instance, Ambedkar seemed convinced that communities in India could never develop feelings of *maitri* among themselves because Hinduism did not lend itself to such a doctrine. Ambedkar considered in this connection the idea of "Brahmanism" (Ambedkar 2014, 3: 284) in Hindu philosophy which Gandhi, for instance, saw as laying the foundations of kinship between humans and between the human and non-human world. Ambedkar admitted that the belief in the idea that "the world is real and the reality behind the world is Brahma" (Ibid., 285) refers to everyone and everything equally. He argued that though the idea of *Brahmanism* had great potentialities to strengthen fraternity and produce a social democracy, it had failed in practice to translate itself in the face of caste. On this view, as all people inhabiting the caste order could not be thought of as equal and as equally infused with the ideal of *Brahma, Brahmanism* failed to contribute towards the ideal of democracy. Ambedkar argued that it was on account of such a failure that Hinduism had never been able to produce beliefs and convictions that could lay the foundation of a true democracy in India.

In a somewhat similar strain, Ambedkar had also rejected Gandhi's *swaraj* as located in a comprehensive (and Hindu) account of the good. Ambedkar did not think of individual freedom as Gandhian *swaraj* a state where the *atman*/higher moral possibilities in the human being rules over the psycho physical organism that goes by the name of the self. The Gandhian self it may be noted achieved true freedom when he/she approached the state analogous to that of the *sthitaprajna* of the *Gita*/the person who was unperturbed by extremes of emotion connected to ordinary life. In its stead Ambedkar offered a purely political account of freedom/liberty along enlightenment lines. Liberty, Ambedkar explained, is both civil and political and he added;

> There is no freedom where there are no means of taking advantage of it. Real liberty of action exists only where exploitation has been annihilated. (Ibid., 98)

The point that this section has sought to make is that Ambedkar's self is as far removed from Gandhi's *atman*-driven self as can possibly be imagined. It is in this conceptual distance that one can perhaps locate the birth of the modern Indian subject born of philosophical developments that shaped the Western world post the eighteenth century. However, this Ambedkarian self does not, as already noted, appear to sit uneasily with religion. Quite to the contrary scholars have argued that Ambedkar took a religious turn to convert to Buddhism and write *The Buddha and his dhamma*. Yet that said it is also important to note that, as he did all these things, Ambedkar completely re-invented 'religion' itself along modern lines. Perhaps one might say that Buddhism had lent itself to Ambedkar's reading of liberal values rather than provided him with a comprehensive general account of the good and a background moral framework. In that sense one might argue that it is modernity itself that takes a new different and perhaps sacred[xvi] turn in the life and work of Babasaheb:

> Once the sacredness of human personality is admitted the necessity of liberty, equality and fraternity must also be submitted as the proper climate for the development of personality. (Ibid., 99)

3.3.2 Ambedkar: On Religion and the Banishment of God

One might now re-visit the question which was raised at the beginning of this chapter. This relates to the argument that Ambedkar's conversion marked a 'religious' turn which spoke to the influence that the debate with Gandhi had exerted upon his ideas. This would imply that, unlike what the first chapter has suggested, the debate between Gandhi and Ambedkar cannot be read in terms of a divergence between fundamentally different world views—ancient and modern. This last reading (which is also the reading in this book) could become difficult if it can be argued that Ambedkar had shared with the ancients (and departed from the modern) by making a commitment to God and to the religious community.

As mentioned in Sect. 3.1, scholars have found it plausible to suggest that Ambedkar's acceptance of Religion and of the religious community might have served to re-instate a transcendental realm to replace the unjust Hindu Gods who (it might be recalled) had been banished from the dalit huts. Scholars have argued that accepting Religion signified that Ambedkar (like Gandhi) accepted a comprehensive and general account of the good, a given (Buddhist) ontology of the human and the idea that there was a standard of evaluation outside of man and independent of the individual's will, desires and all too human ideals. This section will argue that though Ambedkar converted to Buddhism, this conversion did not make, for quite such a departure, from modernity. To the contrary, this (and the next) section will attempt to argue that Ambedkar's conversion was quite in keeping with his radical modernity.

To this end, Sect. 3.3.2.1 will discuss what Ambedkar meant by "religion" and the place he accorded to God as the source of all value. Section 3.4 (with its various sub sections) will go on to argue that Ambedkar's conversion to Buddhism did not signify the acceptance of the comprehensive Buddhist religious account of the good. The section will argue that Ambedkar re-wrote Buddhism as he re-wrote history along the lines of the enlightenment and modernity.

3.3.2.1 Ambedkar on Religion: Articulating Norms to Formulate a "New Religion" for a "New World"[xvii]

While this book opened with Ambedkar's re-writing of history this section considers Ambedkar's *Navayana* and his re-writing of Buddhism. Scholars who have argued that Ambedkar took a religious turn towards tradition at the end of his life refer to his conversion and to his *Navayana*. In this context, mention is made of the fact that Ambedkar wrote *The buddha and his dhamma* between 1951 and 1956 and converted to Buddhism in 1956. It may be recalled that *The buddha and his dhamma* was published posthumously by the People's Education Society in November 1957.

The buddha and his dhamma is an anthology in which material connected with Buddha's actual teaching is put together with the story of his life. Both these are interwoven with explanatory additions made by Ambedkar himself. Apart from these explanatory additions, the text has been compiled from canonical and non-canonical

Buddhist works in Pali, Sanskrit and Chinese and it draws from texts that belong to Theravada *Sarvastivada* and Mahayana schools of Buddhism.

I am no scholar of Buddhism and cannot therefore make a philosophically comprehensive and conceptually useful account of Buddhist teachings and indeed of Buddhist literature here. All that this subsection (and the next) will attempt to do is indicate that Ambedkar's conversion and commitment to a *Navayana* Buddhism did not constitute a departure from modernity.

To begin with one might get a philosophical clue on how Ambedkar understood the term 'Religion' from his own remarks in the Preface that he wrote to *The buddha and his dhamma* in 1956 (but which did not appear in print till 1980). In that Preface, Ambedkar had traced the origin of *The buddha and his dhamma* to the article he had written on "The Buddha and the future of his Religion". In this article (written in 1915), Ambedkar had stated that Buddha was different from Jesus, Krishna and Mohammed in that he (the Buddha) had wanted to base his religion on reason and experience;

> The Buddha claimed no such infallibility for what he taught. In the *Mahaparinibbana Sutta* He told Ananda that His religion was based on reason and experience and that his followers should not accept his teaching as correct and binding merely because they emanated from Him. Being based on reason and experience they were free to modify or even to abandon any of his teachings if it was found that at a given time and in given circumstances they do not apply.He wished, his religion not to be encumbered with the dead wood of the past. He wanted that it should remain evergreen and serviceable at all times. (Ambedkar 2014, 17 Part 2: 98)

It is important to note that Ambedkar was clear that Buddhism was the only religion which a society based on science could accept and without which it could indeed not survive. It is important to recall here that Ambedkar perhaps drew such revolutionary insights from Durkheim's *Elementary forms of Religious life* (1912) and then later from Henri Bergson's *The two sources of Religion and Morality* (1932). It was the last that became crucial to the moral theology of *The buddha and his dhamma*. In "The Buddha and the future of his Religion" Ambedkar spoke in fact of the need for a "new religion" (Ambedkar 2014, 17 Part 2: 104) for the "new world" (Ibid., 105) and proposed a fourfold test to evaluate which of the already existing religions could qualify as such religions for the new world:

> Is there any religion which satisfies all these tests? So far as I know, the only religion which satisfies all these tests is Buddhism. In other words Buddhism is the only religion which the world can have. If the new world—which be it realized is very different from the old-must have a religion—and the new world needs religion far more than the old world did—then it can only be religion of the Buddha. (Ibid., 104–105)

To begin with Ambedkar's emphasis on putting religions through a fourfold test in itself presupposes the modern stance of radical disengagement/the view from nowhere (spoken of by Nagel) which is the distinctive characteristic of modern identity. Such a radical disengagement is (as already noted) the product of the inwardness of the modern subject. The idea that it is the subject who must **choose** the new religion for the new world presupposes that the subject can and must disengage with the world/cosmos outside of itself and that it's own very inwardness is the source of all value. On a contrary note, one might recall here that Scruton had spoken of the religious life as essentially given to one rather than chosen/selected:

> ...the normal tendency of the religious urge is toward membership, by which I mean a network of relations that are neither contractual nor negotiated, but which are received as a destiny and a gift. (Scruton 2014, 14)

Finally, one can note that the substance of Ambedkar's fourfold test suggests that the new religion had to be based upon reason and experience and in line with the paradigm set by modern science;

> I maintain that:
>
> (i)   That society must have either the sanction of law or the sanction of morality to hold it together. Without either, society is sure to go to pieces. In all societies, law plays a very small part. It is intended to keep the minority within the range of social discipline. The majority is left and has to be left to sustain its social life by the postulates and sanction of morality. Religion in the sense of morality, must therefore, remain the governing principle in every society.
>
> (ii)   That religion as defined in the first proposition must be in accord with science. Religion is bound to lose its respect and therefore becomes the subject of ridicule and thereby not merely lose its force as a governing principle of life, but might in course of time disintegrate and lapse, if it is not in accord with science. In other words, religion if it is to function, must be in accord with reason which is merely another name for science.
>
> (iii) That religion as a code of social morality, must also stand together another test. It is not enough for religion to consist of a moral code, but its moral code must recognise the fundamental tenets of liberty, equality and fraternity. Unless a religion recognises these three fundamental principles of social life, religion will be doomed.
>
> (iv)   That religion must not sanctify or ennoble poverty. Renunciation of riches by those who have it, may be a blessed state, but poverty can never be. To declare poverty to be a blessed state is to pervert religion, to perpetuate vice and crime, to consent to make earth a living hell." (Ambedkar 2014, 17 Part 2: 104)

To understand that what Ambedkar meant by "religion" (and by the new religion for the new world) was quite different from religion as it was understood in ancient world views one may also note Ambedkar's comments in *Philosophy of Hinduism* (Ambedkar 2014, 3: 94): Here Ambedkar explained that the "disruption of the Empire of Religion" (Ambedkar 2014, 3: 9) was a "Great Revolution" (Ibid.):

> Students of History are familiar with one Religious Revolution. That Revolution was concerned with the sphere of Religion and the extent of its authority. There was a time when Religion had covered the whole field of human knowledge and claimed infallibility for what it taught. (Ibid., 8)

It is significant to note (in the present context) that Ambedkar points to two revolutions which had substantially altered the meaning of religion itself. At first there was an external revolution which had challenged the ancient dominion of religion over all areas of human life and knowledge. However there was, according to Ambedkar, a more important revolution, an internal revolution in Religion. It was this second revolution which led to a transformation in that which was signified by the term 'Religion'. This understanding led Ambedkar to self-consciously distinguish between his *Navayana* and the religions of the ancients;

> But for ascertaining the norm for judging the philosophy of Religion we must turn to another and a different kind of Revolution which Religion has undergone. That Revolution touches the nature and content of ruling conceptions of the relations of God to man, of Society to man, and of man to man. How great was this revolution can be seen from the differences which divide savage society from civilised society. Strange as it may seem no systematic study of this Religious Revolution has so far been made. None the less this Revolution is so great and so immense that it has brought about a complete transformation in the nature of Religion as it is taken to be by savage society and by civilized society although very few seem to be aware of it. (Ibid., 9–10)

It was this internal revolution which, according to Ambedkar, made for the differences between savage religions and the new religion of a more civilized society. The latter had itself (on this view) lent itself to another distinction which divided it into two kinds:

> The contrast is so big that civilized society has become split into two, antique society and modern society, so that instead of speaking of the religion of the civilized society it becomes necessary to speak of the religion of antique society as against the religion of modern society. The religious revolution which marks off antique society from modern society is far greater than the religious revolution which divides savage society from civilized society. Its dimensions will be obvious from the differences it has brought about in the conceptions regarding the relations between God, Society and Man. (Ibid., 12–13)

It is here (as he speaks of the differences between the religion of the antique society and the religion of modern society) that one can see the philosophical continuities between Ambedkar's "new Religion"/*Navayana* and modernity. Ambedkar lays down a number of differences between "the religion of modern society" (Ibid., 13) and that of antique society.

> The first point of difference relates to the composition of society. (Ibid.)
>
> … in ancient Society men and their Gods formed a social and political as well as a religious whole. Religion was founded on kinship between the God and his worshippers. Modern Society has eliminated God from its composition. It consists of men only. (Ibid., 14)

In a move that put him alongside the most modern of the modern philosophers (recall Nietzsche on the death of God), Ambedkar reaffirmed here the banishment of God, as a father, from the empire of Religion. He explained that this departure of the father effected the conception of "the bond between God and Society" (Ibid.). He explained that in antique society God as a father of the religious community had necessarily to be seen as related to that community. This had made God exclusive to the community of faith and had (as corelative to this) implied that God could not be conceived of as more than a father of the specific community of believers. It followed that the concept of God could, by the nature of the case, never have been conceived in expansive terms as a universal God;

> God had become attached to a community, and the community had become attached to their God. God had become the God of the Community and the Community had become the

chosen community of the God. This view had two consequences. Antique Society never came to conceive that God could be universal God, the God of all. Antique Society never could conceive that there was any such thing as humanity in general. The third point of difference between ancient and modern society, has reference to the conception of the fatherhood of God. In the antique Society God was the Father of his people but the basis of this conception of Fatherhood was deemed to be physical. (Ibid., 15)

Ambedkar argued that in the religion of modern society, God was no longer seen as a father (on the analogy of the family) but now understood as an idea/concept so that human being could perfect individual virtue in the light of the idea of the good/God as it were. This movement from Gandhi's idea of kinship between man and God to Ambedkar's idea of God as perhaps an idea of absolute righteousness (to which humans could aspire) marks the shift from the ancient to the modern world. As already noted in his essay in *Young India* (Gandhi 1888–1948, 36: 4) and at many places in his writing, Gandhi had used the idea of kinship to explain the bonds in society between human beings, and between human beings and the natural world. Gandhi saw man as the silhouette/*pratibimb* of God perhaps because the child alone can be seen as the silhouette of the parent. However, Ambedkar thought of God along different and perhaps Kantian lines. God was for him (after what he described as the internal revolution in religion) no longer seen as the beggotter of the human but as an idea of a being capable of absolute virtue and absolute good;

> This conception of blood kinship of Gods and men had one important consequence. To the antique world God was a human being and as such was not capable of absolute virtue and absolute goodness. God shared the physical nature of man and was afflicted with the passions, infirmities and vices to which man was subject. The God of the antique world had all the wants and appetites of man and he often indulged in the vices in which many revelled. Worshipers had to implore God not to lead them into temptations. In modern Society the idea of divine fatherhood has become entirely dissociated from the physical basis of natural fatherhood. In its place man is conceived to be created in the image of God; he is not deemed to be begotten by God. This change in the conception of the fatherhood of God looked at from its moral aspect has made a tremendous difference in the nature of God as a Governor of the Universe. God with his physical basis was not capable of absolute good and absolute virtue. With God wanting in righteousness the universe could not insist on righteousness as an immutable principle. This dissociation of God from physical contact with man has made it possible for God to be conceived of as capable of absolute good and absolute virtue. (Ibid., 16)

It is significant to bring up here Ambedkar's discussion of the (seventh point of) difference between the religion of antique and modern societies in the same text (*Philosophy of Hinduism*) Ambedkar spoke of this difference in terms of the change that modern inwardness makes in "the place of individual conviction in Religion" (Ibid., 18). He argued here that religion to moderns is no longer seen as the word of God but becomes instead a matter of individual conviction and reasoned belief. Spelling out further points of difference led Ambedkar to conclude that;

> Such is this other Revolution in Religion. There have thus been two Religious Revolutions. One was an external Revolution. The other was an internal Revolution. The External Revolution was concerned with the field within which the authority of Religion was to prevail. The Internal Revolution had to do with the changes in Religion as a scheme of divine Governance for human society. The External Revolution was not really a Religious Revolution at

all. It was a revolt of science against the extra territorial jurisdiction assumed by Religion over a field which did not belong. The Internal Revolution was a real Revolution or may be compared to any other political Revolution, such as the French Revolution or the Russian Revolution. It involved a constitutional change. By this Revolution the Scheme of divine governance came to be altered, amended and reconstituted. How profound have been the changes which this internal Revolution, has made in the antique scheme of divine governance can be easily seen. By this Revolution God has ceased to be a member of a community. Thereby he has become impartial. God has ceased to be the Father of Man in the physical sense of the word. He has become the creator of the Universe. The breaking of this blood bond has made it possible to hold that God is good. By this Revolution man has ceased to be a blind worshipper of God doing nothing but obeying his commands. Thereby man has become a responsible person required to justify his belief in God's commandments by his conviction. (Ibid., 21)

At the centre of the universe and as the modern subject (with Ambedkar) the human being becomes the source of the norm to evaluate religion. Ambedkar spells out this norm clearly;

At one end of the Revolution was the antique society with its Religious ideal in which the end was Society. At the other end of the Revolution is the modern Society with its Religious ideal in which the end is the individual. To put the same fact in terms of the norm it can be said that the norm or the criterion, for judging right and wrong in the Antique Society was utility while the norm or the criterion for judging right and wrong in the modern Society is justice. The Religious Revolution was not thus a revolution in the religious organization of Society resulting in the shifting of the centre—from society to the individual—it was a revolution in the norms. (Ibid., 22)

Ambedkar had suggested that the norm to evaluate the new religion took its birth in modern society, that this norm had emerged from the human beings inwardness and that it pertained to justice;

In the first place the norm must enable people to judge what is right and wrong in the conduct of men. In the second place the norm must be appropriate to current notion of what constitutes the moral good. From both these points of view, they appear to be the true norms. They enable us to judge what is right and wrong. They are appropriate to the society which adopted them. Utility as a criterion was appropriate to the antique world in which society being the end, the moral good was held to be something which had social utility. Justice as a criterion became appropriate to the Modern World in which individual being the end, the moral good was held to be something which does justice to the individual. There may be controversy as to which of the two norms is morally superior. But I do not think there can be any serious controversy that these are not the norms. If it is said that these norms are not transcendental enough; my reply is that if a norm whereby one is to judge the philosophy of religion must be Godly, it must also be earthly. (Ibid.)

As may appear fairly obvious, applying this norm, led Ambedkar to condemn Hinduism as unjust and not fit for the modern world:

It has not the impulse to serve and that is because by its very nature it is unhuman and unmoral. It is a misnomer to call it religion. Its philosophy is opposed to very thing for which religion stands. (Ibid., 92)

It was an application of this same norm which also led Ambedkar to regard the Buddha's *dhamma* (there will be some discussion on the connection between the concept of justice and the notion of *dhamma/dharma* in the ancient Indian tradition in Chap. 5 of this Book) as the only fitting "new religion" for the new world:

> …The religion of the Buddha is perfect justice, springing from a man's own meritorious disposition. (Ambedkar 2011, 166)

As he re-thought Buddhism in *The Buddha and his dhamma* Ambedkar emphasized that belief in *Ishwara* (God) was not essentially a part of *Dhamma* and that the Buddha had rejected the idea of God;

> The question is, did the Blessed Lord accept God as the creator of the Universe? The answer is, 'No'. He did not.There are various grounds why he rejected the doctrine of the existence of God. Nobody has seen God. People only speak of God. God is unknown and unseen. Nobody can prove that God has created the world. The world has evolved and is not created. What advantage can there be in believing in God? It is unprofitable. The Buddha said that a religion based on God is based on speculation.A religion based on God is, therefore, not worth having. (Ibid., 134)

In an interesting discussion Ambedkar had re-constructed several arguments along the line of Buddha's own thoughts against a belief in God. Among these is one pertaining to the meaning of "the religion of modern society" (Ambedkar 2014, 3: 12–13) which referred to his own *navayana*/re-created Buddhism Ambedkar recounts in this connection;

> His (Buddha's) next argument against the doctrine of God was that the discussion about the existence of God was unprofitable. According to him, the centre of religion lay not in the relation of man to God. It lay in the relation between man and man. The purpose of religion is to teach man how to be happy. (Ambedkar 2011, 136)

To my mind what is most significant about Ambedkar's discussion is that it brings out the point that he was absolutely clear that a new more "earthly" (Ambedkar 2014, 3: 22) religion needed to be worked out for a new world on the basis of reason and experience. The source of this religion, which was to be built around enlightenment values, was not to be God but the human being herself/himself who was the centre of the universe. The purpose of formulating such a new religion emerged from more "earthly" considerations. It emerged, in fact, from the conception of religion as serving to keep the community together by building fraternity between the co-religionists thereby creating the conditions for liberty and equality.

As Ambedkar put it himself;

> …it is an error to look upon religion as a matter which is individual, private and personal. Indeed as will be seen from what follows, religion becomes a source of positive mischief if not danger when it remains individual, private and personal. Equally mistaken is the view that religion is the flowering of special religious instinct inherent in the nature of the individual. The correct view is that religion like language is social for the reason that either is essential for social life and the individual has to have it because without it he cannot participate in the life of the society. (Ambedkar 2002, 225)

This idea "that religion like language is social" (Ibid.) was translated by Ambedkar into the need to keep fraternity, liberty and equality in place in human society. In his essay on conversion Ambedkar had argued that;

> Religion emphasizes, universalizes social values and brings them to the mind of the individual who is required to recognize them in all his acts in order that he may function as an approved member of the society. But the purpose of religion is more than this. It spiritualizes them. (Ibid., 226)

It is important to note that the values which were at the basis of Ambedkar's new religion were the same political values of the liberal enlightenment. These were the values which defined the modern subject and modern institutions of political governance;

> Fraternity and liberty are really derivative notions. The basic and fundamental conceptions are equality and respect for human personality. Fraternity and liberty take their roots in these two fundamental conceptions. Digging further down it may be said that equality is the original notion and respect for human personality is a reflexion of it. So that where equality is denied, everything else may be taken to be denied. (Ambedkar 2014, 3: 66)

Ambedkar's understanding of religion seemed to have been that of a set of beliefs which were instrumental to (and conceived as a means of) keeping fraternity, liberty and equality intact in human relations and adhered to across society for the right reasons. Further this social end was thought of along the lines of maintaining a modern democratic society which ensured all the three values—liberty equality and fraternity—to its members. Ambedkar's "religion for modern society" was a product of the needs of modern society. What then of this *Navayana* Buddhism? Could it be said to have signified a religious turn and a departure from modernity?

3.4   Ambedkar's Religious Turn: *Dhamma* and *Adhamma*

As noted at the beginning of this chapter, many have argued that the debate with Gandhi, transformed Ambedkar and led him to recognize the importance of religion and of the religious community to individual identity;

> Committed to denouncing the violence of positive religions, he nevertheless sought another religion of the book (or, indeed, a book for *his* religion), a desire that would culminate in his masterwork, *The Buddha and His Dhamma* (1956). (Kumar 2015, 36)

This section will examine whether (or not) Ambedkar did indeed seek to re-constitute the religious community in the "more traditional sense of religion" (Vajpeyi 2013, 222). In this connection this subsection will emphasize three points/places of departure (from more traditional Buddhist accounts) in Ambedkar's re-telling of Buddha's life and teachings in *The buddha and his dhamma*.

Before moving on to these points of departure in Ambedkar's telling of the story of Buddha's life "in a very untraditional way" (Sangharakshita 2006, 152) one might note that this was not the first volume of selections from Buddhist literature for the benefit of the common reader. In the early ninth century CE, Shantideva had compiled the *Shiksha-samuchchaya*/"Compendium of Instruction" which was mainly a compilation from earlier *Mahayana* Sutras. There were a fairly large number of such compilations which had preceded Ambedkar's and with most of which he was familiar.

Mention may be made of the following; *The Gospel of the Buddha* (Paul Carus 1894), *Buddhism in Translations* (Henry Clarke Warren) which came two years later, *Some Sayings of the Buddha* (F. L. Woodward 1925), *A Buddhist Bible* (Dwight Goddard 1932), *Early Buddhist Scriptures* (E. J. Thomas 1935), *The Vedantic Buddhism of the Buddha* (J. G. Jenning 1947), *Buddhist Texts Through the Ages* (E. Conze 1954) and *The Teachings of the Compassionate Buddha* (E. A. Burtt 1955).

The buddha and his dhamma is in 40 parts 14 sections 248 subsections and has been divided into eight books. About three fourth of the book consists of selections from canonical/non-canonical Buddhist literature and the rest of the book (as already noted) is filled up with Ambedkar's own explanatory passages. This last set of passages are what make for differences between Ambedkar and the more traditional anthologies referred to above. These differences are also the subject of interest in this section of this chapter as they serve to bring out the non- "religious" nature of Ambedkar's turn to Buddhism.

There are three significant points that I would like to bring up briefly in this regards. The first concerns Ambedkar's departure from the traditional Buddhist accounts, enumerating the reasons why Buddha, had left home. The second concerns Ambedkar's singular re-telling of the Buddha's first Sermon where he offers a revised account of the Four Noble Truths. The third relates to the discussion in Part 1 and 11 of Book 1V, on "Religion and *Dhamma*" where Ambedkar argues that what Buddha taught was *Dhamma*/morality which (he argued) was different from Religion. The consideration of these points in this section will be followed by the conclusion (to the chapter) which will argue that Ambedkar's re-writing of Buddhism along enlightenment lines was not only in keeping with enlightenment modernity but that it was a manifestation of the modern expressivist turn in the making of individual identity.

3.4.1 Ambedkar: How a Boddhisatta Became the Buddha

In part 1 of *The buddha and his dhamma* "Siddharth Gautama. How a Boddhisatta became the Buddha" Ambedkar tells the story of Siddharth Gautama's life from his birth at Kapilvastu to his leaving his home and thereafter attaining enlightenment/*nibbana*. However, Ambedkar tells this story of Buddha's life quite in his own way. The reason behind such a re-telling comes from the rejection of the traditional Buddhist account that the Buddha left home because he saw an old man, a sick man, a corpse and a wandering ascetic. Drawing from a passage in the *Sutta Nipata* (an ancient text which belonged to the fifth division of the *Sutta Pitaka*), Ambedkar refers to a version of the conflict between the *Sakya* clan (to whom the Buddha was related through his father) and the clan of the *Koliyas* (to whom Buddha was related through his mother). Ambedkar makes "an imaginative reconstruction" (Sangharakshita 2006, 152) of this conflict to conclude that the Buddha left home because of his opposition to the *Sakya* clan's decision to go to war with the *Koliya* clan. As Ambedkar puts it, Siddharth tells his weeping parents;

…I hope you realize how I have saved the situation… I have not given up the cause of truth and justice, I have succeeded in making its infliction personal to me. (Ambedkar 2011, 21)

Ambedkar goes on to affirm that even after the Buddha received the news that the *Koliya*s and the *Sakya*s had made peace he remained uneasy and asked himself;

He had left his home because he was opposed to war. 'Now that the war is over, is there any problem left to me? Does my problem end because war has ended?' On a deeper reflection, he thought not. 'The problem of war is essentially a problem of conflict. It is only part of a larger problem'…. 'This conflict is going on not only between kings and nations, but between nobles and Brahmins…' 'The conflict between nations is ocassional. But the conflict between classes is constant and perpetual. It is this which is the root cause of all sorrow and suffering in the world'. True, I left home on account of the war. But I cannot go home, although the war between the *Sakya*s and *Koliya*s has ended. I now see that my problem has become wider. I have to find a solution for this problem of social conflict… (Ibid., 41)

In Ambedkar's re-telling of the story of the Buddha's life, the Buddha left home because he wanted to solve the problem of social conflict. This re-writing seems to bring home the earlier point that Ambedkar wanted to provide a "non-comprehensive" (used here purely in the sense specified by Rawls in *Political Liberalism*, 2005) account of Buddhism.

3.4.2 Ambedkar: On the First Sermon of the Buddha and the Four Noble Truths

As Tradition recounts it, the first Sermon of the Buddha, was delivered to the five *Parivrajakas*[xviii] at the deer park in Sarnath, near Benares. In this Sermon, the Buddha explained the important doctrines namely, the middle way, the Four Noble Truths and the Noble Eightfold path. In Book 11 of *The buddha and his dhamma*, Ambedkar describes the preaching of the First Sermon and the conversion of the five *Parivrajakas*, as well as the conversions of "the High and the holy", "conversion of women", "conversion of the fallen and the criminals".

Ambedkar recounts that once the Buddha had received enlightenment and formulated the way he realized that it was not necessary to escape from the world. In his re-telling of the story, Ambedkar clearly states that the reason why the Buddha decided to preach his path to the world derived from the need to ameliorate social conflict (which he saw clearly would lead to suffering and pain). Fiske and Emmirich comment (in this connection) that "where the *Mahavagga* stresses "preaching the doctrine", Ambedkar speaks of "service to the suffering world"" (Fiske and Emmirich 2004, 107). Ambedkar explains that the Buddha had thought that;

What is necessary is to change the world and make it better. He realized that he had left the world because there was so much conflict, resulting in misery and unhappiness, and for which he knew no remedy. If he could banish misery and unhappiness from the world by the propagation of his doctrine, it was his duty to return to the world and serve it, and not sit silent as the personification of inactive impassivity. The Buddha therefore agreed to the request of Brahma Sahampati and decided to preach his doctrine to the world. (Ambedkar 2011, 65)

It is such a reading that leads Ambedkar to depart significantly from traditional Buddhist accounts as he discusses Buddha's first sermon. Ambedkar explains that when the *Parivrajakas* asked the Buddha to expound the path to them, the Buddha agreed;

> He began by saying that his path which is his Dhamma (Religion) has nothing to do with God and the soul. His Dhamma had nothing to do with life after death. Nor has his dhamma any concern with rituals and ceremonies. The centre of his Dhamma is man, and the relation of man to man in his life on earth. This, he said, was his first postulate. His second postulate was that men are living in sorrow, in misery, and poverty. The world is full of suffering and that discovering how to remove this suffering from the world is the only purpose of Dhamma. Nothing else is Dhamma. The recognition of the existence of suffering, and to show the way to remove suffering, is the foundation and basis of his Dhamma… A Religion which fails to recognize this is no religion at all. (Ibid., 68–69)

It is significant to note that Ambedkar's re-interpretation of Buddha's *dhamma* seemed to have been significantly different from the traditional Buddhist understanding of *dhamma* and of other central concepts. To that extent, one must also note, that Ambedkar's understanding of the *Navayana* departs from 'religion' as it had erstwhile been understood in theology and philosophy. The newness in Ambedkar's new faith did not only refer to an innovation/newness in concepts but to the conception of 'religion' itself. Fiske and Emmirich make the point;

> An important interpolation in the text of the *Mahavagga* expresses Ambedkar's basic concept of religion: its end is and must be to remove *dukkha*, its centre is man, the relationship of man to man to earth. Hence, true religion must be without God, soul, life after death, ritual and ceremony. (Fiske and Emmirich 2004, 109)

One of the central doctrines in Buddhism, which Buddha has been said to have put forth in the first sermon, is that of the Four Noble Truths. In his introduction to *The Buddha and his dhamma*, Ambedkar regarded traditional accounts of the Four Noble Truths as inadequate and doubtful;

> The second problem is created by the four noble Aryan Truths? Do they form part of the original teachings of the Buddha? This formula cuts at the root of Buddhism. If life is sorrow, death is sorrow, and rebirth is sorrow, then there is an end of everything. Neither religion nor philosophy can help a man to achieve happiness in the world. If there is no escape from sorrow, then what can religion do, what can Buddha do, to relieve man from such sorrow which is ever there in birth itself? The four Aryan Truths make the gospel of the Buddha a gospel of pessimism. (Rathore and Verma 2011, xxix–xxx)

For Ambedkar the problem with the canonical Buddhist accounts of the Four Noble Truths was that they attributed suffering to the ignorance and craving of the sufferers rather than to the externally controlled conditions of society for which the individual bore no responsibility. According to Ambedkar, it would be helpful, and certainly hopeful, to alter the social conditions that caused suffering to the masses rather than offer religious accounts that convince the sufferers that they could achieve enduring happiness in *moksha/Nibbana* in spite of such social oppression.

This led Ambedkar to radically re-think the Four Noble Truths and related doctrines. In orthodox Buddhist accounts in the first sermon the Buddha had given an account of the Middle Way, the Four Noble Truths and the Eightfold path. However Ambedkar departed significantly from all such accounts.

"Indeed besides being doubtful whether the four Noble truths formed part of the original teaching of the Buddha he is of the opinion that they are "a great stumbling block in the way of non-Buddhists accepting the gospel of Buddhism" (Sangharakshita 2006, 153).

In his account of the first sermon of the Buddha, Ambedkar represents the Buddha as speaking of the way that he had discovered not only in terms of the Middle Way and a revised version of the Four Noble Truths, but also in terms of the path of purity, the path of Righteousness and the path of Virtue. Ambedkar identified the path of purity with the traditional five precepts. The path of righteousness was identified with the Noble Eight fold path (equivalent to the Four Noble Truths) and the path of virtue was taken to be that of the ten traditional *paramitas* or 'states of perfections', including the four *brahmaviharas* or 'blessed abodes'. Apart from this re-interpretation Ambedkar went on to explain that the first step in the *Ashtangamarga Samma Ditti* (right views) had as its object "the destruction of Avijja (Nescience)" (Ambedkar 2011, 70). In his account of the first sermon of the Buddha Ambedkar further recounted that "Samma Ditti requires the giving up of belief in the efficacy of rites and ceremonies…" (Ibid.). and "requires the abandonment of superstition and supernaturalism." (Ibid., 71). Ambedkar emphasized that "Samma Ditti requires a free mind and free thought." (Ibid.) The eighth step of the Eightfold path *Samma Samadhi* was re-defined by Ambedkar to mean that which builds up a "habit to the mind to think of good… Samma Samadhi gives the mind the necessary motive power to do good" (Ibid., 72) rather than the traditional "right concentration." Queen makes the important point;

> The Eightfold path is interpreted not as a means to *nirvana* ("the traditional Theravada Buddhist goal") but as the way "to remove injustice and inhumanity that man does to man." *Dana* and *Karuna* ("generosity"and "Compassion") are directed to the "suffering of the needy and the poor," *maitri* ("loving-kindness") "means fellowship not merely with human beings but with all living beings," and *prajna* ("wisdom") is identified as the "understanding and intelligence" that motivates and rationalizes all acts of virtue. (Queen 1996, 57)

When commenting on the classification of *dhamma* into *dhamma, Not-dhamma* and *saddhamma* Ambedkar had occasion to revisit the Four Noble Truths. In Chap. 3 of *The buddha and his dhamma,* Ambedkar explained that to give up craving is *dhamma.* In a telling passage-where Ambedkar gives his own account of the second and third Noble truths-Suffering's arising (from craving) and Cessation were re-interpreted as social teachings and Buddha was described as propagating a social rather than religious message. Queen comments that in Ambedkar's re-interpretation of Buddhism, "the Buddha speaks of craving-the traditional cause of suffering-but quickly relates it to the violence of class struggle" (Ibid.). Ambedkar writes;

> This spirit of contentment is not to be understood to mean meekness or surrender to circumstances…The Buddha has not said, 'Blessed are they who are poor'. The Buddha has not said that the sufferer should not try to change his condition. On the other hand, he has said that

riches are welcome;…What the Buddha meant when he said that contentment is the highest form of wealth is that man should not allow himself to be overpowered by greed which has no limits…. 'why is this craving or greed to be condemned? Because of this,' said the Buddha to Ananda, 'many a bad and wicked state of things arises-blows and wounds, strife, contradiction and retorts; quarrelling, slander, and lies.' That this is the correct analysis of the class struggle, there can be no doubt. That is why the Buddha insisted upon the control of greed and craving. (Ambedkar 2011, 129)

In the very same chapter (in the *Buddha and his Dhamma),* Ambedkar went on to explain that the Buddha's concept of *Nibbana* or salvation as a *telos* of the religious life was totally different from that of his predecessors;

By Nibbana they meant the salvation of the soul… There was one common feature of the Brahmanic and Upanishadic conceptions of Nibbana. They involved the recognition of a soul as an independent entity—a theory which the Buddha had denied… The Buddha's conception of Nibbana is quite different… There are three ideas which underlie his conception of Nibbana. Of these the happiness of a sentient being as distinct from the salvation of the soul is one. The second idea is the happiness of the sentient being in *Samsara* while he is alive… The third idea which underlies his conception of Nibbana is the exercise of control over the flames of the passions which are always on fire… (Ibid., 126)

Ambedkar suggested that;

Nibbana means enough control over passion so as to enable one to walk on the path of righteousness. It was not intended to mean anything more. (Ibid., 127)

It seems fairly apparent that Ambedkar had indeed radically re-thought the Four Noble Truths and the *Nibbana* of the Buddha and interpreted them along the lines of social reform rather than the religio-moral progress of the individual religious aspirant. Ambedkar had recognized that his own reading of the central conceptions pronounced by the Buddha were at serious variance with the versions given by Buddhist scholars. This led him to argue that those who had regarded that "the essence of Buddhism lies in Samadhi or Vipassana, or Esoterism" had misunderstood that essence;

The question that arises is –'Did the Buddha have no Social Message?' When pressed for an answer students of Buddhism refer to the two points. They say—'The Buddha taught Ahimsa'. 'The Buddha taught peace!' Asked, 'Did the Buddha teach justice?' 'Did the Buddha teach Equality?' 'Did the Buddha teach fraternity?' 'Could the Buddha answer Karl Marx?'. These questions are hardly ever raised in discussing the Buddha's Dhamma. My answer is that the Buddha has a social message. He answers all these questions. But they have been buried by modern scholars. (Ibid., 122).

3.4.3 Ambedkar: On Religion and Dhamma

Book 111 of *The buddha and his dhamma* entitled "What the Buddha Taught" and parts 1 and 11 of Book 1V entitled "Religion and *Dhamma*" are philosophical and concerned with establishing the real nature of Buddha's teaching. This section seeks to discuss these to bring out Ambedkar's distinction between *Dhamma* and Religion which seems to evidence some influence of Bergson's *Two Sources of Religion and Morality* (1932).

This distinction between *dhamma* and religion is philosophically important to the present discussion as it underwrites the point that Ambedkar's conversion to Buddhism did not signify a religious turn as Ambedkar had himself clearly distinguished between religion and *dhamma* and rejected what was ordinarily understood by the term 'religion'. This might have become apparent from the earlier section which had given an account of Ambedkar's notion of the internal revolution in religion. Which last, one might recall, had in turn made way for the difference between ancient and civilized religion and within the latter (within, that is, what he terms 'civilized religion') between religion for antique society and the religion for modern society. One might recall Pradeep P. Gokhale on this point;

'Is Buddhism a religion?' Ambedkar raised this question and answered it by saying that Buddhism is Dhamma and not a religion. (Gokhale 2021, 258)

Locating Ambedkar's Buddhism in the context of its continuities and discontinues with a new engaged/applied understanding of Buddhism and the work of "engaged Buddhist thinkers" (*Ibid.*) across the world Gokhale has argued:

The Buddha's dhamma as presented by Ambedkar is not a religion in its conventional sense, but in an unconventional sense: as a way of life based on rationality and sacred morality. (Ibid., 260)

One might gain a better insight into these remarks by visiting Gokhale's comments made in an earlier essay;

Here, a remark on Ambedkar's use of the word "religion" is necessary. Ambedkar sometimes uses the word in a popular sense, when he wants to contradistinguish it from Dhamma. In this sense, "religion" mainly stands for theistic religion in which, according to him, both morality and rationality are undermined. That which is ordinarily understood by the term "Religion" emphasizes the relation between the individual and God and undermines social relations; it also falls prey to superstition. Dhamma, on the other hand, is essentially moral, social, and rational. But Ambedkar does not always use the word "religion" in a popular sense; he also uses it in the sense of Dhamma, when he says that the purpose of religion (according to the Buddha) is to make the world a kingdom of righteousness. Here the word is used in the sense of the ideal form of religion. So, Ambedkar seems to be making a distinction between religions as they are and religion as it ought to be… and Dhamma is religion as it ought to be… (Gokhale 2004, 126).

However, one needs to put this last statement (and Gokhale's position) in perspective by paying sustained philosophic attention to Ambedkar's own repeated re-iteration, which Gokhale has noted (Gokhale 2021, 260) that the *dhamma* was not religion. It is significant to note that Ambedkar was clear that there had been considerable transformation in the meaning of 'religion' between the ancient and the modern world. It is important that this difference was in fundamentals, making it difficult to use the same term 'religion', to describe the *dhamma* of the Buddha. Ambedkar had argued that theistic religion was about the human being's relationship to a wider order that was recognized to be outside of him/her while the Buddha's *dhamma* was about human beings and earthly happiness in a democratic society:

Here we encounter some of Ambedkar's deepest thinking. Morality, he asserts, has no place in religion, for religion is concerned with the relation between man and God, morality with the relation between man and man. Though every religion preaches morality, morality comes into religion only in order to help maintain peace and order, and is not the root of religion. (Sangharakshita 2006, 156)

To begin with one might note that Ambedkar clarified in Chapter 1V of *The buddha and his dhamma* (Ambedkar 2011, 167–221) that the term "religion" itself is an ambiguous word which has no fixed meaning;

The word 'religion' is an indefinite word with no fixed meaning. It is one word with many meanings. This is because religion has passed through many stages. The concept at each stage is called Religion, though the concept at one stage has not the same meaning which it had at the preceding stage, or is likely to have at the succeeding stage... (Ambedkar 2011, 167).

Commentators who speak of Ambedkar's religious turn bringing him closer to Gandhi (Guha 2012; Pantham 2013; Vajpeyi 2013) would do well to take their clue from Ambedkar himself. For the religious turn, Ambedkar took was a turn that distanced him from ancient religion, as well as, from more recent understandings of, what he called the "religion of antique society" ((Ambedkar 2014, 3: 12–13), see Sect. 3.3.2.1 of this chapter for detailed elaboration of Ambedkar's point that instead of speaking of the religion of the civilized society (as one) it becomes necessary to differentiate the religion of the civilized society into two types, i.e. the religion of antique society and the religion of modern society.)). Kumar speaks of Ambedkar's "'non-negative negation' of religion" (Kumar 2005, 32). This negation of religion becomes all the more evident from Ambedkar's account of the differences between religion and *dhamma* in *The Buddha and his dhamma*. Ambedkar certainly seemed to affirm that what he was rejecting and distancing himself from, was the idea of religion, as commonly understood. Perhaps from the idea of religion as understood by Gandhi;

This is, in short, the evolution of the concept of Religion. This is what it has come to be and this is what it connotes-belief in God, belief in soul, worship of God, curing of the erring soul, propriating God by prayers, ceremonies, sacrifices, and other such activities. (Ambedkar 2011, 167)

Ambedkar seemed to have himself pre-emptively rejected the interpretation of scholars who had argued (much after his death) that his conversion had signified a religious turn which somewhat diminished the conceptual distance which separated him from Gandhi.

As Ambedkar put it;

What the Buddha calls Dhamma differs fundamentally from what is called Religion. What the Buddha calls Dhamma is analogous to what the European theologians call Religion. But there is no greater affinity between the two. On the other hand, the differences between the two are very great... it is better to proceed to give an idea of Dhamma, and show how it differs from Religion. (Ibid., 168)

There are two reasons why Ambedkar's account of the differences between Religion and *Dhamma* become important to the argument of this chapter and of the book.

The first (as already made apparent) is that this account demonstrates that Ambedkar's conversion to Buddhism did not signify that he had come closer to Gandhi or that the distance between them had diminished. The second reason is that Ambedkar's account of the differences between Religion and *Dhamma* brings out the point that his conversion to Buddhism was not a 'religious' move and therefore it does not threaten the central argument of this chapter and indeed of this book. This argument, it may be recalled, attempts to make the point that the debate between Gandhi and Ambedkar rested upon fundamental conceptual differences between their notions of the self and the relationship of that self to the world. On this account, while Gandhi saw the self in continuity with India's *itihaas,* Ambedkar (on the other hand) dedicated himself to the making of the radically disengaged modern Indian self. It is Ambedkar's account of the differences between *dhamma* and religion that establish the consistency between Ambedkar's *Navayana* and the making of modern Indian identity.

There are three important differences that Ambedkar brings out between *dhamma* and religion that need to be emphasized in this connection. The first, as Ambedkar put it himself, is that;

> Religion, it is said, is personal, and one must keep it to oneself. One must not let it play its part in public life. Contrary to this, Dhamma is social. It is fundamentally and essentially so. Dhamma is righteousness, which means right relations between man and man in all spheres of life. (Ibid., 168)

One might see some influence of Bergson at this point. Bergson, one might recall, had spoken of moral obligation as grounded in "the cohesion of the group" (Bergson 1977, 266).

Ambedkar has spelt out what he meant by the idea that *Dhamma* is social by clarifying that "Dhamma is nothing if it is not an instrument of Government" (Ambedkar 2011, 168). He argues in fact that society has only three alternatives to choose from-Society may choose not to have dhamma as an instrument of government resulting in the "road to anarchy" (Ibid.). Secondly it might choose the police and dictatorship as the instrument of government. Thirdly, it might make the best choice that is "Dhamma, plus the Magistrate wherever people fail to observe dhamma" (Ibid.). Ambedkar explains that liberty only survives if society chooses the last option;

> Those who want liberty must therefore have Dhamma. Now what is Dhamma? And why is Dhamma necessary? According to the Buddha, Dhamma consists of Prajna and Karuna...Prajna is understanding. The Buddha made Prajna one of the two cornerstones of his Dhamma because he did not wish to leave any room for superstition... Karuna is love. Because without it, society can neither live nor grow; ...Such is the definition of the Buddha's Dhamma. How different is this definition of Dhamma from that of Religion. So ancient, yet so modern, is the definition of Dhamma given by the Buddha... Such is the difference between Religion and Dhamma. (Ibid.)

The second difference (between *dhamma* and religion) relates to the difference of purpose between them. Recounting two dialogues one between the Buddha and Sunakkhatta and the other between Buddha and the Brahmin Potthapada Ambedkar explains that;

> The two are poles apart. The purpose of Religion is to explain the origin of the world.The
> purpose of Dhamma is to reconstruct the world. (Ibid., 171).

The third difference concerns the role of morality in Religion and in *Dhamma*. Ambedkar argues that religion being primarily about God, the soul, prayer etc. morality comes into religion as, what he terms, "a side wind" (Ibid.). What is perhaps more significant is the sort of answer religion provides to the question of moral motivation. To questions regarding why one should do the right thing by one's fellow beings religion can only offer the answer 'because we are children of the same God'. Ambedkar argues;

> Religion is a triangular piece. Be good to your neighbor because you are both children
> of God. That is the argument of Religion. Every religion preaches morality, but morality
> is not the root of religion. It is a wagon attached to it. It is attached and detached as the
> occasion requires. The action of morality in the functioning of religion is therefore casual
> and occasional. Morality in religion is therefore not effective. (Ibid.)

Ambedkar argues that the *dhamma* is very different from religion/all religions. A powerful way in which this difference is brought home is by considering that in *dhamma* morality itself becomes both the means and the end of the good human life:

> What is the place of morality in Dhamma? The simple answer is, Morality is Dhamma and
> Dhamma is Morality. In other words, in Dhamma morality takes the place of God, although
> there is no God in Dhamma. In Dhamma there is no place for prayers, pilgrimages, rituals,
> ceremonies, or sacrifices. Morality is the essence of Dhamma. Without it there is no Dhamma.
> Morality in Dhamma arises from the direct necessity for man to love man. It does not require
> the sanction of God. It is not to please God that man has to be moral. It is for his own good
> that man has to love man. (Ibid., 172)

Ambedkar had made it absolutely clear that in embracing Buddhism he had embraced the *Dhamma* and in doing so steadfastly kept away from Religion. He had argued that the *dhamma* is morality and explained that morality (such that constitutes the nature of *dhamma*) is not a spirituo-religious experience but one which relates to the more earthly needs of living together in society. One could then say that for Ambedkar *Dhamma* was that which bound society together by supporting constitutional morality and strengthening a commitment to liberal enlightenment virtues (this point was made earlier in the chapter while discussing the relationship between Ambedkar's more modern self and the new Buddhist community). I would like to recall Rawls' argument (which was also brought up earlier in this chapter) that if the political conception of justice is to be stable for the right reasons it must be supported by an overlapping consensus between comprehensive theories of the good (Rawls 2005, xviii). I recall this argument because Ambedkar seems close to it when he argues that a notion of the sacred has to be associated with morality if society is to prevent "discrimination and denial of justice" (Ambedkar 2011, 173).

It seems important to reflect upon Ambedkar's account of the differences between Religion and *Dhamma* (as delineated above) as that account serves to re-iterate and indeed re-enforce the point that Ambedkar's conversion to the *Dhamma* was not a religious move. As he argued himself "similarity in terminology" (Ibid., 178) often becomes an "easy handle" (Ibid.) for misunderstanding. Ambedkar had emphasized that "however much may be similarity of words" (Ibid.) this alone cannot lead to the words being "the same in…connotation" (Ibid.). With regards to the association of *dhamma* with the sacred one gets to see, that though the words are the same, what Ambedkar meant by "sacred" was not the same as what the religious associate with that term. Ambedkar had explained the association of the term "sacred" with any "thing" (or belief) in the following words;

> When is a thing sacred? …In every human society, primitive or advanced, there are things or beliefs which it regards as sacred, and the rest it regards as profane. When a thing or belief has reached the stage of being sacred (pavitra), it means that it cannot be violated… Contrary to this, a thing or a belief which is profane (apavitra), that is, outside the field of the sacred, may be violated… Why is a thing made sacred? Three factors seem to have played their part in making morality sacred. The first factor is the social need for protecting the best. The background of this question lies embedded in what is called the struggle of existence and the survival of the fittest… The struggle is bitter… Would not the weakest, if protected, be ultimately the best for advancing the ends and aims of society? …Then comes, the question what is the way to protect the weak? Nothing less than to impose some restraints upon the fittest.In this lies the origin and necessity of morality.

> This morality had to be sacred because it was imposed originally on the fittest… (Ibid., 172).

> The other two reasons/"factors" (Ibid.) offered (by Ambedkar) in answer to the question "why is a thing made sacred?" were along the same lines. The second reason on Ambedkar's account of it comes from the idea that if morality is "marked by isolation and exclusiveness" it will develop a "anti-social spirit" (Ibid., 173). Ambedkar had argued in this connection that;

> The only way to put a stop to conflict is to have common rules of morality which are sacred to all. There is the third factor which requires morality to be made sacred and universal. It is to safeguard the growth of the individual. Under the struggle for existence or under group rule the interests of the individuals are not safe… (Ibid.).

Relating the notion of the "sacred" straightforwardly with the need to ensure the stability of justice for the basic institutions of society and to the familiar liberal enlightenment values Ambedkar had explained that the "group set-up leads to discrimination" (Ibid.) and that this meant that owners remain owners and "serfs remain serfs" in perpetuity;

> This means that there can be liberty for some, but not for all. This means that there can be equality for a few, but none for the majority. What is the remedy? The only remedy lies in making fraternity universally effective. What is fraternity? It is nothing but another name for the brotherhood of men-which is another name for morality. This is why the Buddha preached that Dhamma is morality; and as Dhamma is sacred, so is morality. (Ibid.)

Conclusion

The sacred, the profane and the modern subject

There are two thoughts that this chapter seeks to leave the reader with -the first (as already obvious) is that Ambedkar's religious turn was not a 'religious' homecoming but a move to set up a new Buddhist community with "common rules of morality which are sacred to all" (Ibid.). The object of making morality sacred and common to all was to make "fraternity universally effective" (Ibid.) thereby securing not only fraternity but also the other enlightenment values, liberty and equality for the new dalit Buddhist community. The establishment of such a new dalit-buddhist community (built along enlightenment lines) was in its turn a basis for the demand of rights and remedial justice for the dalits who were the new converts and members of that community. The second point somewhat related to this, and important to the argument of this book, is that (consequent to this perhaps) Ambedkar's conversion did not make for any discontinuity in his project of the making of modern Indian identity. Rather it was quite in keeping with the spirit of the same.

Looking at the first point that Ambedkar's religious turn was not a 'religious' homecoming I will pick up where the last section closed with Ambedkar's understanding of the sacred. I will counter pose that understanding with Roger Scruton's remarks on the notion of that which is 'forbidden' in/by the term 'sacred'. Referring to the idea (important since Durkheim) that "religion is a *social* phenomenon" (Scruton 2014, 14) Scruton confronts the argument made by Quine and others that the epistemology of religious thoughts must be 'naturalized', so as to provide the empirical explanation of our knowledge rather than some putative *a priori* ground for it (Ibid., 8). Scruton has argued that the real phenomena of faith do not lend themselves to such naturalization.

One might recall that Durkheim (and indeed Ambedkar) had characterized that which is sacred as that which is set apart and forbidden;

> There is truth in Durkheim's view that sacred things are in some way forbidden. But what is forbidden is to treat a sacred thing as though it belonged in the ordinary frame of nature: as though it had no mediating role. Treating a sacred thing in this day-to-day way is a *profanation*. One stage beyond profanation is *desecration*, in which a sacred object is deliberately wrenched from its apartness and trampled on or in some way reduced to its opposite,... (Ibid., 16)

The point which Scruton has made here is that the 'sacred' does not belong to the domain of the day to day, and it is not (unlike what Ambedkar suggests) a part of the socio-political-democratic world. Scruton emphasizes (to the contrary) that the domain of the sacred—certain times, places, objects, words—can only be understood "on the assumption that these experiences mediate between this world and another that is not otherwise revealed to us" (Ibid., 11). On this view in the world of faith;

> The experience of sacred things is, ...a kind of interpersonal encounter. It is as though you address and are addressed by, another I, but one that has no embodiment in the natural order. Your experience "reaches beyond" the empirical realm, to a place on its horizon. This idea is vividly conveyed in the Upanishads, in which Brahman, the creative principle, is represented as transcendental, universal, and also as *atman*, the self in which all our separate selves aspire to be absorbed and united. (Ibid., 24)

Scruton's observation on the mediating role played by the domain of the sacred brings out the important insight that the term 'sacred' does not occupy different places in the world view of Gandhi and Ambedkar but that the world views themselves are completely different. The term "sacred" belongs "to the perspective of the religious believer, for whom this experience is a window onto the transcendental and an encounter with the hidden God" (Ibid., 25) it simply cannot function, as it has been taken to function by Ambedkar, to ensure the stability of a commitment to fraternity (and from thence to the stability of a non-comprehensive purely political conception of justice ensuring remedial justice for the dalit community) in the day-to-day socio-political realm.

One might now take up the second point that this section attempts to make –that Ambedkar's conversion did not make for any discontinuity in his project of—the making of modern Indian identity. It is surely significant to note that Ambedkar himself seemed to have, somewhat decisively, settled this issue of the purportedly religious turn in his life in the negative. For he made it clear that the turn he had taken was a turn towards *dhamma* understood in terms of constitutional/civic morality ensuring a commitment to fraternity in the dalit Buddhist community. Thereby ensuring perhaps that there was a rightful space for that community whenever the stability of justice for the basic structure of society/new nation came to be at issue. The commitment to *dhamma* thus understood seemed to have brought out the rigour of Ambedkar's "constitutional imagination" (Kumar 2015, 8) rather than brought him any closer to the Gandhian (primarily) religious world view.

In this connection, it becomes important to consider the contrary arguments offered by recent commentators on the Gandhi–Ambedkar debate. Kumar (Aishwary Kumar 2015) for instance argues that the move to annihilation was in itself a truly religious act. Kumar speaks in this connection of; "this immeasureable freedom of force whose essence Ambedkar is able to grasp in terms of a "truly religious act", and which he calls "annihilation" (*ucched*)" (Ibid., 10). He explains in an aside "what is "annihilation"…if not a radicalization of the concept of force" (Ibid., 13). However difficult this sounds, on such a view, it was the very erasure/annihilation (by an exercise of force) of traditional religion that came to constitute the "truly religious" for Ambedkar because;

> Religion, he argues, has to be destroyed so that a faith without intermediaries and mediation by the law, freed from ecclesiastical and juridical injunctions, might be reclaimed by the multitude for itself. Indeed, to not destroy a religion bound by rules, to not resist the historic alliance between theology and the majoritarian will to domination …to not revolt against the mystical permanence of the theologico-politico bond, becomes in Ambedkar's schema the most irreligious instance of the multitude's complicity with its own subjugation and defeat. (Ibid., 10–11)

The destruction of an unjust religion in itself, on such a view, made for the experience of the immeasurable freedom of force. Force became the "Pure means" (Ibid., 10) for the new faith/*Navayana*. I have reservations about such an association of "force" with Ambedkar's constitutional imagination and move to annihilate the unjust past. I would consequently suggest that Kumar's use of "force" is a misrepresentation in terms. The annihilation of caste or the burning of the *Manu Smriti* (like Locke's rejection of innate ideas) were in the nature of philosophical moves thought up, as it were, by the modern Ambedkar. These were very much in line with the moments of erasure involved in the making of the modern subject in the history of modern Western philosophy. Consequently I would also suggest that Ambedkar's essay *Annihilation of Caste* or his burning of the *Manu Smriti* were not "truly religious" moments. For however pure the means and however just the end, the new faith, as Ambedkar had argued, was not a 'religion' but *dhamma*/morality. In differentiating between the two Ambedkar had re-defined (perhaps 'naturalized'), the term 'sacred' (consequent to his belief that the epistemology of religious thoughts must be "naturalized" made earthly perhaps) associating that term with the experience of, what was essentially, an enlightenment morality. In Ambedkar it was not religion but modernity itself (with its immeasurable freedom from commitment to that which is located outside the human), which took on the reverence, erstwhile associated, with the realm of the sacred.

This last perhaps also serves to confirm the point (the second of the two that this chapter seeks to close with) that Ambedkar's conversion did not in any manner disrupt the making of the radically disengaged modern Indian self. This might seem evident from a consideration of the point that Ambedkar's move to re-write Buddhism was in keeping with the inwardness of the modern self and in keeping with the idea that such an inwardness was the source of all notions of value. Again Ambedkar's *Navayana* with its emphasis on the alleviation of pain and the idea of *nibbana* as the attainment of earthly happiness were perfectly in line with the emphasis on the value of ordinary life in the making of modern identity.

Consequently (and as noted above), Ambedkar's move towards a radically re-interpreted Buddhism did not quite interrupt his engagement with the making of modern Indian identity. Quite to the contrary the act of conversion was in itself a playing out of the constitutional tension in the modern self (which Taylor has spoken of) the tension between an enlightenment driven need for disengagement and a some-what contrary need for expressive self-articulation. It was perhaps Ambedkar's self-conscious engagement with the conflict (inevitable to/for the modern self) between the need for disengagement and the contrary need for self-expression driven by imagination and feeling that completely distanced him from Gandhi. Ambedkar had embraced the radically disengaged rational stance of modernity rejecting the past as inconsequential to self-identity. This disengagement colluded with the contrary pull, voiced so well, by the Romantics. Consequently, there was the felt compulsion (for Ambedkar as for moderns) to recognize the idea that nature (not reason) drives the human being and that there is some need for self-expression (in art, poetry, emotion) to protest against the disengagement demanded by modern rationality. The product of this tension led Ambedkar to the tremendous drive to express himself by confronting his own lived experience in articulating a new faith (rather than religion perhaps) for a new world. Established firmly in the conceptual predicaments of modernity Ambedkar distanced both himself and the dalit movement from Gandhi's politics located as it was in tradition and in a conceptually incommensurable world view.

It follows that it is possible to say that the distance between Gandhi and Ambedkar cannot really be traversed. Gandhi and Ambedkar cannot come close now, just as they could not come close then, because they were not speaking about the same things when they spoke indeed of the self, of the community and of God. There could be no meaningful dialogue between them because, though they used the same words, they meant very different things by those words. This came to mean that their world views were fundamentally at variance with each other and that Gandhi's debate with Ambedkar brought the old-world Indian mind into conflict with the modern Indian subject. The differences between their world view's and their conceptions of the self; and of the relationship between that self and the world made the differences between Gandhi and Ambedkar "most intimate and irreconciliable" (Ibid., 11).

Notes

i.   The term *dalit* comes from the Sanskrit *dal*– literally "split"/'broken open." It came to represent the condition of being "ground down". By the 1970s, however the term was divested of its negative connotation and adopted as a self-description by ancient India's erstwhile(unjustly designated and) so-called 'untouchable' groups.

ii. The *Bhagavad Gita* also referred to simply as the *Gita* is a religious book for the Hindus. It is a 700 verse text in Sanskrit that is part of the epic *Mahabharata*. The *Gita* narrates a dialogue between the *Kshatriya* prince Arjuna and his charioteer Sri Krishna. At the start of the war between the Pandavas and their cousins, the kauravas; Arjuna is filled with despair and wonders if he should take part in a war against his kinsmen. Sri Krishna's reply to him forms the *Gita*. Krishna counsels Arjuna to fulfill his duty by action without any self-directed desire for results thereof.

iii. The problem with calling them goods is that modern liberal philosophers would not acknowledge them to be goods. Nor would modern philosophers accept a given ontology of the human or a background moral framework. This is because any framework that is referred to to explain our moral choices, must be in conflict with other frameworks. In a situation of pluralism, there is no way of adjudicating between rival frameworks competing for allegiance.

iv. Read the heading "Mere Morality is Not Enough; It must be sacred and Universal" (Ambekar 2011, 172).

v.   See the discussion about Ambedkar's *Navayana* Buddhism as a means to put forth "his own political message" (Rathore and Verma 2011, xi) in the Editor's Introduction to *The Buddha and His Dhamma* (2011).

vi. Rawls explains the difference between a political conception of justice and what he terms a comprehensive moral conception;

> This contrast will be clearer if we observe that the distinction between a political conception of justice and other moral conceptions is a matter of scope: that is, the range of subjects to which a conception applies and the content a wider range requires. A moral conception is general if it applies to a wide range of subjects, and in the limit to all subjects universally. It is comprehensive when it includes conceptions of what is of value in human life, and ideals of personal character, as well as ideals of friendship and of familial and associational relationships, and much else that is to inform our conduct, and in the limit to our life as a whole." (Rawls 2005, 13).

vii. This was originally a lecture delivered while the writer was Principal of Hoogly College between 1928 and 1930.

viii. It might be useful to bringing out the difference of world views between Gandhi and Ambedkar to contrast this notion of the 'rights usurper' with that of Ambedkar's discussion of the notion of the transgressor in the caste system.

ix.   *Prohairesis* is an ancient greek word variously translated as "moral character", "will", "volition", "choice", "intention" or "moral choice". It is a fundamental concept in the Stoic philosophy of Epictetus. It represents the choice involved in giving or withholding assent to impressions (*phantasiai*). The use of this Greek word was first introduced into philosophy by Aristotle in the *Nichomachean Ethics*. For Epictetus nothing is properly considered either good, or bad, aside from those things that are within our own power to control, and the only thing fully in our power to control is our own volition (*prohairesis*) which exercises the faculty of choice that we use to judge our impressions. According to Epictetus *Prohairesis* is the faculty that distinguishes human beings from all other creatures.

x.   In Indian philosophy, the *antahkarana* refers to the internal organ/instrument which is the location or inner origin of thought and feeling. The *antaḥkaraṇa* (meaning 'the inner cause') includes the *buddhi* which is the higher mind/intellect, the *manas* which is the lower mind and the *ahamkara*/ego. The function of the *antah karana* is to unite all the sensations and present them to the *atman* which remains outside of, and is not a part of, the *antah karana*.

xi.   Gandhi was introduced to the *Bhagavad Gita* in England in 1888–89 when he read Sir Edwin Arnold's translation. It made such an impact on his thinking that he went on to engage systematically with it across the next few decades of his life. In 1919 he commented on the Gita in one of the *satyagraha* leaflets. In 1926 he gave a series of almost daily talks on the *Gita* between February and November during morning prayers at the *Satyagraha Ashram*. They were posthumously published under the title *Gandhijijinu Gitashikshan* (Gandhi's Teaching of the Gita). *Gitashikshan* seems to have been translated by the editors of the collected works as "Discourses on the Gita". It was later published in English as a book "The *Bhagavadgita*" (New Delhi: Orient Paperbacks, 1980). Gandhi's Gujarati translation of the *Gita* the *Anasaktiyoga* literally 'the *yoga* of non-attachment' was completed in Yeravada jail in 1929. The *Anasaktiyoga* was a "rendering" of the *Gita* with short glosses on some passages and an additional preface. The English translation of the book by Mahadev Desai was published in 1931 by Navajivan Press under the title "The Gita according to Gandhi". There were also two other publications. Faced with complaints that *Anasaktiyoga* was too difficult to follow Gandhi wrote a series of letters on the *Gita*. These were later published under the title *Gitabodh*. To help readers understand the *Anasaktiyoga* he published a glossary to the terms in it, which was published in 1936 as the *Gitapadarthkosa*.

xii. Gandhi's comments on the *Gita* have been almost entirely neglected by more contemporary philosophers writing on his moral political and religious ideas. An exception is the fourth chapter in Douglas Allen's *Gandhi After 9/11: Creative Nonviolence and Sustainability* (2019) and Chap. 1 in Ananya

        Vajpeyi's *Righteous Republic: The Political Foundations of Modern India* (2013).

xiii.   Gandhi said: "…that prince of yogis Patañjali, gave the first place to *yamas* (cardinal vows) and *niyamas* (casual vows) and held as eligible for yogic practices only those who have gone through the preliminary discipline" (Gandhi 1888–1948, 46: 192). The five cardinal virtues were "…non-violence, truth, non-stealing, celibacy, non- possession." The five casual virtues were "…bodily purity, contentment, the study of scriptures, austerity, and meditation on God…" (Ibid.). The list of *yamas*/cardinal virtues was later expanded by Gandhi to include what could be reconstructed as moral maxims (borrowing the Kantian sense of a maxim as a subjective principle of action) or moral truths which were contextual: "…the five have been expanded into eleven…. They are non-violence, truth, non-stealing, brahmacharya, non-possession, bread labour, control of the palate, fearlessness, equal regard for all religions, *swadeshi* and removal of untouchability" (Gandhi 1888–1948, 95: 190).

xiv.   "The truth is that my ethics not only permit me to claim but require me to own kinship with not merely the ape but the horse and the sheep, the lion and the leopard, the snake and the scorpion. Not so need these kinsfolk regard themselves. The hard ethics which rule my life, and I hold ought to rule that of every man and woman, impose this unilateral obligation upon us. And it is so imposed because man alone is made in the image of God. …And to prove the proposition that man is made in the image of God, it is surely unnecessary to show that all men admittedly exhibit that image in their own persons. It is enough to show that one man at least has done so. And, will it be denied that the great religious teachers of mankind have exhibited the image of God in their own persons?" (Gandhi 1888–1948, 36: 5).

xv.   Jacques Maritain (1882–1973), French philosopher and political thinker, was a scholar of the philosophy of St Thomas Aquinas who later developed principles of a liberal Christian humanism and defense of natural rights.

xvi.   With the *caveat* that 'sacred' in Ambedkar's usage of the term is very different from what that term means for the religious.

xvii.   These are Ambedkar's own words taken from page 104 and 105 of Volume 17 Part 2 of *Dr. Babasaheb Ambedkar writings and Speeches*, 2014. (set of 17 Volumes). New Delhi: Dr. Ambedkar Foundation, Ministry of Social Justice and Empowerment, Government of India.

xviii.   Literally means a wandering ascetic; the term was used to refer to the peripatetic monks of India whether these were Buddhist Jain or Hindu.

References

Allen, Douglas. 2019. *Gandhi After 9/11: Creative nonviolence and sustainability*. New Delhi: Oxford University Press.

Ambedkar, B. R. 2002. Conversion. In *The essential writings of B.R. Ambedkar*, ed. Valerian Rodrigues, 219–238. New Delhi: Oxford University Press.

Ambedkar, B. R. 2011. *The Buddha and his dhamma*. Eds. and Trans. Aakash Singh Rathore and Ajay Verma. New Delhi: Oxford University Press.

Ambedkar, B. R. 2014. *Dr Babasaheb Ambedkar writings and Speeches*, ed. Vasant Moon (set of 17 Volumes). New Delhi: Dr Ambedkar Foundation. Ministry of Social Justice and Empowerment. Government of India.

Bergson, Henri. 1932. *Two sources of religion and morality*. Trans. by R. Ashley Cloudesley and Laura Brereton (1977). Notre Dame: University of Notre Dame Press.

Bhattacharya, K. C. *Swaraj* in ideas. In *Indian philosophy in English: From Renaissance to independence*, eds. Nalini Bhushan and Jay L. Garfield, 103–114. New York: Oxford University Press.

Durkheim, E. 1912. *The elementary forms of religious life*. Trans. Carol Cosman and Mark Sydney Cladis (2001). Oxford: Oxford University Press.

Fiske, Adele and Christoph Emmrich. 2004. The Use of Buddhist Scriptures in B.R. Ambedkar's The Buddha and His Dhamma. In *Reconstructing the World: B.R. Ambedkar and Buddhism in India*, eds. Surendra Jondhale and Johannes Beltz, 97–119. New Delhi: Oxford University Press.

Gandhi, M. K. 1888–1948. *Collected Works of Mahatma Gandhi*: Volumes 1 to 98. Accessed online in May 2021 at https://www.gandhiashramsevagram.org/gandhi-literature/collected-works-of-mahatma-gandhi-volume-1-to-98.php.

Gandhi, M. K. 2010. *Hind swaraj and other Writings*, ed. Anthony J Parel. Cambridge: Cambridge University Press.

Gokhale, Pradeep P. 2004. Universal Consequentialism. In *Reconstructing the World: B.R. Ambedkar and Buddhism in India*, eds. Surendra Jondhale and Johannes Beltz, 120–31. New Delhi: Oxford University Press.

Gokhale, Pradeep P. 2021. Ambedkar and modern Buddhism: Continuity and Discontinuity. In *Classical Buddhism, Neo-Buddhism and the question of caste*, ed. Pradeep P. Gokhale, 257–274. London, New York: Routledge.

Guha, Ramachandra. 2012. Gandhi's Ambedkar. In *Indian political thought: A reader*, eds. Aakash Singh and Silika Mohapatra, 33–38. London: Routledge.

Kolge, Nishikant. 2017. *Gandhi against caste*. New Delhi: Oxford University Press.

Kumar, Aishwary. 2015. *Radical equality: Ambedkar, Gandhi, and the risk of democracy*. Stanford, CA: Stanford University Press.

Lal, Vinay. 2020. Ambedkar and Religion. Speech delivered at *Kerala Literary Festival*, Kozhikode 16–19 January, 2020. Accessible at https://www.youtube.com/watch?v=IgrH6bYjggY

MacIntyre, A. 1988. *Whose justice? Which rationality?* Notre Dame, Indiana: University of Notre Dame Press.

Murdoch, I. 1970. *The sovereignty of good*. New York: Routledge & Kegan Paul.

Nagel, Thomas. 1986. *The view from nowhere*. New York: Oxford University Press.

Pantham, Thomas. 2013. Against Untouchability: The Discourses of Gandhi and Ambedkar. In *Humiliation: Claims and context*, ed. Gopal Guru, 179–208. New Delhi: Oxford University Press.

Parfit, Derek. 1984. *Reasons and persons*. Oxford: Oxford University Press.

Queen, Christopher S. 1996. Dr. Ambedkar and the Hermeneutics of Buddhist Liberation. In *Engaged Buddhism: Buddhist liberation movements in Asia*, eds. Christopher S. Queen and Sallie B. King, 45–72. Albany: SUNY.

Rathore, Aakash Singh and Verma, Ajay (eds.). 2011. Editors' Introduction. *B R Ambedkar: The buddha and his dhamma. A Critical edition*. Eds. and Trans. Aakash Singh Rathore and Ajay Verma, New Delhi: Oxford University Press.

Rawls, J. 2005. *Political Liberalism*. New York: Columbia University Press.

Roy, Arundhati. 2014. The Doctor and the Saint. *Annihilation of caste: The annotated critical edition* B. R Ambedkar, Ed. S. Anand. New Delhi: Navyana Publishing.

Sangharakshita, 2006. *Ambedkar and Buddhism*. New Delhi: Motilal Banarsidas Pvt. Ltd.

Scruton, R. 2014. *The Soul of the world*. Oxford, Princeton: Princeton University Press.

Sorabji, Richard. 2012. *Gandhi and the Stoics: Modern experiments on ancient values.* Chicago: The University of Chicago Press.

Taylor, C. 2001. *Sources of the Self: The Making of the modern identity.* Cambridge: Harvard University Press.

Vajpeyi, A. 2013. *Righteous republic: The political foundations of modern india.* Harvard: Harvard University Press.

Chapter 4
The Insurrectionary Gandhi and the Revolutionary Ambedkar: Caste and *Varna*

Abstract The conflict between Gandhi and Ambedkar was at its worst around the issues of caste and *varna*. This chapter will present and philosophically re-interpret their positions on the proper approach to the abolishment of untouchability, caste and *varna*. It will suggest that Gandhi's *Discourses on the Gita* (and the *Anasaktiyoga*) and Ambedkar's *Annihilation of Caste* present an ideational site for a philosophical encounter between the old-world mind of India and the modern Indian self. The chapter will argue that Gandhi had pre-emptively responded to some of Ambedkar's arguments, even before they had been made in the *Annihilation of Caste* (1936) with eight arguments about equality made across his *Discourses on the Gita* (1926) and the *Anasaktiyoga* (1929).

Keywords Untouchability · Caste · *Varna* · Agency · Personhood · Indictment · Annihilation · *Yajna* · *Bhagavad Gita* · Equality · *Satyagraha* · *Swaraj* · *Samata/*status of equality · *Samadarshana/*having an attitude of equality to things as they are despite inequalities · *Samabhava/*attitude of equality to things as they are/exist

The intimate and irreconcilable nature of the differences between Gandhi and Ambedkar is most apparent when it comes to the notions of caste and *varna*. It is here that the conflicts between Gandhi and Ambedkar seem most pronounced. Gandhi did not make a connection between untouchability and the caste system, and he continued to support the caste system till the 1920s. As late as 1934, Gandhi defended an idealized version of the *Varna* system. However, by the 1940s his position had changed and he decided to challenge caste directly, by accepting and proposing, inter-caste marriage itself. Perhaps taking his *que* from the historian Bhattacharya's (2008)

The terms 'insurrectionary' and 'revolutionary' are intended to highlight the difference between 'insurrection' and 'revolution'. Revolution—from the Latin revolutio, 'a turnaround'—is a fundamental change in political power or organizational structures that takes place through a revolt against authorities occupying power at the time. Insurrection coming from 'insurgere' implies to rise against. This term has the sense of an uprising against a usurper. In this case perhaps, Gandhi saw the usurper (strangely enough) as the orthodox Hindu who had usurped control of the dominant set of meanings of the religious texts of the Hindus. Perhaps, insurrection carries the sense of emerging from within and revolution that of emerging from outside of the group concerned.

chronological account of the debate between Gandhi and Tagore (*The Mahatma and the Poet* 2008), Nishikant Kolge (2017) has made a detailed (and most useful) chronological account of Gandhi's evolving views on caste and *varna*. He has divided this account into five time periods—1915–1920, 1920–1927, 1927–1932, 1932–1945 and 1945–1948 (Kolge 2017, 101) on the basis on the themes (and changes) that emerged in Gandhi's writings during these periods.

This chapter will not attempt a chronological account of the differences between Gandhi and Ambedkar on *varna* and caste. It will present, and philosophically re-interpret, Gandhi and Ambedkar's individual positions, on the proper approach to the abolishment of untouchability, caste and *varna*. Section 4.1 "Ambedkar: On Caste *Varna* and Gandhi" will discuss Ambedkar's critique of Gandhi's efforts to remove untouchability from Indian society across two subsections and four texts. It is important to remember that Ambedkar's insightful understanding of caste and the caste system went through significant changes over the period of his writing. In his initial works, Ambedkar spoke of endogamy as the essential characteristic of caste. However, he later argued that graded inequality was the central feature of the caste system. The solution that Ambedkar proposed (in the *Annihilation of Caste*) was the annihilation of caste and the abolishment of hereditary priesthood. Section 4.2 "Absolute Equality: Gandhi on the *Bhagavad Gita*" will argue that Gandhi had responded to untouchability as early as 1926, and sought to dismantle the basis of both caste and *varna*, in his *Discourses on the Gita* (and the *Anasaktiyoga* which was completed in 1929). A closer reading of Gandhi's *Discourses on the Gita* (and the *Anasaktiyoga* which was completed some three years later) might lead one to argue that Gandhi had pre-emptively responded to some of Ambedkar's arguments in *Annihilation of Caste* even before that text had been written. Gandhi's arguments about absolute equality were characterized by a critical, even insurrectionary, questioning. However, such questioning (albeit insurrectionary) remained powerfully inward looking as it sought to reform Hinduism by challenging the orthodox from within the Hindu tradition.

The last section of the chapter "Gandhi on Caste and *Varna:* Responding to Ambedkar" will (across three subsections) argue that the differences between Gandhi and Ambedkar emerged from a fundamental conflict of world views. This conflict might be best put, as that between the old-world mind of India and the modern Indian self as it *came to be* in the person of Babasaheb Ambedkar. This section will suggest that Gandhi's apparent, and glaring inability, to understand the need of the dalit self to respond (with revolution and rejection) to an essentially oppressive memory of a Hindu past can be located in his alternative understanding of tradition as forming a constitutive part of self-identity. The section will discuss the relationship between *satyagraha* and *swaraj* as the measure of Gandhi's understanding of the relationship between freedom and equality and suggest that Gandhi had privileged the claims of equality over those of freedom. The object of such a discussion is to unpack Gandhi's response to *varna* and argue that, unlike what other commentators have suggested, Gandhi was not purely a "a strategist in his response" (Kolge 2017, 38) to untouchability, caste and *varna*.

4.1 Ambedkar: On Caste, *Varna* and Gandhi

This section will put together Ambedkar's case against Gandhi across two subsections. The first of these (subsections) will discuss Ambedkar's most revolutionary move (while still within the Hindu fold) in 1936, the move to annihilate caste. It will discuss the exchange between Gandhi and Ambedkar at this time. The second subsection will put forth Ambedkar's central arguments against Gandhi made across three texts: *Mr. Gandhi and the Emancipation of Untouchables* (1942); *Ranade Gandhi and Jinnah* (1943) and *What Congress and Gandhi have done to the Untouchables* (1945).[1]

4.1.1 Annihilation Versus Transformation: Gandhi and Ambedkar on the Annihilation of Caste

As is well known, Ambedkar was to have delivered an address to the *Jat Pat Todak Mandal* in May 1936. That address was never delivered, and the rest, as they say, became history and (I would suggest) not *itihaas*. I say this conscious that the idea foremost in Ambedkar's speech (published and not delivered) on *Annihilation of Caste* was that of history as measure and the historian as the judge making a retrospective judgement on the oppressive Hindu past. It is appropriate then that Gandhi should have entitled his response to Ambedkar's undelivered address as "Dr. Ambedkar's Indictment". In this section, I want to briefly discuss the chief parts of that indictment and of the exchange that took place between Ambedkar and Gandhi around that indictment.

As seen in the last chapter, expressivism and self-expression have been somewhat critical to modern identity, and it was indeed so, for Ambedkar. It seemed natural enough for him to have had the speech (which was never delivered) published. As he wrote to Mr. Har Bhagwan of the *Mandal* on 27 April 1936 about the controversy regarding the printing of his address in Bombay, "I thought that it was only fools who were afraid of words" (Ambedkar 2014, 1: 33).[2] Ambedkar's words frightened the *Mandal*, perhaps because they contained, as Gandhi was to put it, an indictment. The indictment delivered by Ambedkar (as historian/juror) in the *Annihilation of Caste* was made in nine parts which might be (very briefly) summarized in the following points:

---

[1] The year mentioned within parentheses against the texts represents their original year of publication. These have been mentioned to show the chronology of the books. However, for the purposes of reference, I have resourced these books from the set of 17 volumes entitled *Dr. Babasaheb Ambedkar Writings and Speeches*, edited by Vasant Moon, 2014, New Delhi, Dr. Ambedkar Foundation, Ministry of Social Justice and Empowerment, Government of India.

[2] Ambedkar, B. R. 2014. *Dr Babasaheb Ambedkar writings and Speeches*, edited by Vasant Moon (set of 17 Volumes). New Delhi: Dr Ambedkar Foundation. Ministry of Social Justice and Empowerment. Government of India.

(1)   A discussion of the path of social reform in India and an examination of the views of the critics of social reform and movements thereof;
(2)   An enumeration and evaluation of the arguments made by those in support of caste;
(3)   A summary of the defects of the caste system;
(4)   An account of the alternative ideal society to be built in modern India after the destruction of caste;
(5)   An evaluation of the *chaturvarna* proposed by the *Arya Samaj*;
(6)   The difference between "castes" among the Hindus and among the non-Hindus;
(7)   A question—Can a Hindu appeal to reason and morality to question the authority of the *Shastra*?;
(8)   Solutions to the pernicious Hindu system of social organization;
(9)   Questions for the Hindus.

To summarize this fairly detailed indictment in a few words is almost impossible. However, one must see Ambedkar primarily as a person who dealt with making possible, what others saw to be impossible, and so it seems only appropriate that the attempt must be made. In the second point (of the nine, in Ambedkar's indictment, as summarized above), Ambedkar dismissed the chief (and untenable) arguments made by the supporters of caste. These were to the effect that caste was economically efficient as a division of labour, and that, it was "eugenic in its conception" (Ibid., 50).

Ambedkar went on (in *Annihilation of Caste*) to make several arguments bringing out the defects of the caste system. These could be summarized briefly as follows: that the caste system had disorganized and demoralized the Hindus so that the very idea of Hindu society had become a myth; that caste consciousness had served to keep the memory of past feuds alive and prevented solidarity (one might note Ambedkar's attempt to create an alternative memory by rewriting history); that it had compromised the condition of the tribals; that the caste system had prevented lower castes from rising to the cultural level of the castes that came higher in the system; that it had prevented Hindus from converting others; that it had made *Sangathan* and common brotherhood/fraternity impossible; that it had discouraged individual independence; and lastly, that it has destroyed the ethics of the Hindus. As Ambedkar was to put it (almost poetically), "virtue has become caste-ridden and morality has become caste-bound" (Ibid., 56).

Ambedkar recommended (as an alternative to the Hindu caste system of social organization) a modern democratic Indian society kept together by enlightenment values, which was "a society based on *Liberty, Equality* and *Fraternity*" (Ibid., 57). In the fourth part of *Annihilation of Caste*, Ambedkar picked up the system of *chatur-varna* or the division of society into four classes based on "guna (worth)" (Ibid., 58) proposed by the *Arya Samajists*. He condemned this last system (among other reasons) on account of its close association with "such stinking labels" (Ibid., 59) as Brahmin Kshatriya, etc. He also pointed out that "…as a system of social organization, Chaturvarna is impracticable, harmful" (Ibid.) and, as he said, it had "turned out to be a miserable failure" (Ibid.).

In the next part of the *Annihilation of Caste,* Ambedkar argued that there was great difference between castes as they existed among the Hindus and as they existed among the non-Hindus. In this connection, he made the significant point that "Caste among the non-Hindus has no religious consecration; but among the Hindus most decisively it has… Religion compels the Hindus to treat isolation and segregation of castes as a virtue" (Ibid., 65). In the seventh part of his undelivered lecture, Ambedkar raised and answered an important question. He asked, if it was even possible for the Hindus, to appeal to reason and morality to question the authority of the *Shastra*? One might appreciate the significance of this question by recalling Kant's famous essay in 1784 "An Answer to the Question: What is Enlightenment?". In this essay, Kant had emphasized that what is required for the enlightenment is "freedom to make *public use* of one's reason in all matters" (Kant 1999, 18). Kant had famously explained that the *public* use of one's reason is "that use which someone makes of it *as a scholar* before …the *world of readers*" (Ibid.). Kant's definition of the enlightenment and Ambedkar's raising this question (almost a century later) were both perhaps equally critical to the making of modern identity in India. Ambedkar asked if the Hindus could appeal to reason and morality to question the authority of the *Shastra*? He answered this question in the negative declaring that the Hindu had no freedom in the use of his/her reason. Such a negative answer made it clear that in Ambedkar's indictment of it, Hinduism could certainly not be a part of the project of the making of the modern Indian self, and consequently that it needed to be relegated to the past. One might recall that Kant's critique of reason had made a critical investigation of the powers of reason itself to determine what were the proper objects of rational enquiry. The coming to be of the modern self was essentially wrought up with the individual and self-conscious avowal of reason as his/her own constitutive ability. Ambedkar's decisive dismissal of Hinduism followed from his answer (to his own question) that reason had no role to play in Hindu religious and (more importantly) moral and social life.

However, striking a somewhat discordant note one could submit that even a superficial reading of Gandhi's comments on the *Gita* could reveal a contrary, almost emphatic insistence, that the *Gita* itself enjoins the duty of re-interpretation of the sacred texts and central terms in them. On Gandhi's view, the *Gita* recommended the re-interpretation of its own central concepts such as *yajna, karma* and *sannyasa* in the light of the demands of reason and morality and with the change in the context in which one found oneself as a reader of that text. Interestingly, Ambedkar seemed not to have paid any attention to Gandhi's arguments (about reason and the re-interpretation of sacred texts), and ten years after Gandhi's *Discourses on the Gita,* he went on to ask, "Is a Hindu free to follow his reason?" (Ambedkar 2014, 1: 72). To re-iterate that which was noted above, Ambedkar answered his own question in the negative saying that "A Hindu must follow either *Veda, Smriti* or *sadachar.* He cannot follow anything else… rationalism as a canon of interpreting the *Vedas* and the *Smritis* is absolutely condemned" (Ibid.). From such an indictment, it followed naturally enough that Hinduism ought to be destroyed as having no role to play (and indeed being positively detrimental) in/to the making of the modern Indian identity.

In the grand tradition of the revolutions of the modern West, the revolutionary Ambedkar suggested the "destruction of Religion" (Ibid., 75) of the Hindus. He explained that "Once you clear the minds of people… and enable them to realize that what they are told as Religion is not but that it is really Law, you will be in a position to urge for its amendment or abolition" (Ibid., 76). By way of such, he recommended both the annihilation of caste and of hereditary priesthood. Before closing his undelivered lecture/published essay, Ambedkar raised questions (and suggested possible answers for the Hindus): "The Hindus must, therefore, examine their religion and morality in terms of their survival value" (Ibid., 79); inspired by Dewey, Ambedkar recommended that the Hindus rid themselves of "the dead wood from the past" (Ibid.); "…. the hindus must consider whether they must not cease to worship the past as supplying its ideals" (Ibid.). Drawing from Dewey once again, Ambedkar remained fascinated with the all too modern engagements with erasure, as not only possible but highly desirable (the last in both the sense of "object of desire" and as carrying normative weight). As he put it (in the words of Dewey), "An individual can live only in the present" (Ibid.).

One might be tempted to respond to Ambedkar's modern obsession with erasure in lay terms, by suggesting that erasure is not always attractive and sometimes (for instance for the old in years) it can happen, and that the past becomes much more real and indeed more meaningful than the present. Ambedkar of course rejects all such nostalgia and goes on to make his most radical move to confine both the Hindu self and its location in time sharply to/in the present;

Nothing is fixed, nothing eternal, nothing *sanatan*. (Ibid.)

Gandhi recognized Ambedkar's retrospective judgement of the past through the measure of history for what it was, an indictment, and replied to him across two **essays**[i] in *Harijan*—one on 11 July 1936 and one on 18 July 1936. As I will argue in Sect. 4.2, some of the arguments made by Ambedkar had already been pre-emptively answered by Gandhi in the 1926 *Discourses on the Gita*. However, what remained most important to this exchange in 1936 (and indeed to posterity) was Gandhi's position on *varna* and Ambedkar's response to it and it is to this that I shall turn here. In responding to Ambedkar, Gandhi accepted the merit of Ambedkar's arguments and indeed the indictment passed on the Hindus and their society by history. Spelling out the content of Ambedkar's indictment, Gandhi wrote "Brought up as a Hindu …he (Ambedkar) has become so disgusted with the so-called Sa*varna* Hindus… that he proposes to leave not only them but the very religion that is his and their common heritage" (Gandhi[3] 1888–1948, 69: 206). Gandhi sought, at this time, to respond to

---

[3] Gandhi 1888–1948, refers to the Collected Works of Mahatma Gandhi. The volume concerned and the page numbers from which citations from Gandhi are drawn have been mentioned within parentheses. These have been mentioned to indicate the exact location of the quotation in the electronic edition of the Collected Works of Mahatma Gandhi. However, for the purposes of reference, it may be noted that I have resourced these volumes from the Collected Works of Mahatma Gandhi : Volumes 1 to 98. New Delhi: Publications Division Government of India, 1999. Accessed online in May 2021 at https://www.gandhiashramsevagram.org/gandhi-literature/collected-works-of-mahatma-gandhi-volume-1-to-98.php.

Ambedkar by re-iterating some of his own arguments from 1926 (in the *Discourses on the Gita*) rejecting the idea that the Hindu scriptures occupied a hallowed space beyond the measure of reason and morality:

> Nothing can be accepted as the word of God which cannot be tested by reason or be capable of being spiritually experienced. (Ibid., 226)

The use of reason for revaluating the Hindu scriptures could not remain a matter of contention between the old-world Gandhi and the modern Ambedkar. However, while Gandhi (in 1936) agreed with Ambedkar's central argument that castes must go stating decisively that "caste has nothing to do with religion" (Ibid.), he did go on to make other problematic claims in his response to Ambedkar:

> *Varna* and Ashrama are institutions which have nothing to do with castes. The law of *varna* teaches us that we have each of us to earn our bread by following the ancestral calling. It defines not our rights but our duties. It necessarily has reference to callings that are conducive to the welfare of humanity and to no other. It also follows that there is no calling too low and none too high. All are good, lawful and absolutely equal in status. The callings of a Brahmin—spiritual teacher—and a scavenger are equal, and their due performance carries equal merit before God and at one time seems to have carried identical reward before man. Both were entitled to their livelihood and no more. Indeed one traces even now in the villages the faint lines of this healthy operation of the law. Living in Segaon with its population of 600, I do not *find* a great disparity between the earnings of different tradesmen including Brahmins. I *find* too that real Brahmins are to be found even in these degenerate days who are living on alms freely given to them and are giving freely of what they have of spiritual treasures. It would be wrong and improper to judge the law of *Varna* by its caricature in the lives of men who profess to belong to a *Varna*, whilst they openly commit a breach of its only operative rule. Arrogation of a superior status by any of the *Varnas* over another is a denial of the law. And there is nothing in the law of *Varna* to warrant a belief in untouchability. (The essence of Hinduism is contained in its enunciation of one and only God as Truth and its bold acceptance of Ahimsa as the law of the human family.) (Ibid., 226–227)

In his reply to Gandhi's reply (to his indictment), Ambedkar had many difficulties to consider, but by far the most important issue was that of *varna*; "When can a calling be deemed to have become an ancestral calling so as to make it binding on a man ? Must man follow his ancestral calling even if it does not suit his capacities, even when it has ceased to be profitable ?" (Ambedkar 2014, 1: 90).

In a fairly telling passage, in his "A Reply to the Mahatma", Ambedkar reminded Gandhi of his own abrogation of ancestral calling:

> Does the Mahatma practise what he preaches? One does not like to make personal reference in an argument which is general in its application. But when one preaches a doctrine and holds it as a dogma there is a curiosity to know how far he practises what he preaches. It may be that his failure to practise is due to the ideal being too high to be attainable; it may be that his failure to practise is due to the innate hypocracy of the man. In any case he exposes his conduct to examination and I must not be blamed if I asked how far has the Mahatma attempted to realize his ideal in his own case. The Mahatma is a Bania by birth. His ancestors had abandoned trading in favour of ministership which is a calling of the Brahmins. In his own life, before he became a Mahatma, when occasion came for him to choose his career he preferred law to scales. On abandoning law he became half saint and half politician. He has never touched trading which is his ancestral calling. (Ibid.)

This issue of *varna* was at the centre of this exchange, and indeed, this issue continues to attack the ire of Gandhi's critics. In that sense, the questions posed by Ambedkar in his reply continue to be relevant today:

> The Mahatma's view of *Varna* not only makes nonsense of the Vedic *Varna* but it makes it an abominable thing. *Varna* and Caste are two very different concepts. *Varna* is based on the principle of each according to his worth-while Caste is based on the principle of each according to his birth. The two are as distinct as chalk is from cheese. In fact there is an antithesis between the two. If the Mahatma believes as he does in every one following his or her ancestral calling, then most certainly he is advocating the Caste System and that in calling it the *Varna* System he is not only guilty of terminological inexactitude, but he is causing confusion worse confounded. I am sure that all his confusion is due to the fact that the Mahatma has no definite and clear conception as to what is *Varna* and what is Caste and as to the necessity of either for the conservation of Hinduism. He has said and one hopes that he will not *find* some mystic reason to change his view that caste is not the essence of Hinduism. Does he regard *Varna* as the essence of Hinduism? One cannot as yet give any categorical answer. Readers of his article on "Dr. Ambedkar's Indictment" will answer "No". In that article he does not say that the dogma of *Varna* is an essential part of the creed of Hinduism. Far from making *Varna* the essence of Hinduism he says "the essence of Hinduism is contained in its enunciation of one and only God as Truth and its bold acceptance of Ahimsa as the law of the human family" ….Why does the Mahatma hedge ? Whom does he want to please ? Has the saint failed to sense the truth ? Or does the politician stand in the way of the Saint ? The real reason why the Mahatma is suffering from this confusion is probably to be traced to two sources. The first is the temperament of the Mahatma. He has …..the child's capacity for self-deception. … The second source of confusion is the double role which the Mahatma wants to play—of a Mahatma and a Politician. …. The reason why the Mahatma is always supporting Caste and *Varna* is because he is afraid that if he opposed them he will lose his place in politics. (Ibid., 91)

Having formulated the problematic in Gandhi's position on *varna*, as somewhat central to the exchange with Ambedkar on untouchability, this chapter will re-construct Gandhi's arguments about *varna* and equality in Sects. 4.2 and 4.3 of this chapter.

4.1.2   Three Texts from Ambedkar: Of Agency and a Critique of Gandhi

The word "person" comes from the Latin "persona", which originally referred to a theatrical mask and thereby to the person who spoke through it. This term was taken up in Roman law to denote the right-and-duty-bearing subject of the law. It should be obvious why this term should have become the most important term in modern philosophy. One might note here that "when Boethius defined "person" as "an individual subject of a rational nature" he brought out the point "that a person is *essentially* a person, and therefore could not cease to be a person without ceasing to be" (Scruton 2014, 29). This statement about personhood seems relevant to any account of Ambedkar's position on untouchability because it speaks to Ambedkar as it perhaps never could to Gandhi. Perhaps, Ambedkar's emphasis on the need to relocate agency for the abolishment of untouchability to the right-bearing dalit subject (the person inside the mask as it were) was at the start and at the end of any understanding of the opposition between their rival approaches to untouchability.

I will digress here to D. R. Nagraj's argument that "The mode of self purification which Gandhi advocated had no role …for the untouchables; the single protagonist it created had to be the upper caste reformer… the untouchable was thereby reduced to the status of a passive object in a holy rite of self-purification" (Nagraj 2015, 100). One of the points at issue in the debate, according to this argument, was that there was space for only one hero and "Ambedkar could never settle for the roles of Hanumantha…" (Ibid., 47). I would argue that Ambedkar's difficulties with Gandhi's approach went beyond those of playing the hero or remaining sidelined. As modern Indian identity came to be, in Babasaheb's own person, his arguments emerged from a sensitivity to the idea that the dalit could not cease to be a right-bearing subject/person without ceasing to be/exist as a person *qua* person in any meaningful sense.

Gandhi's inability to respond to the dalit demand for agency and absolute loss of personhood is the primary sense one might get from Ambedkar's critique of Gandhi's approach to untouchability (caste and *varna*) in the three texts that he wrote around this theme: *Mr. Gandhi and the Emancipation of Caste* (1942)[4]; *Ranade Gandhi and Jinnah* (1943); and *What Congress and Gandhi have done to the Untouchables* (1945) and to these I will now turn.

Mr. Gandhi and the Emancipation of Caste was a paper Ambedkar had presented at a conference in December 1942 at Quebec. As Ambedkar explains in the Preface, the essay was primarily concerned with "the problem of the Untouchables of India" (Ambedkar 2014, 9: 397). One might add that this essay was also perhaps equally concerned with putting together a case against Gandhi's approach to the problem of untouchability in India. In the first part of the paper, Ambedkar contextualized Gandhi's approach to the problem of untouchability within a politics of numbers arguing that the "Politics in India" had "become a matter of numbers" (Ibid., 399). Ambedkar explained that the struggle for freedom from colonialism was merely "a struggle for power" (Ibid., 401) on the part of the self-styled primary agents (or rather those who had usurped all agency) Hindus and Mussalmans. "If there is any cause of freedom in this Indian turmoil for independence it is the cause of the Untouchables" (Ibid.). In Ambedkar's alternative understanding, any approach to the abolition of untouchability was inseparable from the assertion of political, economic and social rights, for and by, the untouchables. Such an assertion, as he noted, had been "a subject matter of great controversy between the Untouchables and the Hindus. Mr. Gandhi, the friend of the Untouchables, preferred to fast to death rather than consent to them…" (Ibid., 407). The central political demand (which Gandhi had famously opposed) was related to the carving out of a separate political identity for the

---

[4] The year mentioned within parentheses against the books represents their original year of publication. These have been mentioned to show the years in which the original works appeared. However, for purposes of reference, I have referred to these books as they have formed a part of *Dr. Babasaheb Ambedkar Writings and Speeches*, edited by Vasant Moon (set of 17 Volumes), 2014, New Delhi, Dr. Ambedkar Foundation, Ministry of Social Justice and Empowerment, Government of India.

untouchables by employing communal rather than territorial electorates. Ambedkar explained that:

> A separate electorate means an electorate composed exclusively of Untouchable voters who are to elect an Untouchable as their representative to the legislature. The Hindus agree that certain number of seats are to be reserved for Untouchables to be filled only by Untouchables. But they insist that the Untouchables who is to be the representative of the Untouchables in the Legislature should be elected by a mixed electorate consisting both of the Hindus as well as of the Untouchables and not by an electorate exclusively of the Untouchables. In other words there is still a controversy over the question of joint versus separate electorates. Here again I want to set out the pros and cons of this controversy. The objection to separate electorate raised by the Hindus is that separate electorate means the fragmentation of the nation. The reply is obvious. First of all, there is no nation of Indians in the real sense of the word. The nation does not exist, it is to be created, and I think it will be admitted that the suppression of a distinct and a separate community is not the method of creating a nation. Secondly, it is conceded—as the Hindus have done—that Untouchables should be represented in that Legislature by Untouchable; then, it cannot be denied that the Untouchable must be a true representative of the Untouchable voters. If this is a correct position then separate electorate is the only mechanism by which real representation can be guaranteed to the Untouchables. The Hindu argument against separate electorate is insubstantial and unsupportable. …Special electorates are devised as a means of protecting the minorities. Why not permit a minority like the Untouchables to determine what kind of electorate is necessary for its protection ? If the Untouchables decide to have separate electorates why should their choice not prevail ? These are questions to which the Hindus can give no answer. The reason is that the real objection to separate electorates by the Hindus is different from this ostensible objection raised in the name of a nation. The real objection is that separate electorate does not permit the Hindus to capture the seats reserved for the Untouchables. (Ibid., 418–419)

This issue revolves around the question of agency and, as stated at the start of this section, is perhaps located around that of personhood. One might better understand what was at stake here if only one were to ask why the untouchables should not have represented themselves by themselves? That is, without a joint electorate where their choice of representatives would be compromised by the *savarna* Hindu voters. Or more importantly, (one might also ask) why Gandhi should have sought to so compromise the coming of age of the dalit subject/person by confining him/her within the electoral exercise (patronage?) of the community of the Hindu voters? Regards the first question, it seems apparent that the modern self first appeared in India in the shape of the so-called out caste/*avarna*. It was natural enough for that modern dalit self to see his/her own identity (and indeed existence itself) as essentially bound up with being a person, i.e. being a subject and a bearer of rights and not of Hindu largesse. For making this movement towards modern identity/personhood (coming to be as a subject of the law), the untouchable felt the need to shake off all association with the oppressor who had denied him/her agency through the ages:

> If the social forces are to be prevented from contaminating politics and perverting it to the aggrandizement of the few and the degradation of the many then it follows that the political structure must be so framed that it will contain mechanisms which will bottle the prejudices…. (Ibid., 424)

> There can be no doubt that the Hindus have all these ages despised, disregarded and disowned the untouchables as belonging to a different and contemptible strata of society if not to a different race. (Ibid., 425)

The second question is more difficult to answer. This (one might recall) relates to why **Gandhi should have sought** to confine dalit identity by keeping the choice of the candidate to represent the dalit community within a joint electorate. Such an electorate became the method of keeping the so-called untouchable within the Hindu fold as far as the choice of political representatives was concerned. Properly speaking, this issue aligns with that of Gandhi's problematic position on *varna* and will be best responded to by the re-interpretation of Gandhi's position on *varna* across Sects. 4.2 and 4.3 of this chapter.

Mr. Gandhi and the Emancipation of Caste (1942) went on to make two more points, important to this debate, about the proper method for the abolishment of untouchability in India. The first of these takes on Gandhi's efforts to bring the village to the centre of the political re-construction of India. Ambedkar has argued here that:

It is the village system which perpetuates Untouchability… (Ibid., 419)

One might consider that the conflict between Gandhi and Ambedkar around villages and the related issue of temples (note the interesting history, and not *itihaas,* of the temple entry bill at the time) cannot properly be understood as a contest about the organization or reorganization of physical spaces alone. When Ambedkar rejected the village, he did not only disregard the village as an antiquated/inadequate physical space to relocate attention to the city (of amenities and buildings) as it were. The point was more substantial, and it served to emphasize the fact that their respective approaches to such physical space—as it housed temples and villages— became critical to bringing out the differences in their approach to the eradication of untouchability. Gandhi thought from within the old-world mind of India as he sought to retain a continuity with the traditional precolonial communities of India. One way to seek such a continuity was to keep the age old organization of physical (and sacred) space intact in the form of villages and temples. One could argue that such physical continuity in the organization of space was (to Gandhi's mind) a source of (both geographical and spiritual) belonging for the self as it faced disorientation (spatial and spiritual) in modernity. It might be recalled that Gandhi was convinced that the self would be unable to draw all value from its individual inwardness and needed to *find* meaning (and belonging) as much from continuity in the organization of physical and spiritual space, as from that of traditional ideas and ideals.

However (in sharp contrast) for Ambedkar, the modern self in its absolutely indi-vidualistic inwardness drew its identity and all value from that very inwardness. Therefore, such continuity, for instance, in retaining the old-world organization of (physical and spiritual) space only served as a continuous source of embarrassment (and worse humiliation) rather than as an *a priori* source of continuity in the self's sense of itself. The modern dalit self (as it came of age in India) sought erasure here, as it did in the case of memory, history and caste, and replaced continuity with anonymity:

India is admittedly a land of villages and so long as the village system provides an easy method of marking out and identifying the untouchable, the untouchable has no escape from untouchability. (Ibid.)

The next important point that Ambedkar made in this text (his first in the trilogy against Gandhi) was that of raising the internal contradiction in Gandhi's struggle for *swaraj*. He argued that the struggle for freedom against colonialism suffered from an internal inconsistency given that it was a war to save the dominion of the Hindus over the so-called untouchables:

> Will Mr Gandhi and Hindus establish establish a new Order or will they be content with rehabilitation of the traditional Hindu India, with its castes and its untouchability, with its denial of Liberty, Equality and Fraternity? (Ibid., 429)

Ambedkar's final point in this text brought up the inter-relationship, between the concepts of agency and self-hood. It was in such a connection that Ambedkar raised problems with the *Harijan Sewak Sangh*. Ambedkar argued that the object of this *Sangh* was simply to distribute largesse in the form of "petty gifts to petty Untouchables" (Ibid., 431). The idea of distributing favours meant that untouchables were "to remain as Hindus… not as partners but as poor relations of the Hindus…" (Ibid.). This implied that Gandhi and the *Sangh* were actively involved in undermining Ambedkar's efforts to rebuild a modern dalit self on the demise of the untouchable Hindu self. The start of such rebuilding naturally involved a self that would consciously assume agency/personhood in coming to the realization that without such agency/personhood there would be no self at all.

The second text in this trilogy (of the indictment delivered by Ambedkar) was *Ranade Gandhi and Jinnah* (1943). This was an address that Ambedkar was able to deliver (unlike *Annihilation of Caste*) on the 101st birth anniversary of Justice Govind Ranade at the Gokhale Memorial Hall, Pune, on 18 January 1943. This address was as much about the unmaking of idols and heroes as it was about the precedence of social over political reform. Interestingly, Ambedkar begun this address with some thoughts about history and the role of great men in the making of history. As this was history and not *itihaas*, it became essential to **find** a measure to determine greatness so that the issue might be decisively settled. Criticizing both Marx and Henry Thomas Buckle, Ambedkar argued that "man …is a factor in the making of history and …environmental forces whether impersonal or social if they are the first are not the last things" (Ambedkar 2014, 1: 213). However, while he agreed that great men could play a role in history, Ambedkar was clear that one needed (retrospectively as a historian perhaps) to provide the measure of the great man. Ambedkar found such a measure in social reform judging its claims higher than those of mere political leadership, while adjudicating the role of great men, in history. As he put it

> A great man must be motivated by the dynamics of social purpose and must act as the scourge and scavenger of society. (Ibid., 215)

The die was decisively cast, and looking at history through this measure, the claims of Ranade to greatness, resting as they did on the claims to social reform, counted much higher than those who had merely been political leaders. Ambedkar responded to the critics who had discounted the claims of Ranade by arguing that Ranade's claims fell short against the measure of nationalism and the glory associated with the lives of those who responded to its demands. Ambedkar argued in Ranade's defence that while he had indeed regarded the presence of the British in India as providential, such a position would be retrospectively judged as necessary (by history) as "he had the wisdom to forsee the evils of a premature revolution" (Ibid., 235). On Ambedkar's reading of it, in fact, history would **find** both Gandhi and Jinnah falling short of Ranade who had given a precedence to social over political reform, given that they carried a "colossal egotism" (Ibid., 226) and more importantly that they had prioritized political over social reform. Such prioritization was not only pernicious (as it carried forward the Nietzschean rule of supermen) but also self-defeating in as much as democracy was "not a form of government it was … a form of society" (Ibid., 222).

The last text from Ambedkar which continues (as the very title suggests) to put together his indictment of Gandhi is *What Congress and Gandhi have done to the Untouchables* (1945). This text "records" across 11 chapters "the deeds of the Congress and Mr. Gandhi from 1917 to date in so far as they touch the problem of the Untouchables" (Ambedkar 2014, 9: Preface, iv). The book brings out Ambedkar's central difficulties with Gandhi's approach to untouchability—the insistence of treating the problem as an internal affair of the Hindus, the denial of agency to the untouchable self by keeping the work of the *Harijan Sewak Sangh* the prerogative of the high castes who became leaders of the so-called reform, the problems with Gandhi's critique of modernity and last (but most important) Gandhi's support for *varna*.

The first of these, Gandhi's insistence on treating the problem of untouchability as a religious problem and as a problem internal to the Hindu society, manifests itself (in this book) across two issues—representation and temples. The first issue was central to the famous clash between Gandhi and Ambedkar over the issue of separate electorates. It is interesting that Ambedkar himself had (in earlier years) argued against separate electorates, though from the perspective of democratic process. One might recall that in his statement before the Indian Statutory Commission in 1928 Ambedkar had argued against separate/communal electorates for the Muslims in the following words:

> ..it is a universally recognized canon of political life that the government must be by the consent of the governed….communal electorates are a violation of that canon. For, it is government without consent. It is contrary to all sense of political justice to approve of a system which permits the members of one community to rule other communities without their having submitted themselves to the suffrage of those communities. (Ambedkar 2014, 2: 354–355)

However, there was a very substantial shift in *What Congress and Gandhi have done to the Untouchables* (1945) in that Ambedkar now wrote that despite the fact that the Poona Pact gave the untouchables 148 seats (though the Communal Award had only given them 78) "…Mr. Gandhi was the most determined enemy of the Untouchables" (Ambedkar 2014, 9: 70). The central argument against joint electorates (at this time) was that "…if the Poona pact increased the fixed quota of seats it also took away the right to the double vote. This increase in seats can never be deemed to be a compensation for the loss of the double vote. The second vote given by the Communal Award was a priceless privilege. Its value as a political weapon was beyond reckoning … With this voting strength free to be used in the election of caste Hindu candidates, the Untouchables would have been in a position to determine, if not dictate, the issue of the general Election" (Ibid., 90).

There seem to have been two issues that Ambedkar had brought in here. The first was that of the political advantage conferred by the double vote—one in a separate electorate and the other in the joint electorate which (by a process of self-closure) could have transformed the untouchables into an independent power group in Indian politics. The second, more fundamental issue, was that of the uniqueness of individual agency and the related idea that the right to choose representatives, both from and for a caste/group, was not an "unrestricted right" (Ambedkar 2014, 2: 348). It only accrued properly to those who had "a certain social attitude as a condition precedent to" (Ibid., 349) the exercise of the right to choose a representative of that caste/group. This second point connects straightforwardly with Charles Taylor's account of the third feature in the making of modern identity (discussed in the last chapter) which, as noted earlier, was expressivism. It is important to recall (from Chap. 3 of this book) that, post the romantics, individual expression was understood as that which "helps to define what is to be realized" (Taylor 2001, 375). It is only by such articulation and by expression that the individual can realize/give a direction to his/her life. This seems to be a quintessentially modern notion. For moderns, an individual can only define and thereafter realize his/her own life by expressing choices/defining values for his/her own self and by his/her own self. Such expressivism leads to arguments about the importance of 'the right to speak' for oneself. It follows naturally enough that there should have been some thinking about restricting the right to choose one's own representatives (or to speak for oneself), as a group, by Ambedkar (and later of restricting the right to speak for dalits by modern dalit scholarship).

In its positive aspect, expressivism (as a defining element in the making of modern identity) defines the relationship between expression and self-identity. In its negative aspect, expressivism rejects as inauthentic the right of others to express what belongs to the unique experience of another. It follows that Ambedkar should have argued in 1945 that the right to vote for those who would serve to represent the interest of the untouchables could only accrue to those who had lived (without choosing to) the unique experience/life of the untouchables.

The second central issue in this text (the third in the trilogy) relates to the role of temple entry as part of the method to abolish untouchability from Hindu society. Ambedkar had declined to support the temple entry movement after September 1932. In explaining why he would not give support to the temple entry bill, Ambedkar had argued that the bill did not recognize untouchability as a "sin" (Ambedkar 2014, 9: 109). It is important to look at Ambedkar's argument explaining the position of the depressed classes towards the temple entry movement at this time:

What the depressed classes want is a religion, which will give them equality of social status….they have made up their mind not to tolerate a religion that will lend its support to the continuance of these inequities…The mere amendment of Hindu religious code by the mere inclusion in it of a provision to permit temple entry for all, cannot make it a religion of equality of social status….What is required is to purge it of the doctrine of Chaturvarna. That

is the root cause of all inequality and also the parent of the caste system and Untouchability…
(Ibid., 111–112).

Ambedkar brought this point home, in the last chapter of this text, titled "Gandhism: The Doom of the Untouchables". He also made several other arguments against Gandhi in this chapter. Notable here was his argument that Gandhi had become a defender of *varna* (since 1925) and that Gandhi's *varna* system was "simply a new name for the caste system" which had retained "all the worst features of the caste system" (Ibid., 297). In fact as Ambedkar explained Gandhi's system was even more pernicious as "with Mr Gandhi *varna* is determined by birth and the profession of a *varna* is determined by the principle of heredity…" (Ibid., 290).

With the coming to age of modern identity in the erstwhile so-called untouchable self, it seems obvious that Ambedkar should also have voiced his opposition of Gandhi's critique of modernity and of machines (as first put forth in *Hind Swaraj*) in this same chapter. Ambedkar dismissed Gandhi's arguments against modern civilization as:

…primitive. It is a return to nature…the practical instincts of men… have found them unfruitful …which society in search of progress has thought it best to reject. (Ibid., 283).

Ambedkar argued that the evils of machinery and modern civilization were "no argument against them" for they would be mitigated by appropriate "social organization" (Ibid.).

This chapter (the 11) of *What Congress and Gandhi have done to the Untouchables* completes the indictment of Gandhi's approach to the problem of untouchability. Ambedkar dismissed Gandhi, stating decisively, that Gandhism had also failed to ameliorate the economic and social condition of the untouchables. He explained that this was natural enough as all that Gandhi had offered was the change from caste to *varna*:

The social ideal of Gandhism is either *caste* or *varna*….there can be no doubt that the social ideal of Gandhism is not democracy (Ibid., 286).

In the same strain, Ambedkar explained that the economics of Gandhism was "hopelessly fallacious" (Ibid., 283). Machinery and modern civilization offered the possibility of leisure and of "emancipating man from leading the life of a brute" (Ibid., 284). Gandhi's trusteeship did nothing to eliminate the class structure of society and was in fact "ridiculous" (Ibid., 286).

Perhaps, Gandhi's indictment is best recalled in Ambedkar's famous last words from this book:

Good God! Is this man Gandhi our Saviour? (Ibid., 297)

4.2 Absolute Equality: Gandhi on the *Bhagavad Gita*

By far, the most disturbing thing about Gandhi (as appears apparent enough from the last section) seems to be the position he took on caste and *varna*. To a superficial reader making a piecemeal study of Gandhi's life and work, Gandhi seemed to have stubbornly insisted upon locating the abolishment of untouchability in the religious domain. As Nagraj has pointed out, Gandhi had tried, by a process of "dual identification" to "identify simultaneously both with caste Hindu society and the untouchable" (Nagraj 2015, 70). Gandhi's insistence on the religious dimension of the problem of untouchability has been read into his retention of a hopelessly idealistic (indeed unrecognizable) form of *varna*. Commentators on the Gandhi–Ambedkar debate have read Gandhi's insistence on such an idealistic reading of *varna* as at best strategic and at worst a conservative/orthodox appeal to *maryada*/limit.

Why should Gandhi's views on caste and *varna* (which as Nishikant Kolge brings out evolved through five stages in his life) seem disturbing? Why, for instance, may we not write him off (in line perhaps with Roy 2014) as an unjust man? For one, this last becomes difficult given his life and practice. Gandhi had abjured all discriminations in his life and practice. He had adopted an untouchable girl as his daughter in South Africa, taken up spinning as a national programme which (one might recall) was an occupation traditionally restricted to lower castes. Gandhi was also, by choice, a skilled scavenger. However, what dismantled the critique of Gandhi most decisively (even perhaps more than Gandhi's practice) were his arguments about equality. Gandhi made his arguments about an equality that comes before freedom in his several comments on the *Gita*. In this section, I will therefore go back to those comments and to the *Gita*. I will argue that far from invoking *maryada*/limits (in the manner perhaps of Tilak in the *Bhagavad Gita Rahasya*) Gandhi counters the orthodox, in these comments, by reading the *Gita* as a text about absolute equality rather than as one about limits/*maryada*. I will suggest that the burden and dominant tone in Gandhi's *Discourses on the Gita*[ii] and the *Anasaktiyoga* are absolute equality and that Gandhi uses his several comments on the *Gita* to make eight arguments about such an absolute equality.

By far, the most important question for those seeking to understand Gandhi is why at all he should have sought for a solution to untouchability by treating it as essentially a religious matter, i.e. as one that required an interpersonal conversation within Hinduism between the oppressed and the oppressors? One could argue (with his critics) that this question could be answered solely in terms of the electoral politics of numbers and the desire to retain untouchable seats within the Hindu fold. However, one might **find** insights that point beyond a politics of numbers, by going back to the arguments in the last chapter, which had unpacked Gandhi's understanding of the self in continuity with tradition. Given that Gandhi did not share the modern understanding of the inwardness of the self as the source of all value, he sought to keep the *a priori* continuity of the self as a part of his/her *itihaas* essentially unbroken. This led him to seek reform rather than annihilation of tradition. In the moral life, such a search for reform of tradition and continuity, expressed itself, as a commitment to *swadeshi* understood as a moral obligation to commit oneself to one's immediate surroundings. Though, often understood in a primarily economic context, *Swadeshi* in Gandhi went very much further. It expressed the keeping of a commitment to one's family, neighbours, district, country, world going outwards in (by now famous Gandhi's) concentric circles. The practice of *swadeshi* as a virtue in one's moral quest committed the human being in matters of religion to a reform of the religion of his/her ancestors rather than attempting its total rejection/annihilation. Such *swadeshi* was only symptomatic of Gandhi's deep philosophical discomfort with the modern understanding of the self with its characteristic inwardness and obsessive individualism. One might profitably recall the argument from Taylor bringing out the sources of modern identity (from Chap. 3 of this book) in this regard.

Why did Gandhi feel the need to comment on the *Gita* as part of his own practice of *swadeshi* in religion? One might see the beginnings of an answer if one would consider that the two texts—Gandhi's *Discourses on the Gita* (and indeed also and by extension Gandhi's *Anasaktiyoga)* and Ambedkar's *Annihilation of Caste*—present an ideational site for the philosophical encounter between the old-world mind of India and the modern Indian self seeking to become a citizen of the republic. Can one then retrospectively adjudicate between these texts and speak of the relative merits of the traditional self-understanding *vis-a-vis* the making of modern identity in India? How, at best, can philosophy itself seek to answer such questions? It might serve here to recall Nagel's insights into the task of philosophy:

> I do not know whether it is more important to change the world or to understand it, but philosophy is best judged by its contribution to the understanding, not to the course of events (Nagel 2002, xiii).

The object here then is not an engagement with the world of events but engagement with the world of ideas. More specifically, with Gandhi's world of ideas; and with attempting to understand why he could possibly have taken the position that he did on caste and *varna*. Section 4.2.1 will look at six arguments about equality made across Gandhi's *Discourses on the Gita* and the *Anasaktiyoga*. Section 4.2.2 will put forth Gandhi's seventh and eighth arguments about equality. In this context, the section will discuss Gandhi's reading of *yajna* or sacrificial action (recommended to the Hindus as bodily labour) and argue that this understanding of *yajna* worked against the traditional understanding of the *varna vyavastha*. The last section of this chapter, "Gandhi on Caste and *Varna:* Responding to Ambedkar", will seek to philosophically unpack Gandhi's position on untouchability and *varna* in all its powerful dissonances from Ambedkar.

4.2.1 Samata, Samadarshana *and* Sambhava*: Six Arguments About Equality*

It might come as a surprise, especially to those familiar with Gandhi's detractors that Gandhi had thought seriously about equality. The insurrectionary Gandhi had sought to challenge the inegalitarianism of the orthodox Hindu (who had usurped the dominant sense of the Hindu text and tradition) by drawing arguments from within Hindu metaphysics and ethics as laid out in sacred texts like the *Gita*. He refused to leave Hinduism to the orthodox, as it were, and sought to challenge them from within the Hindu religious tradition. It is perhaps not surprising that this distanced

Gandhi from the orthodox and eventually perhaps led to his death.[iii] What is ironical, however, is that neither the orthodox nor their severest critics can take Gandhi as one of their own. Note, for instance, that most radical critics of Gandhi align him with Hindu orthodoxy. Aishwary Kumar (2015), for example, argues that Gandhi came to "reconceptualize the relationship between force and obligation, between *bal* and *dharma*, distilling much of it in the 1920s through his *Discourses on the Gita*" (Kumar 2015, 91). The burden of Kumar's argument against Gandhi's treatment of untouchability is built around Gandhi's relationship with the Hindu tradition and texts like *Discourses on the Gita*. Kumar emphasizes that equality, for Gandhi, was aligned with measure/limit and that such measure was provided by *maryada dharma*. Such a confinement of equality within the limits of *maryada dharma* allowed Gandhi, Kumar argues, to think of equality as a civic virtue rather than as a political claim:

> Equality, Gandhi insisted, had to be presupposed rather than viewed as something that had to be fought for; equality was a civic virtue rather than a political claim. Thus, in sharp opposition to the revolutionary energies of young India, against which *Hind Swaraj* was composed, Satyagrahic action remained within the limits of a prohibitive equality, regulated by a firm ethics of measure. Gandhi would subsequently call this obligation to limit *maryada dharma*. (Ibid., 93)

Such an argument (which paraphrases several others made by Gandhi's critics) seems to be absolutely innocent of Gandhi's very serious engagements with equality throughout his *Discourses on the Gita*. It appears innocent of how much that engagement differed from the interpretation of other commentators on the *Gita*, as for instance, the one by Tilak[iv] (with which one might note Gandhi was familiar). I will argue that Gandhi's *Discourses on the Gita* was radical and insurrectionary even if they were not in the "revolutionary" (Ibid., 225) tenor of Ambedkar's *Annihilation of Caste*. The two texts Gandhi's *Discourses on the Gita* (and indeed Gandhi's *Anasaktiyoga* which was written in Gujarati in 1929) and Ambedkar's *Annihilation of Caste* (a decade apart in time from Gandhi's *Discourses*) were concerned with the conflict "between freedom and equality" (Ibid.). As Kumar has pointed out "the revolutionary Ambedkar's most insurrectionary demand" was that "Equality, then, must be made equal to freedom" (Ibid.). One must note that unlike Ambedkar and unlike the liberals (who put the triad—liberty, equality and fraternity together, each "equal" to the other as Kumar put it) the religious Gandhi put equality before freedom. This last might have seemed to **find** some support from the etymology of the term that Gandhi used to think freedom, i.e. *swaraj*/self-rule/self-restraint and his emphasis that such self-rule came before political freedom. However, Gandhi had laid forth his (eight) arguments about absolute equality in his *Discourses on the Gita* (and the 1929 *Anasaktiyoga*) challenging the orthodox proponents of *maryada dharma* at their own turf as it were. I will argue (in this and the next subsection) that Gandhi seemed to have written the commentaries on the *Gita* as part of his own practice of the virtue of *swadeshi*, which committed him as a Hindu to the reform of his religious tradition. The central reason behind Gandhi's writing the several comments on the *Gita*, including the *Discourses*, was perhaps to make conceptual space for the abolishment of untouchability, caste and *varna* from within Hindu *dharma*.

This last seems to **find** support from Gandhi's use of *samata, samadarshana* and *samabhava* (all referring to equality) in his *Anasaktiyoga* and *Discourses on the Gita*. All three terms come from the same Sanskrit root *sama* a word that shares an etymology with the English word 'same' and that has often been translated into English as equal or constant. Though I cannot claim much knowledge of Sanskrit, roughly translated, *samadarshana* means 'to see things with an equal eye despite inequalities', *Samabhava* means having the 'attitude of equality to things as they are/exist', and *samata* refers to 'the status of equality'. Gandhi employed all three of these terms in his arguments about equality in the comments on the *Gita*.

The first argument about equality that Gandhi makes in his *Discourses on the Gita* is that equality requires all individual's to treat others **as** absolutely equal in status/*samata*. Seeing people/things (who are absolutely equal) with an equal eye—*samadarshita*—is a constant theme in Gandhi. As early as 1909 in *Hind Swaraj* Gandhi spoke at length of the thief who came in to rob one's belongings and recommended that the reader should even treat a thief who had come in to rob his belongings as if he was his "father who has come to steal" (Gandhi 1888–1948, 10: 287) or "an ignorant brother" (Ibid., 289). In the *Discourses on the Gita,* Gandhi initiated the discussion on such an absolute equality by re-interpreting Shri Krishna's answer to Arjuna's question in line with *samabhava/* having the 'attitude of equality to things as they are/exist':

> It is important to consider what Arjuna's question was and what the circumstances were in which he raised it… (Gandhi 1888–1948, 37: 80).

It is at the very start of the text, in interpreting Arjuna's question, that Gandhi made his first argument about the absolute equality of the *Gita*. Gandhi recounts:

> Arjuna requests Shri Krishna to station his chariot between the two armies, so that he may see the warriors on the field.
>
> He sees that all of them are relatives and friends, whom one cannot easily bring oneself to kill.
>
> Arjuna says: "I do not see any good in killing one's kinsmen." The stress here is on "kinsmen". He says:
>
> "I would not fight against them, even for the kingdom of the three worlds; how could I, then, fight against them for a few clods of earth?" (Ibid., 79)

Reminding the Hindus, as it were, about the ethical implications of the espousal of a metaphysics of a *vedantic* oneness in sacred Hindu texts, Gandhi makes the observation:

> The first thing to bear in mind is that Arjuna falls into the error of making a distinction between kinsmen and outsiders. Outsiders may be killed even if they are not oppressors, and kinsmen may not be killed even if they are….The *Gita* permits no distinction between one's relations and others. (Ibid., 83)

As suggested, at the start of this chapter, Gandhi seemed (in 1926) to be pre-empting and addressing the arguments that Ambedkar went on to make in the 1936 *Annihilation of Caste*. One might be tempted to reject the idea that Gandhi's response to untouchability (initiated in the *Discourses* in 1926) was motivated by a politics of numbers if one notes that Gandhi spoke to arguments from the much later *Annihilation of Caste* (which came ten years later) as early as 1926. In this context, one might note Ambedkar's comment from the 1936 *Annihilation of Caste*:

> The capacity to appreciate the merits in a man apart from his caste does not exist in a Hindu. There is appreciation of virtue but only when the man is a fellow caste-man... My caste-man, right or wrong; my caste-man, good or bad. It is not a case of standing by virtue and not standing by vice. (Ambedkar 2014, 1: 57)

It might be philosophically useful here to consider one more figure, that of Tilak, only to recall how he had interpreted Arjuna's question in the *Bhagavad Gita Rahasya* his own commentary on the *Bhagavad Gita*. It is surely significant that Gandhi had read Tilak's commentary:

> I went reverently through the Gujarati translation of the Lokamanya's great work. He had kindly presented me with the Marathi original and the translations in Gujarati and Hindi, and had asked me, if I could not tackle the original, at least to go through the Gujarati translation. (Gandhi 1888–1948, 46: 165)

Perhaps, a comparison with Tilak's commentary on the *Gita* (of which Gandhi had clearly made a study and therefore knew he was departing from) might serve to bring out the Gandhi who seemed radically insurrectionary to the orthodox Hindu. It is in the *Discourses on the Gita* that one sees this somewhat critical Gandhi as he dismantles orthodox readings and radically re-interprets the text. One might recall Tilak on Arjuna's despondency and Sri Krishna's advice to him:

> The blessed Lord is telling Arjuna to fight, having regard to what his 'dharma' is,... it is better to die performing one's caste duties; following the duties enjoined on another caste is dangerous. (Tilak 1935, 89)

There is clearly a radical theoretical shift between Tilak's interpretation that Sri Krishna asks Arjuna to shake of his despondency to perform the duties enjoined by his caste and, Gandhi's alternative understanding, that Sri Krishna asks Arjuna to abjure the discrimination between kinsmen and others. It is here that one can perhaps locate the discomfort/threat that the orthodox might have felt with Gandhi. For Gandhi translated the notion of equality, from that of an equality before law to an equality that could be practiced; an equality of regard between one's own and others, by bringing it home to the *Gita*, too close for comfort, as it were. This was the absolute equality which (in Gandhi's understanding) Sri Krishna had spoken about when he had answered Arjuna's question in the *Gita*:

> He (Arjuna) simply raised the question of distinction between kinsmen and others, in the same way that a fond mother would advance arguments favoring her child. (Gandhi 1888–1948, 37: 86)

> To this question whether one ought not to make an exception in regard to relations, he gets an unambiguous answer. (Ibid.)

Gandhi remained emphatic that, in his very first response to Arjuna in the *Bhagavad Gita*, Sri Krishna had enjoined that it was incumbent on the Hindu to see every "other" (human or animal) with *samadarshita/*an equal eye, that is, as an absolute equal and thereby entitled to equal deference/regard. Such an absolute equality was brought home by Gandhi, by bringing in examples from the family and indeed from caste and *varna* in the term "kinsmen" as evidenced in the quotation above. Given the claims that Gandhian *ahimsa*/ non-violence made on an individual's thought, speech and action, Gandhi brought a radical fervour to his arguments about equality when he had observed (somewhat uncharacteristically) in this context:

> …should it be necessary to cut off, with a sword, one's fathers head, one must do so… **if one would be ready to cut off anyone else's head** in similar circumstances. (Ibid., 83) (the highlighting is mine and not present in Gandhi's original text)
>
> You will incur no sin by killing your kinsmen (Ibid., 96).

Making much the same point but interchanging the position of the father and child, Gandhi wrote in the same text:

> Suppose that your father was a teacher, that you and… misbehaved in the same way and your father punished …but not you; would that be right? Arjuna did what even a child like you does. Shri Krishna told him all this long argument of the *Gita* just to explain this. (Ibid., 91)
>
> We should merely cure the fever of a member of our family, but try to discover the cause of the fever from which the whole world is suffering and remove the cause. (Ibid., 214)

This might be the appropriate moment to recall Bernard Williams on equality. In Chap. 14 of *The Problems of the Self* (1999), Williams discusses the idea of equality. The idea of equality (as Williams has explained) is used both in statements of fact, or what purport to be statements of fact—that men **are** equal—; and in statements of political principles or aims—that men **should be** equal, though at present they are not equal, in terms of the way things are in the world. These two are frequently combined as it were, when one argues in favour of bringing about a state in which human beings are treated as what they are (but not yet treated as being) equal. Williams argued that in both these senses, the idea of equality faces difficulties: in the first—that men are equal—the statements in which equality figures are perceived as being too strong, and in the second—that men ought to be equal—as being much too weak. In practice, it is hard to **find** a satisfactory interpretation that lies between the two interpretations. Williams argues that the idea that human beings should be treated as equal is only apparently trivial. Quite to the contrary, it, serves to remind us that human beings share "obvious human characteristics" (Williams 1999, 233) and should be treated as equal on account of their common humanity. By virtue of the fact, for instance, that they share human characteristics and "moral ability or capacity, the capacity for virtue or achievement of the highest kind of moral worth" (Ibid., 234).

In the *Discourses on the Gita*, Gandhi seemed to be making a somewhat similar argument though he made an appeal to existence itself (rather than to obvious human characteristics) as common between **all things that exist**, to the effect, that all things that exist (and not just human beings) should be treated as absolutely equal. Gandhi employed this argument at its most dramatic, of course, using examples from the family and from kinship to bring home the point. He argued, in his *Discourses*, that a person "… a *samadarshi* will …" have an "equal regard for all" (Gandhi1888–1948,

37: 212). It is significant that Gandhi's absolute equality is expressed as a demand for a complete interchangeability in the objects of one's regard. As he argues:

> The yogi is not one who sits down to practice breathing exercises; he is one who looks upon all with an equal eye, sees other creatures in himself. Such a one attains moksha. To look upon all with an equal eye means to act towards others as we would towards ourselves (Ibid., 228).

Perhaps, Gandhi's emphatic insistence that the practice of equality demanded that the individual **finds** herself/himself capable of such an absolute interchangeability between different human beings as objects of one's regard (and indeed between human and non-human objects of one's regard) emerged from the context in which Gandhi found himself. This was a context in which the preponderance of caste and *varna* had made for **discrimination in regard/deference** between those who were one's kin and those outside one's caste/not one's kin.

Gandhi's **second important argument** for equality (in his 1929 commentary on the *Gita* the *Anasaktiyoga*) was no less dramatic, and it connected *samadarshita/* "to see things with an equal eye despite inequalities" with *samabhava* and *samata/* status of equality. In 1929, Gandhi spoke of an "Equimindedness" (Gandhi 1888–1948, 50: 102). Mahadev Desai, the translator of Gandhi's *Anasaktiyoga,* had paraphrased *samabhava* into English as "treating alike". Earlier in his translation of Gandhi's *Autobiography* (into English), Desai had translated *samabhava* as "equability". Gandhi had rendered *samadarshanah* in verse 18 of Chap. 5 of his commentary on the *Bhagavad Gita,*[v] the *Anasaktiyoga,* as *samadrishti/*looking "with an equal eye".[vi] The verse in Gandhi's text goes as follows:

> The men of self-realization look with an equal eye on a Brahmana possessed of learning and humility, a cow, an elephant, a dog and even a dog eater. (Gandhi 1888–1948, 46: 191)

Gandhi explained the verse in the following words:

> That is to say, they serve every one of them alike, according to the needs of each. Treating a Brahmana and *shwapaka* (dog-eater) alike means that the wise man will suck the poison off a snake-bitten *shwapaka* with as much eagerness and readiness as he would from a snake-bitten Brahmana (Ibid.)

The verse above is telling because it speaks of treating alike and brings in the corporeality of touching, in fact, of sucking the poison out. Gandhi adds that this verse recommends *samabhava/*equability. In rendering *samadarshana/* 'to see things with an equal eye despite apparent inequalities' as *samabhava/* 'the attitude of equality to things as they are/exist', Gandhi differed radically from Ramanuja's reading of the *Bhagavad Gita*. In his comments on the *Bhagavad Gita,* Gandhi had been conscious of, and indeed expressed some dissatisfaction with, the readings of other scholars including perhaps the commentaries of Tilak and that of Ramanuja (the renowned scholar of the *Viśiṣtadvaita Vedanta* system of Indian philosophy). He noted, for instance, at one point that:

> Some interpret this verse in a different way, but we shall not go into that. (Gandhi 1888–1948, 37: 104)

   Though as seen above Gandhi had expressed his dissatisfaction with the readings of other scholars, he had not explained the reasons for such dissatisfaction. Ajay Skaria has insightfully suggested that Gandhi might have been dissatisfied with the way in which Ramanuja and others had interpreted the idea of equality in the *Gita*. Drawing on the distinction between different levels of reality made in the *Vedanta* system of philosophy, in his commentary of the *Gita* (the *Gita Bhasya*), Ramanuja says: "A person who has brought his *atman* into yoga, will see similarity in all *atmans* when separated from *prakriti* (material nature); …" (Skaria 2016, 207). In terms of Ramanuja's argument, one could say that equality between human beings rested on the fact that unequal things and persons could be seen to be really the same when abstracted from their present existence and seen at the rarefied level of what may be called the absolute reality/*paramarthika satta*. It seems clear enough that on any such reading of the *Gita* it is the sameness of the *atman/soul* at the level of absolute reality that makes partiality and inequality impossible at the level of everyday existence. Ajay Skaria has suggested that in Gandhi's alternative reading of *samadarshana/*seeing things with an equal eye despite inequalities as *samabhava/*attitude of equality to things as they are, "the equality of the *atman/soul* can no longer comfortably co-exist in separation and abstraction from the inequality of (material nature) to draw on Ramanuja's word" (Ibid., 208). This argument suggests that, for Gandhi, human and non-human beings are absolutely equal in terms of (and **in) the here and now**, and not only, when and if, considered in abstraction as rarefied souls without bodies/*atmans*.
   Gandhi's arguments about equality were clearly meant to counter other, more prominent, readings of the *Gita* in his own time. For instance, as pointed out earlier, the one by Tilak where the theory of *karma* was philosophically employed to argue that present inequality in the material world could be seen as consistent with absolute equality at the level of the *atman/*souls without bodies. Note, for instance, Tilak on *karma* in his commentary on the *Gita*:

   …karma is the activity which is to be seen in the fundamental quality-less Brahman, at the time when the visible world began to be created. (Tilak 1935, 365)

Further "the ordinary rules according to which man has to suffer the results of karma…" (Ibid., 366) harmonize inequalities in the here and now with absolute equality at the level of absolute reality. Tilak explains:

   In the same way, the fact of one person being born a beggar, and another being born in the family of a king, has also to be explained by the theory of karma; and according to some this is the proof of the theory of karma. (Ibid., 368)

Such inequalities in the here and now are inevitable on such a reading simply because:

   …whatever we are now doing is the result of the commenced karma, that is to say, of that portion of accumulated karma, which we have commenced to suffer for. (Ibid., 375)

Gandhi rejects all such arguments and emphasizes that all beings are equal **in the here and now**:

It is only if we have the faith in our hearts that we are all one, though we exist as separate beings, it is only then that we can feel a sense of equality. Otherwise even two leaves are not equal. (Gandhi 1888–1948, 37: 100–101)

Gandhi's **third argument about equality** made in the *Discourses* concerned the deeply contested issue of eligibility for the reading of sacred texts. Since there is an absolute freedom in the world of ideas and texts can pre-emptively answer arguments, even where the arguments have not yet been made, one might move ten years ahead in time to 1936, to Ambedkar's arguments, in the *Annihilation of Caste*. In his Introduction to that lecture, Ambedkar writes:

According to the *Shastras* the Brahmin is appointed to be the Guru for the three *varnas*…The *Shastras* do not permit a Hindu to accept any one as his Guru merely because he is well versed. (Ambedkar 2014, 1: 37)

He goes on to recount that:

The Hindus are taught that the Brahmins are *Bhudevas* (Gods on earth)… Manu says 'If it be asked how it should be with respect to points of the Dharma which have not been specially mentioned', the answer is that which Brahmins who are Shishthas propound doubtless have legal force. (Ibid., 71)

Gandhi seemed to have pre-empted Ambedkar's arguments as he argued in 1926 that the *Gita* had laid down the eligibility of all castes and genders with regard to itself:

The *Gita*…was written not for the learned, but for all the four castes,--rather, all the eighteen castes—to read and understand. It was written for the Sudras, the Bhangis, and the women—in fact, for all classes. (Gandhi 1888–1948, 37: 92)

Moving beyond the issue of mere eligibility to read sacred texts (in making **a fourth** argument about equality), Gandhi rendered the ability to acquire spiritual knowledge in egalitarian terms:

It is stated in the *Gita* itself that everyone, whether a woman, a vaisya or a Sudra can acquire spiritual knowledge if they have devotion to God. (Ibid., 76)

The Lord has given a great assurance to the world in these verses. This is His reply to those learned in the Vedas. Such persons argue that …women, Vaisyas and Sudras cannot attain moksha…Shri Krishna says here that, …Anyone who, …knows the Brahman, and has a pure heart is certain to attain this state. (Ibid., 265)

On Gandhi's understanding of the *Gita*, the *Gita* itself argues that spiritual knowledge does not lie in deciphering the meanings of abstruse passages in sacred texts but lies instead in developing a "yoga of intellect" (Ibid. 105) and in realizing an absolute humility in oneself. This path is one equally open to all, and Gandhi was emphatic in his insistence that "The *Bhagavad Gita* says that women, Vaisyas and Sudras, all classes of people, can win freedom" (Ibid., 121).

Such an emphatic egalitarianism derived from the conviction that "Vyasa has run down the Veda…" he gave "the description of an intellect not fixed on one aim" (Ibid., 101). Gandhi recounted that Vyasa had declared that "Ignorant people, that is people who are learned and yet devoid of knowledge …wrangle over the meaning of the Vedas" (Ibid.). The key to a resolute intellect (in this text) lies instead in the realization of an absolute equality for "Only one who has a spirit of extreme humility" who accords himself no superiority "can be said to have a resolute intellect" (Ibid., 102).

In support of this point, referring to the verse 45 in Chap. 2, that "The Vedas have as their domain the three *gunas*, eschew them, O Arjuna" (Ibid., 103). Gandhi had argued that "Shri Krishna is here talking about the Vedas as expounded by the ritualist pedants" (Ibid.). Unlike other commentators (unlike Tilak for instance), Gandhi had argued that Sri Krishna did not mean to recommend (here) that the devotee should rise above the *gunas,* as in the concerns of empirical life. To the contrary, (Gandhi argues that) Sri Krishna meant to suggest that the devotee must rise **above ritualistic concerns** and the opposition inherent in emotions. Such a reading prompted Gandhi to emphasize that the *sthitaprajna*/person of steady intellect of the *Gita* referred to that person who had overcome extremes of attachment and more importantly of aversion:

> *Sthitaprajna* means a person who has become completely free from attachments and aversions. (Ibid.,126)

Gandhi's egalitarianism extended beyond the eligibility to read the Vedas and the possibility of achieving salvation. It extended beyond limits/measure to the dismantling of the *varna vyavastha* itself as traditionally understood. Though Gandhi remained a defender of the *varna vyavastha* till the last phase [note Kolge's division of the five time periods in terms of which Gandhi's position on *varna* ought to be read (Kolge 2017, 101)], his understanding of the same was far from traditional. It was in the *Discourses on the Gita* that Gandhi made his most insurrectionary (**and fifth**) argument to dismantle the *varna vyavastha* with a radical re-interpretation of the term "varna". One might recall Ambedkar in the *Annihilation of Caste*:

> A close examination of this ideal has convinced me that as a system of social organization, Chaturvarnya is impracticable, harmful and has turned out to be a miserable failure. (Ambedkar 2014, 1: 59)

Gandhi's own re-interpretation of *varna* was initiated in 1926 in the *Discourses on the Gita.* In fact, one might even argue that Gandhi perhaps sought to comment on the *Gita* primarily to reject caste and re-interpret *varna* in the context of the attempt to abolish untouchability. Note that he wrote in 1926:

> …a Kshatriya should have the qualities of a Brahmin, Yudhisthira Ramachandra, etc., were Kshatriyas but possessed the virtues of Brahmins. Bharat was the very ideal of what a Brahmin should be. In this way every individual should display in varying measure, the qualities associated with all … (Gandhi 1888–1948, 37: 323).

Gandhi argued here and elsewhere (in the booklet *Varnavyavastha* that he wrote in 1934, for instance) that each individual presented in herself/himself the qualities of all the four *varna*s. Gandhi might have drawn sources for such a radical rethinking, from the (by then) notorious *Purushasukta* hymn of the *Rigveda*:

> The idea of superiority and inferiority is repugnant to the elementary principles of morality
> …the very first mention of the *Varna* in the Vedas likens the four *varna*s to the four main
> parts of the body. (Gandhi 1888–1948, 65: 92)

Just as the *varna*s were likened to parts of a single body in the *Purushasukta* hymn,
so Gandhi had argued in the September of 1934[vii] (two years before Ambedkar's
Annihilation of Caste) that all the four *varna*s are present in one and the same person,
as/and, to the extent that the person concerned exhibits the characteristic qualities
thereof:

> The four varnas have been compared in the Vedas to the four members of the body, and no
> simile could be happier. If they are members of one body, how can one be superior or inferior
> to another? If the members of the body had the power of expression and each of them were
> to say that it was higher and better than the rest, the body would go to pieces. Even so, our
> body politic, the body of humanity, would go to pieces, if it were to perpetuate the canker
> of superiority or inferiority… (Gandhi 1888–1948, 65: 66).

In the *Discourses* and in his reply to Ambedkar's *Annihilation of Caste*, Gandhi
added to such an idealistic version of *varna* by bringing in the notion of absolute
equality in remuneration (**making a sixth argument for an absolute equality**).
This seemed to initiate a radical (somewhat idealistic) dismantling of the connection
between economic privilege and *varna* dharma. Gandhi writes:

> The *Gita*, therefore, tells us that if, giving up attachment to the ego, we attend to the best of
> our ability to the task which has fallen to our lot, an emperor's work and that of one who
> cleans lavatories will be esteemed of equal worth… (Gandhi 1888–1948, 37: 178)

Taking note of Gandhi's comments in the reply to Ambedkar's *Annihilation of
Caste*:

> The law of *varna* teaches us that we have each of us to earn our bread by following the
> ancestral calling…It also follows that there is no calling too low and none too high. All
> are…absolutely equal in status…and their due performance carries equal merit before God
> and at one time seems to have carried identical reward before man. Both were entitled to
> their livelihood and no more. (Gandhi 1888–1948, 69: 226)

However, by far the most insurrectionary move (and seventh argument) to
dismantle *varna* came from Gandhi's rethinking of the *yajna* of the *Bhagavad Gita*.
The **seventh and eighth** arguments about equality in Gandhi's comments on the *Gita*
will form the subject of the next subsection.

4.2.2   Yajna/*Scavenging for All: Two Additional Arguments About Equality*

This section will argue that Gandhi's **seventh argument about equality** which
served to dismantle the traditional understanding of the *varna vyavastha* was
connected with the recommendation that *karma*/action ought to be performed in
a spirit of *yajna*/sacrifice without any thought for the fruit of the action that had

fallen to one's lot. Gandhi argued that the *yajna*/sacrifice of the *Gita* did not refer to rituals or sacrificial duties falling to the four castes/*varna*s but rather to bodily labour. He argued, in fact, that the *Bhagavad Gita* had enjoined that all human beings ought to perform *yajna*/bodily/manual labour for the sustenance of the body and in service of the most distant 'others'. Such an insistence that work with one's hands was the appropriate task for all (irrespective of the traditional *varna* that each might have been born into) sought to transform the status conferred on those performing bodily labour, and the most important of such labour, scavenging. Gandhi argued at many places that *yajna* of the *Gita* had enjoined bodily labour. He argued that such bodily labour could be best performed by making scavenging obligatory for all. This was Gandhi's most audacious egalitarian move (and the seventh argument in the context of this chapter), for in one sweep, it did away with the occupational division at the heart of the traditional *varna vyavastha*.

Having put together seven arguments about equality in Gandhi's *Discourses on the Gita* (and the *Anasaktiyoga*), one might take a moment to recapitulate Gandhi's understanding of the central argument of the *Gita*. Gandhi was clear that the *Gita* made its argument in three parts/stages:

> The argument of the Bhagavad *Gita* falls into three parts (1) 'whence this weakness?' (Gandhi 1888–1948, 37: 97)

For Gandhi, Sri Krishna's reply to Arjuna's despondency (as already noted) was to tell Arjuna to dismantle distinctions and recommend an absolute equality between one's own kinsmen/fellow caste members/family members and "others".

> (2) Arjuna's questioning (Ibid., 97).

This pertained to the question whether he should kill his kinsmen? This last (Gandhi argued) was answered by Sri Krishna by recommending that all human beings should be treated as if they are absolutely equal and seen with an equal eye. **If one is ready to kill any human being in the same circumstances**, one ought not to **make an exception** for one's kinsmen.

> (3) Krishna explaining that the body and the *atman* are separate. Then follow the practical considerations-'what is one to do?' How is one to proceed having known that the *atman* is different from the body? This is the fourth stage in the argument. (Ibid.)

Gandhi had recounted that Sri Krishna had explained the distinction between the *atman* and the body and moved on to extort Arjuna to work without thought of the fruit/result:

> What type of person is he who works without worrying about the result? To answer this question, Shri Krishna describes the characteristics of such a person in Chap. 2 itself....If such a person still needs to do karma, it is only for serving others and not for his own sake....And so the Lord explains how to do karma, and thereafter he explains the secret of *bhakti*. (Understanding that),one's attachment to the body falls away, the *atman* becomes stronger and awakens more fully day by day, and ultimately one sees it in a divine vision. (Ibid., 341)

Gandhi made conceptual space to bring out the importance of action or *karma* and suggested that Chap. 3 of the *Bhagavad Gita* explains the meaning of *karma*. "It means, then, that the *atman*, joined to the ego, dwells in the body and does things. What we should do then was explained in Chap. 3. 'Service of others brings holy merit to one, and through harassment of others one incurs sin'…" (Ibid., 343). Gandhi went on to argue that performing one's *swadharma*/duty incumbent on oneself in a spirit of *yajna*/sacrifice for the service of others ought to involve bodily labour.

> If I run away from a task in despair,…I weave the bonds of karma round me…In this age, we do not have the means with which to measure ourselves. The *Gita* was composed to help us. It says that we should work like machines and pour our life into our work. (Ibid., 186–187)

Gandhi further clarified that by action which had come to be one's *swadharma* or duty incumbent on oneself the *Gita* had bodily labour alone in mind:

> That person who is described as doing *shariram* karma does not have to suffer the fruits of karma. (Ibid., 190)

> *Shariram* karma means karma for keeping the body alive.…The mind works for the *atman*, and so does the body, but we ought to undertake physical labour to maintain the body. Even the work of teaching cannot serve as a means to this purpose… (Ibid., 191).

It is in this context, Gandhi suggests, that the *Gita* speaks of *yajna*:

> 'Along with *yajna* the Lord created men'. Which type of *yajna* is meant here? Does the term have any special meaning? I think it has. The reference here is not to mental or intellectual work. Brahma did not ask human beings to multiply and prosper merely by working with their minds; what he meant was that they should do so through bodily *yajna*, by working with the body… Thus bodily labour is our lot in life; it is best, then, to do it in a spirit of service and dedicate it Shri Krishna… The verse, commencing with *sahayajna* then, talks of bodily *yajna*… This verse tells us that we should undertake bodily labour to do service. Man simply cannot live without such work. If he had not violated this law, he would not suffer as much as he does, the rich would not have become masters of immeasurable stores of wealth and the millions would not be suffering in poverty. God is a great economist… He wants us, therefore, to provide only for each day… If we want anything the next day, we must labour for it… (Ibid., 135–136).

Gandhi had explained the idea of *yajna* as bread labour:

> It is not recently that I have come to attach this meaning to *yajna*; I have understood it in that sense ever since I first read the *Gita*. What I read about the Russian writer Bondoref's (views on) 'bread labour' only confirmed my idea, …Labour in this context means bodily labour. He alone should eat who has labored for twelve hours…The one universal form of labour is agriculture and it should, therefore be looked upon as *yajna*. (Ibid., 139)

It is surely significant that in Gandhi's own *ashrams* obligatory bodily labour involved the cleaning of latrines. In 1930, he wrote from Yeravda jail:

> Bread labour is a veritable blessing to one who would observe Non-violence, worship Truth… Everyone must be his own scavenger. Evacuation is as necessary as eating; and the best thing would be for everyone to dispose of his own waste… I have felt for years, that there must be something radically wrong, where scavenging has been made the concern of a separate class in society…We should, from our very childhood, have the idea… that we are all scavengers… **Scavenging, …will help one to a true appreciation of the equality of man**. (Gandhi 1888–1948, 50: 59) (The emphasis here is my own and does not belong to the original text)

The last passage seems to make it clear that Gandhi self-consciously employed the connection between *yajna*, bodily labour and scavenging as the seventh argument for absolute equality in his comments on the *Gita*. It is noteworthy to look at another passage that also clarifies that while recommending agricultural labour for all Gandhi was aware that the work of agriculture had been traditionally confined to the *Sudras*:

> …In fact, Krishna tended cows as a boy in Nanda's family and did the work of a Sudra…in course of time those who were engaged in agriculture came to be regarded as Sudras. (Gandhi 1888–1948, 37: 265)

Once Gandhi had argued that the *Gita* had itself directed the Hindu to perform bodily labour every day as a *yajna*, it followed that the very basis of the traditional *varna vyavastha* (where the *Sudra* and the untouchables were those who performed the menial tasks) was discredited and dismantled. Post-1926, then Gandhi rejected caste and offered a completely idealistic version of *varna* linking it with equality of remuneration and often arguing that all the four *varna*s were present in each human being. Every human being, as he argued, was first and foremost a *Sudra* given that he/she had to perform bodily labour as a *yajna* without which he/she would be "a thief" (Ibid., 191).

One might once again appreciate the radical nature of such an understanding of *yajna* as bodily labour "which is done to serve others' good, but without causing suffering to any creature" (Ibid., 133) by returning to Tilak's commentary on the *Gita*, Tilak writes on *yajna*:

> The followers of the Karma-kāṇḍa, that is to say, the Mīmāṃsakas say that the observance of the four months, and of the sacrificial ritual, such as, the Jyotiṣṭoma-yajñá, etc., are the important doctrines of the Śruti religion; and that according to the Vedas, he alone will acquire release who performs that karma. Whoever he may be, he must not give up this sacrificial Karma; and if he does so, he must be taken to have abondened the Śruti religion… (Tilak 1935, 402)

Or as Tilak says:

> It is not that all this karma or sacrifice is to be performed only by Brahmins; and as even women and shudras are competent to perform all other Karma, except the Vedic sacrificial ritual, all the karma performed according to the classification of the four castes made by the writers of the Smṛti—e.g warfare by the kṣatriyas etc.–is also a yajñá (sacrifice); and the word yajñá has been used in this comprehensive meaning in these texts. Manu has said that whatever is proper for anyone, is his religious austerity. (Ibid., 404)

It is important to note that Gandhi was well aware of readings, such as the above, and it was such an awareness which led him to offer a different interpretation of *yajna* in the *Discourses on the Gita*. On a historical aside, one might note that even before Gandhi had written his *Discourses on the Gita* (and the *Anasaktiyoga*) Tilak had taken issue with Gandhi's understanding of the *Gita*. Tilak had also argued against Gandhi's interpretation of war in the *Mahabharata* as a metaphorical depiction of the struggle in individual moral life. He had written to Gandhi in 1920 in this regard saying that; "Politics is a game of worldly people and not of sadhus… and instead of the maxim *Akkodhen jine kordh* (conquer anger by non-anger) as preached by

Buddha, I prefer to rely on the maxim of Shri Krishna… (In whatever way men resort to Me, even so do I render to them). Both methods are equally honest and righteous but the one is more suited to this world then the other" (Tilak quoted in Skaria 2016, 196). On Tilak's reading sacrificial violence was interpreted by the *Gita* as righteous for it would ultimately do good to humanity. On such nationalist readings, the *Gita's nishkamakarma* came to mean disinterested action where violent means were morally transformed by being selflessly directed to the right end.

Gandhi took on all such orthodox views as the *purva paksha* or the opponent's view. He seemed to have Tilak's interpretation of *yajna* in mind, when he suggested that it was misleading to think that the *yajna* of the *Gita* referred to the performance of ritual as prescribed for the four castes or *varnas*:

> I cannot understand the idea that one can perform a *yajna* by lighting a few sticks. It does not do to say that doing so purifies the air. There are many other ways of purifying the air... But this is not the aim behind a *yajna*... If we think of the matter now, we shall see that burning sticks is no longer a form of bodily *yajna*. If we undertake any such *yajna* in this age and in this country, it is spinning... (Gandhi 1888–1948, 37: 137).

One needs to once again counter pose Gandhi's comments (as quoted above) with the very contrary understanding put forth by Tilak as he explains the most important aspect of *yajna*:

> The most important element in a yajñá is the giving up of mine-ness (mamatva) with reference to the object thrown into the sacrificial fire, by uttering the words: '*na mama*' (i.e., 'this is not for me'), at the time of the throwing... (Tilak 1935, 407).

Tilak went on to explain that those who performed karma or *yajna* with a desire for fruit "the pure orthodox ritualists, obtain non permanent reward in the shape of heaven etc., whereas the others, that is, the jnanins who perform all Actions by Jnana or with a desireless frame of mind, obtain permanent reward in the shape of release" (Ibid., 408).

One might argue that Gandhi did not shy away from the radical stance of the insurrectionary reformer though he did indeed fall short of Ambedkar's revolutionary move (in 1936) when the latter spoke of the annihilation of caste. Gandhi's arguments were insurrectionary, but they sought not to throw the baby away with the bath water as it were. Gandhi sought rather to save the Hindu tradition from what he condemned as "sin" (Gandhi 1888–1948, 63: 164), by subjecting it to a radical reform, in the light of the requirements of an absolute equality that had to be practised by each Hindu.

In both the *Anasaktiyoga* and his *Discourses on the Gita,* Gandhi made yet another **(the eighth) argument** about equality by emphasizing the need to follow Vyasa in rethinking the central terms/concepts of the *Gita* and of the *Shastras* themselves in the light of reason and morality. In terms of this argument, once it was accepted that the *Gita* itself had taught the lesson of critical re-interpretation of the *Shastras*, in the light of reason and morality, the reform of Hinduism by the purging of caste and *varna* would no longer be seen as disruptive of the integrity of its belief and practice.

Gandhi seemed to make this clear in the *Discourses*:

Even if Vyasa had defined the words which he used, we would ask why we should accept the meanings given by him... There is no harm in our enlarging the meaning of the word *yajna*, even if the new meaning we attach to the term was never in Vyasa's mind. We shall do no injustice to Vyasa by expanding the meaning of his words... (Gandhi 1888–1948, 37: 134).

Gandhi went on to suggest that it was possible that people in future "may see harm" (Ibid.) in some interpretations of terms as used in the sacred text and that in such a case "we may, and should, attach to it a meaning not intended by Vyasa" (Ibid.).

Gandhi argued that "If a *Shastra* is not supported by truth and non-violence, it may even be the means of our fall. As they say, we should swim in our father's well, not drown ourselves in it" (Ibid., 311).

Gandhi took on the orthodox, headlong, as it were, to argue (**in the eighth argument being considered here**) that re-interpretation of the sacred text was a religious duty of the devout:

So many things were interpolated into the *Shastra*s in the course of time, but we have gone on believing that everything in them is divinely inspired. By doing this we make ourselves mere pedants. *Veda* means to know... Ignorant people... wrangle over the meaning of the Vedas... (Ibid., 101).

Commenting on the other Gujarati readings on the *Gita* opposed to his own, Gandhi suggested that the differences in interpretation (between readings of the *Gita*) had arisen on account of very different understandings of the relationship between the knowledge of religious truths and the experience of those truths in the practice of a good human life. On this view, the problem with many readings was that the interpreters had not read the texts with a view to living out the truths in them. Gandhi wrote "I am not aware of the claim made by the translators of enforcing their meaning of the *Gita* in their own lives" (Gandhi 1888–1948, 46: 166). Gandhi had time and again re-iterated that the proper or rightful manner of interpreting religious texts was by reading the eternal truths in them in the light of being able to live them out in one's moral life. As he said, "We should understand the meaning of the words in the *Gita* not merely to satisfy our curiosity but with the aim of putting its teaching into practise... We should leave alone what we cannot put into practise. It is a misuse of our intellectual energy and a waste of our time to go on reading what we cannot put into practise" (Gandhi 1888–1948, 37: 208). One can get a clear indication of what it was, that was to be put into practice, in order to arrive at the true meaning of the *Gita* by looking at Gandhi's comment in the *Discourses on the Gita*:

Wherever we *find* anyone,...who suffers when others suffer and who practises the supreme *yajna* of maintaining a sameness of attitude towards all, there we may be sure that *Brahman* is present. (Ibid., 141)

In Gandhi's understanding, the test of the text itself (its veracity) laid in putting what it taught into practice and the only way to put it into practice was by growing into a *samadarshita* that comes from the recognition of *samata*. That is from treating all others with a sameness that comes from the recognition that all embodied souls/indeed all things in the cosmos are equal in the here and now. One gets a sense of what might be involved in putting the moral concepts of a religious text into practice, if one reads, Gandhi on Chapter VI of the *Gita*. Gandhi brings in here the distinction between *jnana* and *vijnana*. In this passage, one gets a sense of the constant interrelation between faith, reason (tradition constitutive and tradition constituted and hence analogous, but not identical to, the reason of the liberals) and experience in interpreting religious texts for the practice of a religious and good human life:

> *Jnana* is understanding through reason, and *vijnana* is that knowledge which sinks through reason into experience. *Jnana* is knowledge obtained from the *Shastras*, whereas *vijnana* is knowledge which is part of one's experience. Non-violence will have become direct experience for us in this sense when our whole life comes to be permeated with the spirit of compassion, when non-violence manifests itself in us in its true essence… He whose *atman* is filled to perfect contentment with such *jnana* and *vijnana*… To such a yogi, clay, stone and gold, all are equal… If we shed greed we would look upon all these articles with the same eye. (Ibid., 219)

Gandhi comments on Chap. 6 verse 9 of the *Gita* in the following passage:

> He who has the same regard for friend and foe, for one who deserves to be hated and one who is a kinsmen….as he would have for clay and gold, he may be said to have won the battle of this life. (Ibid., 220)

It is to such *samadarshita* that Gandhi turns again and again to locate the chief teaching of the *Gita* in an absolute equality. He clarifies that the *samadarshi's* "men of knowledge, see all things with an equal eye" (Ibid., 211). Those who question Gandhi's frequent references to the non-human world alongside references to the *Brahmins* and *Sudras* could be referred to the following passage:

> …the yogi (the *samadarshi*) sees himself in others, means the same thing as this. Ganga water in separate vessels is Ganga water after all (Ibid., 211). (The brackets here are my own addition.)

Gandhi's understanding of *varna* then is best put in his own words from *Harijan* 25-3-1933, written three years before the *Annihilation of Caste*.

> …today Brahmins and Kshatriyas, Vaisyas and shudras are mere labels. There is utter confusion of *varna*s as I understand it, and I wish that all Hindus voluntarily call themselves shudras. That is the only way to demonstrate the truth of Brahmanism and revive varnadharma in its true state. Because all Hindus may be classed as shudras, wisdom and power and wealth will not disappear, but they will all be used for the service of not a sectional religion but the service of Truth and Humanity. (Gandhi 1888–1948, 60: 149)

4.3   Gandhi on Caste and *Varna:* Responding to Ambedkar

As brought out in the previous chapter, Gandhi had thought about the relationship between the memory of (racial, religious or caste) oppression and individual self-identity very differently from Ambedkar. For one, he thought that the memory of past oppression should be overcome and the manner of overcoming it should be such that the oppressed must transcend the need to hate and punish the oppressor. Secondly, he thought that *ahimsa* as love, expressed in the act of overcoming hate, would transform not only the oppressor but more importantly the oppressed by truly freeing her/him from the domination involved in the oppressive memory and the obligation to hate the oppressor. One should note here that Gandhi did not speak of the depressed classes forgiving their oppressors, or forgetting their past, but of the oppressed and the oppressors working through the past. It is important to understand Gandhi's appreciation of the moral difficulties associated with asking the oppressed to forgive their oppressors. In this connection, it is also important to note that Gandhi had thought of *ahimsa*/non-violence and love (once emancipated from its passion for a singular object) as the appropriate response to his own experiences of racial and colonial domination. His understanding of *swaraj* as self-rule was constructed around the freedom from the need to resent and hate the oppressive, racial or colonizing, 'other'.

4.3.1 Samabhava *and* Satyagraha *as an Equality of Deference*

Was Gandhi's absolute equality confined (as Ambedkar alleged) to "just words words and words and…no action" (Ambedkar 2014, 9: 266)? Was in other words Gandhi's absolute equality to be confined to his hundreds and thousands of words (and eight arguments about equality) in/on the *Gita*?

This section will argue that Gandhi's conception of *satyagraha* as the means of earning rights/*swaraj*/freedom, his prioritization of self-rule over home rule in attaining such rights/*swaraj* and the inseparability of Gandhian *swaraj* from *satyagraha* spoke of a politics and indeed of a life pervaded by the practice of equality. To begin with, one might consider the younger Gandhi's choice of method. One might note that when he was confronted with discrimination and humiliation Gandhi thought up a method of securing rights and after much discussion chose the word *satyagraha* in 1908 to best describe that method (Gandhi 1888–1948, 10: 292). As Gandhi went on to explain his choice later:

> *Satyagraha* literally means insistence on truth. This insistence arms the votary with matchless power. This power or force is connoted by the word *satyagraha. Satyagraha,* to be genuine, may be offered against parents, against one's wife or one's children, against rulers, against fellow-citizens, even against the whole world. Such a universal force necessarily makes no distinction between kinsmen or strangers, young and old, man and women, friend and foe. (Gandhi 1888–1948, 48: 340)

In Gandhi's understanding of *satyagraha,* while the oppressed stood firm/*agraha* on truth they were equally firm in maintaining **an equality of deference** between their own people and the oppressor. In refusing to discriminate (in terms of being deferent to) between more intimate oppressors (unjust family members for instance) and the racial/caste/colonial oppressors, while resisting injustice, Gandhi and *satyagrahi* Indians (in South Africa and later India) had put the claims of equality over those of freedom/rights. As Gandhi put it in 1916, "the significance of *satyagraha* consists in the quest for a principle of life" (Gandhi 1888–1948, 15: 238) rather than merely a method of protest. Gandhi saw (as he put it) that there were always two ways open for "countering injustice. One way is to smash the head of the man who perpetuates injustice…" (Ibid.) and the other is that in which those seeking rights "alone suffer the consequences…and the other side is wholly spared" (Ibid., 240). The principle on the basis of which the latter way was chosen was perhaps drawn from Shri Krishna's advice to Arjuna in the *Gita*. Namely, the soldier of truth fighting for rights should never depart from an equi-mindedness. That is, he/she should see kinsmen and oppressing others with an equal eye/*samadarshita*. Such an equality of deference or rather equi-mindedness was a constant theme in Gandhi. From the 1909 *Hind Swaraj*, where he spoke of treating the mistakes of the thief as one would treat the thieving of a father or a brother (Gandhi 1888–1948, 10: 287–89), to the 1930, *From Yeravda Mandir*.[viii] The constant use of the example of the thief is perhaps telling, for so much of oppression consists, of stealing what is due to the other. Those who struggle against oppressors are seeking rights from those who are perhaps best seen as dispossessors/thieves of that which belongs to 'others'. Note in this context Gandhi's understanding of the virtue of non-stealing/*asteya*. He had explained that the practice of *asteya*/non-stealing did not only mean that one would not take without another's permission that which belonged to him/her. It went "…very much farther. It is theft to take something from another even with his permission if we have no need of it" (Gandhi 1888–1948, 49: 451). Gandhi connected non-stealing with a freedom from acquisitiveness: "There is besides another kind of theft subtler and far more degrading to the human spirit. It is theft mentally to desire acquisition of anything belonging to others, or to cast a greedy eye on it" (Ibid., 451–52).

In a telling passage from *From Yeravda Mandir*, Gandhi explains that equality is practised by an emotional, almost acrobatic psychological equi-mindedness, which trains the human being to maintain an equi-mindedness while interchanging the objects of his/her regard. It is such a practice that helps one to become at home in an equi-mindedness when deferring to one's own and the distant other—the thief and one's kin, oneself as the victim and the unknown other who becomes a victim of the thief one has been able to harass, and finally the thief and the God within. It must be kept in mind that the terms "thief" and "theft" were connected to any person/act who/which was involved in keeping more than what was needed; provided such a keeping was the result of being acquisitive:

> We punish thieves because, we think they harass us. They may leave us alone; but they will only transfer their attentions to another victim. This other victim is also a human being, ourselves in a different form, and so we are caught in a vicious circle… In the end we see that it is better to endure the thieves than to punish them… By enduring them we realize that thieves are not different from ourselves, they are our brethren, our friends, and may not be punished. But whilst we may bear with the thieves, we may not endure the infliction. That would only induce cowardice. So we realize a further duty. Since we regard the thieves as our kith and kin, they must be made to realize the kinship. And so we must take pains to devise ways and means of winning them over. This is the path of ahimsa. It may entail continuous

suffering and the cultivating of endless patience. Given these…the thief is bound in the end to turn away from his evil ways… we realize the greatness of God-of Truth. (Ibid., 408)

To transform the equi-mindedness/*samdarshita* into a *samabhava/*status of equality understood as an equality of deference (even love) Gandhi never tired of bringing in examples from the family. It is here that one might locate the difference between the practice of protest in our times and Gandhian *satyagraha.* In their practice of protest, modern citizens (of democratic polities) never tire of looking for opportunities of embarrassing the opponent. Gandhi would and indeed did describe such practices as what he called *duragraha.* He recommended and indeed sought always to treat the opposer as one would treat one's erring brother, father or mother. In Gandhi's view, protest did not present an opportunity for the oppressed to discriminate between one's own or oppressive "others". In 1918, he wrote:

We are to apply here the same principle that we follow in a domestic quarrel. We should think of the Government and the people as constituting a large family and act accordingly… (Gandhi 1888–1948, 16: 437).

For Gandhi, since *satyagraha* was an extension of the law of love between families, "There can be no question here of making anyone else suffer" (Ibid., 438).

That Gandhi took *Samabhava/*attitude of equality to its own absolute limit is perhaps evident enough from his recommendation of an absolute interchangeability of the objects of one's regard/deference. One might illustrate this by another interesting passage from Gandhi where he wrote of having an equi-mindedness in the regard for one's nation and one's religion:

A friend asked me the other day whether I shared the opinion often expressed that as between nationalism and religion, the former was superior to the latter. I said…Each was equal to the other in its own place. (Gandhi 1888–1948, 97: 406).

Gandhi explained (in 1947) the need for such an equi-mindedness towards the claims of the nation and of one's own religion, by arguing that the claims of respect/love from different family members are never the same but yet always equal:

Suppose I have mother, wife and daughter. All the three must be equally dear to me in their own places. (Ibid.)

However, Gandhi was not oblivious of the need for the practice (and not merely verbal avowal) of such equality of respect/deference. He argued that the equality of regard to be real had to manifest in an equality of treatment to all—mother daughter and wife; friend or foe; *savarana* or a*varna*:

my central aim… is equal treatment for the whole of humanity … (Gandhi 1888–1948, 30: 396).

Sensitive to the fact that an equality of treatment could not make for **absolute sameness** in one's emotional and physical interactions with every 'other', Gandhi was well aware that relationships often enough made different claims on one's inner life. He did not leave such a practice of equality to the judgement of each *satyagrahi* (somewhat like the exercise of *phronesis* by Aristotle's man of practical wisdom) but spelt out the requirements that such an equality of deference made in terms of an appropriate response to the person and beliefs of conflicting 'others'. Such equal claims—of civility, courteousness, politeness—supervened and over-wrote the more specific and unique claims that emerged from what one owed in one's familial relationships. For the *satyagrahi* (and indeed for every oppressed person seeking freedom), practising such an quality of treatment came to mean that:

> Just as it was necessary for us to be courteous to those who cooperate with the government, so those of us who are imprisoned will also have to behave with civility in the prison... He who holds his self respect dear acts towards everyone in a spirit of friendship, for he values other's respect as much as he values his own. He sees himself in all and everyone in himself, putting himself in line with others. The egotist keeps aloof from others; believing himself superior to the rest of the world, he takes himself to judge everyone and in the result enables the world to have the measure of his smallness. Hence the non-violent ...should regard civility as a distinct virtue and try to cultivate it. (Gandhi 1888–1948, 25: 289–290)

Gandhi explained that the *satyagrahi* (and indeed every oppressed person) could **find** it possible not to be an egoist and judge others. On this view, the *satyagrahi* could learn to extend an equality of treatment to the oppressor by making a distinction between the "wrong doer" and the "wrong done". It was always possible, just as one experienced from one's relationships in the family, to hate the action but not the wrong doing father/brother. Gandhi argued that while "anger wells up" (Gandhi 1888–1948, 39: 227) against the wrong doer or perceived wrong doer; intelligent suffering could direct the victim to "hate the wrong" (Ibid.) rather than hate the wrong doing person. Perhaps, this was an important insight from Gandhi. For one might consider that particular wrong/unjust actions do not, in themselves and in all their perniciousness, completely exhaust the life of the wrong doing person. The evil doer who commits an unjust action might still be a father/son/mother/daughter who lives a life extending beyond that unjust/evil action. Think here of how rare it might be to **find** human persons who become completely evil, so that nothing remains in/of themselves outside of their evil actions, as it were.

The equability which was demanded from the *satyagrahi*/soldier of truth was akin to the absolute equality practised by the *sthitaprajna*/wise person of the *Gita* who was described as being of steady/resolute intellect and thereby able to avoid the extremes of love and aversion. Gandhi wrote of such equability in 1917:

> ..it is seen in all the books that soul-force is the supreme power... Rama stands for the soul and Ravan for the non-soul....Rama..has conquered self and pride. He is 'placed equally in affluence and adversity', he has 'neither attachment, nor greed nor the intoxication of status'. This represents the ultimate in *satyagraha*. (Gandhi 1888–1948, 16: 11).

Gandhi never tired of reminding those seeking *swaraj* that all discrimination in Hindu society was a breach of the principle of life, which principle he spelt out in terms of the requirements of practising *satyagraha* and non-violence. In 1908, he wrote:

> It is only because we do not appreciate the marvel of *satyagraha* that we live in India as a poor and cowardly race...certain customs which are papably evil are kept alive in our country mainly because we lack the spirit of *satyagraha*. Though well aware that certain customs are

bad, we do very little to end them either because of fear, laziness or undue regard for others. (Gandhi 1888–1948, 8 :153)

Gandhi's critics often miss the point that Gandhi's absolute equality (and *satyagraha* as a method of seeking rights) rested ultimately upon his ontological privileging of truth as the only possible name of God. He famously shifted from the traditional equation "God is Truth" to "Truth is God". Note:

> The word *satya* (Truth) is derived from *sat*, which means 'being'. Nothing is or exists in reality except truth. That is why *sat* or truth is perhaps the most important name of God. (Gandhi 1888–1948, 49: 383)

One might consider that Gandhi's privileging of truth or *satya* - which last term, when seen etymologically, comes from '*sat*' or Being- pointed towards the recognition of the divinity of all beings rather than the divinity of a sovereign and single being. This shift formed the background framework for Gandhi's deep commitment to *samabhava* which involved the practice of an equality and sameness of attitude towards all beings.

The *samadarshita* and *samabhava* of the *satyagrahi* were only one aspect of the absolute equality that constituted the spirit of Gandhi's *satyagraha*. As he never tired of saying, *satyagraha* and indeed non-violence, as a method of securing rights by personal suffering, was a method that could be equally practised in any situation (a necessary *caveat* here is **any situation that involved truth**) and was also equally open to all to practice:

> Just as anyone can resort to *satyagraha*, it can be resorted to in almost any situation. (Gandhi 1888–1948, 16: 12)

As Gandhi put it, *satyagraha* could be practised by the weak and the strong even "a child should learn that …it can easily conquer hate by love, untruth by truth, violence by self-suffering" (Gandhi 1888–1948, 14: 218).

4.3.2 *Reconciling the Claims of Liberty and Equality:* Satyagraha *and* Swaraj

Though Gandhi came close to the liberal philosophers,[xi] in as much as he appreciated the importance of rights to the human person, he did not quite endorse the manner in which the liberal philosophers had equated the claims of the enlightenment values— liberty, equality and fraternity. As seen in the last subsection, Gandhi had departed significantly from the liberals in elevating the claims of equality, so much as to insist, that liberty/rights could only be affirmed by means that maintained an absolute equality of deference between the rights aspirant and his/her unjust oppressor.

Gandhi seemed to have given much thought to the conflicts that had become somewhat inevitable given the equivalence between liberty and equality in the liberal conception. He made some effort to reconcile the contrary and often rival claims of these two values by rethinking the meaning of freedom (in fact renaming it by a *Vedic* term *swaraj*) and by proposing a relationship of inextricability between *satyagraha* and *swaraj*. By these two last, fairly dexterous, conceptual manoeuvres, Gandhi reconciled the struggle for political, economic and social liberty with the somewhat (often) contrary need to ensure an equality of deference and treatment to the unjust oppressors.

To begin with, one needs to take note of the manner in which Gandhi's understanding of freedom reconciled the contrariety between liberty and equality as these values had been read in and by the liberal tradition. Gandhi's equality as absolute and as involving *samata, samdarshita* and *samabhava* has already been discussed above. It remains here to look at how Gandhi reconciled such an absolute equality with freedom, and how such a reconciliation demanded a rethinking of freedom as Gandhian *swaraj*.

A central thrust of the *Hind Swaraj* (which was written to explain the freedom of India, or that which Gandhi thought of, as the freedom/*swaraj* for India/*Hind* at any rate) was to dismantle the conceptual and practical contrariety, between freedom and equality. *Swaraj* was discussed in Chaps. 4 and 14 of *Hind Swaraj* in 1909. Gandhi argued, in Chap. 4 of the *Hind Swaraj*, that the *swaraj* of *Hind*/India could not be translated as liberty understood solely in the negative terms of driving out the English from India and attaining rights/political freedom. He was familiar with the liberal understanding and had indeed read Mill's *On Liberty* (2006) and mentioned it by name in the 1920s. Of such an understanding of the liberty of the liberals (which he equated with license), he said:

> I know that in the West there is a powerful trend towards license. But I have no desire to see students in India take to such license…I want to tell you that the man who has not received education for freedom –and you may be sure that this is not to be had by reading Mill on 'Liberty'- cannot be taken to be a free man. (Gandhi 1888–1948, 22: 12)

The word for the freedom of his conception was therefore neither 'liberty' (a term too close perhaps to Mill's *On Liberty*) nor the Western 'independence' but *swaraj*. The last i.e, *swaraj* as Gandhi explained, referred to the state of the self as self-rule; and only secondarily to political self-government/home rule. It followed that the home rule that a country attained would only be in exact proportion to the state of self-rule of its individual members. In Chap. 14 of *Hind Swaraj*, Gandhi went on to explain why swaraj was not something that could be attained by the mere acquisition of political freedom and subsequent securing of political, social and economic rights. To the contrary, for Gandhi to be free, meant to have become self-ruled which involved having been educated into a spirit of *satyagraha* which (as argued in the last section) involved the practice of an absolute equality of deference. There could be no *swaraj* as either self-rule or indeed home rule without an education into the practice of such an absolute equality. Gandhi had argued that the primary requirement for *swaraj* was not freedom as in an absence of restraint (and thereby license) but rather "self-restraint".

Understanding *swaraj* as self-rule and subsequently as home rule and arguing for the dependence of the latter on the former[x] meant that Gandhi's *swaraj* was "…self rule and self restraint, and not freedom from all restraint which 'independence' often means" (Gandhi 1888–1948, 51: 220). This was not a matter of words and just words. Indeed, it was no less than an ideational feat that reconciled the contrary claims of liberty with equality. Note what Gandhi said about such *swaraj* in *Hind Swaraj:*

> It is *swaraj* when we learn to rule ourselves. (Gandhi 1888–1948, 10: 282)

Elsewhere, Gandhi unpacks the idea of *swaraj* as utmost humility and self-restraint:

> It is very difficult-practically impossible-to achieve real freedom without self-denial (Gandhi 1888–1948, 95: 207).

Each and every human being could have an equal opportunity for and equal share in such Gandhian *swaraj.* As Gandhi explained:

> The outward freedom therefore that we shall attain will only be in exact proportion to the inward freedom to which we may have grown at a given moment. And if this is the correct meaning of freedom, our chief energy must be concentrated upon achieving reform from within. In this much-needed work all who will can take an equal share. (Gandhi 1888–1948, 43: 171).

Such an inner reform might be unpacked in terms of moral self-rule, as in the rule over the ego and control over its aggrandizement. Gandhi had argued that true freedom "is in the palm of our hands… But such *swaraj* has to be experienced by each one for himself" (Gandhi 1888–1948, 10: 282). Freedom for Gandhi then was nothing if not an experience of absolute restraint of the self by the self and therefore utmost humility. This experience, it seems apparent, would also be an experience of absolute equality since utmost humility is nothing, if not, the recognition that one is not superior to anything or anyone else. Gandhi (as noted above) had emphasized that such a recognition of equality was a condition of both individual and national freedom:

> National independence is not a fiction. It is as necessary as individual independence. But neither, if it is based on non-violence can ever be a menace to the equal independence of the nation or the individual as the case may be... It has been well said that the universe is compressed in the atom. There is not one law for the atom and another for the universe. (Gandhi 1888–1948 48: 274)

Clearly, Gandhian *swaraj* as self-rule rested on according a higher place to equality over the claims of liberty in the trilogy of the enlightenment values. Gandhi made this point even more strongly by making an inseparable connection between *swaraj* as moral autonomy (self-rule) and *satyagraha* (non-violent resistance). The critical point was that Gandhian *swaraj* as individual self-rule or becoming established in the moral life could be actualized only by progressively and resolutely practising an equality of deference in resolving conflicts with hostile others. It is necessary to understand just how uniquely Gandhi had conceptualized the relation between *swaraj* (as individual liberty and national independence) and *satyagraha* (as non-violent resistance):

This *satyagraha* is India's distinctive weapon. It has had others but *satyagraha* has been in greater use. It is an unfailing source of strength, and is capable of being used at all times and under all circumstances. It requires no stamp of approval from the congress. He who knows its power cannot but use it. **Even as the eye lashes automatically protect the eyes, so does *satyagraha*, when kindled automatically protect the freedom of the soul**. (Gandhi 1888–1948, 16: 127) (The emphasis is mine)

One might recall that Gandhi defines "*satyagraha*" in the following words:

This is the literal meaning of *satyagraha*—insistence on truth, and force derivable from such insistence… We shall *find* too, on further reflection, that conduct based on truth is impossible without love. Truth force then is love-force. We cannot remedy evil by harboring ill-will against the evil-doer (Gandhi 1888–1948, 17: 448–449).

It is surely significant that Gandhi's understanding of what it meant for the self to be morally autonomous or truly free was structured by the connection he made between *swaraj* as moral self-rule and *satyagraha* as the supreme moral duty. That Gandhi should have connected the two notions makes it fairly clear that the Gandhian self could attain freedom (and rights) only by both recognizing his or her supreme moral duty to practise an equality of deference and further by engaging to resist injustice **while at the same time practising such an absolute equality**. In other words in terms of the Gandhian argument, freedom had to be achieved by the essentially social and relational self in the presence of the absolutely equal, sometimes unjust, other. One might conclude this section with the insight that Gandhi had reconciled the contrariety between the values of liberty and equality by an emphatic insistence on putting equality before freedom.

4.3.3 Gandhi on **Varna** and Untouchability: Working Through and Beyond the Past

The last question which must be answered is the one which has persistently appeared in the course of the argument in this chapter. This question appeared to come and go in the form of two issues—*varna* and separate electorates—across and beyond the duration of Gandhi's life. The two issues that divided Gandhi and Ambedkar so sharply, *varna* and separate electorates, were perhaps two aspects of a single problem; that of the divergence between Gandhi and Ambedkar in their conflicting approaches to the problem of untouchability. The fundamental issue here was whether untouchability was to be treated as a problem within the Hindu community or whether the untouchables were to reconstitute themselves as an independent political/social group outside of the Hindu society? Perhaps, one might ask if Gandhi's engagement with the abolishment of untouchability as a problem that needed to be resolved **from within** the Hindu community was at best a sentimental nostalgia and, at worst, an insistence that equality must be confined within the limits of measure/*maryada dharma*.

It was in their very different answers to this issue that one might see the incommensurability between the world views from within which Gandhi and Ambedkar saw the problem of untouchability, the solution to the problem and indeed the cosmos itself. With the coming to age of modern Indian identity, all three aspects (that Taylor had pointed out)—radical inwardness, expressivism and the affirmation of ordinary life—found their perfect expression in the person of Babasaheb Ambedkar:

> Ambedkar's programs were intended to integrate the Untouchable into Indian society in modern, not traditional ways, and on as high a level as possible. (Zelliot 1972, 77)

With the history of a century of liberal philosophy behind him, Ambedkar looked at the very inwardness of the individual as the source of all value. One might note the difference between the inner reflexivity in the notion of the autonomy where the modern self turns around to look upon itself quite as an object and the powerful sense of restraint of the self by the self in Gandhian *swaraj*/self-rule. The Gandhian self engages with itself or rather with its own ego in *swaraj,* only to subdue the 'I' and ego directed passions in order to identify the world within that which is outside it, other selves and the cosmos. By contrast, the inner reflexivity in the modern notion of autonomy turns the self around only to look at itself. In Kant's terms (and in modernity), the self sees/confronts the unity of apperception within itself. Such an understanding of the self- as powerfully inward looking- distanced the modern Indian (and Ambedkar) from a search for authenticity and freedom in unity with the 'other' or indeed with the world outside of his/her inner life. The search for unity- which Gandhi read as a kinship with the 'other' (all creatures of the same father God)- was transformed by Ambedkar into an external fraternity between those who were equal subjects of the law/citizens of the republic.

As noted (in Chap. 3) it was Locke's punctual self who came of age in India in the person of Babasaheb Ambedkar with the erasure of innate ideas and the quest to build anew on the foundations of experience and sensation. In this modern Ambedkarian self there was a privileging of individual emotion, experience and self-expression. Ambedkar saw that the experience of ordinary life in the dalit community shared a suffering that uniquely belonged to such a life and, in the modern way, he sought "to self-minoritize Dalits" (Nagraj 2015, 117) around that very experience of suffering and its expression. It is significant to note that this self-minoritization became a "mode of self-closure" (Ibid., 115). Given the location of modern identity within modern institutions that inevitably accompanied the coming of age of modern identity, Ambedkar was also constrained (at the same time), by the demands of the domain of the political. It might be recalled (from Chap. 3) that the modern idea of the social contract made consent of the group a prerequisite to any act that confirmed that group's acceptance of an act of political belonging to a nation. It seemed natural enough that Ambedkar should have acted upon the realization that "in the context of the modern polity, aggressive self-minoritization was the surest way to stay in the mainstream political institutions" (Ibid., 117). His insistence on the separate electorate as the modern dalit's prior consent to enter the contract (which was to form the nation) was an obvious consequence of such a philosophical lineage in modernity.

One needs to consider that Gandhi could not have been expected to share in such a vision given that he had thought of the self drawing on the idea of the *atman* and the background (and comprehensive framework) of the *Advaita* metaphysics. For

Gandhi the individual self was a combination of the *atman* and body. Like Descartes he saw these elements in a hierarchical relationship. There are always far reaching consequences to how one understands the self and such hierarchies. With Descartes the hierarchical dualism of mind and body, with a prioritization of the first, led to a radical and obsessive individualism and a purely instrumental understanding of that which was outside of the mind and purely extended/physical. With Gandhi it was quite the contrary; as the *atman* dominated his ethics which constantly sought to overcome the empirical body and its demands. On another note, Gandhi's prioritization of the *atman* lead him into a metaphysics of oneness with all others and with all of creation. It therefore seems to have been fairly apparent that Gandhi could not have consistently endorsed the separate electorate with the removal of the so-called untouchables from the Hindu fold, as in his view, both the so-called lower and upper castes were only acting in bad faith so long as they sought such self-closure.

Translating the ontological oneness of the *atman*-Brahman to everyday life Gandhi brought the practice of an absolute equality of deference, to his own conceptions of individual self-worth and self-identity. This perhaps led him to insist on an idealistic and unrecognizable reading of *varna*, in which for instance all the four *varnas* were represented in a single individual; according as such an individual should manifest different qualities at different times. There are three arguments which one might consider in connection with Gandhi's position on *varna* and on the approach most appropriate to the abolishment of untouchability. To begin with the first argument one might note that, as brought out in the very first chapter of this book, Gandhi simply did not and could not accept third-party justice with history providing the measure and passing an indictment on the past and its concepts. One might recall Gandhi from the quotation in the last subsection:

> The egotist keeps aloof from others; believing himself superior to the rest of the world, he takes himself to judge everyone and in the result enables the world to have the measure of his smallness… (Gandhi 1888–1948, 25: 289–290).

As discussed in both Chaps. 1 and 2 in this book Gandhi had rejected the retrospective application of measure as the way to access the truth of the past. In his view such retrospective judgement effectively destroyed any access to the truth of the past as it was or had passed as a set of unique individual happenings. For Gandhi the only way to access the truth of the past was through the memory of it as a passing of all that which had happened in its unique singularity. Such a rejection of measure is perhaps what led Gandhi to reject the retrospective judgement on *varna;* one indeed that had recommended its complete erasure. Gandhi sought instead, to re-interpret *varna*, in his own times and in line with reason and morality.

This takes one to Gandhi's second argument for the rethinking of *varna*. This argument drew from Gandhi's own understanding of reason which was very different from that of the liberals. For Gandhi (in line with the ancients) reason was a tradition constituted and tradition constitutive term. One should note that such a conception of reason (alternative to the liberal one) could and did countenance critique and reform, of all concepts and meanings that constituted a tradition, from within the continuity of the same evolving (never static) tradition (see MacIntyre 1988, 9). On such a

Gandhian understanding of reason the very continuity of the tradition (as essentially evolving and subject to an internal critique) demanded the re-interpretation of its own central concepts in line with morality. *Varna* was no exception and Gandhi recommended its radical re-interpretation rather than complete erasure.

No matter how strange this may sound the third argument which could explain why Gandhi should have insisted on making an idealistic and apparently unrecognizable re-interpretation of *varna* was practical. There were a number of reasons why Gandhi thought that an idealistic re-interpretation of *varna* was paradoxically enough the most practical path to the abolition of untouchability in Indian society. To begin with for Gandhi, not only was rational re-interpretation of *varna* possible, but it was also necessary; as complete erasure of the past (and the concept of *varna* from that past) was not something that he (or other ancients) could choose to undertake or indeed choose not to undertake in practise. Gandhi understood that the old-world Indian simply did not have the modern obsession with erasure. Consequently, Gandhi proposed that the sins of the past had to be worked through rather than wiped out. Such a working out demanded at one level an identification with both sides to the conflict. At another level, it meant that the oppressor and oppressed had both to work through the sins of the past—the oppressor by owning up to the sin and the oppressed by moving ahead and past it. It may be recalled (from Chapter Two of this book) that in Gandhi's understanding of it the memory of the past through a telling of *itihaas*/it so happened in the past (unlike history) called for a giving and working out of what had happened in that past. Unlike history *itihaas* tried to understand all parties in a conflict through the only way in which one could understand, such parties, that is by love. This became possible because the notion of *itihaas* was based upon the idea that one can only understand the conflicts of the past (or any conflicts) with love and not with measure, hence the non-juridical 'it so happened'.

Such an approach that concentrated on working though the wrong doing was also perhaps based on Gandhi's (whether practical or unrealistic) faith in the goodness of every human 'other'. No matter how evil a person appeared, for Gandhi, the good could always be brought forth by moral criticism and voluntary intelligent suffering/*tapasya*. This led Gandhi to attempt a method of dual identification and consequently refuse to caricature the oppressor (religious, caste 'other') in unidimensional terms as radically evil. There was a textured interiority to the oppressor as to the oppressed. The unjust oppressor on such a view had his/her own struggle and the good in him/her could be made to prevail over the evil. Elsewhere Gandhi noted that the sources of untruth /injustice were internal enemies of the moral life: "Our difficulties are of two kinds: those that are imposed from without and those that are of our own creation. The latter are far more dangerous, because we often hug them and are therefore reluctant to remove them" (Gandhi 1888–1948, 21: 470).

Another practical concern brought to bear upon the abolishment of untouchability came from the need to retain the integrity of the oppressed and indeed that of the oppressive self. Perhaps one's approach to problems (like untouchability and *varna*) that plague the community, rests ultimately upon, how one thinks about (or understands) the nature of the self. The question is whether one can think of the self as someone who can retain his/her integrity after the erasure of his/her relation to the community as it is (and was) and its *itihaas*/it so happened? Gandhi thought that this question could only be answered in the negative and therefore recommended that the self needed to work out conflicts with troublesome, messy, unjust others in order to maintain its own integrity (wholeness). Significantly, and in the ancient way, one could not erase the relationships within the community without disrupting one's own self-integrity/wholeness. It is only perhaps in modernity that one can reject the erring father or brother completely by moving away to another country, learning a new language and becoming someone altogether different.

It was perhaps such practical concerns for the integrity of the self (as it confronted conflicting others as part of his/her community) that led Gandhi to speak of the first step in *satyagraha* as involving a conversation between the oppressor and the oppressed so that both the oppressor and the society/public opinion could get educated about the issues involved. To digress a little from Gandhi's approach to *varna* and untouchability and discuss this last point one might recall that Gandhi had recommended that the *satyagrahi* must first put across his/her arguments to the oppressor and seek to educate the public at large about the perceived wrong. Such education and discussion was not just part of resistance but **the first stage** which was essential before resistance/*satyagraha* itself could be carried out. This becomes apparent when one reflects upon the stages in Gandhian *satyagraha*:

> A *satyagrahi*, for instance, must first mobilize public opinion against the evil which he is out to eradicate, by means of a wide and intensive agitation. When public opinion is sufficiently roused against a social abuse even the tallest will not dare to practice or openly to lend support to it. An awakened and intelligent public opinion is the most potent weapon of a *satyagrahi*. (Gandhi 1888–1948, 46: 289)

On this view it was only **after** one had educated not only the wrong doer but the public at large **about the evil** in the position one sought to resist that resistance in the form of dissociation, civil disobedience etc. **could justifiably take place**. One can understand such non-violent mobilization of public opinion against **evil** only in terms of the individual's effort to **work through the wrong doing** with the wrong doer and the community at large. For Gandhi, as for all ancient world views, the oppressed individual was inextricably related to the oppressive human 'other' as to the rest of the cosmos. It therefore became important for the oppressed and oppressor, as so related, to work through wrong doing by engaging with each other and with the community.

The most important aspect to this third and more practical Gandhian argument in support of a re-interpretation of *varna* (and of the Hindu tradition from within itself as it were) as the best possible approach to the abolition of untouchability came from the fact that Gandhi was looking for an absolute equality that could be practised by the community rather than for an equality to be enforced by the law courts/an equality before law. It was the demands of such an equality and of *samata*/status of equality that led Gandhi to re-interpret *varna* and suggest that all the four *varnas* referred to the qualities that were inevitably represented in one and the same person or alternatively that all Indians were, properly speaking, *Sudras*. It was Gandhi's sense of even mindedness that led him (paradoxically enough) to identify with both sides to the conflict by radically rethinking *varna* rather than completely rejecting it. Thereby those who believed that the self could only retain its integrity by seeking a continuity with the tradition (and with *varna*) and those who were modern and did not believe in the necessity of continuity (to integrity) and consequently rejected the ancient interpretation of *varna* as unjust; would both be **equally enabled** to move beyond and work through the injustice of *varna* and untouchability. It was also the same need for continuity and working though the unjust past that led Gandhi to seek joint rather than separate electorates. Perhaps on another aspect of this more practical note (and one true to his own personal *itihaas*/it had so happened, born as he was, into a trading family) Gandhi had realized that where people needed to live together in the same nation (in close proximity) it was practical to work through the hate of the past by both sides to the conflict accepting the radically re-interpreted version of *varna* in the present. One might consider that it might have seemed more practical to Gandhi to seek such radical re-interpretation and indeed choose continuity given that it might not have been possible, to erase *varna* completely from that which had passed or from the time in which he lived.

The difference in approach between Ambedkar and Gandhi was then that of world views, the difference was philosophical, between the ancient and the modern. It could not be retrospectively erased or adjudicated but remained incommensurable and impossible to traverse; just as, the present cannot traverse the distance to the past or to the future.

Notes

i.   Gandhi wrote two responses to Ambedkar's scheduled address to the Jat Pat Todak Mandal in May 1936, which last address was never delivered but later published. These essays entitled "Dr. Ambedkar Indictment-I" and "Dr. Ambedkar Indictment-II" were published in *Harijan* on 11.07.1936 and 18.07.1936, respectively. They are included in (and I have referred to them from) Gandhi 1888–1948, *The Collected Works of Mahatma Gandhi, (electronic edition)*, Vol. 69, pp. 205–207 and pp. 226–227. This set of 98 volumes was published in 1999 at New Delhi by the Publications Division, Ministry of Information and Broadcasting, Government of India. It is accessible online at https://www.gandhiashramsevagram.org/gandhi-literature/col lected-works-of-mahatma-gandhi-volume-1-to-98.php.

ii. In 1926, he gave a series of almost daily talks on the *Gita* between February and November during morning prayers at the *Satyagraha Ashram.* They were posthumously published under the title *Gandhijijinu Gitashikshan* (Gandhi's Teaching of the Gita). *Gitashikshan* seems to have been translated by the editors of the collected works as "Discourses on the Gita". It was later published in English as a book "The *Bhagavad Gita*" (New Delhi: Orient Paperbacks, 1980). Gandhi's Gujarati translation of the *Gita* the *Anasaktiyoga* literally "the *yoga* of non-attachment" was completed in Yeravada jail in 1929. The *Anasaktiyoga* was a "rendering" of the *Gita* with short glosses on some passages and an additional preface. The English translation of the book by Mahadev Desai was published in 1931 by Navajivan Press under the title "The Gita according to Gandhi". However, for the purpose of reference I have referred to these two texts from Gandhi 1888–1948, *The Collected Works of Mahatma Gandhi (Electronic edition)* 1–98 volumes, New Delhi, Publications Division, Ministry of Information and Broadcasting, Government of India, 1999 accessible online at https://www.gandhiashramsevagram.org/gandhi-literature/collected-works-of-mahatma-gandhi-volume-1-to-98.php.

iii.   See Ashis Nandy on the politics of Gandhi's death in *The Intimate Enemy*, Oxford University Press, New Delhi, 2009.

iv.   Bal Gangadhar Tilak (the militant leader prominent in Indian politics since the 1890s).

v.   The *Bhagavad Gita* also referred to simply as the *Gita* is a religious book for the Hindus. It is a 700-verse text in Sanskrit that is part of the epic *Mahabharata*. The *Gita* narrates a dialogue between the *Kshatriya* prince Arjuna and his charioteer Sri Krishna. At the start of the war between the *Pandavas* and their cousins the *Kauravas,* Arjuna is filled with despair and wonders if he should take part in a war against his kinsmen. Sri Krishna's reply to him forms the *Gita.* Krishna counsels Arjuna to fulfil his duty by action without any self-directed desire for results thereof.

vi.   "The men of self-realization look with an equal eye on a Brahmana possessed of learning and humility, a cow, an elephant…." (Gandhi 1888–1948, 46: 191).

vii.   In the Introduction to his (Gandhi's) collection of writings on *Varnadharma* entitled *Varnavyavastha.*

viii.   "Of the discourses on the Ashram vows, which Gandhiji wrote weekly in his letters to Satyagraha Ashram during his detention in Yeravda Prison in 1930. The first in the series was written in July 22, 1930; vide 'Letter to Narandas Gandhi'. These were first published in Gujarati under the title *Vratavichar* and later under the title *Mangal Prabhat*" (Gandhi 1888–1948, 54: 417). It was translated into English from Gujarati by Shri Valji Desai and entitled *From Yeravada Mandir* (Ashram observances) and published by Navajivan Mudranalaya, Ahmedabad, in 1933. In 1932, Gandhi himself wrote the preface of this book and stated: "Shri Valji Desai gave a fairly full translation in English. But seeing me in possession of comparative leisure during the recurrent incarceration, he has sent me his translation for revision. I have gone through it carefully, and touched up several passages to bring out my meaning more to my liking. I need hardly add that, if I was writing anew for the English reader, perhaps I should write a wholly new thing. But that would be going beyond my commission. And perhaps it is as well that even the English reader has the trend of my thought as expressed to the inmates of the Ashram, and in the year 1930. I have therefore taken the least liberty with the original argument" (Gandhi 1888–1948, 55: 104). However, for reference purposes I have referred to these letters and writings from Gandhi 1888–1948, *The Collected Works of Mahatma Gandhi (Electronic)* 1–98 volumes, New Delhi, Publications Division, Ministry of Information and Broadcasting, Government of

India,1999 accessible online at https://www.gandhiashramsevagram.org/gandhi-literature/collected-works-of-mahatma-gandhi-volume-1-to-98.php.

ix.   Liberalism stands for a systematic set of philosophical, moral and political beliefs; and also for a certain set of regulative principles to put socio-economic and sociopolitical arrangements in place in state and society. It is necessary to clarify that I am aware that liberalism is not quite a unitary tradition. There is a divide between the utilitarian versions of liberalism as espoused by Mill and Bentham and the tradition originating in Kant. The former is guided by a comprehensive theory of the good as utility. It is in sharp contrast to the tradition primarily originating with Kant and followed by Rawls which can be termed deontological liberalism and which opposes consequentialism in ethics. It is typically defined in opposition to utilitarianism and bases justice in respect for individual rights independently of utility or of any other comprehensive theory of the good. Within such deontological rights-oriented liberalism, there are libertarian (such as those of Robert Nozick and Friedrich Hayek) and egalitarian (Rawls' being foremost) versions. For the purpose of this chapter (and other chapters in this book), it is not necessary for me to address these internal conflicts in liberalism. It seems clear that liberals in general and across divides agree in largely equating the claims of liberty equality and fraternity.

x.   "Real home-rule is self-rule or self-control" (Gandhi 1888–1948, 10: 310).

References

Ambedkar, B.R. 2014. *Dr Babasaheb Ambedkar writings and speeches*, ed. Vasant Moon (set of 17 Volumes). New Delhi: Dr Ambedkar Foundation. Ministry of Social Justice and Empowerment. Government of India.
Bhattacharya, S. 2008. *The Mahatma and the poet. Letters and debates between Gandhi and Tagore, 1915–1941*, 5th ed. New Delhi: National Book Trust.
Gandhi, M. K.1888–1948. *Collected Works of Mahatma Gandhi*: Volumes 1 to 98. New Delhi: Publications Division, Government of India, 1999. Accessed online in May 2021 at https://www.gandhiashramsevagram.org/gandhi-literature/collected-works-of-mahatma-gandhi-volume-1-to-98.php.
Kant, I. 1999. An answer to the question: What is enlightenment?. In *Immanuel Kant practical philosophy*. Ed. and trans. by Mary J Gregor. General Introduction by Allen Wood. Cambridge: Cambridge University Press.
Kolge, Nishikant. 2017. *Gandhi against caste*. New Delhi: Oxford University Press.
Kumar, Aishwary. 2015. *Radical equality: Ambedkar, Gandhi, and the risk of democracy*. Stanford, California: Stanford University Press.
Mill, John Stuart, 2006. *On liberty and subjection of women*, ed. Alan Ryan. London: Penguin Classic.
Nagel, Thomas. 2002. *Mortal questions*. Cambridge: Cambridge University Press.
Nagraj, D.R. 2015. *The flaming feet and other essays: The Dalit movement in India*, ed. Prithvi Datta Chandra Shobhi. Ranikhet: Permanent Black.
Nandy, Ashish. 2009. *The intimate enemy*. New Delhi: Oxford University Press.

Roy, Arundhati. 2014. The doctor and the saint. In *B. R. Ambedkar annihilation of caste: The annotated critical edition,* ed. S. Anand. New Delhi: Navyana Publishing.

Scruton, R. 2014. *The soul of the world*. Oxford, Princeton: Princeton University Press.

Skaria, Ajay. 2016. *Unconditional equality Gandhi's religion of resistance*. Ranikhet: Permanent Black.

Taylor, C. 2001. *Sources of the self: The making of the modern identity*. Cambridge: Harvard University Press.

Tilak, B. G. 1935. *Sri Bhagavad Gita-Rahasya* or *Karma-Yoga-Sastra* (English Translation), vol. 1, 1 ed. Bombay: Bombay Vaibhav Press.

Williams, Bernard. 1999. *The problems of the self*. Cambridge: Cambridge University Press.

Zelliot, Eleanor. 1972. Gandhi and Ambedkar—A study in leadership. In *The untouchables in contemporary India*, ed. J. Michael Mahar, pp. 69–95. Tucson, Arizona: University of Arizona Press.

Chapter 5
Impartiality and *Samdarshita:*
Ambedkar and Gandhi on Justice

Abstract Moving to the third, of the three concepts, in *The Ambedkar Gandhi Debate: On Identity Community and Justice,* this chapter will argue that differences between Ambedkar and Gandhi on caste, *varna,* separate electorates, untouchability and its eradication, followed from fundamental philosophical differences between their conceptions of justice. The chapter will argue that while Ambedkar followed in the tradition of an enlightenment liberal contractarian approach to justice, Gandhi's conception of justice can be better understood, in continuity with the ancient Indian tradition. Gandhi thought about justice in line with the ancient Indian concepts of *dharma/dhamma nyaya* and *niti.* This chapter will locate the differences between Gandhi and Ambedkar around two important and organizing insights about justice.

Keywords Justice · *Dharma*/righteousness/justice · *Nyaya*/justice · *Niti*/the concerns of institutional justice · Objectivity · Fairness · Closed impartiality · Open impartiality · Equi-mindedness/*samadarshita* · *Swaraj*/self-rule/home rule · *Tapasya*/self-imposed pain

The last chapter had closed by locating the divergences between Gandhi and Ambedkar on *varna* and separate electorates in their philosophically divergent world views. This last, I argued, was a divergence between the ancient and the modern notions of the world and of the self within it. This chapter will take up the discussion where the previous chapter had left it, to move to a related issue, that of exploring Ambedkar and Gandhi's powerfully alternative conceptions of justice. I will argue here that very different understandings of justice perhaps explained and underlay the conflicts between Gandhi and Ambedkar, for instance, those surrounding the issue of separate electorates or that of the proper approach to the eradication of untouchability. The connection of Ambedkar's contract-based constitutional approach to the mainstream discussion of justice within the tradition of the European Enlightenment and its subsequent history is too apparent to be denied. It seems fairly clear that Ambedkar (as the chairman of the drafting committee of the Indian constitution) had thought about justice from within (what Alasdair MacIntyre would describe as) the tradition of liberal modernity (See MacIntyre 1988) and primarily as an institutional virtue. Within such a tradition, Ambedkar seemed to have understood justice primarily in remedial terms and as directed towards historical injustice.

One might easily think (as many commentators have thought) that the last point, by itself, could only serve to bring Gandhi and Ambedkar closer. Note the following sentiment that many but Gandhi's severest critics would share;

> In a very general sense both Gandhi and Ambedkar strived to visualize a community based on justice and fraternity. (Palshikar 1996, 2072)

It may be recalled that Gandhi (like Ambedkar) seemed to have associated justice with redressing the injustice embedded in India's *itihaas* (not of course, in history). Gandhi spoke (at great length and often) of the acceptance of responsibility for "sin" and asked high-caste Hindus to own up to the injustice of the past and make amends for it by eradicating caste distinctions, by undergoing penance and by self-purification. While it is undeniable that they had shared a concern for justice, it is equally undeniable that Gandhi and Ambedkar did not mean the same things when they spoke of justice or indeed of the eradication of injustice.

This chapter will attempt to bring out the differences between what Gandhi and Ambedkar meant by 'justice' by locating such differences around two central issues. The first issue can perhaps be grouped around the divergence in the Indian tradition between *niti* and the alternative set of terms, *dharma/dhamma* and *nyaya*. Amartya Sen brought up this divergence in his discussion on the capabilities approach to justice, referring to the difference between *niti* and *nyaya* (though it is important to note that he did not refer to *dharma/dhamma* in this connection). Though the capabilities approach is far afield from the discussion here, Sen's comments upon *niti* and *nyaya* remain relevant to the distinction between what I have described as, the two approaches, to justice. Sen explains;

> …an important distinction between two different concepts of justice in early Indian jurisprudence– between *niti* and *nyaya*. The former idea, that of *niti*, relates to organizational propriety as well as behavioral correctness, whereas the latter, *nyaya*, is concerned with what emerges and how, and in particular the lives that people are actually able to lead. The distinction …helps us to see clearly that there are two rather different, though not unrelated, kinds of justice for which the idea of justice has to cater. (Sen 2010, xv)

Perhaps one might say, that *niti* is the Sanskrit term analogous to the concerns of institutional justice, that which, for instance, Rawls had in mind when he said that justice was the first virtue of social institutions. The second term *nyaya* is associated with justice understood in a more practical context and in more contextual terms. It can be better understood in conjunction with/in terms of another combine which has had a fairly long history in the Indian political, religious, legal, literary and ethical domains, i.e. *dharma/dhamma*. One might put across the first difference between Gandhi and Ambedkar on justice by saying that while Gandhi understood justice in terms of both *niti* and *dharma/dhamma,* Ambedkar had an institution-centric approach to justice.

The second (and related) difference between Gandhi and Ambedkar emerges from the consideration, that while it is true, that the identification of remedial injustice is central to a conception of justice, a proper understanding of justice itself is not only/entirely about 'our sense of justice and injustice'. Another issue which is

involved in any theory of justice is that of what sort of reasoning ought to count in
our assessment of political and ethical concepts like justice. As Sen puts it;

> In what way can a diagnosis of injustice, or the identification of what would reduce or
> eliminate it be objective? Does this demand impartiality in some particular sense, such as
> detachment from one's own vested interests? Does it also demand re-examination of some
> attitudes even if they are not related to vested interests, but reflect local preconceptions and
> prejudices, which may not survive reasoned confrontation with others not restricted by the
> same parochialism? (Ibid., viii)

Or in MacIntyre's words;

> To know what justice requires, so it may seem, we must first learn what rationality in practice
> requires of us. (MacIntyre 1988, 2)

As in the first, there are powerful differences between Gandhi and Ambedkar
around arguments and positions connected to this second insight about justice.
Gandhi, given his proclivity for the local, could not align himself with liberal institu-
tionalism and indeed impartiality best exemplified in the figure of the judge meting
out justice as the third party to any conflict.

On a deeply contrary note, Ambedkar located himself firmly within the liberal
enlightenment tradition of third-party justice and impartiality;

> Rationality requires, so it has been argued by a number of academic philosophers, that we first
> divest ourselves of allegiance to any of the contending theories and also abstract ourselves
> from all those particularities of social relationship… (Ibid., 3)

One might recall that it was the central aspiration of the enlightenment "an aspiration the formulation of which was itself a great achievement, to provide for debate in
the public realm standards and methods of rational justification… So, it was hoped
reason would displace authority and tradition. Rational justification was to appeal to
principles undeniable by any rational person and therefore independent of all those
social and cultural particularities which the enlightenment thinkers took to be the
mere accidental clothing of reason in particular times and places. And that rational
justification could be nothing other than what the thinkers of the enlightenment had
said that it was came to be accepted, at least by the vast majority of educated people,
in post-enlightenment cultural and social orders". (Ibid., 6).

The soundness of such arguments could not be lost on the modern Ambedkar, when
he thought about rationality and justice and indeed chaired the drafting committee
to frame the Constitution of India along the lines of other liberal constitutions in
the world. Yet paradoxically enough one can still ask if he himself quite took, what
Nagel has picturesquely described as, the "view from nowhere" (Nagel 1986, 70)
when he argued about justice and injustice. Given that appeals to experience (of
suffering/*duhkha* shared by the dalits) were an important aspect of Ambedkar's
insights into justice, it would perhaps not be philosophically misguided to ask if
Ambedkar was entirely free from 'positional sequestering' while making a diagnosis of injustice or, indeed of, any identification of what would reduce or eliminate
it? It might in such a context be useful to recall (for instance) Ambedkar's exchange

with Gandhi about separate electorates at the Second Round Table Conference in London about which more will be said later in the chapter.

The following sections will attempt to bring out the differences between Gandhi and Ambedkar's understandings of justice along these two lines.

5.1   Justice: Two Central Insights

One might argue that whatever be the differences among thinkers (past and present) about how we think about justice or how we might formulate reasons for justice, there is nothing modern about a concern for justice itself which persists over time and connects the ages and the affairs of human beings. Indeed one might forge a connection between the years around 360 BCE and the year 1971 (some 23 hundred years later) in that important treatises about justice appeared in these years. Plato's *The Republic* appeared in approximately 360 BCE and John Rawls' *A Theory of Justice* came in 1971. *The Republic* contained a discussion on justice in line with the views of the ancients and it conceived justice as an attribute of both individuals and of the societies in which they lived (somewhat parallel, though not analogous to, the differentiation between *niti* and *dharma/dhamma* and *nyaya*). Striking a different note, one that set the tone for liberal modernity in our times, Rawls (1971) spoke of justice as the first virtue of institutions drawing from the Western tradition from Rousseau, Kant, Hegel, Marx and those who followed them. Perhaps, this might lead to the humbling thought that no matter how unique and special our times and problems might seem while we suffer them, questions of justice and problems of injustice have always occupied humanity. It is the very same question of justice that both underlies and sets the terms for the debate between Gandhi and Ambedkar uniting them with other ancients and moderns in a concern for justice across spaces, ages and epochs.

The recent set of five volumes on B. R Ambedkar (aptly entitled) *The Quest for Justice* (Rathore 2021a) declares at the start (in the introduction to the first volume in the set) that "Justice is a complex and multi-faceted concept, and none of its components or constituent aspects are necessarily exclusive of all of the others. If we distinguish political justice from social, legal, economic, or gender justice, it is only for the sake of focus and spotlight…" (Rathore 2021a, xxiii). This is saying a lot without saying much for it only tells us how the different aspects of life are inter-connected by concerns of justice and does not throw much light on what is at issue when we claim to have justice on our side. Rathore (in his introduction) fails to ask and answer the question—'what is it that we (or in this case Ambedkar) mean to bring up when we (or he) talk/s about justice?'.

To begin with a primary sense, attached to the term 'justice' is that of getting **what might be due to one** irrespective of whether such a just reward conflicts with the self-interest of oneself or that of others. In that sense, justice often makes demands that an individual put his/her interest behind that of society in general or that of some other person/persons. However, one needs to note that justice can also demand that we perform or refrain from performing actions even when such actions (or refraining from such actions) could undermine the interests of society as a whole. It becomes pertinent then to enquire into the source of the authority/sanctions behind such exacting demands of justice? At the risk of over simplification, one might say that there are two broad types of answers to this question in the history of Anglo American-European philosophy. The first set comes from the works of Mill and Hume, and the second derives from Kant and from Rawls in more recent times. To put things very simply, the first set of answers traces the source of the authority of the exacting demands of justice to utility, and the second argues that the demands of justice derive their authority from the fact that human beings *qua* human beings are ends in themselves and deserve to be treated with respect. Moving on to more contemporary discourse in political philosophy, the term "justice" most often "refers to fairness in the distribution of benefits and burdens in society" (Arneson 2012, 58). It is in such a context perhaps that we can locate the work of a large number of political philosophers nearer to our times.

Following Rawls, contemporary political philosophers assume that principles of justice (relating to the distribution of benefits and burdens) have priority over all other kinds of normative judgments, and that if a society is unjust (in the distribution of benefits and burdens), it ought to be changed to eliminate that injustice. However, this is where the agreement ends, and just about everything else, about fairness in the distribution of benefits and burdens is contested. Note the disputes about what is to count as fair distribution that range from the utilitarians, through Rawls, Nozick's Libertarian doctrine of rights, Ronald Dworkin's Equality of Resources doctrine to the welfarist approach to justice and Prioritism[i] (Parfit 2000) (to mention only the most prominent approaches). This chapter does not seek to enter any such debate to evaluate which pattern of distribution is the most appropriate but rather contends itself with pointing out that there is nothing uncontested in this domain. The chapter seeks to share the thought that there is no unique right answer to what constitutes fairness in the distribution of benefits and burdens in society and things have been said by philosophers on all sides of the conflicts about fairness and distribution.

Taking a philosophical and more fundamental approach, this chapter, seeks rather to highlight two important insights that seem important to understanding justice itself and consequently the debate about justice between Gandhi and Ambedkar. These are insights about what it is at issue, and what might be the appropriate reasons we can bring up, when we proceed to address questions of establishing justice and redressing injustice. It is indeed important to make a note at the start of this chapter that the discussion here remains limited to basic insights about such a task (in terms of its bearing on the differences between Gandhi and Ambedkar on justice) rather than seek to offer resolutions to questions about the nature of perfect justice. The first insight which the chapter (and discussion) seeks to highlight as foundational to any philosophical discussion about justice (as seen earlier) relates to the fact that there can be two aspects/approaches to any discussion about justice which pertain to whether justice is seen as purely an institutional virtue or as both institutional and personal/contextual. The second insight about justice (whether conceived in terms of fairness in distributive concerns or individual rights) pertains to the sorts of reasons which are appropriate to discussions about justice. This is an insight about the kind of reasons that one might give one another for normative conclusions about justice and how **one might have arrived at** such reasons or at identifying and redressing injustice:

> ...we are forced to confront the question: How ought we to decide among the claims of rival and incompatible accounts of justice competing for our moral, social, and political allegiance?
>
> It would be natural enough to attempt to reply to this question by asking which systematic account of justice we would accept if the standards by which our actions were guided were the standards of rationality. To know what justice is, so it may seem, we must first learn what rationality in practice requires of us. (MacIntyre 1988, 2)

5.1.1 Different Approaches to Justice: A Virtue of Institutions or/and Persons

Since the *Bhagavad Gita* has been a continuous presence in Gandhi (and therefrom in this book), I will introduce the distinction between an institution centred and the more individual/contextual perhaps (what Sen describes as a) realization focused approach to justice by going back to the *Bhagavad Gita*. Taking the lead from Amartya Sen (2010, 23–24), it might seem useful to re-visit Arjuna's despondency and difficulties with war in the *Gita*.

> The life within me seems to swim and faint;
> Nothing do I forsee save woe and wail!
> It is not good, O Keshav! nought of good
> Can Spring from mutual slaughter! Lo, I hate
> Triumph and domination, wealth and ease,
> Thus sadly won! Aho! what victory
> Can bring delight, Govinda! what rich spoils
> Could profit; what rule recompense; what span
> Of life itself seem sweet, bought with such blood?
> ...Brothers, and father-in laws, and sons-in-law
> Elders and friends! Shall I deal death on these.... (Arnold 1965, 18)

There had been some occasion to visit the differences between Tilak and Gandhi's interpretations of Sri Krishna's answer to Arjuna's despondency and recommendation to fight in the previous chapter. For now, taking a *que* from Sen, one might consider what implications Arjuna's arguments against taking part in the war might have for the distinction between a more person/realization centred and a more institution-centric approach to justice.

In this context (and at this initiating point into the discussion), one might visit Ashis Nandy's argument that 'politics' is the only category that has remained a constant for the last two thousand years in India (Nandy 1970). One might extend this argument from the term 'politics' and argue for the presence of an *itihaas* of thinking not only about 'politics' but also about 'justice' and its realization in ancient India. Yet in justice, as in politics, of which Nandy had spoken, discussion in twentieth-century India was divided between those who practised politics (and thought about the concerns of justice) in the 'Western' mode, drawing upon concepts and notions from predominantly Western political discourse and those who (theorized about and) practised politics (and thought about justice) through a deep 'emic' set of lenses, i.e. by using concepts which had no equivalents in the Western political vocabulary.

Another related point is that Nandy had assumed and argued that the only source of 'authentically indigenous' concepts was a series of texts produced in Sanskrit in ancient India. This argument somewhat limited the reach of discussions on justice to deep-rooted and culturally specific vocabulary in Sanskrit involving (usually substantive and untranslatable) terms such as *dharma, karma, artha, sannyasa* and the like. While one need not accept Rathore's critique of what he terms the conception of a "thick" (Rathore 2017, 11) *svaraj* in ideas, one might heed the note of caution in his recommendation that scholars need to move towards a more inclusive "thin svaraj that seeks to complete the decolonial ambitions of achieving autonomy and self-determination, but in line with the pluralist and egalitarian strands that also exist within the traditions of …Indian thought and practices,…" (*Ibid.*, 18). In such a context, it is important to note that Velcheru Narayana Rao and Sanjay Subrahmanyam have drawn attention to sources outside Sanskrit as additional resources for a conception of justice. They have argued, for instance, that "a quite substantial and varied body of material can be found in South India between the fourteenth and eighteenth centuries that attempts to theorize politics, while doing so neither in Persian nor in Sanskrit, even if it may bear traces of contact with bodies of material in these two "classical" languages. These materials may be found instead in the Indian vernacular languages…" (Rao and Subrahmanyam 2009, 179).

It seems fairly clear that (though Nandy does not take note of this) there are also rich sources of discussions on "justice" as *niti nyaya* and *dharma* in the various Indian languages. Amartya Sen gestures towards such sources when he argues that one needs to look outside of the Anglo American and predominantly institution-centric approach to justice. He explains that;

> Those who tend to see justice in terms of *niti* rather than *nyaya*, no matter what they call that dichotomy, may be influenced by their fear that a concentration on actual realizations would tend to ignore the significance of social processes, including the exercise of individual duties and responsibilities. We may do the right thing and yet we may not succeed. (Sen 2010, 22).

Sen explains why such a concern (a concern that perhaps drives all institution-centric approaches) might be misplaced saying that a full characterization of realizations "should have room to include the exact processes through which the eventual states of affairs emerge". (Ibid.)

What of the difficulties voiced by Arjuna in the *Bhagavad Gita*? Is this a straightforward conflict (as it is often made out to be) between the deontological perspective (of duty for duty's sake) and that of the process-independent view of the consequentialist? Sen argues that one needs here "to go beyond that simple contrast to examine what the totality of Arjuna's concerns were about the prospect of his *not* faring well. Arjuna is not concerned only about the fact that, if the war were to occur, with him leading the charge on the side of justice and propriety, many people would get killed. That too, but Arjuna also expresses concern, in the early part of the *Gita* itself, that he himself would be doing a lot of the killing…Indeed, the actual event that Arjuna worries about goes well beyond the process-independent view of consequences. An appropriate understanding of social realization-central to justice as *nyaya* -has to take the comprehensive form of a process-inclusive broad account". (Ibid., 24).

This last point (about the social realization of justice as a process inclusive broad account) might have become clearer if Sen had brought up not only the term *nyaya* but also the notion of *dharma/dhamma*[ii] (which I will bring up in the section that follows). For there could be much lost by leaving *dhamma/dharma* out in speaking about a person/realization-centric approach to justice in the Indian tradition. One can argue then that the terms, *niti, dharma/dhamma* and *nyaya,* bear witness to the fact that the Indian tradition incorporated both persons and institutions in reflecting upon justice (and the eradication of injustice). Indeed, the existence of three terms with bearings on legal–moral–political concerns of justice indicates some sophistication in the ideas, in terms of which, the Indian tradition problematized issues concerning justice. If one thought about justice from within that tradition, so to speak, one might have thought about it in a manner so as to include a concern for processes/concrete institutional arrangements as well as practical realization/appropriate behaviour by individuals in particular contexts where justice might be sought. In other words, somewhat closer to the *nyaya/dharma/dhamma/niti* combine rather than in terms of *niti* alone. Velcheru Narayana Rao and Sanjay Subrahmanyam argue that *niti* texts "demonstrate a lively change with time and context as guides to practical wisdom, and strategies of success; and second, that they are not concerned with religion and are therefore mostly 'this-worldly' (*laukika*) or 'secular'…" (Rao and Subrahmanyam 2009, 182). Interestingly, Velcheru Narayana Rao and Sanjay Subrahmanyam contrast *niti* not with *nyaya*[iii] but with *dharma.* They point to the existence of both a sophisticated discipline termed *niti* (with texts in regional languages and in Sanskrit notable here being the *Arthashastra*) and a whole range of texts on *dharma,* the most well known of which was the infamous Manu's *Dharmashastra* (dating perhaps from the early centuries CE).

Manu's text was embroiled in *jati* and *varna* laws and justly discredited (for posterity) on that account. Yet, one often tends to skim over the point that such discredit should not attach itself to the notion of *dharma/dhamma* in itself. Which last, one should note, has a history in both *Brahmanical* and *Sramanic* ideologies, and about which, classical texts were composed in more than one language (Sanskrit, Pali and Tamil).

Major *dharma/dhamma* texts go back to the early Mauryan period and include the Ashokan edicts, *Apastamba Dharma sutra*, Buddhist *Nikayas* from that period. At least, twelve major *dharma/dhamma* texts have been listed (Hiltebeitel 2011, 8) across the early Maurya, later Maurya, *sunga-kanva* and *post-kanva* to early *kusana* period. The term *dharma/dhamma* "takes on discursive breadth and diversity across languages and religious preferences…" (Ibid., 6) in the Indian tradition.

While the term *niti* and therefrom the texts explaining *niti* were concerned with institutions, *nyaya* and *dharma/dhamma* were context bound notions. The historian Ramanujan emphasizes this "context-sensitive nature of *dharma*" (Ramanujan 1989, 47) in the Indian tradition. He connects the context bound notion of *dharma* with (what he has described as) a characteristic that marks the Indian way of thinking, a "pervasive emphasis on context" (Ibid., 53). To recollect the somewhat copious mention of *dharma/dhamma* across traditional texts, one might note that between 300 BCE and 200 CE, concepts and practices of *dharma/dhamma* attained prominence through out India. An important point that bears re-iteration is that it is through the notion of *dharma/dhamma* that *Sramanic* and *Brahmanical* traditions articulate their distinct visions of the good and well-rewarded life. The connection between *niti* and *dharma/dhamma* in the Indian tradition (and in Gandhi as will emerge in the Sect. 5.3 of this chapter) goes powerfully against the liberal understanding of justice as concerned with what it is right to do rather than good to become.[iv] One may note that even as early as Aśoka's Inscriptions (which can be followed through his reign) from the early Mauryan period, the Indian tradition made a connection between justice as a virtue of persons and institutions. This might seem evident from the very fact that Aśoka's Inscriptions which spoke of individual *dharma/dhamma* were meant to broadcast an imperial program. In the twelfth year of his reign for instance, "...Asoka presents the changes he is seeking to implement in relation to his ideas about past and future time..." (Hiltebeitel 2011, 41) in the following edict;

> In the past, over many centuries, killing, violence done to creatures, discourtesy to relatives, and disrespect for Brahmins and Samaṇas have only increased... Promulgation of *dhamma* has increased that which did not exist over many centuries: abstention from killing, kindness to creatures, respect to relatives, respect for Brahmins and Samaṇas, and obedience to mother, father and elders... (Ibid.)

Clearly (as several edicts reveal), Aśoka had realized that if one had to ensure the stability of a conception of justice for a given society one needed, as a correlative, to inspire/encourage individual's to become established in the practice of *dhamma*:

> There are certainly good reasons to emphasize Aśoka's political motivation along with his administrative shrewdness in putting a generalized *dhamma* to imperial work. (Ibid., 43)

If one moves between the *Sramanic* and *Brahmanic* traditions to the *Vedic* history of *dharma* in *Brahmanical* texts starting with the *Rgveda*, "India's oldest textual source, ...the indispensible starting point for a history of *dharma*..." (Ibid., 52). Brereton suggests that the term *dharma* in *vedic* (as in *Sramanic*) sources denotes a thing which supports or upholds, that is, a foundation (Brereton 2004, 450). Consequently, the term *dharma* was translated in the *Sramanic* and *Brahmanic* sources as that which was the foundation of society. It also signified, more generally, that which was the foundational nature of any particular thing (of which I will say more a little later). It is perhaps important to emphasize that it is only in early Buddhism that *dharma/dhamma* becomes a truly vast topic;

> If we extend the notion of early Buddhism through our classical period, we have to consider not only the ways *dharma* is treated and transmitted in the different collections or "baskets"

of texts that comprise the Pāli canon of Theravāda Buddhism but, once we begin to unfold that process, some of the variations in the so-called eighteen schools of "Hīnayāna" Buddhism and some of the important developments in early (not to mention Chinese) Mahāyāna. (Hiltebeitel 2011, 103)

Given that Gandhi explicitly mentioned his relationship to that text, another important text (in terms of the bearing of this issue on the Ambedkar Gandhi debate) is the *Valmiki Ramayana.* In this connection, one might look at how Narada responds to Valmiki's question as to whether there is an ideal man in the world today;

Is there a man in the world today who is truly virtuous… and energetic and yet knows both *dharma* and how to act upon it…? Who always speaks the truth and hold firmly to his vows? Who exemplifies proper conduct and is benevolent to all creatures? …Who is both judicious and free from envy?.... (*Valmiki Ramayana* quoted in Hiltebeitel 2011, 415)

If one is to reflect upon the constant inter-relationship between persons and institutions in the traditional Indian discourse about justice, it seems apparent enough (from the above) that one cannot ignore the conceptual significance of the *dharma/dhamma* combine;

The word '*dharma*' subsumes the English concepts of 'religion' 'duty' 'law' 'right' 'justice' 'practice' and 'principle'. In the Hindu tradition *dharma* has encompassed a wide range of topics- apparently varied- but intimately interrelated in Hindu thought. These include the social obligations and duties of the various castes and of individuals in different stages of life, the proper way for a righteous King to rule, and to punish transgressors in his kingdom, the appropriate social relations between men and women of different castes, and of husbands and wives in the primacy of the home; Birth, death and taxes; cosmogony, karma and rebirth; ritual practices; error and restoration or redemption; and such details of ordinary life as procedures for settling traffic accidents, adjudicating disputes, penances etc. (Doniger 1991, xvii)

While the *Manu Smriti* has brought out (and been associated with) all the injustice that the ancient Indian society had unpacked into the association between the practice of *dharma* and caste distinctions, such injustice should not be allowed to attach itself to the conceptual distinction between justice as a virtue of institutions and persons. One might note here for instance that *dhamma/dharma* had been used in Asoka's many edicts. At the risk of putting it far too simplistically, one could suggest that the *dharma/dhamma,*across the *Sramanic* and *Bramanical* traditions, can be best understood in terms of the demands of righteousness/justice in relation to one's context— as king, as adjudicator, as an individual—in the process of living out one's different roles. That said, the purpose of this very brief philosophical foray into the term has been to make the point that there was indeed a long tradition of speaking about justice in terms of *niti/dharma/dhamma* in ancient Indian texts. Notwithstanding the injustice that came to be associated with the *Brahmanic* interpretations of the demands of *dharma,* Gandhi, reasoning from within the *Sramanic/Brahmanic* combine in the Indian tradition, might have found himself at some variance from an approach to justice such as that adopted by Ambedkar which concentrated on institutions, inspired as it was, from largely Western sources.

In such a connection, this might be the appropriate place to note that while the young Gandhi found Bentham's *Theory of Utility* unreadable Ambedkar emersed himself in the traditions of natural and positive law going on to deliver his lectures on the English Constitution at the Government Law College, Bombay, between 1934 and 1935 (Ambedkar 2014, Vol. 12). A detailed discussion on Gandhi's alternate conception of justice will form the subject of the last section (in this chapter). However, one might note (in passing) that Ambedkar was at sharp variance from Gandhi and seemed to have adopted a Western and predominantly institution-centric approach to justice.

One might emphasize in this context that just as much as he had rejected the Hindu conceptions of *dharma* and *nyaya,* Ambedkar had also completely ignored and failed to make philosophical use of the ancient Buddhist tradition of *dharma/dhamma* as a resource for articulating a conception of justice. One might note here (in line with the discussion in Chap. 3, Sect. 3.3.2.1 of this book) that Ambedkar had spoken copiously about *dhamma* in the context of a "new religion" (Ambedkar2014, 17 Part 2: 104)[1] for the "new world" (Ibid., 105*).* One might recall here that in Part 1 and 11 of Book IV (of *The Buddha and his Dhamma)* on "Religion and *Dhamma*", Ambedkar had argued that what Buddha had taught was *Dhamma*/morality which as (he argued) was different from Religion. In Chap. 3 of this book (Sect. 3.4.3), I have made the point that the distinction between *dhamma* and religion reveals that Ambedkar's conversion to Buddhism does not signify a religious turn. This is because Ambedkar had clearly distinguished between religion and *dhamma* and rejected that which was ordinarily understood by the term 'religion'. Yet it is surely significant that, notwithstanding the writing of *The Buddha and his Dhamma,* the notion of *dhamma* itself does not seem to have played a significant role in Ambedkar's understanding of the demands of justice. In part, this was because (as I argued in Chap. 3) the modern self had come of age in India in the person of Babasaheb Ambedkar. One might consider that for such a self and for liberal modernity itself;

> Government and law are, or ought to be, neutral between rival conceptions of the good life for man, and hence, although it is the task of government to promote law-abidingness, it is on the liberal view no part of the legitimate function of government to inculcate any one moral outlook. (MacIntyre 1981, 182)

Such arguments might indeed have served to keep Ambedkar equidistant from both the *Brahmanical* and *Sramanic* traditions of *dharma/dhamma.* One might note here that Ambedkar spoke in contrast and copiously of inculcating what he termed as "constitutional morality" rather than any conception of the good life or indeed concepts thereof. Ambedkar's response to criticisms that were made against the Draft Constitution of India that "no part of it represents the ancient polity of India" (Ambedkar 2014, 13: 61) ought also to be noted. Ambedkar argued (in response)

---

[1] Ambedkar 2014, refers to the 17 volumes of *Dr Babasaheb Ambedkar writings and Speeches.* The volume concerned and the page numbers from which citations have been drawn have been mentioned within parentheses. These have been mentioned to indicate the exact location of the quotation in the 17 volumes. However, for the purposes of reference, it may be noted that I have resourced these volumes from Ambedkar, B.R. 2014. *Dr Babasaheb Ambedkar writings and Speeches,* edited by Vasant Moon (set of 17 Volumes). New Delhi: Dr Ambedkar Foundation. Ministry of Social Justice and Empowerment. Government of India.

to such criticisms that "T(t)he love of the intellectual Indians for the village is of course infinite if not pathetic". (Ibid.). He expressed satisfaction in having framed a constitution for India which had followed the constitutions of the Western world rather than one that drew upon concepts concerning justice in the Indian tradition. That he had consciously rejected any version of a traditional Indian approach to justice (as both institution and person-centric) finds additional support from the fact that while Ambedkar himself had referred too (and been comfortable with) *niti* texts[v] he had difficulties (fairly natural given the manner in which texts like *Manu Smriti* had used the term *dharma*) when thinking about justice for the basic structure of society to make conceptual use of person-centric concepts like, *nyaya, dhamma* and *dharma,* that had bearings on Hindu and Buddhist conceptions of the good life(or what it might be right to do) for man. Even though *niti* texts (as noted earlier) could be seen as not primarily concerned with the good life for man and in that sense, secular rather than religious, the modern Ambedkar could not take such texts seriously when framing a constitution for India. He was more comfortable with following the lead of a predominantly liberal Western modernity;

> One really likes to ask whether there can be anything new in a constitution framed at this hour in the history of the world. More than hundred years have rolled over when the first written constitution was drafted… what are the fundamentals of a constitution are recognized all over the world. Given these facts all Constitutions in their main provisions must look similar. (Ibid., 59)

Such an emphasis on liberal constitutions already written for nations in the modern world and on Constitutional morality lead Ambedkar to reject, rather than neglect, the ancient Indian traditions of *dhamma/dharma* in connection with justice. In his speech to present the Draft Constitution of India, he made it apparent that constitutional morality on which justice (as set up by such a constitution) was to be based rested upon the details of administration having been explicitly specified in the constitution of the land;

> …the form of administration has a close connection with the form of the Constitution … Constitutional morality is not a natural sentiment. It has to be cultivated… In these circumstances it is wiser not to trust the legislature to prescribe forms of administration. This is the justification for incorporating them in the constitution. (Ibid., 61)

As Chakraborty notes;

> Not only was Ambedkar the principal architect of the Constitution, he was also a staunch advocate of the interventionist modernizing state and the legal protection of 'modern' virtues of equal citizenship and secularism. A liberal to the core, he while seeking to provide a modern constitution sought to address a major contradiction between utopian homogeneity and existent heterogeneity given the prevalance of 'obvious' and also well-entrenched fragments in Indian society. (Chakrabarty 2019, 141)

This might be an appropriate juncture to bring up Bhikhu Parekh's (Parekh 2021) observations on the four limitations in Ambedkar's social and political thought as these might serve to highlight some difficulties with Ambedkar's liberal institution centred approach to justice. These points serve to bring out the insight that though the association between the practice of *dharma* and caste rules discredited the notion of *dharma* itself, such discredit might not justify the conceptual (indeed philosophical) neglect of the role of persons (and the *dhamma/dharma* combine outside of its association with texts like the *Manu Smriti*) in ensuring the stability of justice for the basic institutions of society. Ambedkar though (for good reasons) completely neglected such insights and made liberal modernity at home in India. As I argued in Chap. 3, while it can be said that he changed the manner in which the Indian tradition had thought about (or indeed failed to think about) freedom, equality and justice, he also changed the way liberals themselves had thought about modernity.

That said, it is also important to turn to the limitations of Ambedkar's liberal and institution-centric approach to justice Parekh has argued that; "f(F)irst, Ambedkar relied too heavily on intricate institutional mechanisms and devices to promote the interests on the untouchables, and did not fully appreciate the importance of changing the moral culture of the wider society and Gandhi's role in it" (Ibid., 25). Gandhi, in contrast, as Parekh argues, tried to press for inner change and individual self-transformation. Secondly, Ambedkar tended to create homogenized dalit and caste hindu communities and remained oblivious to internal differences and differentiations. On this view, Ambedkar dismissed other dalit leaders;

> Ambedkar tended to challenge their representative credentials and sometimes dismissed them as Congress stooges or victims of false consciousness. Apart from being unfair, such an approach tended to discourage a vigorous and healthy debate among the untouchables…
> (Ibid., 27).

Parekh argues that Ambedkar showed the same homogenizing tendency towards caste Hindus condemning them as a group incapable of justice "and once even said that no Hindu judge could be trusted to do justice to the untouchables…" (Ibid.)

Making his third point, Parekh argues that "Ambedkar's thought had a strong statist and elitist bias. Like many modernists he drew too neat a contrast between State and society, seeing the former as a rational progressive agency and the latter as reactionary and blighted… The state for him could only play a radical reformist role if it was led by a Westernized elite free from the limitations of the vast majority of fellow citizens and acting in an authoritarian manner" (Ibid., 28). Fourth (and last) Parekh argues that though Ambedkar spoke about fraternity "he gave very little thought on how to develop and nurture it… Equal citizenship facilitated it but it too was not enough…" (Ibid.).

While these comments might well leave the reader unconvinced and content with the insight that justice is the first virtue of social institutions and best kept at a distance from the vagaries of persons and from notions of practical wisdom in the lineage of Aristotelean *phronesis,* Amartya Sen strikes a contrary note. Sen argues for "the interdependent roles of institutions and behavioural patterns in achieving justice in society" (Sen 2010, 77). He re-iterates that there is evidence of both kinds of approaches in the Indian tradition referring to Kautilya's *Arthashastra* and to Asoka's edicts. The one in his view was "a no-nonsense institutional view of advancing justice" (Ibid., 76). The second "focused on the idea that voluntary good behaviour of citizens themselves without being compelled through force" (Ibid.) was important to the realization of a just society.

Sen's argument is part of his wider point that the primarily Western Anglo American philosophical tradition has dominated contemporary discussion about the demands of justice. Perhaps, it should be said that this tradition has come to dominate how we think about justice, as it has dominated, how we think about the self and the relationship between the self and the other. However be that as it may, Sen points out, that this has led, to a serious lacuna in the dominant contemporary liberal approach to justice in that concentration on institutions (in that tradition) has in turn lead to a complete neglect of persons and realizations;

> ...remedial injustice may well be connected with behavioral transgression rather than with institutional shortcomings... Justice is intimately concerned with the way people's lives go, and not merely with the nature of the institutions surrounding them. (Ibid., x)

Sen's point is that there are inadequacies in any approach that concentrates on institutions and neglects persons, behaviour and practical concerns. The problem perhaps emerges from the fact that an institution centred approach (such as that taken by Rawls or in this case by Ambedkar) suffers from a difficulty that emerges from "giving no room to the possibility that some people may not always behave 'reasonably' despite the hypothetical social contract..." (Ibid., 90).

Sen's argument against what he terms "institutional fundamentalism" (Ibid., 83) has to do with his emphasis on the incorporation of a comparative perspective while seeking to understand justice;

> In confining attention almost exclusively to Western literature, the contemporary and largely Western pursuit of political philosophy in general and of the demands of justice in particular has been, I would argue, limited and to some extent parochial. (Ibid., xiv)

I would interject here (in response to Sen and to Parekh) that besides the fact that looking at justice purely though an institution-centric perspective might be inef- fective, in that, people might not act reasonably or quite do what is laid down in the laws and contracts (that are at the foundation of liberal Constitutions), there are more fundamental philosophical issues at stake. These have to do with the difference between the way in which "the relationship between moral character and political virtues is envisaged from the standpoint of liberal individualist modernity and the way in which that relationship was envisaged from the standpoint of ...ancient and medi- aeval traditions of virtues..." (MacIntyre 1981, 182). For Asoka or for the *Ramayana,* one might say (with MacIntyre) that there was a close relationship between "the ability of a practice to retain its integrity" (Ibid.) and "the way in which the virtues can be and are exercised in sustaining the institutional forms which are the social bearers of the practice" (Ibid.) What this means is that in ancient traditions, justice requires both institutional arrangements and some demands on, and reference to, the individual exercise of virtue within institutions. The same argument can be extended to any approach that seeks to remedy historical injustice. Ambedkar endorsed a liberal understanding of justice and this led him to reject Gandhi's approach to justice and to the redressal of injustice focusing as it did on individual virtue and its correlative notion that of individual vice/sin. It might be possible to argue that given that he had thought from within the framework of liberal modernity, Ambedkar could simply not bring himself to share Gandhi's understanding of justice;

> For liberal individualism a community is simply an arena in which individuals each pursue their own self-chosen conception of the good life, and political institutions exist to provide that degree of order which makes such self-determined activity possible. (Ibid.)

Though I do not mean to argue against liberal individualism and its purely institutional approach to justice or indeed in favour of an approach that combines *niti* and *nyaya/dharma/dhamma* (and is in continuity with ancient Indian traditions which made a conceptual distinction between these terms), it is important to emphasize that there are alternative traditions at work in these two approaches. Taking note of such an alterniety between traditions might serve to better understand the divergence between Ambedkar and the old-world Gandhi's understanding of justice and injustice and approach to institutions and persons in that regard.

5.1.2 Practical Rationality and Justice: The Demands of Objectivity and Impartiality

Moving from the distinction between persons and institutions in terms of the bearing of that distinction on justice/injustice, there is another important insight that needs to be brought out in any discussion about justice. Namely that one needs to appreciate, that though an identification of redressable injustice must move us to think about justice that cannot be a "good ending point" (Sen 2010, viii). We need also to "ask what kinds of reasoning should count in the assessment of ethical and political concepts such as justice and injustice" (Ibid.). Even in the face of and besides the insightful criticism made by MacIntyre (1988) and others (e.g. Sandel 2008), I would argue that Rawls was able to raise issues that contain insights somewhat crucial to the connections between rationality, impartiality and justice.

At the start, I must mention that the account of Rawls here is completely elementary. This might seem obvious enough from the fact that Rawls is tertiary (at best) to the central argument of this book but it also follows from the fact that Rawls' theory of justice as fairness is both much commented upon and has been subject to various interpretations. Doing justice to these varied readings of Rawls would take me too far afield from the central interest of this book and indeed of this chapter. My reference to Rawls here is only to remind those, already familiar with his theory, of the bare outlines and to bring out the most important insights about justice that (in my view) his exposition serves to bring out.

This takes me straight to the two fundamental ideas of justice as fairness—the original position and the veil of ignorance. Rawls asks "why introduce the idea of the original position" (Rawls 2005, 22) and answers the question in unambiguous terms;

…we must find some point of view, removed from and not distorted by the particular features
and circumstances of the all-encompassing background framework, from which a fair agreement between persons regarded as free and equal can be reached. The original position, with
the features I have called "the veil of ignorance', is this point of view. (Ibid. 23)

The point is that (for Rawls) the way to think about what would be a just organization of society is to imagine what would be the principles accepted by people who
were placed in situations where they did not have any knowledge about particular
facts about themselves or where they were placed in society. What is important is
that the sorts of reasons which might emerge from the particularities of one's own
position/experiences are simply not relevant to the choice of the principles to govern
the basic structure of society. This led Rawls to suggest that the allocation of rights
and the regulation of the distribution of social and economic advantages should be
understood as that which would emerge from a hypothetical contract which would
be arrived at between persons who were ignorant of the unique particularities of their
own beliefs, experiences and circumstances. One might well ask again 'why should
it be appropriate (even purely as a device of representation) to regard people as ignorant of their position, beliefs and life experiences, while thinking about justice?' The
intuition about justice that is being captured here is that which links justice with
impartiality and positional objectivity;

…one of our considered convictions, I assume, is this: the fact that we occupy a particular
social position is not a good reason for us to propose, or to expect others to accept, a
conception of justice that favors those in this position. Similarly, the fact that we affirm
a particular religious, philosophical, or moral comprehensive doctrine with its associated
conception of the good is not a reason for us to propose, or to expect others to accept,
a conception of justice that favors those of that persuasion. To model this conviction in
the original position, the parties are not allowed to know the social position of those they
represent, or the particular comprehensive doctrine of the person each represents. (Ibid., 24)

The demands of impartiality extends (naturally enough) to the sorts of reasons
that can be offered in arguments/debates about justice/injustice or indeed to remedial
measures to counter historical injustice. Rawls describes the sort of reasons that can
not be offered "on matters of constitutional essentials and basic justice, …" (Ibid.,
224). He argues;

This means that in discussing constitutional essentials and matters of basic justice we are not
to appeal to comprehensive religious and philosophical doctrines- or what we as individuals
or members of associations see as the whole truth-… (Ibid., 224–225)

This argument rests on the founding insight that for the purpose of justice, we need
to regard each person as free and equal to every other person and to think of society
itself as a fair system of social cooperation. This fundamental organizing insight has
to be built into the kind of reasons and arguments we (citizens of liberal democracies)
offer one another while discussing constitutional essentials. One might again ask,
why is it, that the enlightenment overreach on reason, as primary to the reasons and
arguments that might properly be offered to each other concerning justice, seems
convincing? Are not emotions (witness anger, outrage, suffering, humiliation) as
convincing if not more honourable than reason? Why should we accept that reason

should be the ultimate arbitrator of arguments about justice? One insight that might be invaluable here is that which connects justice (and injustice) to objectivity, a difficult notion in moral and political philosophy;

> The important role given to reasoning….relates to the need for objective reasoning in thinking about issues of justice and injustice. (Sen 2010, 41)

The reason that I brought up Rawls in this section was that, he had himself brought up, in perhaps the most powerful way in the history of political philosophy, two intimately related ideas—those of objectivity and impartiality—in terms of their unique conceptual relationship to justice. This relationship becomes even clearer when Sen asks if it would be possible to align Rawls' with Adam Smith's use of the device of the impartial spectator. Posing the question "what would an impartial spectator from a distance say about justice or injustice as a characteristic of an act or institution?", Sen connects Adam Smith with Rawls and Habermas;

> Despite the differences between the distinct types of arguments presented by Smith Habermas and Rawls, there is an essential similarity in their respective approaches to objectivity to the extent that objectivity is linked… by each of them to the ability to survive challenges from informed scrutiny from diverse quarters. (Ibid., 45)

From a Rawlsian position, it seems apparent that Justice derives from fairness, and fairness on its part is linked with objectivity and impartiality in the following manner;

> So what is fairness? This foundational idea can be given shape in various ways, but central to it must be a demand to avoid bias in the evaluations, taking note of the interests and concerns of others as well, and in particular… it can be seen as a demand for impartiality. (Ibid., 54)

Though there are genuinely plural and often conflicting concerns that bear (the debates in the Constituent Assembly on the proposed Constitution of India might come to mind here) on our understanding of what justice demands, if one is to be just at all, one must (on such a view) be impartial between them. This then leads me to the next section on open and closed impartiality and how this distinction is implicated in the debate between Gandhi and Ambedkar on justice and injustice.

5.2   Justice and Impartiality

I will continue to digress from the debate between Gandhi and Ambedkar, as philosophers are wont to do, to speak about closed and open impartiality. It is interesting to note that philosophers like Sandel have argued that Rawls' conception of the original position is misguided as it rests on the idea that the self can be separated from its attributes and viewed purely individualistically. As Sandel puts it; "…the entire account of circumstances of justice is located within the account of the original position, the conditions and motivations it describes are asserted only of the parties to the original position and not necessarily of real human beings" (Sandel 2008, 41). It is in reply to such critics that Rawls clarifies that the original position is simply a device of representation and that it does not involve any metaphysical presuppositions about the self (Rawls 2005, 27). If one recalls the three characteristic features of a political conception of justice and focuses on the first characteristic specified by Rawls, one notes that it is a moral conception worked out for the "basic Structure" (Ibid., 11) of society. Rawls clarifies;

> ...the basic structure is that of a closed society; that is, we are to regard it as self-contained and as having no relations with other societies. Its members enter it only by birth and leave it only by death... (Ibid., 12)

Of course Rawls does speak about the fact that a political conception of justice must, at some point, address the just relations between "the law of peoples" (Ibid.), and Rawls does go on to address such relations (Rawls 1999). Yet Rawls' justice as fairness, like other social contract theories about justice, views the social contract as negotiated within a contracting society and seems to speak of the demands of objectivity as necessarily confined within the pluralistic concerns of the contracting society. Amartya Sen argues that such closed impartiality neglects the organizing insight in Adam Smith's impartial spectator argument which captures that which is most significant about impartiality and its relationship to justice;

> In contrast, in the case of 'open impartiality', the procedure of making impartial assessments can (and in some cases, must) invoke judgements, among others, from outside the focal group, to avoid parochial bias. In Adam Smith's famous use of the device of the 'impartial spectator', the requirement of impartiality requires, as he explains in *The Theory of Moral Sentiments*, the invoking of disinterested judgments of 'any fair and impartial spectator' not necessarily (indeed sometimes ideally not) belonging to the focal group. (Sen 2010, 123)

The point is that a liberal (primarily contractarian) approach to justice proceeds on the notion of maintaining an objectivity between conflicting viewpoints, both in terms of non-subjectivity of comprehension and communication and objective acceptability. However, once such objectivity closes itself conceptually, and practically from the demands of open (rather than closed) impartiality (from the standpoint of the impartial spectator), it might not remain significantly objective at all. Sen captures something very significant about justice when he observes that it is only if the standpoint of the impartial spectator is admitted to evaluate, what we consider appropriate reasons, that one can speak of objectivity and impartiality in any meaningful sense. It is noteworthy that once objectivity (in a demand for closed impartiality) is seen to involve nothing more than a consideration of balance of power between the claims of conflicting and plural minorities and the majority within a target society/group, it might make room for nothing more than prudence/utility (or at best a *modus vivendi*) as a ground for the stability of a conception of justice;

> In this respect, the procedural device of closed impartiality in 'justice as fairness' can be seen as being parochial in construction. (Ibid., 126)

If this is true of Rawls, how might one view Ambedkar on the connection between impartiality and its close connection to justice? Of Gandhi, one can clearly say that he was simply not interested in the view from nowhere situating justice in a very different discourse. One which I shall argue (taking a philosophical lead from MacIntyre 1988) was located within the narrative unity of the Indian tradition and its *itihaas*. Gandhi invoked the language of kinship, and equi-mindedness towards all others, with the argument that one must extend the ties of kinship to the animate and inanimate world. This was a different kind of connection with a universalism of inclusion and one that drew from absolute equality and *ahimsanat*/non-violent equality of deference for the other. The last section of the chapter will attempt to put all such insights together in an alternative Gandhian conception of justice.

However, for the moment, one might turn to Ambedkar's own (what one might term) quagmire/entrapping predicament surrounding the demands of liberal impartiality. One could trace Ambedkar's difficulties with liberal impartiality to difficulties somewhat internal to the liberal understanding of practical rationality, impartiality and justice in itself. Problems which one might say were meticulously brought out by MacIntyre in the aptly titled *Whose Justice? Which Rationality* (MacIntyre 1988). MacIntyre had described the liberal conceptions of practical rationality and the demands of an individualistic conception of justice;

> Consider, for example, one at first sight very plausible philosophical thesis about how we ought to proceed in these matters if we are to be rational. Rationality requires, so it has been argued by a number of academic philosophers, that we first divest ourselves of allegiance to any one of the contending theories and also abstract ourselves from all those particularities of social relationship in terms of which we have been accustomed to understanding our responsibilities and our interests. Only by so doing, it has been suggested, shall we arrive at a genuinely neutral, impartial, and, in this way, universal point of view, freed from the partisanship and the partiality and onesidedness that otherwise affect us. And only by so doing shall we be able to evaluate the contending accounts of justice rationally. (MacIntyre 1988, 3)

The point of divesting oneself from any standpoint derived from the particularities of social relationships situated within inegalitarian societies and traditions, constituted, for Ambedkar, the substance of the appeal of a liberal conception of justice. However, the emphasis that one had, at the same time to be situated in an original position behind a veil of ignorance, and therefore ignorant of the significant features of one's own/ one's community's experience while arriving at a conception of justice and/or of affirmative action seemed (as seen above) deeply problematic to Ambedkar. This quagmire (internal to liberal conceptions of impartiality) perhaps plays out at its most visible in Sen's argument about the difficulties associated with the notions of open and closed impartiality. The point is that (no matter what the differences between them) liberal notions of practical rationality rest on the possibility of the individual abstracting her/him self from traditions of belonging so as to be able to take a disinterested view where questions of justice are at stake. However, if the disinterested view remains confined to the members of the community one enters at birth and exits at death (as in Rawls account of the parties in the original position), there is a **positional sequestering** that rejects the bearing of the point of view of the impartial spectator in matters concerning justice for the basic structure of society. That Ambedkar's position is similarly **positionally sequestered** becomes even more evident from his writing. It becomes apparent, for instance, when one considers his difficulties with the bearing of the point of view of those who had no knowledge of the experience of the dalits while evaluating questions of justice for the basic structure of the Indian polity. It is in this connection that the debate between Gandhi and Ambedkar on separate electorates becomes important to unpacking Ambedkar's own quagmire within a liberal understanding of impartiality.

To begin at the beginning, the history (and not *itihaas*) of the conflict about separate electorates is fairly well known;

> The governing feature of a separate electorate is that in an election through a separate electorate only voters of a community can vote and stand for election. (Ambedkar 2014, 9: 150)

To recount the important moments of the history of the conflict about separate electorates, one might recall that Ambedkar had attended the First Round Table Conference in London in 1930 as a representative of the depressed classes. However, it was not quite then that he put forth the idea of a separate electorate for the depressed classes in India. The Second Round Table Conference in London started on 7 September 1931, and it was only at this session Gandhi and Ambedkar had several clashes around this issue. On 29 January 1932, Ambedkar returned to Bombay but he went back to London in May 1932 to see British parliamentarians before the order on the communal issue was announced. The Communal Award was announced in August 1932. It granted a separate electorate to the "untouchables";

> These seats will be filled by election from special constituencies in which only members of the "depressed classes" electorally qualified will be entitled to vote. Any person voting in such a special constituency will,…be also entitled to vote in a general constituency. ('The Communal Award' quoted in Ambedkar 2014, 9: 80)

Gandhi started a fast unto death against the Award in September 1932. On Thursday 22 September 1932, Ambedkar went to meet Gandhi at Yeravda jail in the evening. The Poona Pact which brought this conflict to an end was signed by Gandhi and Ambedkar on 24 September 1932. This pact provided for a joint electorate with reservations for the depressed classes. However, as Gandhi had agreed to a considerable increase in the number of reserved seats, the pact disappointed the orthodox Hindus as much as it disappointed the depressed classes. It is important to emphasize that Ambedkar had fought for a separate political identity for the depressed classes and his reasons and arguments were concerned primarily with justice and the redressal of injustice. Gandhi on his part had also fought for justice and his reasons drew from the insight that, a universality of inclusion, was what justice and the redressal of injustice demanded.

As I had pointed out in the introduction to this book, Ambedkar was clear that on matters concerning justice the depressed classes could not be represented by anyone who did not share that identity. He had famously declared at the Second Round Table Conference in London;

> I say therefore that whether I am a nominee or not, I fully represent the claims of my community. Let no man be under the mistaken impression as regards that. (Ibid., 65)

And further;

The Mahatma has been always claiming that the congress stands for the Depressed Classes, and that the congress represents the Depressed Classes… To that claim I can only say that it is one of many false claims which irresponsible people keep on making, although the persons concerned with regard to those claims have been invariably denying them. (Ibid.)

Ambedkar took issue with Gandhi's claim to represent a community into which he had not been born. Note the following statement from Gandhi;

I claim myself in my own person to represent the vast mass of the Untouchables. Here I speak not merely on behalf of the Congress, but I speak on my own behalf… (Gandhi, quoted in Ibid., 68)

Criticizing the system that came into operation after the Poona pact (through Gandhi's Intervention) that is, the idea of joint electorates with seats reserved for the depressed classes, Ambedkar explained that;

A candidate whose majority is due to votes of persons other than Untouchables has no right to say that he is a representative of the Untouchables and the Congress cannot claim to represent the Untouchables through him merely because he belongs to the Untouchables and stood on a congress ticket… The only untouchable seats which the Congress can claim to have won are those which it has won, exclusively by the votes of the Untouchable voters. (Ibid., 157)

It seems possible to argue that Ambedkar's arguments in favour of separate electorates could not lend themselves to any conceptual device such as Rawls' device of the original position or the veil of ignorance for they were couched in the particularities of experience;

Let me now take the specific question, namely why it is necessary that in the Indian Constitution the Communal scheme must find its place and why in the Public Services for the Untouchables should be specified and should be assigned to them as their separate possession. The justification of these demands is easy and obvious. It arises from the undeniable fact that what divides the Untouchables from the Hindus is not mere matter of difference on non-essentials. It is a case of fundamental antagonism and antipathy. No evidence of this antipathy and antagonism is necessary… Given this antagonism it is simply impossible to ask the untouchables to depend upon and trust the Hindus to do them justice when the Hindus get their freedom and independence from the British. (Ibid., 425)

The sum of Ambedkar's arguments at this time was;

Untouchability constitutes a definite set of interests which the Untouchables alone can speak for. (Ambedkar 2014, 1: 256)

There are two kinds of arguments (a moral argument and an epistemic one) made by Ambedkar in support of such a positional sequestering. Positional sequestering in Ambedkar might be unpacked as restricting the right to speak for or represent the interest of a community to members of that community in deciding questions critical to securing justice for the basic structure of society of which that particular group is a part. Making the moral argument (in support of such sequestering), Ambedkar suggests that having the moral right to speak about matters concerning justice on behalf of a particular community can only accrue from having shared the suffering/*duhkha* of a community by having been born into such suffering as it were

(One might recall that this argument was preliminarily discussed in the Introduction to the book). In another version of the moral argument, Ambedkar gestures to the fact that justice as giving one another that which is due to others/oneself is contingent on trust between people, which, can be secured by and between members of a community only by virtue of being born into it. In making the epistemic argument, Ambedkar makes an even stronger point which is to the effect that no one who is not born to such suffering/*duhkha* or has shared such an experience can be in a position to know enough (or reliably enough) about it, so as to be epistemically fit, to enter into debates about where justice could lie with regard to questions about rights and distribution of benefits and burdens in so far as they effect that suffering community.

These arguments make it somewhat apparent that Ambedkar could simply not accept the Rawlsian point that the parties in the original position must be ignorant of the suffering of (and everything else about) the citizens they represented. However, the more important problem with a Rawlsian original position in an Ambedkarian framework was that even if the parties in that position were allowed information about the suffering of the citizens whom they represented, this would not make for fairness. The demands on who could represent the citizens of a contracting society for the purpose of the selection of principles of justice went very much further than this. On Ambedkar's view, the party representing the position of the untouchables would need to be a member of that community by birth (not choice) and indeed at no point be unmindful of his/her commitment to that community. A Rawlsian original position, even with the closed impartiality requirement, would simply not work for Ambedkar. Moving away from the requisite qualifications that Ambedkar sought in the parties who could be considered fit to represent the members of the contracting community (peopled by Hindus, Muslims, untouchables, etc.), there are even more fundamental dissonances between Ambedkar's arguments for justice and the liberal demands for impartiality.

Ambedkar, as it were, speaks to the impartial spectator argument made by Adam Smith when he addresses arguments to foreigners (impartial spectators) at several places in his writing. One might consider that impartial spectators always come from outside a sovereign state/focal group and are therefore not discredited by the feelings of antipathy which (in Ambedkar's view) afflicts the insiders. One might recall that Sen had said of the impartial spectators that they;

...come in not as arbitrators but as people whose reading and assessment help us to achieve a less partial understanding of the ethics and justice of a problem, compared with confining attention only to voices of those who are directly involved (and telling all others to go mind their own business). (Sen 2010, 131)

The appeal of open impartiality (and Adam Smith's device of the impartial spectator) derives from the argument that a person's voice can be relevant in matters concerning justice for more than one reason. The most obvious reason is of course that he/she is a member of a group that has experienced historical injustice. Yet this last is perhaps not the only way a voice might be relevant to questions of justice. A voice might also be relevant because of "the enlightenment and the broadening of perspectives that such a voice coming from outside the contracting parties might provide". (Ibid.)

In such a context, it is Ambedkar's arguments about foreigners (as much as Rawls account of the parties in the original position) that become discordant with open impartiality. For they enclose his liberal appeal to a universalism of inclusion within, even a narrower than the closed version of, what Sen later describes as the "closed impartiality" of liberals like Rawls. It is interesting to re-visit some of these arguments here. One might turn to Chapter IX in *What Congress and Gandhi Have done to the Untouchables* (Ambedkar 2014, 9) entitled "A Plea to the Foreignor". Ambedkar opens the chapter with his discomfort with the relevance of the point of view of the impartial spectator to questions concerning justice for the basic structure of a society like that of precolonial India;

> It is a matter of common experience that barring a few exceptions, almost all foreigners who show interest in Indian political affairs take the side of the congress. This quite naturally puzzles and annoys the other political parties in the country, such as the Muslim League claiming to represent the Mussalmans, the Justice Party… claiming to speak in the name of the non-Brahmins and the All India Scheduled Castes Federation claiming to represent the Untouchables, all of whom have been appealing to the foreigner for support but to whom the foreigner is not even prepared to give a sympathetic hearing. (Ambedkar 2014, 9: 199)

Ambedkar explains that the reasons why the foreigner is reluctant to give a sympathetic hearing (to the concerns of the minorities) are related to "the propaganda by the Indian Press in favour of the congress" (Ibid, 199) and on account "…of absence on behalf of the Untouchables to advertise their case" (Ibid., 200). The foreigner on such a view allows himself to be "misled" into confusing "between the freedom of a country and the freedom of the people in the country" (Ibid., 201). Condemning the point of view of the outsider Ambedkar argues;

> There is a tragic side to the foreigner's view of Indian politics to which it is impossible not to make a reference. The foreigners who take interest in Indian politics fall into three groups. The first group is aware of the social cleavages which rend Indian politics, cleavages of majorities and minorities, Hindus and Untouchables and so on. Their main object is not to solve these cleavages by appropriate constitutional safeguards and to open the way to constitutional advancement of India but to use these cleavages to block constitutional progress. The second group of foreigners are those who pay no attention to the cleavages, who care a button what happens to the minorities and to the Untouchables. They are out to support the Congress demand and would fulfil it without bothering about safeguards. The third group consists of tourists who come "to do" India and learn about its politics if possible overnight. All three are dangerous people. But the third group is the most dangerous from the point of view of the ultimate interest of the Indian people. That there should be foreigners of the tourist sort who cannot understand the intricacies of Indian politics and who therefore support the Congress on no other ground except that…—to shout with the biggest crowd—is quite understandable. But what annoys most is the attitude of the leaders of the British Labour Party, heads of radical and leftist groups in Europe and America, represented by men like Laski, Kingsley Martin, Brailsford and editors of journals like the Nation in America, and the New Statesman in England championing the cause of the oppressed and the suppressed people. How can these men support the Congress passes one's comprehension. (Ibid., 234–235)

That these were not isolated comments but rather a well-considered stand against the so-called impartial spectator as someone who did not, rather could not, have access to all the facts of the case/relevant experience becomes evident when we look at another text. In *Mr Gandhi and the Emancipation of Untouchables* (Ambedkar 2014, 9), Ambedkar writes[2];

> Unfortunately this is not the only tragic scene in Indian politics. There is another equally tragic in character. It concerns the friends of the Hindus in foreign countries. The Hindu's have created many friends for themselves all over the world by their clever propaganda, particularly in America, "the land of liberty". The tragedy is that these friends of the Hindus are supporting a side without **examining whether it is the side which they in point of justice ought to support**. No American friends of the Hindus have, so far as I know, asked what do the Hindus stand for? Are they fighting for freedom or are they fighting for power? (Ibid., 428) (The highlighting here is my own addition and not taken from the original text)

Obviously, I am not accusing Ambedkar (or Rawls) of partiality or parochialism which would be absolutely preposterous. The questioning here only relates to the philosophical conception of impartiality which he (like Rawls) uses to arrive at just institutions through both the constitution and through affirmative action. The procedure of recommending measures to redress historical injustice operating in isolation from the world (and treating the view of the Impartial spectator in this case represented by the foreigner with suspicion) is not conducive perhaps to guaranteeing an objective scrutiny of reasons which might for instance be influenced by the particular experience of closed groups. Such absence of scrutiny could make it difficult to avoid parochialism for example in deciding which groups are to be considered as scheduled in the Constitution of India. It is surely significant in this context to note Nagraj's (2015) arguments in connection with the self-enclosing of the dalits and the related breaking of ties between dalit and artisanal communities in India. Speaking specifically of the Beda Jagama and the dalits Nagraj writes;

> The common memory of protest with Beda Jagama …had to be erased… (Nagraj 2015, 117)

This (Nagraj suggests) was a move that drew from Ambedkar's emphasis on self-closure and exclusion of artisan communities from the Dalit communities. Nagraj explains;

> He (Ambedkar) thought that the inclusion of other communities… would weaken the making of the Dalit community. (Ibid., 121)

This point is not restricted to Ambedkar's difficulties with impartiality but seeks to argue that the liberal conception of impartiality is internally in conflict with itself. At one level, liberal notions of practical rationality demand a divesting of oneself from the particularities of one's belief and experience; on the other, there is a need to close out the points of view of those who are not parties to the contract (or representatives of such parties) to arrive at the principles of justice to govern the basic structure of a

---

[2] *Mr Gandhi and the Emancipation of Untouchables* was first published in 1943. However, for the purposes of reference, I have resourced it from Volume 9 in the set of 17 volumes entitled *Dr. Babasaheb Ambedkar Writings and Speeches*, edited by Vasant Moon. New Delhi, Dr. Ambedkar Foundation, Ministry of Social Justice and Empowerment, Government of India, 2014.

liberal pluralistic democracy. If the demands of practical rationality require that one has to divest oneself from positional sequestering why, is the view of the person who has no position in the contracting community (and in this case who is not implicated by the bias' of the parties in the original contracting community), sequestered out of the discussion of justice and injustice? Once a closed impartiality is adopted (as happens in Rawls theory), the loss of the view from nowhere, reverberates though the system and weakens the demands for objectivity on which contractual theories ground their conceptions of justice.

The other equally foundational difficulty is that liberals fail to see that such a quagmire is not conceptually inevitable for there are other notions of impartiality and justice and other understandings of practical rationality outside of the mainstream and dominant liberal tradition which might not suffer from the philosophical dissonances of the liberal notions of impartiality and its connection with justice. MacIntyre for example reminds philosophers that both notions of practical rationality and justice are "specific to traditions of enquiry" (MacIntyre 1988, 401). He argues that the "apparent neutrality" (Ibid., 4) of liberal individualism is "no more than an appearance" (Ibid.). MacIntyre brings out the "deep incompatibility" (Ibid., 400) between "the standpoint of any rational tradition of enquiry" (Ibid.) and the dominant modes of discussion and debate about rationality and justice in "the liberal university" (Ibid.) and liberal polity. He argues that;

> There is no way to engage with or to evaluate rationally the thesis advanced in contemporary form by some particular tradition except in terms which are framed with an eye to the specific character and history of that tradition… (Ibid., 398)

On such an account, liberal notions of both closed and open impartiality are just one specific way of understanding rationality and locating the demands for a universality of inclusion central to matters of justice/injustice. There are ways of doing this within particular traditions of thinking even where these traditions have been most unjust because it is in critiquing them from within the tradition that understandings of rationality (and justice) are formulated and later articulated:

> What the Enlightenment made us for the most part blind to and what we now need to recover is, so I shall argue, a conception of rational enquiry as embodied in a tradition, a conception according to which the standards of rational justification themselves emerge from and are part of a history in which they are vindicated by the way in which they transcend the limitations of and provide remedies for the defects of their predecessors within the history of the same tradition. (Ibid., 7)

MacIntyre's argument makes the much needed philosophical space for turning to Gandhi's alternative understanding of justice which attempted to transcend the limitations of an essentially unjust tradition by a re-thinking of its own categories and concepts such as *samadarshita*/equi-mindedness *tapasya*/self-imposed pain and *swaraj*/freedom. In the process, Gandhi perhaps contributed to an understanding of justice across traditions by securing the objectivity so essential to justice while at the same time avoiding the conflict somewhat internal to the liberal notion of impartiality.

Gandhi did not take the view from nowhere nor did he seek to occupy the position of Adam Smith's impartial spectator given his emphasis on individual responsibility, stress on kinship and emphasis on the particularities of the context concerned with the demand for justice. One might recall Adam Smith on the demand for objectivity to widen the reach of ethical enquiry;

> In solitude we are apt to feel too strongly whatever relates to ourselves... The conversation of a friend brings to us a better, that of a stranger a still better temper... and it is always from that spectator, from whom we can expect the least sympathy and indulgence, that we are likely to learn the most complete lesson of self-command. (Smith 1976 III.3.38, 153–4)

Gandhi thought that one could arrive at a diagnosis of injustice or what could be done to eliminate it by employing the alternative idea of equi-mindedness/*samadarshita* and its derivative an *ahimsanat* **individual** sense of deference to the "other" whether friendly or hostile. It was such *samadarshita* and deference (as argued in Chap. 4) which served as the basis of *satyagraha/*firmness on truth as an attempt to secure justice for oneself while always being just to the conflicting other. Did Gandhi's *samadarshita/*equi-mindedness serve to secure (to the individual) a freedom from positional sequestering? One needs here to consider, if and to what extent, equi-mindedness can (in fact) better secure the results sought from ethical objectivity/impartiality when questions of justice and injustice are at stake.

The next section will seek to answer such questions and bring out the alterniety of Gandhi's understanding of justice.

5.3   Gandhi: An Alternative Understanding of Justice

This section will argue that Gandhi had not only spent his life in practical engagements to secure justice for victims of colonial and racial discrimination but that he had thought seriously about justice and the appropriate approach to redress historical injustice. Indeed, I argue here (and have argued elsewhere) that the ethics of Gandhi's politics was constituted by an overriding concern for justice. That said, it is also true that Gandhi rejected all the presumptions of a liberal contractarian account of justice. One might locate these presumptions in the points of agreement between differing liberal accounts of justice which, whether they emphasized utility or rights, largely accepted justice as primarily a function of a consent-based state authority, the rule of law through third-party justice and an abstract equality before the law. Ambedkar (as noted above) as a liberal constitutionalist was in agreement with the basic aspects of such an understanding of justice.

One might add a note here that in the preface to lectures on the Indian constitution (which he had delivered to the students of the Government Law College in 1934–35), Ambedkar had stated that Dicey's Treatise on the English Constitution "suffers" (Ambedkar 2014, 12: 155) from defects in that the Indian student "fails to grasp the full import of such fundamental principles as supremacy of the rule of law or the role of conventions in the working of the Constitution" (Ibid.). Ambedkar said of his own lectures in 1936 that;

They constitute a revision of Dicey's Treatise on the English Constitution with a view to remove its defects and to adapt it to the needs of the Indian students. (Ibid., 156)

This seems to indicate that as a "a(A) lawyer of repute… an authority on Constitutional law…" (Ibid., 150). Ambedkar was clear (even in the early 1930's) that justice could be best understood in liberal contractarian terms and on the model of the English Constitution. One might also note that in *The Untouchables and the Pax Brittanica* (Ambedkar 2014, 12) also probably written in the 1930s (during his visits to England for the round table conferences), Ambedkar emphasized that it was from the British constitution that Indians had enhanced their own understanding of justice. He also referred to the British as having brought to India an indispensable and fundamental abstract equality before the law;

What good has British conquest done to the Untouchables? In education, nothing; in service, nothing; …With all this, the principle of equality before law has been a special benefit to the Untouchables… The principle of equality before law …has cleansed the air and the Untouchable is permitted to breath the air of freedom. This is a real gain… and having regard to the ancient past it is no small gain. (Ibid., 147)

Ambedkar both understood and celebrated the rule of law and wrote copiously on law (Ibid., Part IV). When it comes to his role as presiding over the drafting committee for the Constitution of India, it seems fairly clear that Ambedkar remained "stuck to his ideological faith in liberalism". (Chakrabarty 2019, 153). As Chakrabarty explains;

…his role as the chairman of the Committee was most crucial in providing an ideological direction to what finally became the Constitution of India. What is noticeable is the imprint of liberal values in the text of the Constitution which Ambedkar held so dear throughout his life…, the twin influences of John Dewey and Goerge Grote provided Ambedkar with arguments to defend his distinctive liberal approach to democratic experimentalism in India. (*Ibid.*)

Interestingly Gandhi had studied law and was as familiar (as Ambedkar) with its execution through the British courts of law. Yet Gandhi unequivocally rejected the idea that it was only, or even primarily, the rule of law that could guarantee an access to justice. He argued against third-party justice and replaced an abstract equality before the law by the notion of absolute equality (*samata, samabhava* and *samadarshita*[vi]). Situating himself within the Indian tradition and in continuity with the *itihaas* of the term *dharma,* Gandhi suggested that the stability of justice as a virtue of social institutions could only rest upon an equi-mindedness/*samadarshita* which ensured an *ahimsanat **individual*** sense of deference to the "other"—whether major or minor-oppressed or colonizing oppressor.

This section will attempt to put together an alternative Gandhian understanding of justice in terms of its powerful divergence from Ambedkar. It will unpack that difference to bring out Gandhi's alternative conception of justice by using the two insights about justice brought out in the first section of the chapter. Accordingly, Sect. 5.3.1

will look at the intimate inter-relationship between justice as a virtue of institutions and persons in Gandhi. Section 5.3.2 will discuss Gandhi's *samadarshita*/equi-mindedness as seeking to capture the best part of the liberal insight into the connection between impartiality and justice. Section 5.3.3 will dwell into the question of sanction. In this context, it will argue that the sanction for justice in a Gandhian conception (of it) was neither that of utility nor that of inviolable human rights belonging to human beings *qua* human beings. Rather, the ultimate sanction from which claims of justice could draw their authority in a Gandhian framework was *tapasya* or the individual capacity to undergo intelligent and self-imposed pain for the sake of justice. Section 5.3.4 will gather the different strands of the argument and attempt to put together the central points of an alternative Gandhian conception of justice.

5.3.1   Unpacking the Alternative Gandhian Conception of Justice

5.3.1.1   Justice: Institutions and Persons—*Niti* and *Dharma*

In a sense, this section brings me back to where I started (perhaps an indication of just how much integrity one must look for in Gandhi) to Gandhi's distinction between history and *itihaas*. In Chap. 2, I had argued that history provides a measure to make a third-party adjudication of the past and one might reject such measure/history (as indeed Ambedkar did) by proposing a different measure. What of *itihaas*/the it so happened of the past? Can one (just as easily) reject how **the it so happened of the past in the form of life of the community** (in all its complex ways) leads one to problematize concepts in the world? Perhaps in the modern way, one can choose to reject and erase such an erring past. Gandhi, we have seen, was not a modern and this erasure did not come as easily to him. Gandhi could not **chose to** erase (or indeed **choose not to** erase) the past in thinking about justice (as in his thinking about most things), and this led him to think of justice in an alternative way as lying in the intimacy of the individual and the institutional. He thought about justice as it were **from within** the long tradition (as noted in the previous section) of *niti* and of the *dharma/dhamma* combine of ancient India. In accordance with MacIntyre's understanding of justice and rationality, one might see Gandhi as seeking to articulate conceptions of, rationality and justice, which emerged from an *itihaas* within the Indian tradition in which these conceptions were vindicated by the way in which they had transcended the limitations of, and provided remedies for, the defects of their predecessors in the same tradition. This section will attempt to re-construct such a tradition-situated and alternative Gandhian understanding of justice.

That Gandhi should have re-constructed justice in line with the Indian tradition and thereby in the intimacy of *niti* and the *dharma/dhamma* combine might seem apparent from the consideration that he unequivocally rejected the distinction between the private and the public—the sphere of the individual and the *socius/politicus*. Consequently, one can argue that justice in the public sphere could (for Gandhi) be no different from the **properly just** human life. It seems to follow from here that Gandhi should have thought about the state/the institutions governing the basic structure of society, relationship between citizens and of relations between states using metaphors of kinship. The ideas of *Ramrajya* as the ideal state and of citizens being bound not by fraternity (even in Ambedkar's somewhat enhanced reading of it) but by extended ties of family certainly seemed to be alternative to the predominantly liberal conception of the relationships of reciprocity between citizens seen as reasonable. On an aside, one might note that Ambedkar (like Rawls) had used the terms "reasonable" and "prudent" (rather than examples from kinship- of siblings, parent or child) in the context of the relationships between citizens in a democratic state (Ambedkar 2014, 13: 394).

Turning now to the first of the two insights about justice that I had raised at the start of the chapter as important to delineating the differences between Ambedkar and Gandhi on justice; as already apparent, Gandhi had rejected the idea that justice could be purely institutional and some part of his difficulties with separate electorates as the primary approach to securing justice for the depressed classes derived from such a rejection. In Gandhi's view, the redressal of justice could be secured by an approach which involved both institutions (as for instance representation in legislatures for the depressed classes) and transformation of persons (by a change of heart of the oppressor). It is important to note that Gandhi was also opposed to the structure of liberal institutions meting out justice against the concept of measure. In this connection, one must recall *Hind Swaraj* where Gandhi had most famously rejected the idea that justice could be purely institutional and meted out by the judge as the third party in a court of law. Gandhi self-consciously situated himself within the Indian tradition when thinking about justice, and this runs deeper than has been ordinarily understood.

At one level, one can say that Gandhi's thinking about justice was opposed to that of the liberals because he thought about justice as a virtue of both institutions and persons. Consequently, Gandhi brought up both the figure of the *panch*/village elder (situated within the idea of the premodern village Republic) and the notion of individual *swabhawa/dharman/*foundational nature into a discussion about justice. However at another level, one might argue that in sharp contrast to the liberals, Gandhi accorded a primacy to persons over institutions when seeking the foundations of justice for the basic structure of society. In such a context, Gandhi emphasized individual *dharma/dhamma* (over institutional arrangements/*niti*) in thinking about justice; rendering *dharma/dharman* as the *swabhava*/foundational nature of the human being and the foundation of justice for the basic institutions of society. One might note in this context that Gandhi had connected self-rule with home rule by making philosophical use of the etymology of *swaraj* as 'swa' (self) and 'raj' (rule). In a similar manner, Gandhi unpacked *dharma/dharman* as the foundational nature/special property of a thing and made a correlation between the *dharma* of the individual and justice as the foundation of society. In this case (as in that of *swaraj* where self-rule was connected to home rule), justice as the first virtue/foundation of society (*niti*) was based on the *dharman/swabhava/*foundational nature of the individual human being.

The contrast between Gandhi and the liberals might become sharper if one were to recall that in his famous opening words in **A Theory of Justice** (1971), Rawls had said that "justice is the first virtue of social institutions" (Rawls 1971, 3). He had emphasized that "the sense of justice as applied to practices" (Rawls 1958, 165) was the "basic one" (Ibid.). On this view, "Justice as a virtue of particular actions or of person's" (Ibid., 164–65) would go "quite easily" (Ibid., 165) once the basic sense of justice as applied to institutions had been understood (Ibid., 165). One needs to digress a little here to unpack Gandhi's philosophical (and copious) use of *dharma* establishing a continuity with both the *Brahmanic* and *Sramanic* portions of the Indian tradition. One needs to note specifically that the term *dharma/dharman* (as mentioned above) has been used as both the foundation of society and as the special property essence/foundation of a thing—heat for instance is seen as the *dharman/*special property/foundation of fire. In what follows, a long commentarial tradition *dharma/*actually *dharman* is usually translated as "nature" "property" or "foundational nature" of a thing. Radhakrishnan (1953) following Shankara speaks of *dharman* as *laksana* "mark, trait, feature" (Radhakrishnan 1953, 285) of something. Speaking from within this tradition, Rabindranath Tagore explains, that the term *dharma* "in its technical sense means the virtue of a thing, the essential quality of it; for instance, heat is the essential quality of fire". (Tagore 2008, 144).

It is in this sense that Gandhi had himself translated the *sadharana dharma/*universal code of conduct common for all humanity in terms of the *khaas lakshana/*distinguishing feature of being human and his understanding of justice itself rested on such an understanding of the essential quality or the *dharma/khaas lakshana* of being human. Gandhi had explained that;

> *Dharma* is a quality of the soul and is present, visibly or invisibly, in every human being. Through it we know our duty in human life and our true relation with other souls. It is evident that we cannot do so till we have known the self in us. Hence *dharma* is the means by which we can know ourselves. (Gandhi 1888–1948, 36: 475)[3]

One might get a sense of what led Gandhi to re-iterate the ancient Indian connection between *dharma* and the essential/foundational nature of the human being (or the distinguishing quality of being human) if we refer to a conversation between Gandhi and his Guru and friend Rajchandra bhai Mehta the Jain mystic and philosopher. Rajchandra Bhai had explained the connection between *dharma* and man's *swabhava,* as it were, in the following words;

---

[3] Gandhi 1888–1948, refers to the *Collected Works of Mahatma Gandhi.* The volume concerned and the page numbers from which citations from Gandhi are drawn have been mentioned within parentheses. These have been mentioned to indicate the exact location of the quotation in the electronic edition of the *Collected Works of Mahatma Gandhi.* However, for the purposes of reference, it may be noted that I have resourced these volumes from the *Collected Works of Mahatma Gandhi*: Volumes 1 to 98. New Delhi: Publications Division Government of India, 1999. Accessed online in May 2021 at https://www.gandhiashramsevagram.org/gandhi-literature/collected-works-of-mahatma-gandhi-volume-1-to-98.php.

The soul's existence in its natural state, that is, in freedom from karma and purely as the *atman*, that it is, is the state of being Ishvar. That which has the *aishvarya* of knowledge, etc., may be described as Ishvar. This *Ishvarhood* is the natural state of the *atman*, which is not revealed when it is engaged in karmas. When the *atman* however, realizes that being engaged in karma is not its real nature and fixes its attention on itself, then alone do omniscience, power etc., manifest themselves in it and we can see nothing among all the objects in the universe with greater power than the *atman's*. It is, therefore, my positive belief that *Ishvar* is another name for *atman* and does not signify a different Being of greater power. (Ibid., 502)

Gandhi had more to say about the natural/*swabhavika* state of the soul (that which made the human in the image of the divine) which helped to unpack the *dharma* of the human being and made for just relations with other human beings. In this context, he wrote an essay in *Navajivan*, on 13–6–1926 on "what is natural to man" (to which I have referred more than once in the preceding chapters). This essay drew from the idea that the *dharman*/essential nature of the human being must be that which distinguishes the human from other beings. Gandhi argued that man's *dharma*/foundational nature was *ahimsanat*/non-violent, and it was such a *khaas lakshana*/special property which distinguished the human being from other species;

Man's nature then is not *himsa*, but ahimsa, for he can speak from experience, his innermost conviction, that he is not the body but *atman*, and that he may use the body only with a view to expressing the *atman*, only with a view to self-realization. And from that experience he evolves the ethics of subduing desire, anger, ignorance, malice and other passions, puts forth his best effort to achieve the end and finally attains complete success. Only when his efforts reach that consummation can he be said to have fulfilled himself, to have acted according to his nature. (Gandhi 1888–1948, 35: 357–358)

Gandhi's argument about the *khaas lakshana*/distinguishing feature of being human is linked to Shankara's interpretation of *dharman* as *laksana* the "mark, trait, feature" (Radhakrishnan 1953, 285) of something. Gandhi went on to write (in 1926) in response to a criticism from a reader who had argued that *himsa*/violence and not *ahimsa*/non-violence rules man "that a species is recognized and differentiated from the rest by its special characteristics" (Gandhi 1888–1948, 36: 4). Gandhi explained that if a human being lost his/her special characteristic/*khaas lakshana*/*dharman*, he/she would no longer be able to share the general status of being an animal;

Therefore, it would be wrong, I presume, to say that a horse is animal first and horse after. He shares something in common with the other animals, but he dare not shed his horseliness and yet remain an animal. Having lost his special virtue, he loses also his general status. Similarly, if a man lost his status as man and began to grow a tail and walk on all fours, lost the use of his hands, and, more than that, lost the use of his reason, would he not lose with the loss of his status as man his status also as animal? Neither the ox nor the ass, neither the sheep nor the goat will claim his as theirs. (Ibid.)

Gandhi had explained (in this essay) the *khaas lakshana*/*dharman* or foundational nature of the human being in terms of duty, in fact, as the unilateral obligation to own kinship with the human and the non-human other. On this view, by virtue of being true to his/her own *swabhawa* or innermost nature, the human being essentially *ahimsanat* upheld the foundations of the basic structure of society by performing the unilateral obligation of owning kinship with human and non-human others. Such an owning of kinship (as I argued in the last chapter) meant that an individual was to respond to all others with equi-mindedness **as if** such others were members of his/her kith and kin. In other words, the *khaas lakshana*/distinguishing feature of human beings was to respond to human and non-human others with kinship and by virtue of such kinship by an equi-mindedness and *samabhava*/equability. One might note that kinship involves equi-mindedness/*samadarshita* as one responds with an equality of deference to all of one's family members. As Gandhi had explained;

> The truth is that my ethics not only permit me to claim but require me to own kinship with not merely the ape but the horse and the sheep, the lion and the leopard, the snake and the scorpion. Not so need these kinsfolk regard themselves. The hard ethics which rule my life, and I hold ought to rule that of every man and woman, impose this unilateral obligation upon us. And it is so imposed because man alone is made in the image of God. (Ibid., 5)

It was such a unilateral obligation of kinship that constituted the "possession of that additional quality" (Ibid.) by all human beings which gave them "such enormous hold upon God's creation" (Ibid., 6).

A far cry from the charge that the Indian tradition had no adequate account of justice one might consider that the Indian tradition had brought the notion of *dharman*/foundational nature as the *khaas lakshana*/distinguishing feature of the human being into harmony with *dharma* as the just foundation of society through the *niti* texts and through the notions of the duties of the king. The king, one might note, had unilateral obligations to act from an equi-mindedness to all human and non-human others in the state both by virtue of being a human being and as representative of the basic structure for the administration of justice in society. It could be useful to note Gandhi's use of the metaphor of *Ramrajya* as standing for the reign of Rama who dispensed justice from such a position of equi-mindedness and equability;

> By 'Ramrajya' I do not mean Hindu Raj... Whether Rama of my imagination ever lived or not on this earth, the ancient ideal of Ramrajya is undoubtedly one of true democracy in which the meanest citizen could be sure of swift justice without an elaborate and costly procedure. Even the dog is described by the poet to have received justice under Ramrajya. (Gandhi 1888–1948, 47: 41)

Going back in time (as noted earlier), one might find precursors in Asoka's edicts, which also illustrated the ancient Indian inter-relationship, between institutional arrangements and individual *dharma* to ensure the stability of justice for the basic structure of society. Asoka's edicts (as already noted) were administrative orders resting upon the inter-relationship between justice as a virtue of the state and the requirements of individual *dhamma*. Gandhi reconciled his own understanding of justice as the unilateral obligation to defer to all human and non-human others (which follows naturally enough from owning kinship with such others) by recommending institutions of justice which might be modelled along the lines of the family and along the lines suggested by kinship between human beings. It was perhaps in such a spirit that Gandhi sought to set up a network of *Panchayats*[vii] with the village elders;

...every village will be a republic or *panchayat* having full powers. (Gandhi 1888–1948, 91: 325)

The central organizing idea for Gandhi was that of setting up a basic structure of the nation state in concentric circles. (see Prabhu & Rao 2007, 374) around relationships between the people at a local level;

> In this structure composed of innumerable villages, there will be ever-widening, never-ascending circles. Life will not be a pyramid with the apex sustained by the bottom. But it will be an oceanic circle whose center will be the individual always ready to perish for the village, the latter ready to perish for the circle of villages... (Gandhi 1888–1948, 91: 326).

For Gandhi, such an oceanic circle view of the nation state would make it possible to keep individual responsibility in plain sight as it were. On such a view, individuals would each be responsible for the fulfilment of their unilateral obligation to treat all human and non-human others as if they were members of the same family. It is interesting in this context to note the constant interlay between institutions and persons/realizations in Gandhi's understanding of justice by recalling his comments made in the context of the kheda *satyagraha*;

> In disobeying an order of the Government, one thing must be remembered. We cannot claim with certainty that the order in question is unjust; though we may think it so, it may in fact be just. Therefore, as in private dealings, so a difference between a Government and its subjects should be settled through a *panch*. This is what our ancient kings used to do... The ultimate result, ...is the same as in arbitration of the usual kind. Government cannot be carried on without taking into account public opinion... (Gandhi 1888–1948, 16: 434).

5.3.1.2   Gandhi: Securing Rights and Individual Liberty

The last section might leave the reader with the thought that Gandhi concentrated overwhelmingly on the obligations of persons at the expense perhaps of their rights/liberties. The values of liberty and equality one might note were at the heart of all liberal theories of justice. Such reflections could, for instance, emerge from Gandhi's idea that the *dharma/swabhava* (or innermost orientation) of being human obligated human beings to own up to the unilateral duty of kinship with the human and the non-human world. This might lead those who emphasize the importance of institutions (to a proper conception of justice) to argue that overmuch pre-occupation with individual and unilateral duties might lead one into difficulties. On this view, such an over emphasis on unilateral duties might lead one to ignore the significance of social processes on the one hand, and on the other, to neglect the guarantee (by a rule of law) of liberty/rights and equality as critical to the realization of justice for the basic structure of society.

It is such considerations perhaps that led liberals like Rawls to declare that justice is the first virtue of social institutions. It is interesting in this context to keep two points about Gandhi's conception of justice in mind. The first is that Gandhi was interested in both the values of equality and liberty of the liberals though he considerably re-thought them in line with his own tradition. In the last chapter, I had brought out the manner in which Gandhi had demurred from the liberals in re-thinking the equality before law as an absolute equality. Following a parallel argument, this section will emphasize that Gandhi was equally interested in liberty/rights and *satyagraha* was conceived as a method of securing individual rights;

> Passive resistance is a method of securing rights by personal suffering. (Gandhi 1888–1948, 10: 292)

However, as with equality, Gandhi considerably re-thought both the notion of individual liberty/rights and the method of securing such liberty/rights.

The second point to note in connection with Gandhi's re-interpretation of liberal rights/liberty is that while Gandhi fought for rights for the dispossessed throughout his life, he thought of rights in conditional terms. It is surely significant in this context that Gandhian rights did not accrue to the human person *qua* person and were conditional on the rights aspirant having fulfilled his/her own unilateral duties to human and non-human others. A word on both these points might be in order here.

In a classical liberal, emphasis on rights Rawls (in 1971) had formulated the first principle of justice in terms of an uncompromising respect for individual liberties. One might think that Gandhi's emphasis on the primacy of the unilateral one sided obligation of the human being *qua* human being to own kinship with the human and non-human world put him at some conceptual distance from any such emphasis on liberty. Yet one needs only consider that Gandhi's own life took a distinct turn towards a realization of the importance of rights to human dignity ever since he found himself thrown out of a train at Petermaritzburg railway station in South Africa. Everything Gandhi did in his struggle for rights against racial and colonial others could be spelt out in terms of a respect for the rights of the dispossessed. One might argue that Gandhi's 1931 resolution on *Fundamental rights and Economic changes* (framed in collaboration with Nehru) could be considered a precursor in the lineage of Rawls' first principle of justice.[viii] This resolution was framed by Gandhi with Nehru and passed in the 1931 session of the Indian National Congress (Gandhi 1888–1948, 51: 327). The preamble to this resolution stated that one of the chief aims of this resolution was to "enable the masses to appreciate what *swaraj* … will mean to them" (Ibid.). The resolution stated;

> The congress, therefore, declare that any constitution which may be agreed to on its behalf should provide, for the following;... (Ibid.)
>
> 1. Fundamental rights of the people, including;
>
> a) Freedom of association and combination.
>
> b) Freedom of speech and press
>
> c) Freedom of conscience and free profession and practice of religion, subject to public order and morality.
>
> d) Protection of culture language and scripts of minorities
>
> e) Equal rights and obligations of all citizens without any bar on account of sex;…
>
> 2. Adult suffrage
>
> 3. Free primary education

4. A living wage for industrial workers, limited hours of labour, healthy conditions of work, protection against the economic consequences of old age, sickness and unemployment. (Ibid., 327–328)

Yet it is important to note that notwithstanding this resolution and his engagements in several efforts to secure economic, political and social rights for the dispossessed Gandhi's emphasis on liberty was not quite that of the liberals. This difference will emerge from the consideration of the second point that follows.

The second point which I seek to make about Gandhi connects with the first and indeed it serves to spell out this difference. One might emphasize that though Gandhi fought for the rights/liberties of the dispossessed in South Africa and in India (after 1917), he thought of rights as contingent on the performance of duties. In his lesser known response to the UN Committee engaged in drafting 'the universal declaration of human rights', Gandhi made his famous correlation between rights and duties. One might feel constrained here to point out that such a correlation had also been made by classical and contemporary liberalism, the social contract tradition and contemporary human rights discourse. Yet it is significant that these theories had made the correlation between rights and duties **in a reciprocal arrangement** of an equitable distribution of mutual freedom **between people**. One needs to note that in a liberal understanding of justice, a right for one represents a perfect/imperfect obligation for another. In complete contrast in a Gandhian understanding of justice, any right has co-relates in duties primarily in the person seeking that right and only after that in the others who need to restrain themselves from encroaching on that right. The second set of duties can, on the Gandhian view, only come into effect after the right aspirant/ bearer performs his/her unilateral obligations as a human being *qua* human being to become a 'fitting recipient' for those rights. One might note Gandhi's reply to the United Nations committee in this context;

All rights to be deserved and preserved come from duty well done. Thus the very right to live accrues to us only when we do the duty of citizenship of the world. From this fundamental statement perhaps it is easy enough to define the duties of man and woman and correlate every right to some corresponding duty to be first performed. Every other right can be shown to be usurpation hardly worth fighting for. (Gandhi 1888–1948, 95: 137)

The same sentiments were expressed to the framers of India's new constitution;

Fundamental rights can only be those rights the exercise of which is not only in the interest of the citizens but that of the whole world… Rights cannot be divorced from duties. This is how *Satyagraha* was born, for I was always striving to decide what my duty was. (Ibid., 353)

It is surely significant to the differences between Gandhi and a liberal understanding of justice that Gandhi should have introduced into the discourse of human rights various terms quite alien to the liberal way of speaking about rights. Terms such as the following; "usurpation of rights" (Gandhi 1888–1948, 19: 449 And, 32: 343); "encroachment upon just rights" (Gandhi 1888–1948, 75: 180); "dispossessing a usurper" (Ibid.); doing "justice to rights that accrue to" (Ibid., 178) one; and the idea that rights result from the due "performance of duty" (Ibid., 178–79).

In rejecting the liberal idea that rights are due to the human being *qua* human being simply by virtue of being human Gandhi was, in fact, going against the entire Anglo American, predominantly liberal, position on rights coming down through (to mention a few) Mill, Locke, Rousseau and Kant. For Gandhi, anyone who had not performed the duties of world citizenship in being a responsible member of the integrated cosmos could not be a fitting recipient of rights. I would suggest that the duty that Gandhi had in mind as the qualifying duty to become a fit recipient for human rights was that which he had specified in terms of the unilateral obligation that accrued from the *dharma/swabhawa/*special nature of a human being. This was that of treating the rest of the world[ix] and indeed the cosmos as if it were one's own kin.

The points discussed in this chapter (and the last) about Gandhi's re-interpretation of the liberal values of liberty and equality (in their bearing on justice) might leave readers with insights into a possible reconciliation of the somewhat contrary pulls of these liberal values. For Gandhi, one might suggest, the relationship between an individual's rights and duties ensures that human beings become eligible for rights, only to the extent that, they treat all others with an equi-mindedness that comes from an acceptance of absolute equality. This leads us once again (as a re-iteration of the findings of the last chapter) to the understanding that Gandhi conceptually reconciled the liberal contrariety between liberty and equality by according a primacy to the claims of equality.

This also serves to set the stage, as it were, for a consideration of *samadarshita/*equi-mindedness, impartiality and its connection to justice in Gandhi which will be the subject of the next subsection.

5.3.2 Justice; Samadarshita/Equi-Mindedness Objectivity and Impartiality

Moving now to the second of the two insights which I have argued (in this chapter) serve to explain what exactly it is that one points towards when one invokes 'justice'. This insight was discussed in Sect. 5.1.2 (of the present chapter) which suggested that invoking justice and seeking redressal for injustice is not the end of the matter when one speaks about justice. One has also, as seen earlier, to think about the appropriateness of the reasons that might be offered in arguments about justice and injustice. At the risk of repetition, one might recall that there is some need to "ask what kinds of reasoning should count in the assessment of ethical and political concepts such as justice and injustice" (Sen 2010, viii).

It was in such a context that I had noted in a previous section that Ambedkar shared (what I have described as) the quagmire somewhat internal to the liberal notion of impartiality. Put simply this is what Sen has spoken of as the conflict between open and closed impartiality. Liberalism requires human beings to step away from attachments, beliefs and communities of belonging, to take a view from nowhere to become free from parochialism when discussing matters of justice. Yet though this seems to invoke the figure of the impartial spectator (recall Adam Smith) and open impartiality as central to liberal notions of justice, in practice, liberals enclose the demand for impartiality within the limits of the contracting communities. This was also the quagmire/entrapping predicament which (as discussed above) afflicted Ambedkar's discussion on justice.

What of Gandhi? Well one can certainly say that Gandhi was not interested in (and clearly rejected) the standpoint of the third-party/impartial spectator when speaking about justice:

> It was certainly a sign of savagery when they (human beings) settled their disputes by fighting. Is it any the less so if I ask a third party to decide between you and me? The parties alone know who is right. (Gandhi 1888–1948, 10: 276)

One might understand Gandhi's reasons for thinking that the parties to a dispute alone know on which side the right/truth lies if one considers that Gandhi was opposed to the idea of measure itself as essentially in conflict with truth. One might note in this connection that the liberal notion of justice with law as the measure brackets away the search for truth (from matters of justice) in a search for facts. This is because measure by the nature of the case cannot be interested in what is singular about particular events and must be interested instead in what is specific about them. That which is specific about the particular, i.e. shared by other particulars can be recorded in history and becomes a precedent. Gandhi thought that the judge/jury applied a specific measure (as the rule of law) noting what was specific (not singular/truthful) to the situation between the parties to pass a third-party judgement in the interest of securing justice.

Gandhi perhaps well understood that the liberals had replaced the search for truth as something that lay outside and between the parties by the application of measure. Such an application did away with truth and replaced it by law. On a deeply contrary, understanding of justice Gandhi thought that it was important to think about justice as concerned with the truth between parties to a conflict, and therefore, he argued that justice ought not to be inalienably associated with the measure of positive law;

> …In England, in South Africa, almost everywhere, I have found that in the practice of their profession, lawyers are consciously or unconsciously led into untruth… (Gandhi 1888–1948, 40: 433).

Gandhi believed that in third-party justice measure mediated the relationship between the judge and the conflict; and that this choice of measure prevented the judge from looking at that which happened at the time in its essential singularity. This was inevitable because measure (as noted above) has no interest in the singularity of events/conflicts on account of the immeasurability of singularity. This implies that third-party justice like history is necessarily pre-occupied with what can be measured and consequently with that which is specific (rather than singular) about events and conflicts and thereby lends itself to be measured;

> If we were not under the spell of lawyers and law courts, and if there were no touts to tempt us into the quagmire of the courts and the appeal to our basest passions, we would be

leading a much happier life than we do. Let those who frequent law courts-and the best of
them-bear witness to the fact that the atmosphere about them is foetid. Perjured witnesses
are ranged on either side, ready to sell their very souls for money or for friendship's sake.
(Gandhi 1888–1948, 21: 332)

Such a complete rejection of the third party who as the judge played the role of an
impartial spectator (with the necessary *caveat* that in most contractual constitutional
societies impartiality functioned as closed rather than open) leaves one with important
questions. One could ask 'Did Gandhi's understanding of justice have any concern
with impartiality?' Or 'Did Gandhi's conception of justice take any account of the
presence of bias' in the reasons that might be offered by interested parties when it
came to questions of justice (and injustice) for the basic institutions of society?'.

It would be useful to return to MacIntyre (*Whose Justice? Which Rationality?*,
1988) who, in his critique of liberalism, brought out the point that there can be alternative notions of rationality (and thereby impartiality) and justice within traditions; and
further, that both justice and rationality are tradition constituted and tradition constitutive terms. MacIntyre has argued that terms such as "rationality" and "justice" are
constituted as members of a community engage with and rethink central concepts
within the framework of that tradition so that the standards of rational justification
and thereby notions of justice themselves emerge from, and are part of, a history in
which they are validated/justified by the way in which they overcome the limitations
and defects of that which happened or came to pass before them within that tradition.
It is in such a context that Gandhi re-visited the notions of *samadarshita, samabhava* and *samata* which I discussed at some detail in the last chapter. Gandhi spoke
of *samadarshita*/equi-mindedness in terms of looking at all human and non-human
others along the lines of one's own family. The reference to kinship in Gandhi is
meant to gesture towards an absolute equality of regard and treatment towards all
others just as perhaps a parent (as the head of the family) maintains an equality of
regard and treatment between his/her dutiful and not so dutiful/even erring children.

I will argue that Gandhi's absolute equality of regard set up a universalism of
inclusion without bringing in liberal notions of rationality and impartiality. These,
it may be recalled, involved abstracting oneself from the particularities of kinship
and indeed involved abstracting oneself from any kind of sharing or belonging to a
community and its system of beliefs. These last constituted bias' that would, on the
liberal view, prevent one from rationally and impartially accessing that which was
specific about events and which consequently could be measured and serve as the
standard for evaluating matters of justice and injustice. While the liberals sought to
ensure fairness and removal of bias by using conceptual devices such as the point
of "view from nowhere" (Nagel 1986, 70), Gandhi took a somewhat contrary route.
He distinguished between being positioned and being positionally sequestered by
arguing that being positioned could be inclusive of all (human and non-human)
others if only one did not alter one's position of equi-mindedness towards all when
confronted with those who might be near or distant from oneself. Note Gandhi's
interpretation of Sri Krishna's advice to Arjuna in the *Bhagavad Gita* at this point;

The first thing to bear in mind is that Arjuna falls into the error of making a distinction
between kinsmen and outsiders. Outsiders may be killed even if they are not oppressors,

and kinsmen may not be killed even if they are… How should I act as editor of *Navajivan*? Would it be right for me to proclaim with beat of drum the theft committed by an outsider's child and say nothing about a boy of my ashram, who may have misbehaved in the same way? Certainly not. The *Gita* permits no distinction between one's relations and others. If one must kill, one should kill one's own people first. Sri Krishna asks Arjuna: 'What is this you are saying about people being your relations?' The Gita wants to free him from this ignorant distinction of some people being his relations and not others. (Gandhi1888–1948, 37: 83)

What needed to be shifted on the Gandhian view was not one's point of view or position in order to take the view from nowhere (or the position of the impartial spectator) but the objects of one's attention which needed to be amenable to constant inter-change. Arjuna needed on such a view to be ready to kill his own relatives if he had been ready to kill those of others. Gandhi therefore recommended that a human being maintain an equi-mindedness through as complete an inter-changeability of the subjects/objects of his/her regard as possible—one's son and the child of another, an ashram inmate and someone outside the ashram, one's father/brother and a thief who had come in to steal one's belongings (see Gandhi 1888–1948, 10: 287–89).

This was an inversion of the route that the liberals took to impartiality. For the liberals, it was the individual who needed to change his/her position between matters concerning the family and matters concerning justice for the basic structure of society. To arrive at a position free from bias or sequestering, on the liberal view, individuals needed to take a view from nowhere when it came to matters related to selecting the principles of justice for the basic structure of society. Rawls of course put this point at its utmost clarity in speaking of situating oneself, in matters of justice, behind a veil of ignorance about all actual or even possible positions that one might ever occupy. Leaving aside doubts about whether a Rawlsian veil of ignorance makes metaphysical assumptions about personhood which might or might not be possible to realize in practice (Sandel 2008, 54), there is the question of an inconsistency internal to the notion of impartiality itself in terms of its use by liberal contractarians. This is the difficulty between open and closed impartiality that I had explained in the earlier sections of this chapter.

Gandhi did not endorse the liberal recommendation of rejecting a position (for instance that of a brother or father) in favour of a view from nowhere as the only method of being able to arrive at a universality of inclusion that could free individuals from parochialism. Gandhi sought freedom from parochialism and bias in matters of justice by recommending that an individual maintain an equi-mindedness making for an almost acrobatic inter-changeability of objects of regard:

Now we shall take the example given by you of the thief to be driven out. I do not agree with you that the thief may be driven out by any means. If it is my father who has come to steal, I shall use one kind of means. If it is an acquaintance, I shall use another, and, in the case of a perfect stranger, I shall use a third. If it is a white man, you will perhaps say, you will use means different from those you will adopt with an Indian thief… (Gandhi 1888–1948, 10: 288)

Gandhi was clear that such diversity of means was simply mistaken and recommended instead that "…your duty is *not* to drive away the thief by any means you like". (Ibid., 287–88).

Note that Gandhi had recommended that one ought to be equi-minded between the objects of one's attention and that this involved an agility to inter-change objects of such attention with equability. In the instance quoted above, for example, Gandhi had argued that one ought to be able to inter-change between the thief who was a stranger and one's father or brother who could be put in the position of that thief and respond to all of them from within a position of absolute equi-mindedness. The critical point was to maintain the position of familial regard no matter if the thief was a brother acquaintance or complete stranger;

> You set this armed robber down as an ignorant brother; you intend to reason with him at a suitable opportunity… Instead of being angry with him, you take pity on him. You think that this stealing habit must be a disease with him… (Ibid., 289)

Gandhi took the example of the thief often enough for it to have become very significant. In the *Discourses on the Gita,* he wrote;

> No one has yet succeeded in laying down a universal rule about how we should act towards a thief. We should, however, bear in mind that however we act we should be inspired by love for him. We must think and find out how we may win him over with love. We should assume that it is not in human nature to steal. Even as rational beings we should be convinced that there is no human being in the world who is beyond all hope of change. Love is a kind of force of attraction…That is why Mirabai sings about the bond of love. That bond is much stronger than that of a slender thread can ever be. Why should we be filled with passion or get angry whenever we lose anything? (Gandhi 1888–1948, 37: 167)

As apparent from the recommendation to treat the thief with the love one might feel for one's own brother—Gandhi seemed to have recommended—as absolute an interchangeability between the objects of one's equi-minded deference as possible. This was an alternative to a liberal, somewhat acrobatic shift within the individual, from the bias inherent in a familial position to a view from nowhere. On Gandhi's alternative view, it was the sequestering/barracading of positions (of affection around members of the family for example) rather than the taking of those positions (of familial regard for instance) in themselves that made for the bias and parochialism involved in/of positional sequestering. Speaking about the basic assumptions of *Satyagraha* in 1938, Gandhi argued that equi-mindedness and dismantling of the barriers around one's love was only an extension of the love that had hitherto remained confined within human families;

> I have argued from the analogy of what we do in families or even clans. The human kind is one big family. And if the love expressed is intense enough, it must apply to all mankind. (Gandhi in Murti (ed) 1970, 42)

Gandhi's sought to make emotional use of the powerful empathy and love that was natural to taking the position of a member of the family towards all human and non-human others;

I wish only to show that only fair means can produce fair results, and that, in the vast majority
of cases, if not, indeed, in all, the force of love …is infinitely greater than the force of arms.
(Gandhi 1888–1948, 10: 289)

Thinking from within the mind of India, as it were, Gandhi sought to employ a
samadarshita/equi-mindedness between all human and non-human beings to make
for the stability of justice for the basic structure of society. This move might have
made for the stability of justice on surer foundations than those of an "overlapping
consensus" (Rawls 2005, 133) of a Rawlsian kind. Note Gandhi's use of love in
responding to all human and non-human others from such a position of familial
regard and kinship;

Love is a rare herb that makes a friend even of a sworn enemy and this herb grows out of
non-violence. What in a dormant state is non-violence becomes love in the waking state.
Love destroys ill will. We should love all-whether Englishmen or Muslims… We should act
only though love…Treat all enemies and friends with love… (Gandhi 1888–1948, 16: 378).

In refusing to discriminate (in terms of being deferent towards and extending
affection) between more intimate oppressors (unjust family members for instance)
and the racial/caste/colonial oppressors, while resisting injustice, Gandhi (in South
Africa and later India) put the claims of equality over those of freedom/rights:

Let us describe some instances of equal regard for all. One is that of the elephant and the ant.
Second, if an enemy and a friend arrive at his place together, both hungry, the *samadarshi*
will offer food first to the enemy. He would feel that to be justice. He would be afraid lest
there be some hatred for the enemy lurking in his heart, and he would satisfy him first. The
friend, too, would appreciate his motive. (Gandhi 1888–1948, 37: 212)

Enough has been said of Gandhi's *samadarshita* in the last chapter so it seems
sufficient here to point out that it secures a freedom from bias while avoiding the
conflicts somewhat internal to the liberal notion of impartiality. Gandhi's thinking
about justice it might be argued is in line with MacIntyre's insights about justice and
rationality as tradition constituted and tradition constitutive terms. This is also born
out by Gandhi's understanding of what might constitute the appropriate sanction that
could lie behind the exacting demands of justice. This shall form the subject of the
next subsection.

5.3.3 *The Great* Tapasvi; Tapas, *Individual Responsibility and a Sanction for Justice*

While justice provides the framework that regulates the play of competing values
and ends in society and is therefore a virtue of social institutions and practices, it is
also true, that it must have a sanction independent of the ends and values that men
actually seek. While Rawls located that sanction in the principles chosen by persons
in a hypothetical original position, utilitarians located it in the principle of utility.
Gandhi located such a sanction firmly in the human capacity to undergo self-imposed

pain/*tapas* for the sake of truth and in the related state of self-restraint/*swaraj* from which such a capacity might develop;

> A people amongst whom brute force is the sole arbiter resorts to violence and seeks justice with arms. My own experience is that this method is futile… The straightforward course is to disobey the order and submit patiently and without anger to the consequent suffering. (Gandhi 1888–1948, 16: 434)

Gandhi brought in the idea of *tapas*/self-imposed pain as a means to transform the otherness of the 'other' in order to secure rights and seek redressal of injustice. Interestingly, it was Tagore (of whom I will speak a little in the conclusion to this book) who had first emphasized the significance of *tapasya*/self-imposed pain in the ethics of Gandhian politics. In the third phase of the Gandhi Tagore debate in the 1930s, the idea of *tapasya* became a subject of debate between them. On 10 June 1933, the *Harijan* carried an editorial note on the significance of Gandhi's third fast against the evil of untouchability. It was in this note that Tagore had referred to Gandhi as the *"the great tapasvi"* (Bhattacharya 2008, 145) who had "courted death with the determination of equalizing the high and the low" (Ibid., 14).

A clarification about the meaning of *tapasya*/self-imposed pain in Gandhi might be in order. *Tapasya* has an *itihaas* (not history) in the Indian tradition, and the earliest reference to this term is in the *Rgveda*. The *Yoga Sutra* translates *tapas* from the root *tapah* which has been rendered as "austerity, penance, heat" (Ranganathan 2008, 130). Accordingly through *tapasya,* a yogi can "burn off" or prevent accumulation of negative energies. Such *tapas* "purifies the body and thereby purifies the mind" (Ibid., 133) clearing a path towards a spiritual evolution. Here, as in the rest of his thinking about justice, Gandhi drew from the *itihaas* of *tapasya* in the Indian tradition.

> In the morning we repeat the names of innumerable *rishis* and *satis*… And for what? To get inspiration from their lives… You went to the Collector, you went to the Commissioner and then to the Bombay Government and gave up the effort at last when you failed everywhere. If that is the truth, I must say that to submit in this helpless fashion is to behave in the manner of a beast. We may find our happiness either in killing or being killed. The first way is that of beasts, the second that of man. The soul of a beast is ever asleep, a man's ever awake. We can never prosper till we are fully grown and awake in our souls. I shall tell you a story from the Puranas. There was a certain *rishi*; the fire emitted from between his brows put an end to all suffering. The point of this text is that, when the soul becomes alive, all miseries end and so the injustices perpetrated by the government will be no more when we become alive in our soul. I want to put this truth to you in the plainest terms. We want happiness in place of the present misery; if so we should suffer voluntarily and lay down our lives for the sake of truth. (Gandhi 1888–1948, 16: 414)

Why should Gandhi have invoked the ancient category of *tapasya* which he picturesquely described using the powerful metaphor of fire between the *yogi's* brows? As mentioned above, *tapasya* had an *itihaas* in the Indian tradition and in Patanjali's *Yoga sutra* (with which Gandhi was familiar and to which there is fairly copious reference in the Collected works) as the voluntary and intelligent acceptance of pain understood as an awakening of the soul to claim its own latent strength. Gandhi re-thought this category as a sanction to ensure rights and justice to the dispossessed. He advised Indians (and indeed humanity);

> ...let them (*ravanias*) dispossess you of all you have; be as fakirs but do not budge an inch. This is the *dharma* for a man...This is the legacy we should leave to posterity... (Ibid.)

Gandhi's argument for *tapas* as the ultimate sanction on which justice in a society ought to rest was twofold. The first part of the argument suggested that one could not locate the sanction for justice in anything that went contrary to man's *dharma*/foundational nature/essential property. This meant that Gandhi could not accept anything that went contrary to human nature as the sanction for justice for the basic structure of a human society. This lead him to reject the *aswabhavika*/unnatural demand that for selecting principles of justice, the human being needed to abstract from relationships of kinship to take a view from nowhere. The second part of Gandhi's argument suggested that while seeking justice and the redressal of injustice, one could not loose sight of the priority of the claims of equality over those of liberty. I will unpack both these points briefly in the following two subsections (That is in 5.3.3.1 and 5.3.3.2, respectively).

5.3.3.1   Locating the Sanction for Justice: *Tapas, Swabhawa* and Kinship

The last chapter and the previous sections of this chapter have made many references to Gandhi's emphasis on that which came naturally to the human person that which was *swabhavika*/natural/innermost orientation. Gandhi had argued that *ahimsa*/ non-violence not *himsa*/ violence was natural to man and that the special virtue/*dharma*n/foundational nature of man lay in the unilateral obligation to own kinship with the human and the non-human other. This meant that the liberal move to select principles of justice from a point of view that abstracted from the human beings foundational attachments to 'others' was *aswabhavika*/unnatural and went against human nature. If impartiality derived from a position of taking a view from nowhere was unnatural to man, the sanction for justice could not be derived from principles selected in an original position of a Rawlsian kind. Still less could the human being depart from kinship (to the rest of the cosmos as it were) to define relationships with others solely against the measure of utility.

In a Gandhian framework, it was the human beings ability (like that illustrated by the ancient story of the *rishi*) to undertake *tapas* (as the fire between the *rishi's* eyes) or voluntary pain upon him/her self in the interest of justice which alone could serve as the sanction for justice. On such a view if justice was withheld (if historical injustice needed to be redressed), the human being (alone or in a group) could use the power of the soul, the capacity to undergo intelligent suffering, "austerity, penance, heat" (Ranganathan 2008, 130), to evoke a just response from the erring other. Gandhi extended such a sanction from what he described as the law in the family. One might begin to understand the role of *tapas* as the sanction of justice if one reflected on how (for Gandhi) the power of the soul to undergo intelligent suffering could indeed serve to transform both oneself and the other. It is perhaps important to recall that in the *itihaas* of *Yoga,* the "practice of *tapas*" has been seen "to have a genuinely transformative power" (Ibid., 134).

To begin with the imposition of austerity/penance on oneself (when confronted by injustice) could become a transformative experience as such austerity/penance could serve to diminish all *himsa*/violence against unjust others which arises from anger and passion. It was in this connection that Gandhi resurrected the ancient Indian tradition of fasting as a method of directing attention away from hostility and anger and thereby doing away with the sources of violence against the conflicting other. This, in his view, made it possible for the afflicted party/victim of injustice to be able to see the unjust other from outside of an ego directed anger. Such a position free from anger was a stance that made for the possibilities of arriving at a truthful evaluation of the position between the self and the other. On the other hand, the sight of the voluntary self-imposed pain/penance in the interest of truth made it possible for the conflicting other (on his/her part) to understand the plight of the victim of injustice. It was in such a connection that Gandhi invoked the transformative power of love as a response to *tapasya* between people (in a conflict) as a source for such transformation. This led Gandhi to undertake fasts against the evil of untouchability with a view to transform hearts rather than concentrate solely on legal solutions for the redressal of the injustice of that which had so happened in the past/*itihaasic.*

Gandhi spoke of *tapasya* as the sanction of justice and argued that it was only taking *tapah*/austerity/penance on oneself (as in his famous fasts) that could secure rights, justice and the redressal of injustice. The Gandhian methodology of *Satyagraha*/firmness on truth was (as mentioned above) an extension of the non-violent deference which guided an individual's resistance to his/her unjust kin in the family. In the last chapter, there was some discussion on the connection between *satyagraha* and *swaraj.* That discussion has bearings on the connection between *tapas* and justice. This connection invoked the issue of individual freedom/*swaraj* and its relationship to authority. On Gandhi's view of it, justice was secured primarily **between** individuals by the selfgrowing into a form of personhood/*swarajya*/self-rule that deferred to 'otherness'. Such a form of personhood was conceived as self-restraint or self-control.

This strain of thinking led to a strange consequence; which was, that the stability of justice in a Gandhian state, could not be secured by the state through a consensus about its institutions alone. One may recall Kant's argument in *The Metaphysics of Morals* (2009) here as representative of the liberal tradition and consent-based accounts of authority. In Kant's view where none exist, citizens have a basic obligation to join with others to create political institutions for these alone make justice possible and allow each person to enjoy his rights. In general, consent-based liberal accounts of authority, that drive most versions of the social contract tradition share the concern to reconcile individual freedom with state authority that ensures the simultaneous freedom of all. Gandhi certainly accepted consent-based accounts of authority recommending a decentralized version of democracy based on direct participation of citizens at the local level. However on Gandhi's understanding, individual freedom as self-rule/*swaraj* (and the related ability to undergo *tapah*) lead to the development of a form of personhood that then empowers the citizen to exercise his/her natural sense of justice and regulate state authority and its exercise of arbitrary power. Gandhi made this clear enough;

> Real *swaraj* will come, not by the acquisition of authority by a few, but by the acquisition of the capacity by all to resist authority when it is abused. In other words, *Swaraj* is to be attained by educating the masses to a sense of their capacity to regulate and control authority. (Gandhi 1888–1948, 30: 159)

In 1918, Gandhi spoke of such suffering to *satyagrahi's* at Vadod;

> I hope all those who have not paid up the land revenue will go the meeting and see what the Commissioner advices… He may tell you that, despite the failure of crops, it is the people's duty to pay the Government the land revenue… say: 'You may cut off our heads, if you please, but we will not pay the land revenue. We shall not submit to the Government's injustice.' (Gandhi 1888–1948, 16: 412–414)

This might seem to suggest that concerns of a sense of justice as constituting the innermost orientation of man *qua* man influenced Gandhi's conception of freedom. Since freedom as political self-governance was contingent upon the individual self-rule or self-control; consent-based authority could not secure freedom to all **independently of** such individual self-rule/*swaraj* or of the related capacity to undergo self-imposed austerity/penance /*tapas* for the sake of justice. In Gandhi's view, there was also perhaps a certain sense of *swaraj* which came from the root *se* which meant 'of one's own most orientation' or 'that which came naturally to oneself *qua* human person'. In that sense, a person could only be free if he/she was able to live out a form of personhood that came naturally to him/her. In Gandhi's case, this was a form of personhood where the human being lived out his/her *khaas lakshana*/distinguishing property by an equi-mindedness that came from owning kinship with all 'others' just or unjust.

This meant that Gandhi was equally concerned with the simultaneous freedom of the major and minor in Indian society as also the freedom of the oppressor/ the colonizer. He said;

> If I want that freedom for my country, I would not be deserving of that freedom if I did not treasure the equal right of every other race, weak or strong to the same freedom. (Gandhi 1888–1948, 53: 364).

It is surely significant that the Gandhian methodology of securing rights through *satyagraha* and *tapasya* was meant to contest domination without seeking to set up a new dominating major/centre. The concern for a simultaneity of freedom through the individual practice of an equi-mindedness, equality of deference to all others and engagement in intelligent suffering meant that individual freedom/*swaraj* in Gandhi was also a freedom from the individual's own need to dominate and exercise arbitrary power. Gandhi argued that;

> "Men aspiring to be free can hardly think of enslaving others. If they try to do so, they will only be binding their own chains of slavery tighter" (Gandhi 1888–1948, 94: 191).

That Gandhi thought that individual freedom/self-rule was a freedom from the need to dominate the other and a freedom from the subjection to domination by the other might become evident if one examines Gandhi's insights about the nature of freedom/ *swaraj. Swaraj* as home rule was conceived as a freedom from economic, political and social domination by the 'other'—whether state or oppressing major. *Swaraj* as self-rule—the primary sense of freedom in Gandhi—was concerned with two things. First, with self-discipline as a progressive freedom from fear and acquisitiveness. These and other passions could lead the self to accept an invigilation of his/her choices by the oppressor. In the context of the *swarajya* or self-rule of the *satyagrahi,* Gandhi made it clear;

> A satyagrahi enjoys a degree of freedom not possible for others, for he becomes a truly fearless person. Once his mind is rid of fear, he will never agree to be another's slave. Having achieved this state of mind, he will never submit to any arbitrary action. (Gandhi 1888–1948, 8: 151)

Secondly, *swaraj* was a form of self-discipline as a freedom to exercise choices that came **naturally** to man. Gandhi had argued that it was man's own most orientation to own kinship with all others, to remain *ahimsanat* and defer equally to just and unjust others. Man was free/*swarajya* when he was free from the domination of internal obstacles posed by an exaggerated sense of self which obstructed him from living out such an *ahimsanat/*non-violent form of personhood that came naturally to the human person *qua* person. Such egoistic obstacles led a human being into a form of inauthentic personhood which instigated him/her to go against his/her sense of justice and dominate the other by invigilation, violence or interference. True *swaraj* was an inner freedom from such inauthentic desires and the need to dominate the other.

Gandhi had also recognized that there could be cases of conflicts about justice **within** the self. Conflicts perhaps caused by a part of the self-turning towards the inauthentic/*aswabhavika.* This could happen both within the specific individual self or the larger collective self. For instance, within a collective, there could be a turning away from the individual and unilateral obligation to defer/be non-violent towards the other. This could lead to a crisis of individual responsibility within the self who was a part of such a collective. This kind of crisis called for a special form of *satyagraha.* Gandhi had explained that;

> The time may come for me to offer Satyagraha against ourselves... But I know how to offer resistance against ourselves as against the rulers. What kind of Satyagraha can I offer against ourselves on such occasions? What penance can I do for such sins? The Satyagraha and the penance[4] I can conceive can only be one and that is for me to fast and if need be to give up this body and thus to prove the truth of Satyagraha. (Gandhi 1888–1948, 17: 412).

5.3.3.2 *Tapas* as the Sanction Behind Justice: Equality Before Liberty

At the start of Sect. 5.3.3, I had argued that Gandhi's argument that *tapas* was the only proper sanction for justice was supported by two insights. The first insight (which has already been discussed in 5.3.3.1) suggested that one could not locate the sanction for

---

[4] In Gujarati *tapasya.*

justice in anything that went contrary to man's *dharma*/foundational nature/essential property. This subsection will turn attention to Gandhi's second insight about *tapas* as the only proper sanction for justice. This Gandhian insight specified that while one presses for the redressal of injustice, one cannot loose sight of the priority of the claims of equality over those of liberty.

For Gandhi (as seen in this and the last chapter), it was *swabhavika*/innermost orientation/foundational nature for human beings to treat human and non-human others as if they were kith and kin, i.e. with absolute equality understood as an uncompromising commitment to *samadarshita*/equi-mindedness. The claims of such an absolute equality necessarily trumped those of freedom, and freedom to protest was no exception to the priority of equality in Gandhi. While injustice called for a response, such response needed to maintain an absolute equality between oneself, one's father or brother, and the erring unjust other. This lead Gandhi to argue that imposing austerity/penance/*tapas* on oneself rather than on the other was the only method of responding to injustice and seeking rights. For *tapas* was the only way in which a right's aspirant could both respond to injustice and at the same time maintain an equality of deference between herself/himself and the erring kin or indeed unjust caste/racial/religious other. On this view to use force against one who appeared unjust was to disregard his/her right to life and bodily integrity thereby assigning him/her (as unjust) to an unequal position. Therefore, Gandhi argued that non-violent *tapas* alone rested on an absolute egalitarianism and a respect for the equal rights of all just/unjust human others;

> Everyone admits that sacrifice of self is infinitely superior to sacrifice of others. Moreover, if this kind of force is used in a cause that is unjust, only the person using it suffers. He does not make others suffer for his mistakes. Men have before now done many things which were subsequently found to have been wrong. No man can claim to be absolutely in the right, or that a particular thing is wrong because he thinks so, but it is wrong for him so long as that is his deliberate judgement. It is, therefore, meet that he should not do that which he knows to be wrong, and suffer the consequences whatever it may be. This is the key to soul force. (Gandhi 1888–1948, 10: 292)

This chapter has argued that a commitment to justice constituted the ethics of Gandhi moral politics and that it lay in the strong concern for responding to others with an equi-mindedness drawn from concepts such as *samata, samadarshita* and *samabhava* in the Indian *itihaas*. It was *swabhavika* for man *qua* man to be ruled by *ahimsa* as the law of the human species in his/her relationships with his/her own kin and equally in relationships with hostile others. With the invocation of *tapas*, Gandhi brought home the point that the sanction for justice lay in the individual assuming responsibility for the stability of justice for the basic structure of society while maintaining an equi-minded regard for the absolutely equal albeit unjust other.

5.3.4 An Alternative Gandhian Understanding of Justice: Some Insights

It may seem appropriate at this point to bring together some alternative Gandhian insights about justice which have emerged from the preceding sections:

1. The first thing to note about Gandhi's conception of justice is that Gandhi thought of justice as a tradition constitutive and tradition constituted term. Locating himself within the Indian tradition of *niti* and *dharma/dhamma* Gandhi thought that justice as *niti*/institutional could not abstract from that which was the *swabhawa*/innermost orientation/foundational nature of the human being. Building upon the root, *se*/natural in *swa*/self-Gandhi thought that the demands of justice could only rest on that which came naturally to the human being. It is important to emphasize that in unpacking the special weight of considerations of justice in terms of the *swabhavika*/natural human sense of a 'unilateral obligation' of kinship to 'otherness', Gandhi went against a dominant strand in the Western tradition of thinking about justice. Gandhi conceived that which came naturally to human beings on the analogy of that which seemed natural to them in their private space. He put together insights about justice for the basic structure for society on the analogy of that which happened in families.

    This went against a dominant strand of thinking about justice which can indeed be traced back to antiquity and goes back at least to the Greek sophists. This strand locates the weight of considerations of justice in prudence and a balance of power. Such thinking regards the acceptance of principles of justice as a compromise/*modus vivendi* between persons of roughly equal power who would enforce their way on others **if only they could do so**. On such a way of thinking about justice, it is only prudence that prevents the parties in a conflict from the use of force. It may be recalled that while Rawls builds on the idea that human beings are both rational and reasonable and thereby differs in significant respects, from such a way of thinking about justice, he still locates the concept of justice in "the conditions of reciprocity" (Rawls 1958, 183–84) between "rational and mutually self-interested parties" (Ibid., 183). Gandhi's idea of unilateral obligation/*farj* natural to human beings is a complete rejection of the idea that justice is grounded in an acceptance of conditions of reciprocity or those of a balance of power.

2. In the same strain, Gandhi not only rejected the liberal "fundamentalism about institutions" (Sen 2010, 83) but also the liberal institutions themselves as inadequate for securing justice for the basic structure of society. *Hind Swaraj* articulates Gandhi's critique of liberal legislative and judicial institutions. On Gandhi's view (as argued above), Justice could not be secured by institutions like Parliaments which were built upon the notion of general rather than individual responsibility. Neither could justice rest upon the measure of positive law. For justice was an irreducibly particular and uniquely contextual experience of arriving at the truth in situations of conflict while (all the time) remaining equi-minded to the unjust other. Locating himself squarely within the *itihaas*/it so happened of

the age old communities of India Gandhi spoke of individual responsibility and the mediation by the near—the next to kin—the village elders or the *panch.*

3. While one might say (as the historian Ramanujan argues) that if there is a Indian way of thinking, it is that Indians gravitate towards the contextual, Gandhi's gravitation had to do with the idea that justice was inseparable from *satya*/truth. It was such a connection to truth that led Gandhi to replace the impartiality of liberals with *samadarshita*/equi-mindedness. Gandhi sought freedom from bias in an equi-mindedness towards all others rather than in an abstraction from one's context to take a view from nowhere. The equality involved in the Gandhian deference to all others was, in an important part, an equality of deference to the possibility that the truth could also lie in the position and beliefs of the contending *other.* Since truth could only be arrived at (in cases of conflict) between the parties at the site of the **supposed** injustice, Gandhi's treatment of justice was essentially contextual. It was this aspect of justice—as inseparably connected with the search for truth—that Gandhi meant to bring out when he used the metaphor of man as the image of God. This will become clear if we recall that Gandhi had famously equated truth with God saying that truth is the best name of God (Gandhi 1888–1948, 66: 112).

4. Mention must be made of Gandhi's emphasis on the inseparable relationship between means adopted and end sought. It was on account of this intimate relationship between means and end that Gandhian justice—political, economic, social or individual—could not be secured without the employment of pure means, i.e. means that gave others their due. Such an insight into the connection between means and end led Gandhi to argue that one could not redress injustice by unjust means. The only suffering that could serve as a pure means on such a view was that which could be imposed on oneself. This meant that the only way that a rights aspirant could seek justice from an oppressive other would be by a non-violent *agraha* or insistence on *satya* or truth.

5. The Gandhian *satyagrahas* and Gandhi's conception of justice shared the liberal concern with the freedom of the individual and nation. However Gandhi thought of such freedom differently in terms of *swaraj*/self-rule. Gandhian *swaraj* was conceptualized both as political self-governance and individual self-control. Gandhi's quest for freedom was philosophically alive to the liberal concern for the simultaneous freedom of all humans as equality. However, Gandhi transformed the liberal abstract equality before the law that relegated actual inequalities to the private realm into an absolute equality that could be **practised**—an equality of deference to all human and non-human others.

5.4 Concluding Remarks

The purpose of attempting to construct an alternative Gandhian understanding of justice has been to bring out the deep dissonance between that understanding and Ambedkar's notion of justice. Located within the framework of a liberal contractarian approach to justice Ambedkar was as far from Gandhi as one could imagine. It seems clear enough that their positions could never meet and that Ambedkar would find Gandhi's attempts to secure justice for the untouchables befuddling.

The solutions one seeks in philosophy are often simply those which are related to clarity and it seems important that we understand that Gandhi and Ambedkar were both truthfully seeking justice and that the differences between them did not emerge because either of them was insincere or acting out of bad faith as it were. No matter what Gandhi's detractors might think, both Gandhi and Ambedkar shared a concern for justice, only they thought about justice in very different ways. The burden of this chapter has been to make this point and to emphasize that justice as a function of the relationship of an equality of deference between individuals was the first virtue in Gandhi and that such a concern for justice made for the ethics of Gandhian politics.

Notes

i.   "Equality or Priority?" was delivered as the Lindley Lecture at the University of Kansas, 21 November 1991. It is included in *The Ideal of Equality*, edited by Matthew Clayton and Andrew Williams, pp. 81–125 (2000).

ii.   *Dhamma* holds the same sense as *dharma* and is the term used by Buddha and the Buddhists. At the risk of putting it far too simplistically, one could suggest that the *dharma/dhamma*, across the *Sramanic* and *Bramanical* traditions, can be best understood in terms of the demands of righteousness/justice in relation to one's context.

iii. *Nyāya* (Sanskrit: न्याय, *nyā-yá*) literally means "justice", "rules", "method" or "judgement".

iv.   "It is significant that the idea of goodness (and of virtue) has been largely superseded in moral philosophy by the idea of rightness, supported perhaps by some conception of sincerity" (Murdoch 2001, 52).

v.   One might recall that Ambedkar did refer to Kautilya's *Artha Shatra* in connection with gender justice. It can be useful to read Chap. 6 in Chakrabarty (2019) for a more detailed discussion of this last point.

vi.   All three come from the same Sanskrit root *sama* a word that shares an etymology with the English word "same" and that has often been translated into English as same, equal or constant. Though I do not claim to be a scholar of the Sanskrit language roughly translated *samadarshana* means 'to see things with an equal eye despite inequalities', *Samabhava* means having the 'attitude of equality to things as they are/ exist' and, *samata* refers to 'the status of equality'.

vii. The *panchayat* was an elected council of five village elders serving to govern a village unit in the simultaneous form of the legislative executive and judiciary.

viii. "Each person is to have an equal right to the most extensive basic liberty compatible with a similar liberty for others". (Rawls 1971, 60).

ix.   "Only when all the nations of the world seek their welfare with a sense of kinship among themselves as among members of a family…" (Gandhi 1888–1948, 18: 116).

References

Ambedkar, B.R. 2014. *Dr Babasaheb Ambedkar writings and Speeches*, Ed. Vasant Moon (set of 17 Volumes). New Delhi: Dr Ambedkar Foundation. Ministry of Social Justice and Empowerment. Government of India.

Arneson, Richard J. 2012. Justice. In *The oxford handbook of political philosophy*, ed. David Estlund. Oxford: Oxford University Press.

Arnold, Edwin. 1965. *The song celestial*. New York: Heritage Press.

Bhattacharya, S. (Comp. and Ed.). 2008. *The Mahatma and the poet. Letters and debates between Gandhi and Tagore, 1915–1941*. New Delhi: National Book Trust.

Brereton, J.P. 2004. Dharman in Rgveda. *Journal of Indian Philosophy* 32 (5/6): 449–489.

Chakrabarty, Bidyut. 2019. *The Socio-Political Ideas of B. R. Ambedkar: Liberal constitutionalism in a creative mould*. New York: Routledge.

Doniger, Wendy, ed. 1991. *The Law of Manu*. With an Introduction and Notes Translated by Wendy Doniger with Brian K Smith. London: Penguin books.

Gandhi, M. K.1888–1948. *Collected Works of Mahatma Gandhi*: Volumes 1 to 98. New Delhi: Publications Division, Government of India, 1999. Accessed online in May 2021 at https://www.gandhiashramsevagram.org/gandhi-literature/collected-works-of-mahatma-gandhi-volume-1-to-98.php.

Hiltebeitel, Alf. 2011. *Dharma: Its early history in law, religion, and narrative*. New York: Oxford University Press.

Kant, I. 2009. *Groundwork of the metaphysic of morals*, H. J. Paton (Tr.), Harper Collins.

MacIntyre, A. 1981. *After Virtue: A study in moral theory*. London: Duckworth.

MacIntyre, A. 1988. *Whose justice? which rationality?* Notre Dame, Indiana: University of Notre Dame Press.

Murdoch, I. 2001. *The Sovereignty of good*. London: Routledge.

Murti, V. V. Ramana (ed). 1970. *Gandhi: Essential writings*. New Delhi: Gandhi Peace Foundation.

Nagel, Thomas. 1986. *The view from nowhere*. New York: Oxford University Press.

Nagraj, D. R. 2015. *The flaming feet and other essays: The Dalit Movement in India*, ed. Prithvi Datta Chandra Shobhi. Ranikhet: Permanent Black.

Nandy, Ashis. 1970. The culture of Indian politics: A stock taking. *The Journal of Asian Studies* 30 (1): 57–79.

Palshikar, Suhas. 1996. Gandhi-Ambedkar interface: When shall the Twain meet? *Economic and Political Weekly* 31 (31): 2070–2072.

Parekh, B. 2021. The Intellectual and Political Legacy of B. R. Ambedkar. In *B. R. Ambedkar: The quest for justice*, Vol. 1 (set of 5 volumes), ed. Aakash Singh Rathore, 1–30. New Delhi: Oxford University Press.

Parfit, Derek. 2000. Equality or Priority. In *The ideal of equality*, ed. Matthew Clayton and Andrew Williams, 81–125. London: Macmillan. (Delivered as the Lindley Lecture at the university of Kansas in 1991).

Prabhu, R.K., and U.R. Rao, eds. 2007. *The mind of the mahatma*. Ahmedabad: Navajivan Publishing House.

Radhakrishnan, S., ed. 1953. *The Principal Upanishads*, edited with Text Translation and Notes by S. Radhakrishnan, The Muirhead Library of Philosophy. London: Allen & Unwin Ltd.

Ramanujan, A.K. 1989. Is There an Indian Way of Thinking. *Contributions to Indian Sociology*. 23 (1): 41–58.

Ranganathan, S. 2008. *Patañjali's Yoga Sūtra*. Delhi: Penguin Books.

Rao, Velcheru Narayana and Subrahmanyam, Sanjay. 2009. Notes on Political Thought in Medieval and Early Modern South India. *Modern Asian Studies* Vol. 43, No. 1, (Expanding Frontiers in South Asian and World History: Essays in Honour of John F. Richards Jan., 2009), 175–210.

Rathore, Aakash Singh. 2017. *Indian political theory: Laying the groundwork for svaraj*. London, New York: Routledge.

Rathore, A. (ed). 2021a. *B. R. Ambedkar: The quest for justice*, Vol. 1 (set of 5 volumes). New Delhi: Oxford University Press.

Rathore, A. 2021b. Introduction. In *B. R. Ambedkar: The quest for justice*, Vol. 1 (set of 5 volumes), ed. Aakash Singh Rathore, xxiii–xxxviii. New Delhi: Oxford University Press.

Rawls, John. 1958. Justice as fairness. *The Philosophical Review* 67 (2): 164–194.

Rawls, John. 1971. *A theory of justice*. Cambridge, Massachusetts: Harvard University Press.

Rawls, John. 1999. *The law of peoples: With the idea of public reason revisited*. Cambridge, Massachusetts: Harvard University Press.

Rawls, John. 2005. *Political Liberalism*. New York: Columbia University Press.

Sandel, Michael J. 2008. *Liberalism and the limits of justice*, 2nd ed. New York: Cambridge University Press.

Sen, A. 2010. *The Idea of Justice*. London: Penguin Books.

Smith, Adam. 1976. *The theory of moral sentiments* (1759, 1790); Republished and ed. D. D. Raphael and A. L. Macfie Oxford: Clarendon Press.

Tagore, R. 2008. The Religion of Man. In *The English writings of Rabindranath Tagore*, Vol. III, Ed. S.K. Das, 83–190. New Delhi: Sahitya Akademi.

Chapter 6
In Conclusion: Owners and Authors.
Of Surplus, Generosity and Trust

Abstract This chapter moves beyond a discussion of the conflicts and the incommensurability between Ambedkar and Gandhi's contrary understandings of the self, community, justice, history and the 'it' so happened of *itihaas*. The chapter brings out insights about why it might be necessary to countenance the theoretical and practical possibilities for extending the understanding of suffering/*duhkha* from those born into the community which suffers to all those to whom such an experience is at the very least intelligible. Moving between the debate between Gandhi and Ambedkar, and the much later essays put together by Professor Guru and Professor Sarukkai (2012), this chapter will suggest that the possibilities of generosity lie both in the realm of theory and those of polity. In the context of theory, one can argue that it is necessary to make ideas about experience/reality available as theory which can be applied to understand experiences no matter to whom such experiences might (or might not) belong. In the context of polity, the chapter suggests that one can break out of the circle of suspicion only by locating something to trust. In this connection, it brings in arguments from Rabindranath Tagore as an ever present third in the debate between Ambedkar and Gandhi.

Keywords Incommensurability · Dalit writing · The right to theorize suffering · Vulnerability · Social sciences · Theory · Owners · Authors · Surplus · Generosity · The religion of man · man the great · Art · Harmony · Music · House of songs

This book has attempted to bring out the incommensurability between Ambedkar and Gandhi's notions of the self, community, justice and their conflicting understandings of the relationship between the past and present of individuals and communities. This chapter will not dwell on such an incommensurability or indeed end on a somewhat stultifying note on their conflicting world views. It will go back to the *duhkha*/suffering spoken about in the introductory chapter and bring out the reasons why it might be necessary to countenance the (theoretical and practical) possibilities for extending the understanding of the experience of suffering/*duhkha* from those born into the community which suffers to all others who seek to understand it. In this connection, this chapter will speak both about the debate between Gandhi and Ambedkar and the much later set of essays put together by Sundar Sarukkai and Gopal

© Springer Science+Business Media Singapore 2022
B. Puri, *The Ambedkar–Gandhi Debate*,
https://doi.org/10.1007/978-981-16-8686-3_6

Guru (Guru and Sarukkai, 2012a) to which there was some reference in the Introduction to this book. This might seem fitting because the conflicts between Ambedkar and Gandhi continue into the present as they inspire both contemporary dalit writing and dalit activism in different and sometimes interrelated ways.

What then about the experience of *duhkha*/suffering and the ownership thereof? To answer this question, it might be interesting to go back to arguments about who owns suffering and from there naturally enough to questions about who has the right to speak and theorize about the *duhkha*/suffering, and by extension, the experience of another. This is because, as has been preliminarily explored in the Introduction to this book, confrontations between Gandhi and Ambedkar on the right to speak about (and on behalf of) the experience of the depressed classes have lingered on in the Indian mind and imagination. These arguments resonate in debates in contemporary social sciences in India about the legitimate owners of the suffering of communities and at another level about "what is important for doing theory: ownership or authorship of experience?" (Guru 2012c, 109).

At one level, this chapter is interested in making space for conceptual generosity in academic writing and theorizing about experiences. However at another, it is interested in a slightly more practical question; one of locating moments of trust between people in drawing upon "models of widening emotional concern" (Nagraj 2015, 64). Since one has to begin somewhere, it might be best to begin with theory and then move on to practices of identification with parties at the opposite ends of conflicts and indeed to the source of reasons, for the practices of emotional identification, lived out by Gandhi. Accordingly, Sect. 6.1 of this concluding chapter will focus on the arguments about the right to theorize about the experiences of the 'other'. Section 6.2 will discuss Rabindranath Tagore's reasons for recommending that all indignity and insult is an "insult to our own humanity" (Tagore 2012b, 326) just as all challenges to victimization belongs to "man the Great in all humanity" (Ibid., 333).

6.1 Guru and Sarukkai: The Right to Speak and to Theorize

The Cracked Mirror (Guru and Sarukkai, 2012a) is an important book, one indeed, that addresses arguments about "the right to theorize" (Sarukkai 2012a, 29) about dalit experience in the contemporary social sciences in India. The metaphor of the cracked mirror somewhat graphically brings out the distortions that confront the dalit in accounts of his/her experience in the social sciences. The metaphor suggests two things—one that the dalit cannot identify with the representation of his/her experiences and consequently does not feel that these reflections promote self-understanding/or help others to understand the experience better. Two that the dalit is suspicious of all such theorizing. The book that provides the theme for my reflections, in the conclusion to this consideration of the Gandhi–Ambedkar debate, makes two points. The first is that the dalits can make better sense of their experience if they realize that theorizing about their experience is an inner necessity and that it is also a "social necessity in order to become the subject of their own thinking rather than becoming the object of somebody else's thinking" (Guru 2012a, 25). It is equally important for the owners and thereby legitimate subjects of their own experience "to realize doing theory as an inner moral necessity" (Ibid., 27). The second important point (at least in terms of the discussion in this chapter and this book) is that distortions in theories about dalit experience must provoke the dalit and the reader to raise a question about "the right to theorize" (Sarukkai 2012a, 29).

To reiterate a point which was made in the **Introductory chapter** and Chap. 3 of this book, the view that the dalits (or any other tormented people) has a necessity to speak about their own experience perhaps derives from the very inwardness of the modern self and from the third facet of modern identity that of "the expressivist notion of nature as an inner moral source" (Taylor 2001, X). The correlative to this, as noted earlier, is that non dalits (those who are not born into the *duhkha* of the dalits) ought not to "appropriate" or parachute into the experience (and expression of such an experience) of the dalits by attempting to theorize about it. This raises the more general question; one of theorizing about the experience of another which might be put simply as follows—"Is it ethically correct to parachute into somebody's experience?" (Guru 2012c, 123).

It seems certainly and undeniably the case that as a community dalits (tribals, racially discriminated against persons, indigenous persons, the religiously persecuted as also other tormented people) ought to become the primary subjects of their own experience and that this can only be effected in any meaningful sense by becoming authors of theory. In other words by seriously engaging with their own first-person experience and thereby making it available to scholars who are intellectually interested in that experience. The sufferers are also at a vantage point or better placed than anyone else, in a certain sense, to theorize about that experience. However, some difficulties could begin to appear when these propositions are related to the ideas of the ownership of experience and the relationship between such ownership and the "right to theorize"; and when it is decisively concluded that non dalits should be denied such a right or perhaps should chose to restrain their "'free' curiosity" (Sarukkai 2012b, 135). The section which immediately follows will raise these and related issues about the central arguments of/in *The Cracked Mirror* (Guru and Sarukkai, 2012a).

6.1.1 Theory: Adequate/Inadequate and Right/Wrong

The right to think and to reflect in a certain way is the basis of the practice of the social sciences. Professor Sarukkai has explained such practice;

> While all thinking is not theorizing, there is a particular mode of thinking that characterizes the act of theorizing. Some of the characteristics of theory, such as subsuming particulars under universals, unification of diverse phenomenon, description(thick description, mathematical description and so on), or explanation(particular structures of explanation) are all

illustrative of this particular mode of thinking. One could view theorizing as a particular 'style' of thinking. (Sarukkai 2012b, 129–30)

If these are some processes that are involved in theorizing it certainly appears possible to say, that while a theory may offer adequate or inadequate descriptions and explanations of what it seeks to understand and simplify, it seems to make little sense to use normative language. To say for instance that a theory like a human being can be normatively evaluated—perhaps praised for being 'right' or condemned for being 'wrong'. Sarukkai argues, however, that social scientists must seriously consider the ethical norms that ought to govern their acts of theorizing. Such an expanded set of norms would indicate that theoreticians not only need to address epistemological issues, but they also need to ask themselves normative questions. Questions such as 'whether they have the right to theorize about certain experiences?'.

On reflection, there are three important points involved in Sarukkai's argument. The first is that the owners of experience must be authors of theory because they alone have the 'lived experience' that 'authenticates' the theory. The second, that the choice of concepts at the level of experience, or at the level of doing theory, is not only an epistemological choice but also an ethical one. The third point is that the social scientist legitimizes his/her exploration of problems by invoking the notion of 'curiosity'. However, it follows (on this point of view) that curiosity (like gossip where it is malicious) about the experience of 'others' is/can be 'intrusive'. This chapter will argue that there are problems with all three of these propositions, and these will be explored in the following three subsections.

6.1.2   Owners and Authors

The first point in Professor Sarukkai's response to Professor Guru's argument raises the notion of "lived experience" (Sarukkai 2012a, 34) and the related notions of ownership, authorship and authenticity. Sarukkai supports Guru's argument that "theorizing" about dalit experience "should be limited only to the Dalits" (Ibid., 30) and that non-dalits have no moral right to theorize about dalits by arguing that experience cannot be "materialized/commodified and transferred without taking the subject of experience into account" (Ibid., 34). Sarukkai argues that what makes lived experience authentic and different from what he calls "vicarious experience" (Ibid., 35) is that "Lived experience" (Ibid., 34) refers only to "those experiences that are seen as *necessary,* experiences over which the subject has no choice whether to experience or not…Even if the experience is unpleasant, there is no choice that allows the subject to leave or even modify it" (Ibid., 35). This qualification of having no choice in the matter of what constitutes one's lived experience is important. For what it comes to mean is that the term "lived experience" cannot be used, for instance, to describe an outsider's attempt to live with dalits or *adivasis*/tribals. One must make a note here to recall Gandhi's efforts to identify with and indeed live out the life of the dalits as an adopted son (as he put it himself). Sarukkai's qualification specifying that all theory about the dalits must begin and end with "Lived experience" (Ibid., 34) rules all such adopted experiences out of the picture. *"Lived experience is not about freedom of experience but about the lack of freedom in an experience"* (Ibid., 36). It is about being insiders in fact *"being them,* in the sense that you *cannot* be anything else" (Ibid.). A related way to justify the nature of the experience and indeed theoretical reflection about the experience is by bringing in the notion of ownership of experience and the moral (which in terms of this argument is also the epistemic) authority to speak about it. Sarukkai paraphrases Guru's claim about owners and authors saying "that only those who experience can theorize implies that only an owner can be an author" (Ibid., 38). Sarukkai brings in the binary between emotion and reason to support Guru's position. He argues that theory should relate the epistemological with the emotional. On this view, theory cannot be legitimated by establishing a distance from experience. If theory is at a distance from experience it will be "vicarious" (Ibid., 35) in two senses—first by vicariously appropriating the "others" experience and then by trying to do theory vicariously as a site to "distribute… guilt" (Ibid., 44) about what one has done to the "other" who has been one's victim.

It is possible to suggest that this position may be mistaken at several levels. To begin with, one should ask if it makes sense to speak about a theory being right or wrong according as the author is the owner/or not of the lived experience which he/she seeks to understand? On reflection, one might consider that this question can be answered by reflecting upon the idea of the ownership of experience. There can be different ways in which individuals may be related to their experiences in general and to their experiences of emotions in particular. The first significant point to make in this connection is that on Guru and Sarukkai's view, it seems difficult to extend the ownership of an experience even from one dalit subject to another individual dalit. Consider the following:

> The experiencer comes to the experience not as a subject who has some control over that experience but as one who *will* have to live with that experience. (Ibid., 35)

Or again;

> …the first prerequisite for an experience to be considered as lived experience is that it is an experience of what it means to *be* the subject who experiences. (Ibid., 36)

It seems clear that each individual dalit subject is the owner of his/her singular experience as it can by definition be **the necessary experience** only of that one person. It follows from this that an individual dalit subject can own his/her unique individual experience but not quite share the experience of other dalits. This position creates problems; for it means that as an individual subject of experience, each dalit person must theorize only about his/her own individual experience which **he/she owns**. However, if one thinks about this, it might become apparent that theory or even language used to do theory would involve more than one experience and more than one language user. However, the problems of this argument only become more compounded; for, besides the idea that the experience of suffering belongs only to the one person whose experience it **necessarily is** there are also the following additional (and fairly untenable) claims made by Guru and Sarukkai: (i) no one outside

the Dalit community—specially those who might have been involved in the humiliation and annihilation of the self-respect of the dalits—can share the experience;
(ii) an outsider cannot therefore articulate the experience in an authentic way; (iii)
the outsider is necessarily seen as someone who becomes incapable of theorising
about the dalit experience in order to make that experience generally intelligible;
(iv) attempts to theorize about the dalit experience of suffering by the outsider; must
therefore be necessarily vicarious, hypocritical or self-deceptive; (v) such attempts,
therefore, must attract moral suspicion, if not moral condemnation.

In the light of these points, one might consider (as noted above) that, if in line with
Guru and Sarukkai's argument, one thinks that lived experience is the experience
which belongs necessarily to the person, as in, to the person who has no choice
with respect to having it, then lived experience is (by definition) private to the one
individual whose experience it is and who has no choice about living/or not living it. In
that sense only one person can be an owner of an experience. For only one person **can
be that and nothing else**. There cannot be a joint ownership of the same experience
though two people (or more) can have different experiences of the same situation.
This is important for if we reflect on this it will become clear that no dalit person can
really be the owner of **another** dalit person's experience, no tribal person can be
the owner of **another** tribal person's experience for he/she can only speak for a
singular experience, the one over which he/she has **no choice** (about having it) and
thereby owns. On a similar note, no one who looses a loved one (in the context of the
present pandemic perhaps) can share the experience of the intense *duhkha*/suffering
with another for he/she owns that particular uniquely felt experience of grief as no
one else ever can. It seems to follow that the relationship which an individual dalit
subject has to the experience which he/she owns is different from the one he/she has
to another dalit's experience. On this view, it follows necessarily that only the one
individual person whose experience it is (who has no choice over whether or not to
have that experience) can own that experience and thereby be in a legitimate position
to theorize about it.

Let us now consider something that we, and indeed Guru and Sarukkai have, so
far been taking for granted and that is simply what is meant by an emotion and how
might social scientists seek to understand an 'emotion' the one that is owned or not
owned by the author. It becomes important to raise the question about what it might
mean to have an experience of an emotion? It seems apparent that an emotion is a
complex mental phenomenon: it is not just a sensation or mere feeling—fleeting or
passing like the pleasure in eating an ice cream or delight in buying a new watch.
An experience of an emotion, for instance that of suffering, must have a structure
surrounding it—a feeling/sensation say of pain or an experience certainly more or less
complex—but an experience embedded in a structure of thought and beliefs which
enables it to be articulated and thus rendered intelligible and assessable. Given that
an emotion has such a structure in which it is embedded and which makes it possible
for us to theorize about the experience of the emotion, it becomes difficult to say the
two things that have been said. One that it can only be understood by the one whose
experience it necessarily is and two that only an owner ought to be an author. This
is a difficult position because an individual dalit or tribal person can only theorize

about his/her own experience of an emotion by unpacking the structure of beliefs and practices in which that emotion (for instance suffering and the sensation of pain) is embedded. Such beliefs and practices are essentially public as beliefs *qua* beliefs and practices *qua* practices must be. Consider Wittgenstein's so very well known and much-cited argument about how even the articulation of sensations like pain make sense only so far as they have a place in a "language game" (Wittgenstein 2009 # 288, 105e) in which all the users of that language participate and the rules of which are known to them all;

> if I assume the abrogation of the normal language game with the expression of a sensation, I need a criterion of identity for the sensation; (Ibid.)

Consider that the readers need to know what "pain" is, for any theory about the experience of suffering authored by the owner of the experience (in terms of this argument) by the dalit social scientist, to be at all intelligible to them;

> It is, one would like to say not merely the picture of the behavior that belongs to the language-game with the words "he is in pain" but also the picture of the pain. Or, not merely the paradigm of the behavior but, but also that of the pain—It is a misunderstanding to say "The picture of pain enters into the language-game with the word 'pain'". Pain in the imagination is not a picture, and *it* is not replaceable in the language game by anything we'd call a picture.—Imagined pain certainly enters the language game in a sense; only not as a picture. (Ibid. #300, 108e)

What then of the practices and beliefs in which emotions and not sensations are embedded? Such practices, beliefs and indeed experiences can make sense only in forms of life in which a number of people (language users for one) participate;

> The word "language-game" is used to emphasize the fact that the speaking of language is part of an activity, or a form of life. (Ibid., 15e)

One might also recall here MacIntyre's account of what might be meant by practices within which emotions and experiences of emotions are embedded;

> By a 'practice' I am going to mean any coherent and complex form of socially established cooperative human activity through which goods internal to that form of activity are realized in the course of trying to achieve those standards of excellence which are appropriate to, and partially definitive of, that form of activity; …In the ancient and medieval worlds the creation and sustaining of human communities—of households, cities, nations—is generally taken to be a practice in the sense in which I have defined it. (MacIntyre 1981, 175)

One might argue that it is in comprehending the structure of beliefs and practices in which the first person experience of suffering is necessarily embedded that any one at all—whether this be the experiencer herself/himself or anyone else (within or outside of the dalit community)—can find the experience of that dalit suffering intelligible. Consider that even while occupying a position from within the community a dalit subject must put the first person experience of another dalit subject into perspective; perhaps by understanding the practice and beliefs from within which that first person suffering arises before he/she can theorize about it. However, one might now ask how it can be argued that such an understanding and the putting into perspective of the suffering, in the context of the beliefs and practices from within which it arises, should be subjected to the strict limitation; that only the experiencer himself/herself or at most a member of the experiencer's community can unpack that structure?

It seems apparent enough that those who are not owners of what, Sarukkai has described as the "lived experience" of suffering, can at the very least understand/make epistemic sense of the experience of suffering or indeed of any other emotion. For the very articulation of the experience as one of "suffering" involves the users of the language game in which words become intelligible to others just as, and just when and indeed how, they become intelligible to oneself. Further, the unpacking of that suffering within a discriminatory set of practices and beliefs also makes sense only so long as it is part of a practice public to the community concerned. Since there are possibilities that the suffering can be understood by others the second part of the question raised by Guru and Sarukkai might be the one which makes for questions of legitimacy. One might then ask—not whether—others **can** understand the experience or whether it is intelligible to those other than the experiencer; but rather whether those **who are not owners** ought to be considered morally fit to speak about the experience of another?

There are two points that I would like to make here in connection with the right to speak about the experience of the other. To begin with the first point, one might note that on Guru and Sarukkai's view, only the single experiencer owns the experience so only that person can indeed theorize about the experience. However, since theory must involve more than one experience, there seems to be some extension in allowing those from the same community the right (normative and not legal of course) to theorize about experiences they cannot own. However, one might consider that human beings *qua* human beings can sympathetically extend themselves emotionally not only because they have experienced a similar sensation embedded in the same set of beliefs and practices on account of coming **from the same community**, but also because they are all equally exposed to suffering deriving from the **shared mortality and vulnerability (to pain) of the human condition**. In this context, one might make a comment upon the points made by both Guru and Sarukkai about Gandhi's relationship to dalit experience. On the above account suffering is private and Ambedkar's suffering in being thrown out of a lodge in Baroda and Phule's experience of being thrown out of an upper-caste marriage procession in nineteenth-century Pune (Guru 2012c, 123); were very different from Gandhi's experience of being thrown out of a first-class compartment (of a train) at Petermaritzburg station, while in South Africa. On the account of Guru and Sarukkai, the three cases were completely different. The first two were cases of caste discrimination the last of racial discrimination. However, one might well wonder why it should happen that while Ambedkar could understand Phule's experience (and both could legitimately speak in the plural about 'the dalit' experience of suffering) Gandhi should not have been able to understand Ambedkar's experience. It seems plausible that Gandhi having had the experience of not being allowed to be in the same space with whites in South Africa, might thereby, have been able to extend that understanding to the oppression suffered by the dalits in India. The point is that if one owns one's lived experience, by virtue of it being a necessary experience to oneself alone, i.e. an experience that one cannot opt out of, there is only one owner of each experience. One might put this in another way and say that there is only one person for whom a particular sensation is such that, it is necessarily his/hers and he/she has no way out of it. It follows that fellow members of a community can only theorize about experiences (in the plural) of particular sensations such as pain by using reason and sympathetic imagination to understand the beliefs and practice that surround that particular sensation of the 'other'; because each has had similar sensations embedded in structures of beliefs and practices—which might differ in details—but which share the same causal relationship as that between their own selves and the bringing about of the sensation. However, 'similar' is not tantamount to 'same', and the two experiences discussed here are similar but not identical. If one is to proceed consistently, these principles of reason and of sympathetic imagination can perhaps also be used (and in the same way) to justify the outsider to the community employing his/her sympathetic imagination to understand (rationally) the sensation of a person and the experience of the community as being similar to some experience that another group (and the outsider concerned) has had. It might then be possible to argue that there is some case for making a disconnect between owners and authors.

The second point I want to make is that there are two additional ways (other than the one specified by Guru and Sarukkai where there is only one authentic way in which an experience can belong to the experiencer) in which a person can be related to an experience. The first is the relation between a person and an experience which he/she could have chosen not to have but has actually and self-consciously chosen to make his/her own. In terms of the argument in this book, this experience is not owned by the individual concerned, but he/she tries to have it by parachuting into the 'others' lived experience. Sarukkai and Guru describe those who seek to live among others and live out their experience in order to theorize about it as authors, as borrowing or "simulating" (Sarukkai 2012a, 35) the experience of the 'other'. So if a person takes, for instance, to voluntary poverty, he/she "has a choice to leave" (Ibid., 36) and stop participating in that experience because it is not his/her lived experience, that is, the sensation of hunger in a borrowed experience of poverty does not belong to the person who has chosen poverty because it is not **necessarily** his/hers. This implies, in terms of the argument made by Guru and Sarukkai (at least), that the relationship of the person to the borrowed experience is inauthentic and that he/she cannot engage in any theory about such an experience. What Guru and Sarukkai mean by invoking inauthenticity here can be better understood if one looks at an example which Guru has employed to indicate the sort of inauthenticity that can come up in connection with those who are not owners of experience seeking to be authors of theory about the experience.

Guru gives the example of a "dancer" (Guru 2012c, 125) who borrows the experience of a devadasi[i] in this connection. The example brings out the third sort of relationship a person can have to an experience. This third type of relationship is (different from the second because it is) lived out by borrowing the experience of another without acknowledging that it has been borrowed. In the case of Guru's example of the dancer, this has been done by reconstructing it in performance and theory as the dancer's own experience to talk about or depict. Guru speaks in this context in

The Cracked Mirror of "the upper-caste woman" (Ibid.) who "does not acknowledge that her dance originated and developed in the Devdasi (temple dancer) tradition" (Ibid.) and instead she "de-contextualize and de-historicized it to a "Krishna-Gopi" version" (Ibid., 126) in order to perform it on the stage. Guru argues that in this "Krishna–Gopi version", the performer "can walk in and walk out of the experience whenever she chooses" (Ibid.). The performance may be excellent, but it is a representation of another's experience and the person performing is an actor, a dancer but not a *devadasi*. On Guru's account, such a performance is inauthentic, in the sense of what the existentialist would perhaps, describe as bad faith. "The non-dalit seems to be acting to get the pure experience of being a devadasi through access to the concept of a devadasi and her narratives and the truth that is rendered visible only through textual material" (Ibid.). There are two levels of deception in the dancer's relationship to the dance. Firstly, she does not acknowledge the genesis of the dance that she has performed in the *devadasi's* experience and the second that she tries to appropriate that experience (essentially private) by simulating in on the stage. This dance performed by "the upper-caste woman" (Ibid., 125) is perhaps twice removed from lived experience. Consequently, the dancer's representation of experience in art (dance) is inadequate and also "wrong". This last is of course a normative judgement.

In discussing this example of the relationships between theory and experience, Guru and Sarukkai are arguing that in such cases there is a departure from the normative demands that ought to govern theory. In this context, Guru argues that when Gandhi spoke about the dalits he was reflecting on the experience of the 'other'. He was making categorizations to help to understand something of which he could never have a lived experience. Guru argues that Gandhi's effort to simulate the experience of the dalit was voluntary and Gandhi could have exited from it at any time. Therefore, it could not be a lived experience by the nature of the case. This leads to the fairly important conclusion that since Gandhi could not have a lived experience as a dalit Gandhi's categorizations were not only inadequate to understand dalit reality but inauthentic as well. For Guru, this inadequacy and inauthenticity can be brought out if we take note of the differences between Gandhi's categories and those employed by Ambedkar. For instance, the difference between "Social justice, self-respect, and nation" (Guru 2012b, 89) in Ambedkar and Gandhi's use of "non-cognitive categories such as seva, trusteeship, care, and co-operation to produce historical conjuncture" (Ibid., 88). Guru argues; "…it is the *achar* (practise) and *anubhava* (experience) mostly of others, in Gandhi, and the authentic *anubhava*, in Ambedkar, that have formative impact on their respective thought" (Ibid.). The absence of having had the lived experience, the *achar*/practise and *anubhava*/experience, become, as it turns out, fairly serious lacunas. In Gandhi, for example, it leads to "non-cognitive" (Ibid.) categories like *seva*/service which do not go to "the roots of the problem" but only "prune its rough edges" (Guru 2012d, 215). The inauthenticity leads Gandhi, on this view, to representations which are theoretically inadequate (and morally impermissible) to throw light on the dalit experience.

It seems possible to make two interventions at this point; and these interventions might have a possible bearing on Guru's example of the inauthenticity of borrowed experience and arguments about the illegitimacy of authorship of theory about experience which one does not own. Firstly, one might note that Gandhi had tried to identify himself in sympathetic imagination with the dalit experience by attempting to live the experience of the dalit subject. This meant that Gandhi tried to situate himself in the surrounding structure of belief and practice even though he might not have been able to have an identical set of emotions whatever this might mean or whether it means anything at all. Consider what it means to talk of a pain as an experience which only the person having it can understand and speak about;

> What would it be like if human beings did not manifest their pains (did not groan, grimace,..)? Then it would be impossible to teach a child the use of the word 'toothache'.—Well, let's assume that that the child is a genius and invents a name for the sensation by himself!—But then, of course, he could'nt make himself understood when he used the word.—So does he understand the name, without being able to explain its meaning to anyone?—But what does it mean to say that he has 'named his pain'?—How has he managed this naming of pain? And whatever he did, what was its purpose?—When one says "He gave a name to his sensation", one forgets that much must be prepared in the language for mere naming to make sense. And if we speak of someone's giving a name to a pain, the grammar of the word "pain" is what has been prepared here; it indicates the post where the new word is stationed. (Wittgenstein 2009 # 257, 98e)

Going back to Guru's argument, he reiterates that Gandhi had a choice and that this choice made his experience of poverty, cleaning latrines, wearing only a *dhoti*,[ii] etc., different from "lived experience" (Guru 2012a, 23; 2012b, 75). Such experience could not legitimize Gandhi's pretensions to theorize about dalit experience. One could consider, however, that Gandhi's experience of living the life of the dalits by adopting voluntary poverty, weaving his own clothes, adopting the act of scavenging as obligatory by taking a *vrata*/vow to practice it (as an appropriate form of the virtue/*niyama* of bread labour) was not such that it was necessarily his. However, it did not **for that reason** become an experience that he could **choose to exit from**. In this sense, one might consider how Gandhi's *vrata*/vow to undertake daily scavenging was different from that of the upper caste dancer who could leave the stage at the end of the performance. Gandhi chose to have certain experiences, but once he made the initial choices, he could no longer exit from those experiences, if and when, they became painful. This was because he, unlike the dancer (in Guru's example of an inauthentic relationship to the experience of another), chose to take vows to make it impossible to exit from such experiences. He also undertook to make such vows obligatory by taking them in/with complete transparency. Transparency in this case truthfulness/*satya* was ensured, for instance, by writing to the public at large about having taken the vows- of truthfulness, of obligatory scavenging every day, of daily spinning (and other such vows)–once they had been taken. Perhaps one of the reasons that Gandhi shared (with the nation at large) the taking of personal vows making some experiences obligatory on himself, was so that, he could ensure that he would himself perhaps no longer be able to exit from such experiences. This was perhaps the reason he took vows to perform bread labour, to practice non stealing/*asteya* non-possession/*aparigraha* and *brahmacarya*/celibacy.

One can certainly question Professor Guru's conclusion that the voluntary experiences of poverty and scavenging as an obligatory form of the daily practice of bread labour were unable to authenticate Gandhi's efforts to speak about the dalit experience. Could the self-imposed necessity of Gandhi's borrowed experiences not validate the authenticity of his claims to understand such experiences? I would argue that the authenticity came from the fact that Gandhi chose to put himself in a line of experiences over which **he thereafter had no control** as an act of taking responsibility for the oppressive experiences of the dalit subject over which the dalit had no control. Taking responsibility for the experiences of the oppressed "other" by choosing to impose both the experience and its necessity (as the structure of belief and practice) on oneself could perhaps be seen to play some role if one was to justify speaking about the experience of the other. In this context, one could add to the contrast between self-respect and *sewa*/service by pointing to the other Gandhian category that of *tapasya*/self-imposed pain discussed in the last chapter.

The next subsection will deal with the second of Sarukkai's points made in support of Guru, namely that the normative demands on theory should take cognizance of the fact that the choice of concepts is not only epistemological but ethical.

6.2   Breaking Out of the Circle of Distrust

6.2.1   The Choice of Concepts—Epistemological and Ethical

In his essay "Ethics of theorizing" (Sarukkai 2012b), Sarukkai has constructed an argument in support of Guru's normative concerns about doing theory. In exploring the relationship between experience, theory and ethics, Sarukkai has drawn upon philosophical discussions (Indian and Western) which look at the place of concepts in perception and sensation. Sarukkai has argued for;

> ...the impossibility of having an experience, of being aware in any sense of the term, without it being influenced by certain beliefs and ideas (if not 'concepts'). It is not just our perception that is 'concept laden'—or, as an extension, 'theory laden' but also our experience. (Ibid., 146)

On this view, it follows that when we choose concepts to make sense of our experience in a particular way there is an ethical component to our choice as we choose the kind of concepts we use to describe those experiences. This can sometimes mean that we can choose our concepts in a manner such that we oppress others "by not allowing certain kinds of a conceptual reordering of experiences. One can continue to subjugate people if certain kinds of concepts are not chosen and made available to those who are oppressed and subjugated" (Ibid., 150). For Sarukkai, this is the problem of the social sciences in India in general since the social scientist continues to choose concepts that are borrowed from the Anglo American and continental traditions. The significant point is that this is "no longer an epistemological issue; it is primarily an ethical one... it is about the practice of Indian social scientists who continue the myth that theoretical structures from the West have as good, if not better, a capacity to describe Indian experiences as compared to 'indigenous' concepts, histories, and narratives." (Ibid., 151).

This argument convincingly reiterates Edward Said's central concern about knowledge as representation and its relation to power. Sudipta Kaviraj perhaps went further than Said when he highlighted the theoretical absences in Indian social sciences making the point that while modern European systems completely disqualified everything associated with "earlier systems" (Kaviraj 2005, 132) the complete (and sweeping) rejection of the traditional Indian knowledge by modern Western knowledge did not follow the same procedure. Modern Western knowledge systems rejected non-Western traditional knowledge systems, "wholesale, in a far more comprehensive fashion—that is ideologically" (Ibid., 133). Raghuramaraju has perhaps changed the tone of this debate by making the point that ignorance also generates power;

> Merely leaving the critique of orientalism at the level of knowledge as representation would eventually make them as perspectives or only as subjective standpoints. It is necessary to take this formula outside the knowledge/power nexus and replace knowledge, with something like, in this context, ignorance that can also generate power. These combinations of ignorance/power provide a qualitatively different combination to knowledge/power, brilliantly illuminated by Foucault. (Raghuramaraju 2009, 4)

Professor Raghuramaraju's point is that one must distinguish between ignorance, falsity, truth and knowledge as having different relationships to power. He argues that "…we can assert here that colonial scholarship may not be considered as knowledge…" (Ibid.) and that "for instance, it would have established an active intellectual agency for postcoloniality… to take on an incorrect interpretation rather than spend a lifetime to prove it wrong" (Ibid., 5). The point that Raghuramaraju has made is perhaps that it is not enough for social scientists to criticize the ideological domination of Western knowledge systems or as in the case under consideration upper caste authors of social science theory. The post-colonial theoretician or the dalit social scientist has to assume active intellectual agency by engaging with other knowledge systems using concepts reconstructed from traditional dalit knowledge systems or by developing new concepts from contemporary experiences of social reality in the post-colonial world. It certainly does not seem enough to say that the theoretician at home in the western knowledge systems cannot be an author because he/she is not an owner of certain experiences. One has instead to examine the theory and take on what is incorrect about it rather than raise concerns about owners and authors if theoretical interventions are to be intelligible to readers who seek intelligibility and not legitimacy.

However, to revisit the argument that this concluding chapter is directly concerned with and to return to Sarukkai's essay "Ethics of theorizing" (Sarukkai 2012b); one might consider that (taking off from Guru's point about the absence of dalit voices in Indian social sciences) Sarukkai has emphasized the importance of indigenous concepts by employing an argument from lived experience, to express the need, for an ethics of theorizing in general. On this view for theory to be 'right' (in a normative sense), the theoretician has not only to be an insider to the experience, such as a set of practices of a group, but an owner of the lived experience. Certainly from Wittgenstein's arguments about languages and forms of life, Said's (1994) arguments and responses to Said, from the work by anthropologists with the tribes, from the work of philosophers on religions and cultures, it is clear that to theorize about a group one must take a perspective from 'within' the experience one wants to understand. In anthropological or sociological research, for example, it is important for the anthropologist or sociologist to understand what the practices of a group mean to those who are insiders to the community. In this sense, the right to theorize is legitimated by being an insider. However, Sarukkai and Guru's point is much stronger—only one who owns a lived experience has the right to theorize about it.

It would be worthwhile to reflect a little here on what is meant by being an 'insider'. One can ask for instance, that while an insider is well placed to reflect on the beliefs and practices of a group, is the insider always and necessarily the best placed to do so? Consider for example what happens in the act of reflection. When a social scientist reflects on experience he/she puts the experience at a certain distance in order to be able to understand it, bring it under rules that simplify experiences of that sort or perhaps, and if it is an experience that departs from such rules, form his/her ideas about it and articulate what can be said about it clearly. One ought to record here that anything one says can be intelligible and understood by all the language users and all practitioners of social science theory no matter whether one is an insider/outsider to the experience. One might now consider that if the social scientist who is indeed theorizing about his/her lived experience would remain absorbed in having the emotion (which constitutes part of the experience of suffering, for instance) he/she would be too close to the sensation of the emotion to make sense of the experience. Too close perhaps to understand the surrounding structure of belief and practice within which that emotion is embedded; for instance, how such an emotion might relate to other emotions in similar experiences. If the theoretician thought that what mattered to doing theory was only the fact that the author owns the experience, that it belongs to her/him and that it was a part of his/her very being the theoretician concerned might not be the best placed to articulate his/her ideas about that experience. At least not in a manner in which the experience could become intelligible to, and illuminate, the understandings of others. Such 'others', one should note, need to learn from the theory about the experience and not simply **respond** to the owner and author's sensations about his/her own experience. It is clear that the act of reflecting and theorizing should involve the perspective from inside, but at the same time, one must also put oneself as a social scientist/philosopher at some distance in order to reflect about it. Consider the difference between the following two questions, 'who has the right to theorize?' and 'why do we theorize at all?'.

In answering the second question "why do we theorize at all?", one might consider that one theorizes perhaps to reflect on experiences, seek to understand them by looking at them in the plural, seek for patterns, place them in systems, or instead single them out as unique/singular, and share insights with others in a dialogical space. An important part of doing theory is to invite criticism, to debate and to rethink a particular understanding in the light of criticism so that a better understanding of experience is put out in a public theoretical space. One might also reflect a little on what is involved in theorizing in the social sciences. To theorize about experiences and practices is part of an academic exercise that by the very nature of the case is shared with others. Social science and natural sciences and knowledge systems in general cannot be solipsistic[iii] for by definition theory involves communication and exchange with other practitioners of the intellectual craft concerned, as it were. This should make it clear that social scientists do not theorize only to own an experience. Consequently, it might begin to appear that it might not be a requirement of doing theory that the theoretician should own an experience in order to adequately describe it. In fact part of what it means to reflect is that one should not exercise ownership over ideas and experiences but share insights in a dialogical space which allows for debate and discussion. If, as it has been argued by Guru and Sarukkai, there is a normative requirement imposed by the ethics of theorizing which demands that only owners of experiences can be authors of theories, the practice of social science would have to be understood almost as a purely solipsistic exercise. However, it is surely meaningful to ask if it is not the purpose of theorizing in general, and in the social sciences in particular, to escape solipsism by sharing ideas, insights and understanding with others? The task of the social scientist involves making ideas about reality available as theoretical tools that can be applied to understand a range of other experiences **no matter to whom they belong**.

The theoretical space is a space where insiders and outsiders can debate their insights with each other. This exercise in itself helps to understand social reality. While concepts which come from the reflection of insiders to the lived experience of a group are critical to such a theoretical space, does this mean that one **has to be an insider** to theorize about the experiences of a person or a community? This question is important for there is a sense in which one can be too close to an experience to be able to reason about it. Going back to Sarukkai's use of the binary between emotion and reason (Sarukkai 2012a, 40), one can consider the point that insiders to a community or owners of lived experience could find emotion obstructing the sort of exercise of reason that is a prerequisite for becoming practitioners of a theory. While we are emphasizing the relationship between theory and experience/emotion, we also need to keep the relationship between theory and reason in perspective. This relationship requires some distance between the lived experience and theorizing about it. There was some discussion on impartiality and its close connection to justice in the last chapter. This discussion might seem to make it apparent that preconceptions and bias can be contrary to the exercise of reason (one might add here that social science theory as it is practised in the academy is governed by liberal notions of procedural rationality) in both social and natural sciences (consider how playing favourites with hypothesis' might actually disrupt the knowledge game in the natural sciences). Dispassionate and disinterested reflection is required to be able to make sense of an experience. The insider has to play the role of an outsider—see things as they really are outside of her strongly felt emotional responses to the experience—and equally of the conceptual baggage dictated by who he/she already is. Otherwise, theory would only reiterate what he/she and his/her group believe to be the case. It might then appear that owners need to play the role of observers before they can be authors. Outsiders in turn need to play the part of insiders before they can be authors.

Indeed if Guru's conditions about the right to theorize is extended, it will make us reject most of contemporary social science as non-indigenous and as inauthentic. One would have to do away in Indian social science with, for instance, any reference to Marx. Marx would be doubly problematic for the ethical concerns of doing social science theory regarding dalit reality or the experience of the work force in India. For his work was both Western, and it rested upon an account of experience which was inauthentic and borrowed. One might note that Marx did not have the lived experience of being an Indian, a dalit or even a worker.

6.2.2 Curiosity and Interest

The third argument made by Sarukkai, in support of Guru's position, is that social science theory legitimizes the intellectual exploration of problems by invoking the notion of "'free' curiosity" (Sarukkai 2012b, 135). He argues that curiosity about the "others" experience can certainly be "intrusive" (Ibid.). Therefore, only those who have experiences can theorize about them.

In Sect. 6.2.1 of this chapter note was made of the difference between two questions, 'who has the right to theorize?' and 'why do we theorize at all?'. It is in response to the latter that Sarukkai invokes the notion of curiosity to explain why pure and social scientists work on a research problem. Borrowing this notion from pure science Sarukkai argues that.

> Social scientists can choose any problem to work on. Why? Because they are curious about or 'interested' in that problem. In principle, there is nothing problematic in invoking curiosity or interest to legitimize exploration, but there is an ethical cost to this 'free' curiosity. Where the curiosity argument really fails is when it is confronted with the category of experience. One's experience is not outwardly open to another's curiosity and thus is fundamentally insulated from the intrusive tool of curiosity. (Ibid.)

Sarukkai suggests that concerns about the ethics of theorizing should lead to an evaluation of theory by norms which are not only epistemological but also ethical. Some part of such norms should lead the social scientist to realize the difficulty with theorizing about the lived experience of 'others' to satisfy his/her 'free' curiosity. Sarukkai does not say why there is no ethical concern about the curiosity driving the pure scientist to speak about any research problem that interests him/her. He makes the point that it is social scientists alone who should subject their theoretical curiosity to ethical evaluation. This is perhaps primarily on account of the nature of the experience with which the social scientist deals. At the level of theory (unlike in the natural sciences), this is often the lived experience of someone with a history and a memory of the past. Owners of experience who have a history and memory respond to their own experience in complicated ways. The social scientist who is not an owner of the experience about which he/she seeks to theorize has to reflect on that experience without taking the subject into account. This means that such a social scientist must necessarily (by the nature of the case) pry into the rubric of the past and into the practices and beliefs of the experiencer because he/she is curious. However, this curiosity is about someone's life, feelings, practices, historical memories, unpleasant experiences and pain. Sarukkai argues that this curiosity is irresponsible. Perhaps it seems to him somewhat like that of an idle gossip who seeks to pry into what the different 'other', unfortunate 'other' or unhappy 'other' does and feels.

However, is intellectual curiosity a free irresponsible curiosity in the sense in which gossip is sometimes irresponsible curiosity? Sarukkai paraphrases curiosity in terms of interest saying above that the social scientist is "curious about or 'interested'" (Ibid.) in a problem. Perhaps one might see why intellectual curiosity as interest would be different from curiosity seen as intrusive by bringing in a third term 'gossip'. Perhaps 'Interest' might seem a more appropriate word to use in connection with the intellectual curiosity of the social scientist and it may also incidentally serve to bring out the difference between the irresponsible curiosity of a gossip and the interest or intellectual curiosity that motivates the theoretician. To do theory is to have an intellectual curiosity about a problem, a desire to engage with it, bring out its different aspects, relate it to other problems, etc. This is what is involved when, for instance, a philosopher has an interest in suffering. It is not that the philosopher who perhaps uses concepts to discuss the choices made by one who is presently suffering—the responsibility for the choices (seen often as belonging to 'others') that lead to the present suffering, the absence/presence of a sense of anxiety and guilt, an experience of bad faith etc.—is irresponsibly curious about the suffering like a disturbed and sadistic voyeur. The philosopher's questions and curiosity is responsible to the norms of adequacy that govern theorizing. This responsibility transforms the intellectual curiosity into sustained academic interest, and such interest perhaps prompts him/her to write a paper which helps to bring what he/she thinks of as a theoretical problem into a space where people (from the academy) can engage with suffering/*duhkha* outside of the feelings of victims and perpetrators of injustice/pain. It is important to remember that this space is valuable. For it provides, as Kant put it, for man's "original vocation" (Kant 1999, 18), the freedom to think and make public use of one's own reason.

Sarukkai's arguments in support of a normative evaluation of theory on the basis of an examination of the feelings which prompt the theoretician—irresponsible curiosity or inner need—to understand experience as an author might have overlooked the importance, indeed even the ethical value, of the 'interest' that sustains all academic practice and engagement.

6.2.3 The Hermeneutics of Suspicion—'Creating the Space to Communicate'

The importance of space to experience and theory is brought out by Guru, in this discussion, in an essay on "Experience, Space and Justice" (Guru, 2012b). This essay "involves an epistemological claim in as much as it suggests a concept of space embedded in experience as the source both for the formation of thought and thoughts articulation" (Guru 2012b, 70). Guru argues that "space provides this necessary condition for the tormentor, who then uses these spaces for producing a particular kind of experience that can morally paralyze a victim. The tormentor reconfigures spaces accordingly, so as to seek the ultimate regulation of the victim into hegemony and domination of the former" (Ibid., 73). This makes it urgent for the victim to "reconfigure spaces" (Ibid., 73) of confinement by discovering herself/himself as an "active or reflective agency" (Ibid., 74) by cultural and intellectual mobilization.

It is in the context of the relationship between space, experience and the theoretical representation of experience that Professor Guru brings in the debate between Gandhi and Ambedkar. Though (on this view of the debate) both Ambedkar and Gandhi shared the belief that experience provides a vantage point for "making epistemological moves and also for ideological and political mobilization of the masses" (Ibid., 75), Guru locates a "fundamental difference" (Ibid.) between them. In that, Gandhi experimented with the experience of "others" so much so that "…the experience of Ambedkar and his community becomes an object of Gandhi's experiment" (Ibid.). The contrast between the two relationships to experience, one that of representing one's own lived experience and the other that of representing the experience of the other, comes out for instance in the manner in which they handled sacred space.

Professor Guru has spoken in this connection of the significance of the difference between Gandhi and Ambedkar on temple entry. While Ambedkar spoke of temple entry in terms of entitlement and rights Gandhi "On the contrary …puts emphasis on the moral duty of the high-caste Hindus to allow the untouchables to enter the Hindu temples" (Ibid., 97). Ambedkar used the language of "entitlement" (Ibid.) deriving from the principle of the recognition of "the labour contribution" (Ibid., 95) of untouchables "for constructing and later protecting the Hindu temple" (Ibid.) to generate an argument about the right to enter the temple. Gandhi however spoke of temple entry in alternative terms belonging to the language of morals by using words like "penance" (Gandhi 1888–1948, Vol 59: 60, 98, 108, 131, 231, 423, 430, 433),[1] "sin" (Gandhi 1888–1948, 59: 231), "atonement"[iv] (Gandhi 1888–1948, 59: 503) and others of that brood.

Perhaps this might lead one to think (like Guru) that for Gandhi the temple entry movement seemed to be akin to "a sacred ritual of self-purification" (Nagraj 2015, 45). It was meant perhaps to provide opportunities for the atonement of upper caste guilt. On such an interpretation, the temple entry movement in itself would be seen to be an experiment that responded to the needs to the upper castes to become more comfortable with the consequences of what they had done to the untouchables.

---

[1] Gandhi 1888–1948, refers to the *Collected Works of Mahatma Gandhi*. The volume concerned and the page numbers from which citations from Gandhi are drawn have been mentioned within parentheses. These have been mentioned to indicate the exact location of the quotation in the electronic edition of the *Collected Works of Mahatma Gandhi*. However, for the purposes of reference, it may be noted that I have resourced these volumes from the *Collected Works of Mahatma Gandhi*: Volumes 1 to 98. New Delhi: Publications Division Government of India, 1999. Accessed online in May 2021 at https://www.gandhiashramsevagram.org/gandhi-literature/collected-works-of-mahatma-gandhi-volume-1-to-98.php.

However, before settling down to such cynical distrust, one might need to look at Gandhi's arguments for the removal of the prohibitions on temple entry more closely. Gandhi understood the symbolic nature of the movement for temple entry. He understood perhaps that "notwithstanding physical closeness, communities also live in insulated and isolated universes" (Ibid., 62). This led Gandhi to the idea that removing the prohibition on temple entry was important not because the untouchables wanted to enter temples but because it was important to make good the sins of the past. Gandhi one might recall had (often enough) made arguments like the following;

> … the caste Hindus who recognize that untouchability is a blot on Hinduism have to atone for the sin of untouchability. Whether, therefore, Harijans desire temple entry or not, caste Hindus have to open their temples to Harijans, precisely on the same terms as the other Hindus. (Gandhi 1888–1948, 59: 231).

It is important to add that Gandhi did recognize that "economic and educational" (Ibid., 276) rights were important to the movement for the removal of untouchability which (he recognized) could not have been abolished by entry into temples alone. However, Gandhi believed that the "the betterment" (Ibid.) of the political and economic condition of *harijans* would be more effectively brought about by rights **accompanied by** a change of heart in the caste Hindus (*savarnas*) which would necessarily involve the recognition of "Religious equality" (Ibid.). Certainly while speaking to upper-caste Hindus Gandhi had used the language of self-purification, penance, chastisement, etc. As theoreticians, this ought not to be sufficient to make us completely suspicious of Gandhi and see him as parachuting into the dalit experience. Perhaps it is such distrust that can be read into the conceptual moves to reconstruct Gandhi's religious attempts as being purely ritualistic and solely about the displacement of guilt. However, there is surely some theoretical room to examine moral arguments made by Gandhi differently. One can, for instance, take note of arguments (such as the one quoted above) where he tried to bring home the enormity of what he saw as the "sin" (Gandhi 1888–1948, 63: 164) of untouchability and the need to assume moral responsibility for it. One needs to think carefully about whether this was a vicarious playing out of guilt as a "larger- than- life hero" (Nagraj 2015, 67) in a high caste drama or whether Gandhi was evoking, assuming and locating moral responsibility for injustice and the wrong done.

The point is that there might still be some room for looking at Gandhi at face value. In Guru's story of the upper-caste appropriation of the *devadasi's* dance form without acknowledgement, there was some deception. This was because, in that example, there was no acknowledgement (regarding the cultural origin of the dance form in the dalit experience) from the upper-caste dancer. Surely, we can distinguish that case from Gandhi's categorizations of dalit experience. There may be at least some room for a little doubt about whether Gandhi was subconsciously playing out upper-caste guilt. We might even, on reflection, think that in Gandhi's attempts to reflect on the experience of the dalit there was no self-conscious deception. This is part of a more general point about the hermeneutics of suspicion in oppressed groups. While there is much reason for distrust in practices of upper-caste domination, orientalism in theory and racism; that should not mean that one can no longer make distinctions between sincere and self-motivated gestures and theory. By the nature of the case, one can only break out of the circle of suspicion by locating something to trust.

One can of course ask, why, the oppressed should break out at all from the circle of distrust? In practice and in theory, surely one can settle down to a suspicion that prevents engagement with what the 'other' does and says at face value. However, when one speaks about the relationships between dalit theory and practice, the meaning of engaging in the discussion itself, is perhaps that of creating a platform for reflection on the respective roles played by experience and reflection in engaging with such theory. It seems apparent that theory must (by definition) involve communication between social scientists. For theoreticians in the domain of the social sciences seek to engage with, and influence, the practice of the social sciences in the academy. In a sense such communication cannot proceed without some space for trust. At the very least, it seems important to listen to what the other is saying and take it at face value. The theoretical space becomes important to breaking out of a circle of suspicion because theorizing involves taking what the other says seriously and engaging with it, if necessarily, only to disagree. What might be needed then is a theoretical space that creates opportunities for debate between dalit and non-dalit perspectives on dalit experience. Consequently, it might be self-contradictory for an ethics of theorizing to restrict the right to theorize so that debate between such perspectives no longer remains theoretically possible.

Moving on from theoretical space for trust to the concerns of the practical. One might consider that the more practical political space involves living together peacefully with diverse others. It might seem evident that even if what is being sought is a minimalist liberal quest for the stability of a political conception of justice, where the constitution provides the text of that conception, some trust between conflicting people living in "contexts of intimate enmity" (Ibid., 62) might be required to ensure such stability. It seems possible to locate Gandhi's practices of "dual identification" (Ibid., 68) with parties on both sides of a conflict and "the widening of emotional concern" (Ibid., 62) as part of the quest for moments of trust in conflicting polities.

6.3   Owning the Rise and Fall of Man: Rabindranath Tagore on the *Surplus* in Man

The last section closed on a note reiterating the need to break out of suspicion by locating a moment of trust in theoretical and in practical space. One might note that liberal reasons for the stability of justice, for instance, those derived from an overlapping consensus of a Rawlsian kind (Rawls 2005, 133) are only slightly more substantial than those which make for a *modus vivendi*/balance of power. Striking a somewhat contrary note, this section will bring up a very different set of arguments to make space for the stability of justice and for trust between conflicting parties in society. It will bring up a vision of interrelationship between human beings and indeed between such beings and the cosmos that envisions a far more substantial trust between those in any conflict than that which could be drawn from a minimalist liberal concern for the stability of justice. Such a contrary note brings this concluding chapter to the figure of a silent interjector in the Ambedkar–Gandhi debate that of the poet and song writer Rabindranath Tagore. As already mentioned, Tagore and Gandhi had been engaged in a series of conflicts for 26 long years between 1916 and 1941. During this time, Tagore had raised arguments against *satyagraha*, the non-cooperation movement, boycott of government schools, the burning of foreign cloth and Gandhi's connection between spinning and *swaraj.*[v] Though Tagore's connection with the debate between Ambedkar and Gandhi is perhaps less well known, he had been silently involved in this debate, both as Gandhi's friend and as his critic and interlocutor. One might recall that Tagore had exchanged letters and telegrams with Gandhi over the conflicts surrounding the Communal Award (Tagore 2012b, 326–335). It seems clear enough that Tagore was acquainted with the differences between Gandhi and Ambedkar and indeed perhaps understood that it was difficult for those in the realm of the political to understand Gandhi;

> ...the reason of their failure is mainly owing to the fact that the language of Mahatmaji is fundamentally different from their own. (Tagore 2012b, 327)

One must not (of course) take the fact that Tagore understood Gandhi better than most others (including perhaps Ambedkar) to mean that he always agreed with what Gandhi thought, did and said. Though he understood Gandhi, Tagore disagreed with him, on important issues. As referred to earlier, some of these issues concerned the meaning of freedom and the method and the goal of the national movement for the freedom of India. Tagore had also disagreed with Gandhi about some issues at stake between Gandhi and Ambedkar. Yet such differences not withstanding Tagore had left for Poona with Surendranath Kar and Amulya Chakravarty and was at Gandhi's side when he broke the famous fast over the communal award in the September of 1932. Tagore had in fact sung a song from the Gitanjali to an "improvised tune" (Ibid., 332) as that fast was broken. Tagore's thoughts on Gandhi's epic fast become important to this discussion on the Gandhi and Ambedkar debate for they set the tenor, for his own, very different arguments for the dissolution of untouchability and indeed for the dissolution of all conflicts no matter whether these were conflicts within Indian society/polity or between human beings at large or indeed between the human and the non-human world;

> His (Gandhi's) great life which today luminously reveals itself on a large background has brought to us the message of discovering man the Great in all humanity. May this message be fulfilled. The true path to emancipation lies in unity; (Ibid., 333) (The parenthesis in the above quotation have been my own addition and are not in the original text)

It was Tagore's idea of the divine understood in terms of "man the Great" (Ibid., 333) and represented (as perhaps such an idea necessarily would be) in all human beings that provide the key to his understanding of the religion of man and to his notion of the *surplus* in human nature. These two ideas present arguments which could explain why it might be possible to move beyond a "politics of rage" (Nandy 2015, xv) and find a moment of trust even in the most oppressive of experiences such as that of untouchability in Indian society. It is on a musical note from the great poet of India then that this book closes on itself and on the incommensurability it has traced across the last five chapters.

6.3.1 *The* Surplus *in Man: To Rise and to Fall Together*

In Chap. 3, there was some discussion of Ambedkar and Gandhi's incommensurable notions of the self which lay at the heart of their very different positions on untouchability. That chapter had brought out the philosophical divergences between Ambedkar and Gandhi on the nature of the self and agency. One might recall that Gandhi had understood the self along the lines of the ancients as a dualism of the empirical mind–body continuum and the *atman*/soul. Ambedkar, however, had a more modern understanding of the self as purely empirical—a body with a mind— as it were. Tagore brought a very different conception of the self and thereby very different resources to bear on the problem of untouchability and on possible arguments that might be drawn upon to locate trust between conflicting persons (and conflicting communities). These resources drew from Tagore's understanding of the individual self, and it is in that understanding that one can locate the idea of the *surplus* in human nature. For Tagore, the *surplus* within the human being (and thereby essential **to being** human) is that which is in excess of what such a being might need for his/her biological survival. Such a notion can become relevant to the conflicts between Gandhi and Ambedkar and indeed to conflicts (discussed in the first two sections of this chapter) about owners and authors. For by invoking the *surplus* in human nature, Tagore philosophically and poetically unpacked the generosity somewhat internal to the human person *qua* human person This generosity, though so often forgotten, was, for Tagore, a constitutive aspect of human nature. It was perhaps as much a part of the modality of being human as is the experience of suffering and indeed as it is inevitable for the human being to be subject to mortality;

> But the most important fact that has come into prominence along with the change of direction in our evolution, is the possession of a Spirit which has its enormous capital with a surplus far in excess of the requirements of the biological animal in Man. Some overflowing influence led us over the strict boundaries of living, and offered to us an open space where Man's thoughts and dreams could have their holidays. Holidays are for gods who have their joy in creation…But above the din of the clamour and scramble rises the voice of the Angel of Surplus, of leisure, of detachment from the compelling claim of physical need… (Tagore 2012a, 99).

Tagore's notion of the *surplus* becomes significant to the debate (between Gandhi and Ambedkar) because it reminds us (thereby striking a completely different note from the arguments considered in the previous sections of this chapter) that the individual has resources to understand the suffering of the 'other' simply by virtue of the generosity somewhat internal to being human. In emphasizing the constitutive generosity of the human self, Tagore perhaps distanced himself from Ambedkar and came somewhat closer to Gandhi. For he had suggested that the experience of plenty within the human person (which does not depend on economic, political or even social rights from without) is the source of a constitutive generosity which unites all human experiences. Whether these experiences be of creative accomplishment or of moral failure (and grief) human beings *qua* human beings have the ability to appreciate (from within their constitutive plenty as it were) that they each rise and fall together, according as, individual persons elevate or degrade their own humanity. Such an understanding of the human person and the divinity within that person leads Tagore to argue that all such individual defects and achievements drag down or elevate (respectively) man the great/divinity as manifested in every individual human being. For Tagore, in fact, there was sense in speaking of the divine only so long as the divine was understood as manifested within the individual to the extent that every human being could advance or destroy the project of such divinity in his/her own being;

> All things that had seemed like vagrant waves were revealed to my mind in relation to a boundless sea. I felt sure that some Being who comprehended me and my world was seeking his best expression in all my experiences, uniting them into an ever-widening individuality which is a spiritual work of art.
>
> To this Being I was responsible; for the creation in me is his as well as mine. It may be that it was the same creative mind that is shaping the universe to its eternal idea; but in me as a person it had one of its special centres of a personal relationship growing into a deepening consciousness. I had my sorrows that left their memory in a long burning track across my days, but I felt at that moment that in them I lent myself to a travail of creation that ever exceeded my own personal bounds like stars which in their individual fire-bursts are lighting the history of the universe. It gave me a great joy to feel in my life detachment at the idea of a mystery of a meeting of the two in a creative comradeship. I felt that I had found my religion at last, the religion of Man, in which the infinite became defined in humanity and came close to me so as to need my love and co-operation. (Ibid., 122)

Tagore's emphasis on a creative comradeship between divinity and individual human beings lead him to part company from Gandhi as much as from Ambedkar. Such a parting of ways was inevitable given that Tagore never sought a *vedantic* union or an experience of oneness with the divine. In its stead Tagore thought of a creative comradeship in which the individual had to engage with his/her own life very much in the nature of a project which could either elevate or destroy the idea of man the great (an idea as much within as outside of the human person) according as such an engagement would elevate or degrade his/her humanity;

> Are we deaf by nature, or is it that we have been deafened by the claims of the world, of self-seeking, by the clamorous noise of the market place? We miss the voice of the Lover, and we fight, we rob, we exploit the weak, we chuckle at our cleverness, when we can appropriate for our use what is due to others; we make our lives a desert by turning away from our world the stream of love which pours down from the blue sky and wells up from the bosom of the earth. (Ibid., 127)

What then of the oppressive memory of the injustice of the past and of the suffering thereof? One might ask if Tagore was oblivious to this unjust degrading past and find a contrary note in the narrative of that past in his play *The Kingdom of Cards* (2011). This play tells the story of a merchant and a prince ship wrecked in mid sea. The two had been "washed ashore in an alien land" (Tagore 2011, 434). In the new land, they found themselves amongst a new monolithic "people flat in shape, walking in stiff geometrical gait,…" (Ibid., 435). These were people or as Tagore described them "Humans mimicking cards…" (Ibid., 456) who were living a life "in strict adherence to the codes of the Card-dynasty"(Ibid., 439) of which Tagore in the guise of the prince in the play pronounced;

> …realize that none of this is real. This is all made-up, imposed from above, a shell fabricated by the pundits of this country….We'll shatter the shell. Then, you'll be amazed to see the fresh uninhibited spirit that will emerge, resplendent in all its natural splendor. (Ibid., 435)

The cards believed themselves bound to such codes from the time that they had been created by "Grandfather, Brahma, in the early stages of creation…" (Ibid., 440). The prince and the merchant "strangers from a distant land" (Ibid., 458) went on to school (or rather perhaps de-school) the inhabitants of the "card-island" (Ibid., 459) with "a strong gust of wind from alien shores" (Ibid., 456) into the "power of the will" (Ibid., 450) which transformed them into human beings at last. Tagore's play *The Kingdom of Cards* (Ibid.,) perhaps expresses his own response to caste, *varna* and the injustice of past tradition as it ends with the words of the Prince;

> Smash all dams; smash them all!
>
> Free the imprisoned spirit,
>
> Let life's endless joys flood the dry river-bed,
>
> Sing the victory-song of the spirit of destruction.
>
> Let everything tattered and traditional be washed away.
>
> We have heard the clarion call of the nameless new.
>
> No fear of the unknown can impede our march
>
> Let's ram down the bolted gates of an unexplored world. (Ibid., 462)

It is significant to note that for Tagore it was from within the *surplus* and therewith from within the generosity constitutive of human nature that individual beings could wash away the "tattered and traditional" (Ibid.) and move beyond "meaningless days" (Ibid., 452) to overcome not only "bondage of inertia" (Ibid.) but also the hate of the rule driven sorrowful past.

6.3.2   The Truth of Interrelationship and Harmony: Tagore's Religious Argument Against untouchability and Conflict

Tagore was clear that his religion "the religion of man" (Tagore 2012a, 122) as he termed it was a "a poet's religion, and neither that of an orthodox man of piety nor that of a theologian" (Ibid., 121). In fact he had declared that his own mind had been "brought up in an atmosphere of freedom –freedom from the dominance of any creed that had its sanction in the definite authority of some scripture…" Ibid., 120).

It seems apparent enough then that Tagore's religion should have drawn its "unity of inspiration" (Ibid., Preface, 85) from both within the human being and from outside the human being, in nature and perhaps the infinite beyond nature;

> When that one mind of ours which wanders in search of things in the outer region of the varied, and the other which seeks the inward vision of unity, are no longer in conflict, they help us to realize…the ineffable. The poet saint Kabir has also the same message when he sings:
>
> By saying that Supreme Reality only dwells in the inner realm of spirit, we shame the outer world of matter; and also when we say that he is only in the outside, we do not speak the truth. (Ibid., 163)

It was in this interrelationship between the human and the divine, between human beings and nature, and indeed among human beings themselves that Tagore's religion of man lay. It becomes important to bring up Tagore and his understanding of the religion of man in this concluding chapter not only because Tagore was (as somewhat apparent from the above) a **not so silent interjector** in the conflicts between Ambedkar and Gandhi; but also because he had made space for a poet's arguments, for (what Nagraj has described as) the widening of emotional concern and identification with parties on both sides of human conflicts. Tagore had located the religion of man in just such a space of interrelationships between human beings (and between such beings and non-human others), and it is to a consideration of his arguments that this concluding section will turn.

There are three points which I seek to bring up in this section in connection with resources for generosity and for locating moments of trust between human beings. First, a consideration of the place of interrelationships in Tagore's religion of man; second Tagore's insight that divinity rests within the *surplus* in the human person "in Man and not in the temple, or scriptures, in images and symbols" (Tagore 2012a, 129); and lastly, the place that Tagore makes for music and rhythm in the *surplus* within the human being and from thence in the religion of man.

To begin with the truth of interrelationship in Tagore's conception of the religion of humanity, it is significant that he spoke of three kind of interrelationships—of the human being with nature, with the divine and with other human beings. Tagore explained what he meant by saying that the religion of man lies in the truth of interrelationships most clearly;

> The divine principle of unity has ever been that of an inner inter-relationship. This is revealed in some of its earliest stages in the evolution of multicellular life on this planet. The most perfect inward expression has been attained by man in his own body. But what is most important of all is the fact that man has also attained its realization in a more subtle body outside his physical system. He misses himself when isolated; he finds his own larger and truer self in his wide human relationship. His multicellular body is born and it dies; his multipersonal humanity is immortal. In this ideal of unity he realizes the eternal in his life and the boundless in his love. The unity becomes not a mere subjective idea, but an energizing truth. Whatever name be given to it, and whatever form it symbolizes, the consciousness of this unity is spiritual, and our effort to be true to it is our religion. (Ibid., 88)

It is perhaps worth noting that Tagore's notion of a multi-personal humanity does not find its natural termination at the boundaries of the human world. It goes beyond the human and relates the human world with nature. Tagore's poetry and music expresses such a relationship between the human and natural world. This relationship leads Tagore to speak of nature in personal terms as comforting the individual in his/her moments of suffering and of the seasons and moods of nature as sharing in an individual's joy and grief;

> The wonder of the gathering clouds hanging heavy with the unshed rain, of the sudden sweep of storms arousing vehement gestures along the line of coconut trees, the fierce loneliness of the blazing summer noon, the silent sunrise behind the dewy veil of autumn morning, kept my mind with the intimacy of a pervasive comradeship. (Ibid., 121)

It was by virtue of this very same pervasive comradeship with the human person that nature, became a third party, mediating a relationship between the human and the divine and removing, when it so chose, the "invisible screen of the commonplace" (Ibid.) to intensify the individual's experience of "the super-personal world of man" (Ibid.). Tagore thought of this comradeship with nature not only as a source of friendship but also as a source of revelation often bringing spiritual illumination to human life. He suggested that like the human being, nature had resources within itself, and could convey "a direct message of spiritual reality" (Ibid.) to the human person. It is perhaps in such a context that one might read Tagore's "The Awakening of the Waterfall" (Ibid.);

> The waterfall, whose spirit lay dormant in its ice-bound isolation, was touched by the sun and, bursting in a cataract of freedom, it found its finality in an unending sacrifice, in a continual union with the sea. (Ibid.)

Tagore had emphasized that nature could bring "a… breeze of religious experience" (Ibid.) to human life. This experience could help an individual break out of his/her own ice-bound isolation and like the waterfall find the realization of "a mysterious unity of inter relationship" (Ibid., 101) with the sea of humanity. This reflection perhaps moves naturally enough to a consideration of the second point (mentioned above) that of, Tagore's insight, that the sources of unity with the cosmos lay very much within the human person. Tagore had argued that divinity/"the infinite" Ibid., 122) itself becomes "defined in humanity" (Ibid.) and is located in the *surplus* in human nature;

> What is purely physical has its limits like the shell of an egg; the liberation is there in the atmosphere of the infinite, which is indefinable, invisible. Religion can have no meaning in the enclosure of mere physical or material interest; it is in the surplus we carry around our personality—the surplus which is like the atmosphere of the earth, bringing to her a constant circulation of light and life and delightfulness. (Ibid., 100)

This last is perhaps the most important insight that Tagore brings to the issues surrounding the Ambedkar–Gandhi debate. Those, for instance, about the relationship between human beings and the relationship between the unjust past and present of such beings. Locating religion itself within human nature or in human personality Tagore makes two points which become relevant here: the first (as already mentioned) that all achievements and all moral lapses belong equally to every person. They belong indeed to "the world-spirit of Man" (Ibid., 104), and we each have an equal share in the good and the bad of human achievement and moral fall. The second point is that the human present needs in its turn to overcome "the miserliness of the present need" (Ibid., 100) and embrace both the past and the future. Tagore had argued that human nature has within it the inherent generosity to accommodate both the good and the bad memories of the past and its manifold injustice and pain;

> For our physical life has its thread of unity in the memory of the past, whereas this ideal life dwells in the prospective memory of the future. In the records of past civilizations …we find …efforts to make their memories uninterrupted through the ages… For we mortals must offer homage to the Man of the everlasting life. In order to do so, we are expected to pay a great deal more than we need for mere living, and in the attempt we often exhaust our very means of livelihood, and even life itself. (Ibid., 106)

Tagore had in fact argued that the human past (across different peoples and ages) was a repository of answers to the eternal question regarding "what Man truly was as man" (Ibid., 107) and he had emphasized that any answer to this question "whatever may be its character" (Ibid.) belonged "not only to any particular people but to us all" (Ibid.).

The last point (from Tagore) which becomes important to the resources to inspire trust between deeply divided people lies in the close interrelationship (Tagore had forged) between art, music and the religion of man. Tagore was not oblivious to, and indeed he had owned up to, the "irrational repressions and …accumulation of dead centuries" (Ibid., 134) in/of the Indian past. He had seen such repression as an immense loss not only for India and for Indians but also for the entire human race and for the divine/man the great;

> For Reality is the Truth of Man, who belongs to all times, and any individualistic madness of men against Man cannot thrive for long. (Ibid., 140)

For Tagore any "individualistic madness" (Ibid.) could not prosper for long because it broke the truth of interrelationship just as it dragged down man the great in humanity. It also went against the human being's essential generosity and did violence to the *surplus* in human nature. It was perhaps in virtue of such a *surplus* that Tagore suggested that human beings were (essentially and) constitutively creative beings and indeed were artists. He had explained that it was in an engagement with his/her *surplus* that the human being could respond to the real by "a continual adaptation, a transformation of facts into human imagery, through constant touches of …sentiments and imagination" (Ibid., 139). For Tagore, as essentially an artist, the human person could not be constrained to respond to things passively. Feeling necessitated as it were by the needs of the purely material to "passively and accurately…" (Ibid.) take that which happened as "…a physical representation of things around" (Ibid.) him/herself. Tagore perhaps, like Gandhi, believed that the facts compiled by the historian juror and the conflict and hatred born of them could not overcome (or exhaust) the human being who was an artist (and not a judge) by nature;

> The animal has the geography of its birthplace; man has his country, the geography of his personal self. The vision of it is not merely physical; it has its artistic unity, it is a perpetual creation. In his country, his consciousness being unobstructed, man extends his relationship, which is of his own creative personality. In order to live efficiently man must know facts and

their laws. In order to be happy he must establish harmonious relationship with all things with which he has dealings. Our creation is the modification of relationship. (Ibid.)

In Tagore's understanding of human nature the human being had a constitutive ability to modify relationships and create them anew because such a being abided in his/her own *surplus* and was essentially an artist and music maker. This understanding of human nature brings into focus the human ability to attune discordant notes into harmony in a song or in a piece of music. This last is perhaps the most significant insight which Tagore brings to the Ambedkar–Gandhi debate. This is also the insight with which this book seeks to close on itself on a note of generosity. It seems most appropriate indeed to end this book in the words of Tagore locating the possibilities of trust between India's past and present (and between Ambedkar and Gandhi and those who come after them on both sides of this conflict) in the *surplus* in human nature and in the human being as an artist and music maker;

> The end of the fight …is in the House of Songs, in the symphony of spiritual union…The detailed facts of history, which are the battle-ground of the learned, are not my province. I am a singer myself, and I am ever attracted by the strains that come forth from the House of Songs. (Ibid., 119)

Notes

i.   In India, a *devadasi* was a female artist who was dedicated to worship and serve a deity or a temple for the rest of her life. The dedication took place in a ceremony somewhat similar to a marriage ceremony. In addition to taking care of the temple and performing rituals, these women also learned and practised classical Indian artistic traditions such as Bharatanatyam, Mohiniyattam, Kuchipudi, and Odissi. Their social status was high as dance and music were an essential part of temple worship.

ii.   A *dhoti* is an article of dress. It refers to a loose piece of clothing wrapped around the lower half of the body, worn by men from different parts of India.

iii. Relating to or characteristic of solipsism means the belief that only your experiences and existence can be known or are important.

iv.   There are numerous instances where Gandhi used these words (mentioned in the *Collected Works of Mahatma Gandhi*). For reference purpose, I have mentioned a few of them.

v.   See Puri (2015) *The Tagore Gandhi debate on Matters of Truth and Untruth.*

References

Gandhi, M. K.1888–1948. *Collected Works of Mahatma Gandhi*: Volumes 1 to 98. New Delhi: Publications Division, Government of India, 1999. Accessed online in May 2021 at https://www.gandhiashramsevagram.org/gandhi-literature/collected-works-of-mahatma-gandhi-volume-1-to-98.php.

Guru, Gopal. 2012a. Egalitarianism and the Social Sciences in India. In *The Cracked mirror: An Indian debate on experience and theory*, eds. Gopal Guru and Sundar Sarukkai, 9–28. New Delhi: Oxford University Press.

Guru, Gopal. 2012b. Experience, Space, and Justice. In *The Cracked Mirror: An Indian Debate on Experience and Theory*, ed. Gopal Guru and Sundar Sarukkai, 71–106. New Delhi: Oxford University Press.

Guru, Gopal. 2012c. Experience and the Ethics of Theory. In *The Cracked Mirror: An Indian Debate on Experience and Theory*, ed. Gopal Guru and Sundar Sarukkai, 107–127. New Delhi: Oxford University Press.

Guru, Gopal. 2012d. Archeology of Untouchability. In *The Cracked Mirror: An Indian Debate on Experience and Theory*, ed. Gopal Guru and Sundar Sarukkai, 200–222. New Delhi: Oxford University Press.

Guru, Gopal, and S. Sarukkai, eds. 2012a. *The Cracked Mirror: An Indian Debate on Experience and Theory*. New Delhi: Oxford University Press.

Guru, Gopal, and S. Sarukkai. 2012b. Introduction. In *The Cracked Mirror: An Indian Debate on Experience and Theory*, ed. Gopal Guru and Sundar Sarukkai, 3–8. New Delhi: Oxford University Press.

Kant, I. 1999. An answer to the question: what is Enlightenment? In *Immanuel Kant Practical Philosophy*. Translated and ed. Mary J. Gregor. General Introduction by Allen Wood. Cambridge: Cambridge University Press.

Kaviraj, Sudipta. 2005. The sudden death of Sanskrit Knowledge. *Journal of Indian Philosophy* 33 (1), 119–142.

MacIntyre, A. 1981. *After virtue: A study in moral theory*. London: Duckworth.

Nagraj, D. R. 2015. *The flaming feet and other essays: The Dalit Movement in India*, ed. Prithvi Datta Chandra Shobhi. Ranikhet: Permanent Black.

Nandy, A. 2015. Foreword. D. R. Nagraj's *The flaming Feet and other essays: The Dalit Movement in India,* ed. Prithvi Datta Chandra Shobhi. Ranikhet: Permanent Black.

Puri, Bindu. 2015. *The Gandhi Tagore debate: On matters of truth and untruth.* Sophia: Studies in Cross-cultural Philosophy of Traditions and Cultures, Vol. 9. New Delhi: Springer.

Raghuramaraju, A. 2009. *Enduring colonialism: Classical presence and modern absences in Indian philosophy*. New Delhi: Oxford University Press.

Rawls, John. 2005. *Political Liberalism*. New York: Columbia University Press.

Said, Edward W. 1994. *Culture and imperialism*. London: Vintage.

Sarukkai, S. 2012a. Experience and Theory: From Habermas to Gopal Guru. In *The Cracked Mirror: An Indian Debate on Experience and Theory*, ed. Gopal Guru and Sundar Sarukkai, 29–45. New Delhi: Oxford University Press.

Sarukkai, S. 2012b. Ethics of Theorizing. In *The Cracked Mirror: An Indian Debate on Experience and Theory*, ed. Gopal Guru and Sundar Sarukkai, 128–156. New Delhi: Oxford University Press.

Tagore, R. 2011. The kingdom of cards. In *The essential Tagore*, ed. F. Alam and R. Chakravarty, 429–462. Santiniketan: Visva-Bharati.

Tagore, R. 2012a. The Religion of Man. In *The English writings of Rabindranath Tagore*, Vol. III, ed. S. K. Das, pp. 83–190. New Delhi: Sahitya Akademi.

Tagore, R. 2012b. Mahatmaji and the Depressed Humanity. In *The English writings of Rabindranath Tagore*, Vol. III, S. K. Das, 326–335. New Delhi: Sahitya Akademi.

Taylor, C. 2001. *Sources of the self: The making of the modern identity*. Cambridge: Harvard University Press.

Wittgenstein, L. 2009. *Philosophical Investigations*. Translated by G. E. M. Anscombe, P. M. S. Hacker and Joachim Schulte (revised 4th edition). Oxford: Wiley Blackwell

Glossary

adiaphora an ancient Greek term for the cultivation of indifference to the vicissitudes of life; detachment from things that are not of enduring value

adivais tribals

advaita non-dualism, monism; designation for one of the six orthodox schools of Indian philosophy

agraha insistence/firmness

ahimsa non-violence, non-injury, harmlessness; abstention from any hostile thought, word or act; Gandhi often used the term interchangeably with love

ahimsanat non-violent

antah karana in Indian philosophy, the *antahkarana* refers to the internal organ/instrument which is the location or inner origin of thought and feeling. The *antahkaraṇa* (meaning "the inner cause") includes the *buddhi* which is the higher mind/intellect, the *manas* which is the lower mind and the *ahamkara*/ego. The function of the *antah karana* is to unite all the sensations and present them to the *atman* which remains outside of, and is not a part of, the *antah karana*

artha one of the four ends/aims of human life in Indian philosophy. The word *artha* literally translates into "meaning, sense, goal, purpose or essence"

Arthashastra an ancient Indian *niti* text on statecraft, economics and military strategy. Kautilya also identified as Vishnugupta and Chanakya, is traditionally credited as the author of the text

Arya samaj literally stands for "Noble Society". It is a monotheistic Hindu reform movement which promotes values based on the belief in the infallible authority of the *Vedas*. The movement was founded by Maharishi Dayanand Saraswati on 10 April 1875.

ashram a spiritual fellowship or community

asteya non-stealing

aswabhavika non-natural

atmabal force of the soul. Gandhi often used the term for the force of love

ātman self/spirit

aufklarung enlightenment

avijja ignorance

© Springer Science+Business Media Singapore 2022
B. Puri, *The Ambedkar–Gandhi Debate*,
https://doi.org/10.1007/978-981-16-8686-3

bhasya commentaries on canonical texts

bhava chakra the wheel of existence

brahmacharya celibacy; refers to the first (and necessarily celebate stage) of the four stages/*ashramas* into which a person's life was divided according to the Hindu tradition.

Brahman the Absolute Reality. The ground/basis of the world

Brahmanism refers to the early *Vedic* religion, emphasizing the status of the Brahman, or priestly, class

charkha spinning wheel

chaturvarna The fourfold vision of ancient Hindu society based upon idealised occupational groupings. The concept is generally traced to the *Purusha Sukta* verse of the *Rig Veda*

dalit "the oppressed"; name preferred by "untouchables" for themselves. The term *dalit* comes from the Sanskrit *dal,* literally "split"/"broken open". It came to represent the condition of being "ground down". By the 1970s, however, the term was divested of its negative connotation and adopted as a self-description by ancient India's erstwhile "untouchable" groups

dhamma *dhamma* holds the same sense as *dharma* and is the term used by Buddha and the Buddhists. It stands for morality, tenet, doctrine, custom, law, religion, virtue, thing

dharma *dharma* has roots in the Sanskrit *dhr-,* which means *to hold* or *to support*; (n.) morality, ethics, ethical thing, item identified by a moral theory, that is, a normative theory selected for its social implications; (adj.): ethical, moral. The term *dharma* also stands in general for righteousness

dharman denotes a thing which upholds or supports, or simply a foundation

Dharmashastra range of texts on *dharma*

dohas stanzas

duḥkha (in Sanskrit) or *Dukkha* (Pāli) Pain, suffering, misery, unhappiness

duragraha persistence in wrong doing

dvija **or** *dwija* twice born; appellation of the upper castes of Hindu society whose initiation is considered a second birth

ekpakshi farj unilateral/one-sided obligation

farj obligation

Gita/Bhagavad Gita the *Srimad Bhagavad Gita* also referred to simply as the *Gita* is a religious book for the Hindus. It is a 700-verse text in Sanskrit that is part of the epic *Mahabharata*. The *Gita* narrates a dialogue between the *Kshatriya* prince Arjuna and his charioteer Sri Krishna. At the start of the war between the *pandavas* and their cousins, the *kauravas* Arjuna is filled with despair and wonders if he should take part in a war against his kinsmen. Sri Krishna's reply to him forms the *Gita*. Krishna counsels Arjuna to fulfil his duty by action without any self-directed desire for results thereof

gunas qualities

harijan the term *Harijan,* or "children of God", was coined by Narsinh Mehta, a Gujarati poet-saint of the *Bhakti* tradition, to refer to all devotees of Krishna irrespective of caste, class or sex. Mahatma Gandhi, an admirer of Mehta's work, first used the word for the dalits in 1933

himsa violence

himsanat violent

Īśvara God; the perfect person

Itihaas thus it happened'/it so happened

Jajmani *jajmani* system or *yajman* system was an economic system most notably found in villages of India in which lower castes performed various functions for upper castes and received grain or other goods in return

Jati a caste or subcaste

Jnana in Indian philosophy, *Jnana* means knowledge. The idea of *jnana* centres on a cognitive event which is recognized when experienced. It is knowledge inseparable from the total experience of reality, especially a total or a divine reality

karma from its earliest sense of "ritual act", it later came to be associated with the sense of "the law of *karma*" which related action and its results to reincarnation

khaas lakshana special characteristic

laksana mark, trait, feature

Mahabharatha the *Mahābhārata* is one of the two major Sanskrit epics of ancient India, the other being the *Rāmāyaṇa*. It narrates the struggle between two groups of cousins in the Kurukshetra War and the fates of the Kaurava and the *Pāṇḍava* princes and their successors

manuski a Marathi term used by Ambedkar to signify humanness

Manusmriti the ancient work of Indic jurisprudence considered unimpeachable in Hindu moral and political culture

maryada is a Sanskrit term meaning "boundary". It usually stands for "propriety of conduct"

maryada dharma conduct within the boundaries of propriety

mīmāṃsakas the followers of the orthodox/*astika* Mīmāṃsa school of Indian philosophy

mokṣa liberation/spiritual freedom

muknayak literally *muk Nayak*/leader of the voiceless. It was also the name of a Marathi fortnightly started by B. R. Ambedkar on 31 January 1920

prakriti nature

navayana literally "new vehicle"; the term was used by B. R. Ambedkar to describe his radically re-interpreted and socially engaged Buddhism on the eve of his own conversion to Buddhism in 1956

nibbana extinction; the Buddhist term for salvation

nikāya is a pali word and means "volume". It is often used to mean "collection", "assemblage", "class" or "group" in both Pāli and Sanskrit. It is most commonly used in reference to the Pāli Buddhist texts of the *Tripitaka*, namely the *Sutta Pitaka*, the *Vinaya Pitaka* and the *Abhidhamma Pitaka*

nishkamakarma the desireless action recommended by the *Bhagavad Gita*. The term signified action which ought to be performed without any thought for the fruit or result thereof *niti* literally political skill or craft; moral code pertaining to social ethics; the concerns of institutional justice

niyama casual virtue/observances (one of the "eight limbs" of *yoga*)

nyāya literally means "justice", "rules", "method" or "judgement"; it is the name of one of the six orthodox/*astika* schools of Indian philosophy

panch a village elder elected to the village council (situated within the premodern traditional Indian village republic)

panchayas an elected council of five village elders serving to govern a village unit combining the role of the legislative executive and judiciary

paramarthika satta the *Adavita Vedanta* (one of the six *astika*/orthodox schools of Indian philosophy) spoke of three grades of *satta*/levels of reality. Of these, the *Paramarthika satta* was the term used to signify the level of absolute truth/reality

parivrajakas literally means a wandering ascetic; the term was used to refer to the peripatetic monks of India whether these were Buddhist Jain or Hindu

phronesis a Greek word used by Aristotle usually taken to mean practical wisdom

prakriti material nature

pratibimb silhouette (in Gujarati)

prohairesis is an ancient Greek word variously translated as "moral character", "will", "volition", "choice", "intention", or "moral choice". It is a fundamental concept in the Stoic philosophy of Epictetus. It represents the choice involved in giving or withholding assent to impressions (*phantasiai*). The use of this Greek word was first introduced into philosophy by Aristotle in the *Nichomachean Ethics*. For Epictetus, nothing is properly considered either good, or bad, aside from those things that are within our own power to control, and the only thing fully in our power to control is our own volition (*prohairesis*) which exercises the faculty of choice that we use to judge our impressions. According to Epictetus, *prohairesis* is the faculty that distinguishes human beings from all other creatures

Ramrajya literally the Kingdom of Lord Ram; golden age; ideal polity; signified a perfectly just state

rgveda the earliest of the four *vedas* and one of the most important and sacred texts in the *Sruti* tradition of the Hinduism

rta order; equilibrium; cosmic moral order

sabda pramana verbal testimony

sadachar customary moral law

sadharana dharma universal code of conduct common for all humanity

sahishnuta tolerance

samabhava having the attitude of equality to things as they are/exist

samadarshana to see things with an equal eye despite apparent inequalities

samadarshi one who see's everything with an equal eye

samadarshita equimindedness

samadrishti looking at everything and every person with an equal eye

samata the Status of equality

sanatan ever existing, beginningless or endless; eternal

sangathan organization

sanyāsa the last stage in the Hindu life cycle

sat being/Absolute reality

satya truth; Reality

satyagraha nonviolent resistance; truth-force or soul-force; firmness (*agraha*) in adhering to the truth (*satya*)

savarna term for the communities which belonged to one of the four *varnas* or idealized occupational groupings in Hindu society, i.e. *Brahmin, Kshatriya, Vaishya* and *Shudra*

sewa service

shastra came from "shas" which means to teach; it includes *vedas, smritis* and *puranas*

shudra the fourth and lowest of the four *varnas*, or occupational groupings in Hindu society

smriti is a term derived from "*smri*" which means to remember. *Smriti* is literally "that which is remembered" and refers to a body of hindu texts usually attributed to an author which were traditionally written down. This set of texts was different from the Sruti's (the Vedic literature) which were considered authorless and were transmitted verbally across generations

sramanic literally means one who labours, toils, or exerts themselves (for some higher or religious purpose). It also meant a seeker who performs acts of austerity. During its later semantic development, the term came to refer to several non-brahmanical ascetic movements parallel to but separate from the Vedic tradition. The *Śramaṇa* tradition included Jainism Buddhism and others such as the *Ājīvikas, Ajñanas* and *Cārvākas*

sthitaprajna the person of resolute intellect spoken about in the *Gita*.The term signified one who had overcome extremes of attachment and aversion

swabhava innermost nature/foundational nature

swabhavik natural, or of one's own orientation

swadeshi pertaining to one's own country; self-reliance

swadharma practicing own *dharma* which includes an individual's unique duties, responsibilities and righteousness

swaraj self-rule; self-government; home-rule

tapas austerity/penance

tapah from the root "tapa", which means, among other things, to cause heat, pain, discomfort

tapasvi ascetic; one who has accumulated much merit through self-mortification

tapasya self-imposed suffering/Austerity, penance, focusing of energy and self-purification

upanayana literally means "the act of leading to or enlightment or near the eye (or eyesight/vision/third eye/Pineal gland)"; it is a ceremony in which a *guru* (teacher) accepts and draws a child towards knowledge and initiates his/her second birth, that is, of the young mind and spirit

Valmiki Ramayana *Ramayana* is one of the great epics of Hinduism written by Valmiki. It contains 24,000 sloka's in 7 *kanda's* and 500 *sarga's*. *Ramayana* is the story of Rama (Lord Vishnu's *avatar*/reincarnation), whose wife Sita was abducted by the demon king Ravana

varna the ideal unit of a functionally divided Hindu society; a single unit of the fourfold occupational division of Hindu society

varna vyavastha traditional Hindu division of the society into four *varnas* (*Brahmins*, *Kshatriyas*, *Vaishya* and *Shudras*) on the basis of occupations; a system where duties are performed according to the system of *varnas* (fourfold hierarchical division of Hindu society)

Veda the *Vedas* are considered the oldest Hindu texts. Scholars believe that they were written down some 2500 years ago. There are four *Vedas*, namely *rig-veda, yajur-veda, sama-veda and atharva-veda*

Vedānta the term *Vedanta* means the "conclusion" (*anta*) of the *Vedas* and originally meant the *Upanishads*; one of the six systems (*darshan*) of Indian Philosophy

vijnana *vijñāna* (Sanskrit) or *viññāṇa* (Pali) means consciousness, life force, mind or discernment. The term *vijñāna* is mentioned in the early *Upanishads* where it has been translated by terms such as understanding, knowledge and intelligence

Viśistadvaita qualified non-dualism; school of *Vedānta*; name of one of the six orthodox schools of Indian Philosophy

vrata vow

yajña sacrifice

yama rule of moral conduct (one of the "eight limbs" of *yoga*)/Gandhi defined *yama* as a cardinal virtue or disposition of character

yugadharma *dharma* prevalent in a specific time/generation

Printed in Great Britain
by Amazon

49449022R00159